Society and the Supernatural in Song China

Society
and the Supernatural
in Song China

Edward L. Davis

UNIVERSITY OF HAWAI'I PRESS
HONOLULU

06   07   08   09   10   11   7   6   5   4   3   2

Library of Congress Cataloging-in-Publication Data

Davis, Edward L.

Society and the supernatural in Song China/ Edward L. Davis.

p.   cm.

Includes bibliographical references and index.

ISBN-13: 978-0-8248-2398-6 (pbk. : alk. paper)

1. China—Religious life and customs.   2. China—History—
Sung Dynasty, 960–1279.   I. Title.

BL1802 .D38 2001

299'.51—dc21   00–064893

Designed by Integrated Composition Systems
Printed by The Maple-Vail Book Manufacturing Group

To my sea-strewn ʻohana—
Mother and Dad,
John, Elizabeth, and Michael,
and Kazuyo,
who still squeals with delight.

Contents

Acknowledgments

ROGER T. AMES • POUL ANDERSEN • COCO ANDERSON • BEVERLY BOSSLER • PHILIPPE BUC • GERARD CASPARY • DANIEL COLE • PATRICIA CROSBY • MEI-LAN FRAME • MARK HALPERIN • IHARA HIROSHI • LIONEL JENSEN • **DAVID JOHNSON** • TERRY KLEEMAN • KEITH KNAPP • LIVIA KOHN • MATSUMOTO KŌICHI • JOHN LAGERWEY • SUSAN MANN • JOSEPH MCDERMOTT • SUSAN NAQUIN • RICHARD NETTELL • PETER NICKERSON • CYNDY NING • IRWIN SCHEINER • KRISTOFER SCHIPPER • VICTORIA SCOTT • LEE SIEGEL • MICHEL STRICKMANN • BUZZY TEISER • TU WEI-MING • TSAO JR-LIEN • GIOVANNI VITIELLO • **FREDERIC WAKEMAN** • **STEPHEN WEST** • YAO DA-JUIN • YUE MING-BAO. WITH LOVE AND APPRECIATION.

Abbreviations

HY   *Combined Indices to the Authors and Titles of Books in Two Collections of Taoist Literature: Harvard-Yenching Institute Sinological Index Series* No. 25. Weng Tu-chieh, ed. (Peking, 1925). Taipei: Ch'eng-wen reprint, 1966.

Stein   Stein Collection of Tun-huang Manuscripts. British Library, London.

T.   *Taishō shinshū daizōkyō.* Takakusu Jinjirō and Watanabe Kaikyoku, eds. (Kyoto, 1905–1912). Tokyo: Daizōkyōkai, 1924–1935.

Z.   *Dai-Nihon Zokuzōkyō.* Kyoto: Zōkyō shoin, 1905–1912.

I

Introduction

This book takes its title seriously. Its overwhelming concern is the relation of Chinese society with the supernatural and with the experience of the supernatural as an aspect of social relations. More specifically, it focuses on the experience of the supernatural in its most palpable and dramatic form—the descent of gods, ghosts, or ancestors, and their habitation within a human body. It focuses, in other words, on what we call "spirit-possession" and what Chinese writers of the Song period (960–1276) denoted by the term *"pingfu."*[1] I understand this experience both to be occasioned by a crisis in social relations and to be in itself an occasion for a transformation of these relations.

Spirit-possession is necessarily a social experience. It has been succinctly defined as a "trance of identification," and this identification—of the subject with a spirit—cannot be made except in the company of others.[2] Moreover, far from being a sign of the private anguish of mental illness, spirit-possession was a means of avoiding it. Spirit-possession was both a role assumed in public and a shared and universally recognized idiom that allowed an individual person to convert emotion into culture, and symptoms into symbols.[3]

In an article written several years ago, Piet van der Loon asked us to examine and expose the "shamanic substrate" of all Chinese religions.[4] Yet what is exposed by any such examination is the weakness of "shamanism" as a description of either China's indigenous religion or the "substrate" of her religions. If there is a common basis of Chinese religious practice, then that basis has more to do with forms of trance associated with spirit-possession than with shamanism. Moreover, if spirit-possession—and particularly the possession trance of the spirit-medium (*wu*)—has informed the religious practice of Daoist and Buddhist priests, then the textual and ritual traditions of China's two organized religions have done just as much over the course of centuries to transform the practices of her spirit-mediums. By the Song dynasty, it becomes as difficult to talk about the "substrate" of Chinese religion as it is to trace the "origin" of a particular religious practice, belief, or divinity.

Recent attempts to unearth the "shamanic substrate" of Chinese religion employ the term "shamanism" in such a loose way that it becomes almost meaningless, and therefore useless, as a category of historical and cultural analysis. In a chapter on the shamanic substrate of the Chinese Buddhist figure Mulian, Stephen Teiser relies on those authorities who identify shamanism and spirit-possession as more or less the same thing:

> Some scholars have tried to make historical and typological distinctions between two forms of mediumship, defining the first as mere "spirit-possession" and the second as true "shamanism." See, for example, Eliade, *Shamanism*, pp. 58, 499–507. But this distinction does not appear valid even for Central Asian spirit-mediumship, to which the distinction was first applied. As Ioan M. Lewis, *Ecstatic Religion*, pp. 55–56, writes, "the Tungus evidence makes nonsense of the assumption that shamanism and spirit-possession are totally different phenomena, belonging necessarily to two different cosmological systems and to separate stages of historical development."[5]

Yet the Tungus evidence makes nonsense of no such thing. The analysis of the central funerary rituals of the Gold of Manchuria reveals that the Tungus shaman is master of the spirits in his journey to the underworld. He employs his auxiliary spirits as his guides, his servants, his means of transportation, his interlocutors. He converses with them and occasionally even imitates them, yet in all cases the subject of trance—the shaman—coexists with the guardian spirits.[6]

Possession, in contrast, is a trance of identification in which the persona of the divinity is substituted for, and does not coexist with, that of the subject. The possessed subject does not converse with or imitate the divinity; he (or she) is the divinity! Although it is true that shamanism and possession are both representations of trance behavior, these representations, as Gilbert Rouget has demonstrated, oppose and contradict each other at every point of comparison:

> The difference between shamanism and possession trance thus seems to rest on three factors: the former is a journey made by man to visit the spirits, the latter is a visit by a spirit (or divinity) to the world of men; in the former the trance subject gains control over the spirit embodied within him, in the latter the reverse is true; and lastly, the former is a voluntary trance whereas the latter is an involuntary one.[7]

It seems perverse to deny any typological distinctions between shamanism and spirit-possession when such distinctions are so stark. A strong case could be made, though I will not make it here, that such distinctions do in fact correspond to, and indeed reflect, differing ecological, sociological, and cosmological systems. To invoke "shamanism" as the substrate of Chinese religion is nothing but a substitute for the serious analysis of everything that is not Buddhism or Daoism, and is not much better than the use of the term "animism" by nineteenth- and early twentieth-century ethnographers. My point here is not to deny that Central Asian shamanism had some influence on China's indigenous religion, but only to note that the search for it will go, for the most part, unrewarded,[8] whereas the evidence of spirit-possession in middle-period China is overwhelming.

For the Song, the *Yijian zhi*, or *Record of Hearsay*, by Hong Mai (1123–1202) includes close to two hundred descriptions of spirit-possession. For purposes of analysis, these descriptions can be organized along the lines of ritualized and nonritualized possession. The accounts of ritualized or religious possession can be further broken down into three groups:

1. Cults of possession proper, exemplified above all by village spirit-mediums who would become possessed by an earth-spirit or other tutelary divinity (occasionally these spirits might stray from the trees or stones in which they were thought to lodge and, as incubi, possess women who, if they were not cured, might become in turn recruits for spirit-mediums);

2. Exorcisms by Daoist priests or Buddhist monks employing or directing one or more boys who would become

possessed by the spirit afflicting the patient or by a tutelary divinity of the exorcist; and

3. Rites for the dead during which relatives of the deceased
   (wife, son, grandson) would become possessed by the
   deceased and converse with the living.

Nonritualized possession includes all those cases where someone becomes harassed and ultimately possessed by a divinity or demon in the
context of family life. In these cases the subject is considered to be suffering from an exogenously caused illness, and the family normally
calls in an exorcist who may be a spirit-medium, Daoist priest, or Buddhist monk. The *Yijian zhi* is particularly rich in accounts of nonreli-
gious possession, and these accounts present an exceptional view of
family relations and private life in the Song.

The chapters of the present volume are organized around the ex-
egesis of cases of ritualized and nonritualized possession in the Song.
The point of this example of microhistory, however, is not simply to
understand spirit-possession and exorcism in their own right.[9] Nor is
it simply to demonstrate how fundamental these phenomena were to
Chinese religion and society at a particular time. Rather, my aim is to
examine the religious interactions and social functions of the Daoist
priest, Buddhist monk, Ritual Master, and spirit-medium in local society during the twelfth century, and to present a description of Song
religious life richer than any available to date. In so doing, I also hope
to say something significant about the major themes that have emerged
in the historiography of the culture and religion of the Song dynasty.
The remainder of this chapter is taken up with a discussion of these
themes.

Historians, Sinologists, and the Song Dynasty

For several years—perhaps for as long as I have been studying middle-
period China—I have been dissatisfied with current explanations for
the great transformation of Chinese culture that scholars believe to
have crystallized in the Song dynasty. In particular, I am uncomfort-
able with the view that the Song elite, not to mention the society
in general, can best be understood (a) from the perspective of what

was to become in later centuries the dominant ideology—namely, Neo-Confucianism, and (b) by focusing on those individuals who were particularly strong in articulating that ideology.

In its extreme form, such a view is often conceived negatively, in terms of the decline of Buddhism and Daoism. According to this thesis, these intellectually moribund, socially ineffectual, and politically irrelevant religions lost the allegiance of the Song elite to a new and vibrant reformulation of the classical tradition; moreover, it was this elite that would for all intents and purposes define, from the Song on, the social, cultural, and political direction of Chinese society. Thus it was the Confucian, whether in office or out, who would be the repository of value in this society and—if one follows the implications of some recent interpretations—the embodiment of the sacred or holy as well. Scholars may disagree as to when this became a reality, but all appear to subscribe to its inevitability. The decline of Buddhism and Daoism and the success of Confucianism were, ostensibly, ensured in the Song by (1) the examination system, which channeled the intellectual talent of the empire into government service by means of a Confucian education; (2) the sale of monk and priest certificates of ordination and the (consequent) moral decline of monastic or clerical integrity, offices, and institutions; (3) the intellectual assault on Buddhism and Daoism by Neo-Confucians; and (4) a new syncretic tendency, primarily defensive and apologetic, that diluted the intellectual substance and power of those religions and confirmed the fact that their philosophical vibrancy had peaked long before.

For almost forty years, this view has both informed the historiography of Song China and to a great extent determined historical inquiry. It is still evident in some of the recent and best work of Song historians and is proverbial wisdom in almost any textbook of premodern Chinese history. The thesis owes its remarkable vitality to many factors, only a few of which I mention here: first, an abiding, essentialist, and largely nonrational conviction that Chinese civilization and culture are synonymous with something called "Confucianism"; second, a tendency to define religion as a matter of individual belief rather than as a community of behavior; and third, a complete failure to consider the enormous evidence preserved in the Daoist and Buddhist canons and in the miscellaneous writings of Song literati.

There is, however, another approach, that takes a noticeably hostile attitude to the victors of the first (the Neo-Confucians) but that, paradoxically, concludes by leaving their victory fully intact. This is the approach of European sinology, which has had the difficult task of helping us grasp more easily the complexity of China's arcane religious traditions. Despite, or perhaps because of, these sinologists' very success, their understanding of these traditions is often narrowly textual— an "unfolding" of (to borrow a word from their adversaries) or, at best, an endless dialogue with, an equally unexamined construct known as China's "shamanic substrate."

In its extreme form, the sinological view sees the patronage or hostility of the state as the only mechanism for change in China's unbroken religious traditions. Thus it posits a fateful split between the bureaucratic class of early imperial China and Chinese religions,[10] a parting of the ways that was exacerbated by an unholy alliance between Confucianism and Christianity. In the name of Confucius, "the Philosopher of the Chinese," the Jesuits of the sixteenth century denied the religious reality of the state cults and decried the religious validity of Daoism as an "aberrant belief" (*mixin*).[11] In the meantime, the bureaucratic class, reeling from the fall of the Ming, which it blamed on sectarian revolt (i.e., religious fervor), took refuge in "Han Studies," which, among other things, sought to excise Daoist books from the imperial library; to force the abandonment of the Daoist canon, which had until then been a necessary confluence of imperial patronage and literati involvement; and generally to deny the Chinese their entire religious patrimony.[12]

Those historians today who ignore the Daoist and Buddhist canons are, in more ways than one, the heirs of this grand repression. In the nineteenth century, Confucians and Christians ultimately joined hands to defeat the Taipings, who, in the name of the Christian God, did the work of the bureaucratic class by laying waste to hundreds of Daoist temples. This Confucian-Christian iconoclasm continued among the Reformers of 1895, Christian warlords in the South, and proponents of the New Life movement in the Republican period. The Cultural Revolution was merely the final blow: "Ce qui, au XVIe siècle, n'était qu'un vœu pieux a fini par se réaliser: la religion chinoise, comme notre religion antique, a pour ainsi dire cessé d'exister, et le monde n'en a rien su."[13]

In statements like these, the sinologist sees himself as the guardian and caretaker of Chinese culture, which has been in decline since the end of the Ming. Like the historians of Confucianism, moreover, he claims, quite explicitly, to represent the "real China." Over and against "le pays officiel"—the state and its Confucianism—he places "le pays réel": "la religion" and, more specifically, "the unique, local structures which express themselves in regional cults and nonofficial religion" (i.e., Daoism).[14] And like the Confucian historian again, the sinologist may find in his real China some of his most cherished Western values: autonomy, liberty, even science and democracy.[15]

Instead, I would like to suggest that we abandon the linear and teleological view of the Tang-Song cultural transition as a succession of metaphysical systems and as a way station in the Confucian elite's march to social and moral preeminence in the Ming and Qing dynasties. We should not immediately replace this thesis with another, equally comprehensive one, but with a tension in which the categories Confucianism, Buddhism, and Daoism find themselves in a very different configuration.

I characterize this tension as a tension among three groups placed along a vertical axis. At the top we find a group broadly defined to include the emperor, the court, and the bureaucratic and religious hierarchies (civil and military officials and their families, Daoist priests, and Buddhist monks); at the bottom are village spirit-mediums and Buddhist acolytes, local landowners (large and small), tenants and servants, and sub-bureaucratic servicemen and functionaries. In the middle I place a new and expanding group of lay Daoist exorcists called "Ritual Masters" (*fashi*), Esoteric Buddhist monks, doctors, ritual experts and religious specialists (*shushi, xiangshi, daoren*, etc.), and those who passed one or more of the examinations but were without official posts (*shiren*). At times the tension between the three hierarchically arranged groups can and will be drawn along urban and rural lines, at other times along the lines of state and local society, or along those of written and martial culture. However we characterize the tension among the groups for purposes of analysis (more on this shortly), the three groups themselves are best conceived of as overlapping or embedded sets, and there are many circumstances in which a member of one group may become a member of another.

The point of this scheme is not an exhaustive or even accurate representation of hierarchies of status or class in Chinese society of the Song period. Rather, the point is to avoid both the inevitable contradictions that arise from the analysis of Chinese culture and society in terms of the categories of the "Three Teachings" (Confucianism, Buddhism, and Daoism) and all prejudicial statements that assume, rather than demonstrate, a necessary relationship between a particular cultural category (e.g., Confucianism), and a particular social category (e.g., officialdom). To take just one example, bureaucratic officials and Daoist priests belonged to the same social milieu in the Song. To be a Daoist priest (*daoshi*) was, above all, to be a "literatus" (*shi*) trained in the classical language and to hold an "office"—that is, to be an administrator of the divine world who dealt with that world by bureaucratic procedure and endless paperwork.[16]

This book focuses on relations between one particular cross section of the three groups outlined above: Daoist priests (group 1), Daoist Ritual Masters and Tantric exorcists (group 2), and spirit-mediums (group 3). I have described the relations among the groups as a tension precisely because these relations were simultaneously symbiotic and antagonistic. On the one hand, we will see the Daoist Ritual Master as an officiant of village spirit-mediums, but also as a traveling exorcist serving an elite, urban clientele; we will see officials as lay exorcists and Daoist exorcists as clerical officials; and we will see increasing ritual exchange, interaction, and accommodation among priests, exorcists (both Daoist and Buddhist), and spirit-mediums. On the other hand, we will find a fierce and protracted conflict with magistrates and "official" and "clerical" exorcists on one side and spirit-mediums and local society on the other. This conflict, which is explored in Chapter 3, is the more obvious theme, and the one that presents itself more easily to historians. Symbiosis is, however, the more difficult and important theme, and deserves not only more attention but a considerably greater degree of analytical subtlety and imagination.

Symbiosis and antagonism are prominent themes in the historiography and ethnography of Daoism. They may be seen, in fact, to emerge out of two quite distinct views of the nature of Daoism and of its relation to "popular religion." One of these views I associate with the work of Michel Strickmann; the other, with that of Kristofer Schipper.

Strickmann's rather consistent views on the nature, origin, and function of Daoism are found throughout his wide-ranging work. They have never been so forcefully argued, however, as in his unpublished study, "Magical Medicine: Therapeutic Rituals in Medieval China." Here Strickmann maintains that "Daoists ancient and modern all agree that the basic raison-d'être of Daoism was to supplant the local cults with

which China teemed: to replace 'shamanism,' 'spirit-possession,' 'ecstatic religion.' Whichever of these terms one chooses, such rites were
the long-established means of responding to disease, disaster and the
shadowy world of the spirits."[17] These rites attempted to "coax or ca-
jole" the gods by "wild music," "lascivious dancing," and "copious
sacrifices." They were the established pattern of curative ritual in ancient China, a pattern to which the Daoists hoped to put a definitive
end. "The first step in the Daoist program . . . was to unmask the so-
called 'gods' worshipped by the people," to show that these gods were
not gods at all but spirits of the dead—ghosts or demons—which in
fact caused the diseases they were meant to cure or which brought
upon their votaries delirium, madness, and premature death. In
Strickmann's reading, what the Daoists sought to rectify was not simply the rites and sacrifices of popular religion but, more fundamen-
tally, a kind of false consciousness. He concludes:

> From all this it is clear that Daoism really amounted to a religious re-
> formation in the China of Late Antiquity. Here the standard histories
> of China, which have neglected Daoist primary sources, have got it quite
> wrong. The chief rival of early Daoism was not Buddhism, and not even
> the so-called "Confucian" State. Rather, it was the despised and ne-
> glected "nameless religion" of the people, the scores of local deities and
> the hundreds of practitioners who invoked and embodied them. For
> Daoists, the distinction between their own faith and these cults was and
> remains quite simply a matter of life against death: the celestial Dao
> against the ill-omened, unhallowed dead and everything connected with
> them.[18]

Kristofer Schipper appears to accept Strickmann's formulation of
the problem, while finding the essence of Daoism somewhere else
entirely:

> Daoism always situates itself in relation to Chinese popular religion and
> not in opposition to Buddhism or Confucianism. The antagonism is sys-
> tematic. Daoism denounces popular cults and shamanism with an in-
> sistence that in the end appears suspect. Doesn't this need to separate
> itself betray a fundamental ambivalence? Doesn't it translate the likely
> confusion of two aspects [of Chinese religion] only seemingly contra-
> dictory? Even before Daoism had become, by assimilation of local cults,
> the religion of townspeople in the Song period, the distance that sep-
> arated the two had already been breached. The revelations of Highest
> Purity Daoism, among other examples, recognized as their patron

saints the Mao brothers, local divinities in the region of Danyang, and put into practice a form of mediumism that while difficult to identify precisely, seems very close to vernacular shamanism. The actual situation of Daoism confirms this *rapprochement*. Often on the occasion of community festivals, two forms of rituals unfold simultaneously: that of the Daoist priest in a sacred space inside the temple, and that of the magical Masters, *fashi*, who practice outside the temple in public. The ritual of the *daoshi* is in the classical language; that of the *fashi* in the vernacular. An entire range of complementary oppositions differentiate the Daoist black-hats from the shamanistic red-hats, but the links between them are numerous.[19]

This was written in 1983. Since then Schipper has elaborated on the complementary oppositions differentiating the black-head from red-head priests, and on the rapprochement between Daoism and popular cults.[20] In his strongest formulation to date, Schipper has defined Daoism as "the written tradition of Chinese indigenous cults."[21] To him, Daoism was never "a religion that became institutionally defined by attaining autonomy from its social background of local cults."[22] It was and is, rather, the "specific and articulated expression of Chinese religion, of its *shehui* or 'assembly of the Earth God.'"[23]

There is a great deal to unpack in such statements. Here I want only to point out that the conclusions of Strickmann and Schipper appear to offer two contradictory assessments of the nature of Daoism. Where Strickmann sees Daoism as a kind of new dispensation that sought to permanently replace the old, eradicating its shamans and local cults, Schipper sees Daoism as a sublimation of shamanism and as a structuring expression of its cults.

Strickmann's view, it seems to me, is deeply colored by the apocalypticism of the late fourth- and fifth-century texts with which he worked. Little consideration is given to the rhetorical nature of these texts. The Manichaean struggle that imbues the *Luxiansheng daomen kelüe*—one of Strickmann's foundational texts—embodied a precise rhetorical strategy to win the favor of an emperor who had good reason to be suspicious of Daoism, having just defeated the Celestial Master-inspired rebellion of Sun En. This text, therefore, seeks not only to distance Daoism from popular religion in the strongest terms but also to distance it from the actual state of affairs and contemporary practice of Celestial Master Daoism itself.[24] Who is to say that the actual state of affairs of Daoism should not be as much a part of what

Daoism was or is as the highly pressured definition given by those who sought to reform it? Perhaps, as Schipper surmises, the insistence with which Daoism denounces popular cults is suspect and betrays a fundamental uneasiness about its origins.

Schipper's view, in contrast, is deeply colored by years of fieldwork on the actual state of contemporary Daoism and on how Daoism fits in with "Chinese religion in its entirety." When Schipper talks about what Daoism is, he is often talking about what Daoism has become, and he occasionally describes what Daoism was in terms of what it is, or identifies "the enduring aspects of Daoism" as the most salient ones historically. Moreover, when Schipper speaks about the rapprochement and complementarity of the *daoshi* and the *fashi*, this is not exactly analogous to Strickmann's contrast between Daoists and "possessed mediums." To refer to red-head priests as "têtes-rouges chamanistes" is either a sleight-of-hand or requires a lengthy historical explanation. Schipper admits elsewhere that when one talks about *daoshi* and *fashi*, one is talking about two traditions within Daoism.[25] In any case, the rapprochement and complementarity that characterize the modern-day relationship between these two figures took a millennium to work out.

If immersion in the texts of Six Dynasties Daoism and prolonged observation of Daoist priests in contemporary Chinese society produce very different notions of Daoism's nature and function, both these views capture an essential truth about Daoism's historical development and its relation to its rival—what Strickmann (following A. R. Stein) refers to as "the nameless religion" and what Schipper (following Piet van der Loon) refers to as "le sustrat shamanique." Daoism's antagonistic and symbiotic relationship to its rival is particularly evident during the Song dynasty, a period that is, not coincidentally, exactly at the midpoint of Strickmann's and Schipper's respective periods of expertise. The Song was a time when Daoism still aspired to define imperial ideology, still managed to capture the attention of large portions of the official and literati class, and still served as a marker of social distance as great as any Confucian paideia. Yet the Song was also a time when, as Schipper remarked above, Daoism became, by assimilation of local cults, the religion of the townspeople. It is, in fact, the assimilation of local cults by Daoism that produced the Daoist Ritual Master (*fashi*, or red-head priest) who, I will argue, mediated between Daoism and the possessed mediums of local cults and village religion.

The Chinese of the Song period were the beneficiaries of a major shift in the center of gravity of their religious institutions, especially of the *she*, or biannual religious celebrations held at the altar of the earth-spirit. By the eleventh and twelfth centuries, the nature of the *she* would shift away from a spring and autumn festival dedicated to various nature or agricultural spirits—a festival exclusive in membership, dominated by a few local families, and overlaid first with Buddhist (sixth-eighth centuries) and then with Confucian (ninth-tenth centuries) activities. The center of gravity moved to a basically urban festival dedicated to one of hundreds of new anthropomorphic or human deities on the god's "birthday"—a festival open in membership, paid for by solicited contributions, dominated by those who could afford the most, and accompanied by processions, theatrical performances, and especially by large-scale Daoist or Buddhist liturgies of renewal and exorcism.[26]

To participate in these new celebrations, generally called "*shehui*," the surrounding towns and villages would bring their own gods (and their spirit-mediums) to serve as subordinate deities (and as subordinate priests) in the rituals. In the urban *shehui*, members of the urban elite (both official and mercantile), together with the clerical elite (Daoist or Buddhist priests), were confirmed in their power in the city and in their control over the hinterland. It is in the urban *shehui* that we can locate the structural context for the symbiosis or rapprochement among Daoist priests, Ritual Masters, and spirit-mediums. The participation of the smaller towns and villages of the hinterland in these urban celebrations established a natural hierarchy in which all these practitioners could be seen to be working together, in succession or simultaneously, inside and outside the temple. This hierarchy was reproduced throughout those areas, particularly in the South, where cities, market towns, and villages were tied together by commercial exchange, and it continues to define the relations among Daoist priests, red-head priests, and *tangki* (spirit-mediums) on Taiwan and elsewhere today.

The emergence of the urban *shehui* after the tenth century did not mean the disappearance of the rural *she*. In the landlocked and mountainous villages, newly opened up by an expanding population and adventurous landlords, a particularly archaic name—"*congci*"—came to designate the altar of the earth-spirit. Here unpredictable and highly sexed spirits were worshipped—the "Spirits of the Five Penetrations" (*wutong shen*) and their ilk, akin to the *nats* of Burma and the *jinn* of Islamic Morocco. These spirits were invariably embodied by a spirit-medium who, as we shall see, was defended by the villagers against all attempts from inside or outside the village to encroach upon his or her autonomy.

By the twelfth century, the contradiction between what I see as the centripetal forces of commercialization and urbanization (forces represented in the urban *shehui*) and the centrifugal forces of demographic and geographic expansion (forces represented in the proliferation of rural *she*) gave new intensity to the old conflict between Daoism and local cults. The Spirits of the Five Penetrations and similar deities of natural villages became the particular bêtes noires of Daoist priests and Daoist Ritual Masters. These "gods" head the list of any Daoist demonology in the twelfth and thirteenth centuries, while the Daoist ritual texts are replete with methods for destroying their altars and the "black magic" of their spirit-mediums. Whereas the villagers thought that these gods brought them life and prosperity, the Daoist knew that they brought only disease, madness, and an early death. In exorcisms the Daoist priest attempted to impose this interpretation on his clients. This interpretation was shared by the official and literati class, and many members of this class linked hands tightly with Daoism and Daoist exorcists in the attempt to eradicate these "demons." I should add parenthetically, however, that even these gods of the village *she* felt the gravitational pull of the urban *shehui*. In the twelfth century, in some areas, the Spirits of the Five Penetrations were reinterpreted so as to better fit the theological expectations of Daoists, officials, and the rest of the literati. Safely transformed or redefined, these gods garnered their own urban temples and *shehui*.

Themes of the Book

All this may be said to constitute the structural backdrop for the themes of symbiosis and antagonism, of ritual convergence and social conflict, that pervade the chapters of this book. Chapter 2 examines a significant body of textual material in the Daoist canon, numbering in the thousands of pages, that is attributable to scores of Daoist lineages that were active in South China during the twelfth and thirteenth centuries. The concern of these lineages was overwhelmingly therapeutic and exorcistic. In addition to a historical and textual study of the

Rites of the Celestial Heart, the Rites of the Five Thunder Gods, and other ritual complexes identified with the new lineages of the twelfth century, this chapter analyzes how these lineages represented a significant break with the orthodox and classical lineages of Daoism and with older, dominant Daoist notions of religious community, sin, and healing. Each of these lineages was defined by a particular method or rite (*fa*), and their practitioners were addressed as Ritual Masters (*fashi*) or Ritual Officers (*faguan*).

These Ritual Masters are examined in Chapter 3. The twelfth-century Ritual Master was a lay (nonclerical) or clerical exorcist who mediated between the Daoist priesthood on the one hand and village spirit-mediums on the other. Chapter 3 examines the Ritual Master's mediating function in terms of the nature of his recruitment, ritual practice, divine pantheon, and working relationship with priests and spirit-mediums. Thus it demonstrates that the Ritual Master was a product of the great historical confrontation between Daoism and local cults, and that he represented a new vernacular culture that stood between the classical, literary culture of priests and officials and the largely martial culture of village spirit-mediums and their cults. This chapter also demonstrates the popularity of the new Daoist lineages among the Song bureaucratic elite. The Rites of the Celestial Heart, the Rites of the Five Thunder Gods, and so forth found fervent devotees among officials and their sons, some of whom actually practiced these exorcistic rituals in the course of their official duties. The Daoist Ritual Master and the Song magistrate linked hands in the twelfth century not only in curing their patients and subjects of demonic obsessions but in ridding them of their demonic cults as well, particularly the cults and temples of local spirit-mediums. The confrontation between Daoist and "official" exorcists and local cults was a unique episode in a more global strategy to suppress spirit-mediums by the representatives of the Song state. This chapter concludes by taking up the strategies and local alliances that permitted the spirit-medium to contend with the pressures of external control, and by considering the elements in the relation between the state and religion that actually mitigated and counteracted the state's repressive policies. One of the many elements working against a European-style inquisition was the fact that the Daoist exorcist had entered into a profound and lasting ritual relationship with the spirit-medium himself.

Chapter 4 looks at the cult to the Black Killer, a god who was honored by the first Song emperors as a guardian of the dynasty and as a guarantor of its possession of the "Mandate of Heaven." In the twelfth century this fierce martial deity would become one of the central divinities of the new therapeutic lineages of Daoism, yet its tenth-century priest already reveals all the characteristics of the twelfth-century Ritual Master.

Chapters 5, 6, and 7 examine the exorcist at work in local society. Chapter 5 analyzes the most characteristic therapeutic ritual of the Daoist exorcist, the Rite of Summoning for Investigation, and demonstrates that this rite was not an exorcism at all but a ritual of spirit-possession in which the demon afflicting the patient was encouraged to possess either the patient himself or a young male surrogate acting as a spirit-medium. These rites are shown to have been particularly compelling because of how they intersected two other institutions in the Song—the judicial trial and the theater.

In Chapters 6 and 7, the focus shifts to Buddhism and to a complex of esoteric therapeutic rituals performed by a class of monks who were in many ways counterparts of the Daoist Ritual Master. These Tantric rituals, like the Daoist ones, involved the possession of a child-medium. In fact, even the Daoist priest and the lowly spirit-medium were performing similar rites, and it is the purpose of a long analysis here to demonstrate that not only the rites but the devotional cults of the four major figures in the Song religious landscape—the Daoist priest, Ritual Master, Buddhist monk, and village spirit-medium—were all converging in the twelfth century.

Chapter 8 takes up Daoist and Buddhist funerary rituals that became in the Song, contrary to much scholarly opinion, a necessary staple of filial expression for the bureaucratic elite. This chapter offers a detailed analysis of the historical development of the Daoist Retreat of the Yellow Register and the Buddhist Retreat of Water and Land. It demonstrates that the structure and purpose of these Daoist and Buddhist mortuary rituals were converging in the Song. The central event of these rites, moreover, turns out to have been the possession of a child-medium (in these cases often a son or grandson of the deceased who transmitted the words of his dead relative or family member). I see in these rituals (1) a co-optation of the traditional ancestor seance of the spirit-medium by the Daoist and Buddhist priesthood; (2) a reinterpretation of archaic Chinese funerary rites that employed someone known as the "corpse-representative"; and, most importantly, (3) a structural convergence with the Rites of Summoning for Investigation. Rituals for the dead were, in fact, exorcisms. In a final example of convergence, these Buddhist and Daoist rites for the dead also came to be performed at the conclusion of the previously examined therapeutic rituals, as a way of satisfying an ancestral spirit who had afflicted a descendant.

Chapter 9 offers an outline of the "syncretic field" of Chinese religions and locates the practitioners and practices within this field.

Methodological Issues

The major methodological innovation of this work lies in its juxtaposition of religious texts (the ritual literature of the Daoist and Buddhist canons) with the miscellaneous writings of Song literati, especially Hong Mai's *Yijian zhi*.[27] A second generation of post-war Daoist scholars is turning increasingly to the texts of Tang and Song Daoism, and thanks to their efforts we are now able to locate many of these texts within a precise matrix of time and space.[28] To this matrix I hope to add a deeper sense of social milieu. My own approach to these texts takes very seriously some of the comments made by John Lagerwey in a review of the principal categories of Daoist ritual texts—namely, those that concern the "offering" (*jiao*), "merit" (*gongde*), and "methods" (*fa*).[29] Lagerwey's remarks all emphasize in one way or another that "a Daoist liturgical text is not a Daoist ritual." He argues first that "all liturgical material in public collections such as the *Daozang* (Daoist canon)—whether imperially sponsored or privately compiled—are farther removed from real performance than are the manuscript texts in possession of hereditary priests." Next, he insists that these materials "would be incomprehensible—and hence useless—if we could not compare [them] with their living counterparts," and finally, he provides numerous reasons why "the gap between texts and performances is even greater in the case of Daoist ritual than that of Chinese opera," and therefore can only loosely be compared to a theatrical script.[30] The gap is particularly formidable in the case of the "method" texts (those devoted to small-scale rituals to solve specific problems, such as exorcisms) that are the principal texts used in my study. According to Lagerwey, the method texts are the most laconic with respect to the rituals to which they refer, and vary not only from region to region but from priest to priest.[31]

Given the fact that this work focuses on a period in the remote past for which we cannot roam the countryside collecting manuscripts or observing ritual performances, are our efforts to use or understand the ritual texts of the Daoist canon condemned to futility? Fortunately, I believe, the close reading and the creative use of the literary anecdotes that make up Hong Mai's *Yijian zhi* can bring us as close to historical fieldwork as we will ever get in using a text of pre-modern China. The *Yijian zhi* is not a scientific, Western-style ethnology. It is, however, unique in the genre of "miscellaneous notes" for its overwhelming concern with the ritual practices and religious expectations of both the lower and upper strata of Chinese society. This concern represents neither the eccentric tastes of the author nor the timeworn obsession of literati with the strange and extraordinary. If one isolates only those anecdotes in the *Yijian zhi* that concern Hong Mai's family, we find that its members included lay initiates in Daoist mysteries, apprentices to spirit-mediums, guardians of Daoist texts, demoniacs, habitual employers of Daoist and Buddhist exorcists, and devotees of Daoist and Buddhist divinities. Although this family boasted numerous high-degree holders, officials, and erudite classicists, its feet were firmly planted in the rich soil of China's religious traditions. Such easy commerce between Song literati and China's religious patrimony was, I believe, more typical and revealing of Song culture than the defenders of an exclusivist Neo-Confucianism are wont to admit.

Although we find useful discussions about—and occasional insights into—the nature and compilation of Hong Mai's massive work, attempts to characterize it as a whole have been less than satisfactory. To state, for example, that "the simple, sometimes monotonous, structure of the tales and their frequent repetition of the same themes testify persuasively to their origin as folktales"[32] seems to me an utterly fallacious inference; to accept that "by identifying his informants, Hong Mai places himself squarely in the *zhiguai* ['strange tale'] tradition"[33] may blind us to serious and substantive differences; to quip that the *Yijian zhi* was "the 'Ripley's Believe It or Not' of the late twelfth century"[34] only trivializes a very complex work.

Given a rigorous definition of the folktale, I believe that very few of the anecdotes in the *Yijian zhi* can be said to so derive. The anecdotes of the *Yijian zhi* range from hagiography to high-placed gossip, from reportage to the generic reconfiguration of the events related, from outside to inside styles of narration. The distinction between outside and inside styles of narration—between what G. Genette calls "heterodiegesis" and "homodiegesis," respectively[35]—is a distinction between narrative postures. It has been elaborated on by John Winkler.[36] In heterodiegesis, the narrator is outside the story; he or she is a purveyor of fiction, a sheer storyteller. Not many of the anecdotes of the *Yijian zhi* are heterodiegetic. In homodiegesis, the narrator does not tell a story but tells what happened and belongs to the same world as the characters, whatever part he or she played or did not play in the events. In homodiegesis, there are degrees of insidedness. The narrator may claim to know something directly because he or she was there at the events (intradiegesis), or he or she may know something from others who were there (extradiegesis).

In the *Yijian zhi* the degrees of insidedness are even more attenuated and refined. Extradiegetically, Hong Mai may also know something from a colleague, kinsman, friend, or neighbor of someone who was there, or he may know something because he read a private account of someone who was there—a diary, perhaps, or commemorative poem. One distinction between the "strange tale" (*zhiguai*) tradition and the *Yijian zhi* is that in the former homodiegetic techniques ("I saw this," "I heard this from . . .") serve the largely heterodiegetic end of sheer storytelling, whereas in the latter the homodiegetic aim of telling what happened is, on occasion, shaped by heterodiegetic forms.

Any attempt to say something significant about the character of the *Yijian zhi* as a whole emerges only from a sustained analysis of its individual anecdotes and from the strength of the interpretive use to which that analysis is put. This book focuses on a well-defined group of homodiegetic narratives that concern spirit-possession and therapeutic ritual. In all cases we must be sensitive to those occasions when Hong Mai's reasons either for telling what happened or for declining to name an informant or participant serve distinctly political or social ends. We must also be sensitive to the weight of literary genre on a particular attempt to tell what happened—the weight of the "demon story," say, on an account of an exorcistic ritual. This is by no means easy to sort out because the structure of the "demon story" itself had long been determined by the structure of exorcistic ritual.

Yet the evidentiary status of the *Yijian zhi*, its usefulness as a document of social history, does not ultimately rest on our ability to distill the prejudicial or the generic from any given anecdote. The *Yijian zhi* is primarily a record of subjective experiences, a document of private life that contrasts with such public documents as historical biographies, eulogies, and grave inscriptions, all of which mark out a lifetime in terms of the objective symbols of bureaucratic and family advancement. This still begs the question, however, because most of the anecdotes in the *Yijian zhi* do not record the subjective experiences of Hong Mai or his family, but the experiences of others that were reported to him or that he otherwise obtained. On what basis, then, can we trust the factualness of the anecdotes in the *Yijian zhi*?

In terms of the subject of this study—namely, the social history of spirit-possession and exorcism in the twelfth century—we can begin to establish trust by juxtaposing a carefully arranged sequence of anecdotes with a large body of canonical ritual texts that refer to exactly the same events. Almost every anecdote I have selected records ritual processes that can be confirmed down to the smallest detail by independent sources. Even those elements that appear to us as quite fantastic—elements that are often related to the representation of the behavior of demons—become decidedly less so in light of the canonical texts. For example, when demons are described in the anecdotes as appearing as objective entities, this usually corresponds to the precise moments in the ritual texts when the demons are visualized by the priest, and when demons are described as speaking, this corresponds to the moments in the texts when they possess the patient.

Now, if the *Yijian zhi*, or at least the anecdotes from it that I employ, are consistently correct about extremely esoteric matters of ritual, should we not also take seriously their evidence about the setting of these rituals—that is, the social relations of the priests, monks, and other exorcists, and of the families who hired them? It is difficult, if not impossible, to settle the question of factualness definitively. But in addition to building up trust by comparing anecdotes and canonical ritual texts, the anecdotes I have chosen appear to be believable based on everything I know and can learn about Song society. For instance, thanks to the work of social historians such as Patricia Ebrey and Gudula Linck, we have learned that in the twelfth and thirteenth centuries a woman's legal, economic, and personal ties to her natal family persisted long after marriage and with greater intensity than in earlier or later dynasties. Can it therefore be an accident that the issue raised over and over again in the cases of psychosomatic illness in the *Yijian zhi* is precisely the trauma that women experienced when trying to maintain these ties in the face of separation?

In this work, I have wherever possible translated rather than paraphrased or simply referred to the anecdotes that are important for my subject. I have done so for a very precise reason. In the paraphrase, the historian tends to discard what seems superfluous (supplemental), so that what is included serves the overarching, teleological narratives of history and historiography. Paraphrase, in other words, tends to close off interpretation and fails to release what Joel Fineman finds to be the unique potential of the anecdote to "effect the real" and to provide "an opening to history."[37]

2

Therapeutic Movements in the Song: Texts

The emergence in the twelfth century of a class of exorcists called "Ritual Masters" (*fashi*) coincides more or less with the appearance of a large corpus of textual material, preserved in the Daoist canon, that was the patrimony of a plethora of new Daoist lineages active in South and particularly Southeast China during the twelfth, thirteenth, and fourteenth centuries. The overwhelming concern of these lineages was therapeutic and exorcistic. Each specialized in a particular method (*fa*), and their practitioners are addressed in the texts as either "Ritual Master" or "Ritual Officer" (*faguan*). The most important of these new lineages, or at least the ones we encounter most frequently in the twelfth century, were those that specialized in the "Rectifying Rites of the Celestial Heart" (*Tianxin zhengfa*) and in the "Rites of the Five Thunder [Gods]" (*Wulei fa*). Because we will refer to these lineages over and over again, I first provide a summary but detailed account of their histories.

The Rites of the Celestial Heart

Thanks largely to Poul Andersen, we now have a better understanding of the "Rites of Tianxin" than of any other therapeutic movement of the Song. Andersen's meticulous analysis of the provenance and transmission of the texts of the *Tianxin zhengfa* and its derivatives allows us to outline the history of this movement with both confidence and economy.[1]

Although this Daoist lineage would come to center in Jiangxi, the putative and, I believe, probable patriarch of its rites was a tenth-century Daoist priest from Quanzhou (Fujian) named Tan Zixiao. While serving the fourth ruler of the state of Min in Fuzhou (Wang Chang, r. 935–939), Tan was asked to interpret a set of talismans unearthed by Chen Shouyuan, a politically influential spirit-medium at court.[2] Based on his understanding of these talismans, Tan announced that he had obtained the Rectifying Rites of Tianxin of Zhang Daoling, the late Han founder of religious Daoism. Lu You (1125–1210) states in his *History of the Southern Tang* that practitioners of the *Tianxin zhengfa* in his time all considered Tan Zixiao to have been the founder of their lineage.[3] Although we have no idea about the nature of these talismans, what would distinguish this Daoist lineage from others was, in fact, a precise set of talismans, one of which embodied the divinity Heisha, or the Black Killer, of whom Tan was a fervent devotee.[4] Tan's collaboration with a spirit-medium, moreover, is significant because spirit-mediums would come to play an important role in the continuing revelation of talismans to, and in the therapeutic rituals of, twelfth-century practitioners of the Rites of Tianxin.[5]

After the fall of the state of Min in 944, Tan Zixiao fled to Lushan in northern Jiangxi, where he acquired over a hundred students. One of these was Rao Dongtian, a former minor official in Linchuan, Jiangxi, who had retired to Mount Huagai in central Jiangxi.[6] One evening in 994, Rao was led by a heavenly light to a particular spot on one of the summits of Huagaishan. There he discovered a bookcase filled with the "Secret Formulas of Tianxin." At the suggestion of a spiritual being, Rao apprenticed himself to Tan Zixiao, who initiated him in the Rites of Tianxin. Tan also recommended that Rao seek further counsel from the Lord of the Eastern Marchmount (Dongyue jun, i.e., the god of Taishan), who endowed him with an array of spirit-soldiers (*yinbing*) as protection.[7]

The Rites of Tianxin passed from Rao Dongtian through four generations of masters to a man named Deng Yougong. Deng lived on or around Mount Huagai during the latter half of the eleventh century. He composed *The Rectifying Rites of the Celestial Heart of Highest Purity* (*Shangqing Tianxin zhengfa*, HY 566). Based on internal evidence, Poul Andersen argues that Deng's preface to this work was written before 1075, but that the seven chapters of the canonical text are an expanded mid-twelfth-century version of a work composed by Deng sometime before 1100.[8] Deng's work lays out the fundamental talismans of the therapeutic rituals of Tianxin. These include the Talisman of the Three Luminosities (*Sanguang fu*), the Talisman of the Black Killer (*Heisha fu*), the Talisman of the Guideline of Heaven (*Tiangang fu*),[9] and nine additional talismans, transmitted by Zhang Daoling, known collectively as the "Spinal Numinous Writ" (*Gusui lingwen*).[10] These talismans and the exorcistic rituals that employed them were intended to embody the power of the various divinities that I will discuss at length in connection with the early Song Ritual Master Zhang Shouzhen—namely, the Emperor of the North, who presides over the Department of Exorcism, and his spiritual agents Tianpeng, Heisha, and Zhenwu, among many others.[11] An anonymous Southern Song work entitled *The Rectifying Rites of the Celestial Heart of the Northern Pole of Highest Purity* (*Shangqing beiji Tianxin zhengfa*, HY 567) expands on the internal meditations and circulation of pneumas involved in the writing of the talismans.[12]

Sometime before 1116, Deng Yougong also edited a text that he attributes to Rao Dongtian and identifies with "the secret writings" discovered by Rao on Mount Huagai. This is entitled *The Demon Code of the "Spinal Numinous Writ" of Highest Purity* (*Shangqing Gusui lingwen guilu*, HY 461) and is based on five different versions that Deng himself collected from various Daoist abbeys in northern Jiangxi.[13] The text includes a set of regulations governing the behavior of demons and spirits, which is the Demon Code itself; regulations for clerical initiation, called "Jade Models" (*yuge*); and lists of clerical titles and documentary forms under the rubric "Rituals and Formulas" (*yishi*). Rao Dongtian, having been an official himself, ostensibly based this code on "the laws and regulations of secular administration."[14] Deng mentions in his preface that similar but inadequate "Demon Codes" were currently in the possession of lay (i.e., unordained) masters (*sushi*).[15] I will have more to say about these "lay masters" and their "Demon Codes" later on.

About the time Deng was completing his edition of Rao's *Demon Code*, a man named Yuan Miaozong was performing exorcisms for the people of Nanyang. In 1115, Yuan was summoned to the capital in Kaifeng to take part in the compilation of texts for a new, printed edition of the Daoist canon. To redress what he saw to be a marked deficiency in therapeutic texts, Yuan began work on *The Secret Essentials of the Totality of the Perfected, of [Lord Lao] the Most High, for Assist-*

ing the Country and Saving the People (*Taishang jiuguo jiumin zongzhen biyao*, HY 1217), which was submitted to the throne in 1116. *The Secret Essentials* is the largest compendium of, and our principal source for, the exorcistic rituals of Tianxin. Yuan traces the Tianxin tradition back from Rao Dongtian and Tan Zixiao to Zhang Daoling. The relation of the *Tianxin zhengfa* to the Orthodox Unity tradition begun by Zhang is an issue I address later on. Because I refer to this text over and over again, there is no need to review its contents here, except to point out the overwhelming coherence between its talismans, seals, divinities, and rituals and those of its textual antecedents.[16]

The Rites of the Five Thunder Gods

The history of Thunder Magic in the Song presents difficulties entirely different from that of the Rites of Tianxin. First, the compilation of a textual tradition was a somewhat belated event with respect to the practice of Thunder Magic. The relation of the early practitioners and what they practiced to the textual tradition is problematic. Second, there is no basic text or set of texts that can be granted priority—that is, from which others derived or by which they were influenced in part. Thunder Magic was a kind of generic practice that could be and was adopted by many Daoist lineages, including the one that practiced the Rites of Tianxin. There were as many styles of Thunder Magic as there were Daoist lineages. This, along with the sheer volume of textual material, goes a long way toward explaining why few scholars have undertaken its systematic study; when they have studied it at all, the results have often been confusing or unsatisfying.[17]

As a natural phenomenon, thunder had long been perceived as both a beneficial and a harmful force, a welcome sign of rain and an unexpected cause of fire. In accordance with this archaic perception, Thunder Magic was simply a human attempt to ritually harness the benevolent and destructive power of this spectacular cosmic manifestation in order to bring relief in times of drought and destroy demons in the event of illness. The divinization of thunder was already well established in classical times.[18] By the Tang, the focus of the cult had shifted to a Thunder God temple in Leizhou (Guangdong),[19] which spawned many temples throughout the South.

Magicians who summoned thunder and lightning to various ends appear in the sources as far back as the Han.[20] Only one of these pre-

Song examples seems to be relevant with respect to the Daoist thunder rites of the twelfth and thirteenth centuries. Du Guangting's *Shenxian ganyu zhuan* (HY 592) includes a biography of a late Tang native of Xinzhou, Jiangxi, named Ye Qianshao.[21] As a youth, the Lord of Thunder (Leigong) appeared to Ye during a rainstorm, and on the following day transmitted to him a single scroll that enabled its possessor to bring down thunder and rain and to cure sickness for the benefit of mankind. The scroll actually contained rites for summoning the five Thunder Gods, brothers of the Lord of Thunder himself and obvious forerunners of the Prime Marshals of the Five Thunders (Wulei yuanshuai) central to the Thunder Magic schools of the Song. Evidently they were so violent that the Lord of Thunder warned Ye that these divinities could not be summoned except in the most calamitous circumstances. Their violence would continue to present problems for devotees in the Song.[22] Ye soon found an opportunity to demonstrate their destructive power when he was arrested for drunken rowdiness in the marketplace of Jizhou, Jiangxi, and taunted with insults by the local prefect (*taishou*). After forcing this person to submit ignominiously to a thunderous assault, Ye's reputation carried him throughout the towns south of the Yangzi (Jiangzhe), writing and transmitting talismans, exorcizing demons, and making rain. It is said that Ye neither kept a vegetarian diet nor cultivated the Dao.

The career of Ye Qianshao is paradigmatic of the unmediated relationship with a divinity, the peripatetic lifestyle, and the therapeutic activities of the lay Daoist exorcist of the Song, whom we will examine shortly in great detail. Although we cannot yet speak here of Daoist Thunder Magic as it evolved in the Song, a significant segment of those who practiced the Rites of the Five Thunder Gods in the twelfth century cannot be said to have practiced it with any more sophistication than Ye Qianshao and were quite ignorant of its theoretical and ritual elaboration.

It is precisely this elaboration that came to define Daoist Thunder Magic proper in the Song. The summoning of Thunder Gods to bring rain and to exorcise demons came to be supported by a vast ethical, cosmological, and ritual scaffolding.[23] First, the destructive power of thunder became ethicized. Long thought to be an expression of heavenly anger, particularly with respect to unfilial behavior,[24] thunder became, in its divinized and personified form, the executor of heavenly punishment. And the Daoist practitioner who embodied and directed its power on behalf of Heaven was, above all, an administrator of justice, upholding orthodox values against evil demons and the cults that lay behind them. It was this function that would highly recommend Thunder Magic to Song magistrates.

Second, thunder became bureaucratized and cosmologized. On the one hand, the various schools of Thunder Magic created complex systems of imperial courts, departments, and prisons, infinitely tesserated hierarchies of officials, spirit-generals and -soldiers, and mythic genealogies linking all these to the supreme divinities of the Daoist heavens. On the other hand, thunder was transformed from a manifestation of nature into the controlling power of the cosmos itself, the pivot of Heaven and Earth and the power of transformation behind the continuous alternation of *yin* and *yang*. The point of Thunder Magic, therefore, was to plug into this cosmic force and, as one text says, literally to "hold the power of transformation in the palm of one's hand." To do so, Daoists erected a vast ritual apparatus defined above all by the complex meditations of internal or physiological alchemy (*neidan*). Using these meditations, which vary endlessly with respect to the school and task, the practitioner learned to reproduce and store thunder within his own body, to generate and summon the Thunder Gods, and to create, vitalize, and project the talismans that embody their power.

Hung Mai's *Yijian zhi* confirms the ubiquity of Daoist masters of the Rites of the Five Thunder Gods throughout the twelfth century. The person who is generally acknowledged to have made an early and formative contribution to the development of the Daoist tradition is Lin Lingsu (1076–1120). Lin was born to a poor family in the port city of Wenzhou in southern Zhejiang. His remarkable career ultimately brought him to Kaifeng as part of the emperor Huizong's general call for participation in the project of publishing a Daoist canon. Lin distinguished himself from others, first as the revealer and sponsor of a new scriptural tradition identified with the gods of a heretofore unknown part of the cosmos, the Divine Empyrean (*Shenxiao*), and second as the inspiration for the emperor's self-proclaimed incarnation as the "Great Monarch of Everlasting Life" (Changsheng dadi), the central divinity of this most sublime of Daoist heavens.[25]

The school spawned by Lin's revelation passed from Zhang Ruhui in the first generation to Chen Daoyi in the second, Lu Ye in the third, and Liu Yu in the fourth. Liu Yu and his teacher, Lu Ye, were responsible for compiling *The Great Rites of the Divine Empyrean of the Golden*

Flame Celestial Stalwart, in which the Thunder Gods are given a prominent role.[26] The history of Daoist thunder ritual and cosmology is, in fact, inseparable from the texts inspired by Lin Lingsu's revelation of the Divine Empyrean. This is evident in such theoretical works as *The Jade Scripture of the Thunderclap,*[27] as well as in such large ritual compendia as *The Great Rites in Purple Script of the Most High Divine Empyrean.*[28] Although Lin Lingsu is credited as both a master of Shenxiao and as a practitioner of Thunder Magic, his role in the process of integrating the two traditions is far from certain.

According to Lin's biography in *The Comprehensive Mirror of Immortals,* when Lin was traveling in Shanxi as a young man, he encountered a holy man (*daoren*) later identified as Zhao Sheng, a disciple of Zhang Daoling.[29] Zhao transmitted to him a three-volume, nineteen-chapter work entitled *The Jade Book of the Heavenly Altars of the Divine Empyrean,* which included spells and talismans for controlling thunder and lightning in order to exorcise demons and cure illness. Zhao subsequently conferred upon Lin the titles "Master of the Teaching of the Divine Empyrean" and "Great Judicial Officer of the Thunderclap." The more contemporary but unflattering account of Lin preserved in the *Bin Tuilu* places this mysterious encounter in Sichuan, and states that from this time on Lin practiced the "Rites of the Five Thunders." The *Song History* also emphasizes Lin's mastery of Thunder Magic. There he is described as a devotee of the popular Thunder God cults of the Southeast and as ultimately seeking instruction in Daoism from Zhang Jixian, the thirtieth Celestial Master, on Mount Longhu in Jiangxi.

The Divine Empyrean, Thunder Magic, and the Celestial Masters are brought together in another passage in Lin's biography in *The Comprehensive Mirror.* After Lin arrived at court, he was asked to collect and submit to the throne the various works on thunder ritual (*wulei fa*) for inclusion in the Daoist canon. Apparently, the first Celestial Master had possessed a certain *Thunder Book of the Divine Empyrean* (*Shenxiao leishu*) in twenty volumes. Ten volumes of this work had been transmitted by the eighth Celestial Master to the present, while the rest had disappeared. Five of the lost volumes, it was now discovered, had been revealed to the early Song Ritual Master Zhang Shouzhen by the Perfected Lord "Protector of Sageliness" (i.e., the Black Killer), and the remaining five were now mysteriously revealed to Lin himself by the Emperor on High.[30]

All this is quite fantastical, and, needless to say, I can find no trace of such a book in Daoist bibliographies or the Ming canon. Moreover, though it is not impossible that Lin was a popular practitioner of Thunder Magic—though even here I have my doubts—it seems more probable that the integration of the Rites of the Five Thunders and the Rites of Shenxiao was a gradual process that Lin Lingsu was belatedly honored as having established willy-nilly. Lin left his mark on only one text in the Ming-dynasty canon, *A Song of the Flaming Bell of the Three Emanations of the Divine Empyrean and the Celestial Stalwart of Metal and Fire.*[31] He was, I believe, an inspired cosmographer and poetic visionary, but the textual elaboration of Thunder Magic by the school he founded was primarily the work of others.[32]

One of these was another first-generation disciple of Lin Lingsu named Wang Wenqing (1093–1153). Like Lin, Wang was from Wenzhou and was summoned to the court in Kaifeng. Yet unlike Lin, we have confirmation of Wang's practice of Thunder Magic in a non-Daoist source, the *Yijian zhi.* One anecdote states that "Wang Wenqing's disciple Zheng the Daoist Priest (Zheng Daoshi) obtained from him the Rites of the Five Thunder [Gods]";[33] another, that "Wang's technique was none other than the Rites of the Five Thunder [Gods]";[34] and still another, that "when Fu Xuan became the Assistant Regional Governor of Jiangxi, he invited Wang Shichen [i.e., Wang Wenqing] from Linchuan to come to Yuzhang and studied Thunder Rites (*leifa*) with him."[35] Wang, moreover, produced numerous disciples[36] and was responsible for several basic texts on Thunder Magic in the canon.

Chapters 56 through 100 of the *Daofa huiyuan* (*Corpus of Rites of the Dao*), for example, appear to constitute a coherent, or at least related, tradition of Thunder Magic attributed to the Tang-dynasty Fire Master (*huoshi*) Wang Zihua.[37] Many of the texts in this group invoke one or more of three spirit-generals, the Celestial Lords Deng, Xin, and Zhang. Wang Wenqing was responsible for the prefaces, and perhaps the texts themselves, of chapters 56 and 61, for a theoretical discussion of thunder cosmology in chapter 67, for all of chapter 69, and for the editing of chapter 70.[38]

The *Daomen shigui* (*Ten Statutes for Followers of the Way*), a Ming text, states that the Shenxiao (Divine Empyrean) lineage itself was founded by Wang the Fire Master *and* Wang Wenqing, from whom it was passed to Zhang, Li, Bo (Yuchan), Sa (Shoujian), Fan (Songnian), Yang

(Jingchang), Dang, Mo (Yueding), and others.[39] Indeed, when we review the contents of chapters 56 through 100 of the *Daofa huiyuan*, we find that, among these so-called Shenxiao masters, Bo Yuchan wrote a commentary to chapter 70, the preface to chapter 76, and all of chapter 82; Sa Shoujian composed another theoretical treatise on thunder and ritual instructions in chapter 67; Fan Songnian and Yang Jingchang are mentioned as the authors of chapters 80 and 81; and Mo Yueding transmitted "the oral instructions for writing talismans" in chapter 77. Can we not conclude, then, that the "Shenxiao" lineage described in the *Daomen shigui* is none other than the very same lineage attributed to the Fire Master and associated with forty-four chapters from the *Daofa huiyuan?*

Although Wang Wenqing evidently played a formative role in the development of the practice and theory of Daoist Thunder Magic, the constitution of this textual tradition began, I suspect, with Bo Yuchan and those who followed him. Bo Yuchan (1194?–1229) was born in Minqing county in Fujian, trained in Qiongzhou on Hainan Island, and focused his pedagogical activities on Mount Wuyi in northern Fujian.[40] By his own account, Bo was a major beneficiary and organizer of the Divine Empyrean and Thunderclap traditions, as well as a practitioner of Thunder Magic and an astute and critical genealogist of its various schools.[41] He wrote, moreover, some notes (*ti*) on the major text integrating Thunder Magic and Shenxiao cosmology, namely, *The Jade Scripture of the Thunderclap*, examined superficially above.[42] According to his notes, this scripture was circulated by a man named Zhang Yuanduan on Mount Wuyi and passed to Bo by Zhang's son. If Bo Yuchan played a central role in the editing of this and other important texts on Thunder Magic,[43] then this would provide additional evidence to support the notion that, in contrast to the Tianxin tradition, the center of gravity of the textual canonization of Thunder Magic should be placed in the early thirteenth century. Recall that Liu Ye and Lu Yu, the third- and fourth-generation disciples of Lin Lingsu, occupied the most important editorial positions in the textual compilation of Lin's tradition, again highlighting the first half of the thirteenth century. It was during the same period, finally, that a third great textual tradition of thunder ritual was formed under the rubric "Qingwei" (Pure Tenuity).

The Qingwei was the ultimate accretionist tradition, unifying all the great lineages of middle-period Daoism and assimilating the cosmology of the Divine Empyrean, elements of Tantric Buddhism, and various local exorcistic cults. Thunder Magic is a prominent feature of the Qingwei ritual texts, which occupy the first fifty-five chapters of the *Daofa huiyuan*. The legendary founder of the Qingwei tradition was a late ninth–early tenth-century female adept named Zu Shu. The compiler of the tradition, however, was Huang Shunshen (b. 1224), a native of Jianning (Fujian) and an official in Guangxi.[44] From Huang, the Qingwei tradition was apparently transmitted north by Zhang (Shouqing) of Mount Wudang (Hubei), and throughout the South by Xiong (Daohui) of Mount Xi (Jiangxi).[45] There is no need to pursue this any further here. In addition to the Divine Empyrean, Fire Master, and Pure Tenuity styles of Thunder Magic, there were others, represented by individual chapters in the *Daofa huiyuan*.[46]

The Rites of Tianxin and the Rites of the Five Thunder Gods were clearly the most popular, but by no means the only, new therapeutic movements of the twelfth and thirteenth centuries. Many more are represented in the 268 chapters of the *Daofa huiyuan*, a fourteenth-century compilation of ritual, theoretical, and legalistic texts that were circulating among various southern Daoist lineages during the preceding two centuries.[47] I refer to the content of this collection repeatedly in the course of this book. For the moment, what needs to be said is that each of these lineages was associated with one or more martial deities generally referred to as "Generals" (*jiangjun*), "Prime Marshals" (*yuanshuai*), or "Spiritual Officers" (*lingguan*). The Daoist practitioner—the Ritual Master (*fashi*) or Ritual Officer (*faguan*)—controlled these deities by means of registers, talismans, spells, and seals in order to dispel demons from an individual, family, or community. Many lineages formed around cults to individual deities such as Ma Sheng, Zhu Yan, or Chen Danian.[48] Some of these, as well as others, were distinguished by the transformation of the Ritual Master into the divinity itself and by his use of a spirit-medium, a young boy to whom was transferred the demon afflicting the patient. At this level of generalization, these texts should be read as the literary residue of a creative confrontation and accommodation between Daoism and local cults or village religion. The Ritual Master was at one and the same time midwife and human precipitate of this confrontation.

To some scholars, the appearance of the lineages represented by the Rites of Tianxin, Thunder Magic, and the texts of the *Daofa huiyuan* marks a profound shift in the history of Daoism itself. In a conference paper several years ago, Michel Strickmann argued that as late as the eleventh century, Daoism "was epitomized in the official and popular mind not so much by its urban temples as by its great mountain centers of pilgrimage and ascetic practice" (i.e., Maoshan in Jiangsu and Gezaoshan and Longhushan, both in Jiangxi).[49] Citing the contents of the *Yunji qiqian*, the great Daoist *summa* published sometime after 1028, and the overwhelming dominance of the Maoshan lineage in official and court circles during the Tang and Northern Song, Strickmann saw a continuity of meditational and liturgical practice from the fifth century until Emperor Huizong (r. 1101–1125) turned his attention to some of the new revelations outlined above. Strickmann perhaps placed too much emphasis on imperial or official patronage in drawing the broad contours of Daoist history; he thereby managed to finesse the problem of the historical relation between the new Daoist lineages and the great medieval traditions, especially the Celestial Master tradition, whose therapeutic concerns and involvement in local society ran long and deep. If, as Strickmann says, the new Daoist lineages posed a direct challenge to the older orders, then the Celestial Masters could best meet this challenge by claiming many of these new lineages as their own (more on this later).[50]

Still, Strickmann's recognition of a sea change in Daoist history was both prescient and insightful. First, the focus of these new revelations and lineages was overwhelmingly therapeutic and exorcistic, rather than liturgical, meditational, or related to a personal and graduated ascesis. Second, their pantheons were dominated by martial, humanized, and historicized deities rather than by cosmic powers, immortals, or emanations of the Dao. Third, their texts often reflect the practices of an unorganized class of lay Daoist practitioners, some living within the communities or among the families whom they served, others traveling throughout the villages and towns of South China, performing exorcisms. Many of these exorcists existed outside the Daoist religious organization and hierarchy.

The Daoist priest (*daoshi*), like the Buddhist monk, was subject to a process of examination, ordination certification, and temple affiliation and residence, all administered by the Board of Rites. The extent to which the Daoist priesthood ever conformed to the ascetic or monastic model envisioned by this policy is questionable, however. The Southern Song Daoist exegete Jin Yunzhong remarked critically on the number of priests in his day who had obtained Daoist registers yet who still lived and practiced within the boundaries of family life (*zai-jia*). What does distinguish the Daoist priest is precisely these registers (*lu*), the transmission of which was controlled ostensibly by the priests and ordination centers of Maoshan, Gezaoshan, and Longhushan. In the Song, there were seven types of registers corresponding to seven levels of initiation, though instruction in and transmission of the first, the "Register of the Authority of the Covenant of Orthodox Unity" (*Zhengyi mengwei lu*), was sufficient to grant the acolyte the clerical title of "*daoshi*."[51] The lay exorcist, in contrast, eluded this formal initiation, acquiring his registers, talismans, and texts by a variety of unorthodox means: in visions, by revelation, pursuant to mysterious encounters with holy men, or simply by windfall or purchase.[52]

The anecdotes in Hung Mai's *Yijian zhi* explicitly refer to the lay practitioner of the Rites of Tianxin or Rites of the Five Thunder Gods as a "*fashi.*" This is also the title conferred upon the practitioner who is addressed in the canonical texts, which is not to suggest that the person so addressed was not a Daoist priest (*daoshi*). Daoist priests were clearly the compilers of, and the intended audience for, many of these texts. The *fashi* was simply a master (*shi*) of the rites (*fa*) of a particular exorcistic tradition the instructions for which were conferred upon the acolytes along with a corresponding register. *The Jade Models of the Celestial Altar of Taishang* asserts that if the priest is to practice the Rites of Tianxin, he must first receive the "Register of All Merit of the Three and the Five" (*Sanwu dougong lu*); if he is to practice the Rites of Thunder, he must first receive the "Register of the Divine Empyrean of the Most High" (*Gaoshang Shenxiao lu*); and so forth. The passage goes on to mention eight other exorcistic traditions and their corresponding registers. The list reveals no particular hierarchy of initiation, and, as we shall see, a priest could launch an entire career based exclusively on his expertise in one or another of these exorcistic rituals. At the same time, however, it is clear that by the Song period, the term "*fashi*," or "Ritual Master," had also come to denote a class of lay exorcists who were explicitly distinguished from Daoist priests. The relation between these lay and clerical exorcists was nonetheless extremely fluid, and many of the latter were hardly distinguishable from their unordained counterparts. Exploring the contours of this relationship will occupy most of the next section.

The term "*fashi*" has a long and intricate history in the context of medieval Daoism. It figures prominently, for example, in *The Scripture of the Spirit-Spells from the Abyss of the Most High* (*Taishang dongyuan shen-zhou jing*, HY 335), which has been studied by Christine Mollier.[53] The first ten chapters of this text had their origins among the members of a Daoist community in fifth-century Jiangnan. This popular apocalyptic movement existed at the margins of the Celestial Master sect. Its leaders were individuals called "Preceptors of the Three Caverns" (*Sandong fashi*), the Three Caverns being, in this context, a euphemism for Daoism.[54] These "preceptors" were proselytizing and itinerant ritual therapists whom Mollier contrasts with the hierarchical and hereditary clergy, or "libationers" (*jijiu*), of the Celestial Master sect. Similarly, Mollier has identified two scriptures dedicated to the Emperor of the North (Beidi) with another apocalyptic community in the lower Yangzi region during the fourth and fifth centuries. The priests of this community were called "Preceptors of Samādhi of the Emperor of the North" (*Beidi sanmei fashi*). They, too, were itinerant exorcists who performed large-scale communal exorcisms in addition to private cures at the homes of their devotees.[55]

Mollier suggests that the idea of a missionary priesthood may have been borrowed directly from Buddhism.[56] This suggests to me, in turn, that the title of these priests may also have been borrowed from Buddhism—from the "Dharma Master" (*fashi*), or "Preacher of the Law," to whom *The Lotus Sūtra* devotes an entire chapter. It is clear from numerous studies of the early development of Mahāyāna Buddhism in China that the term "*fashi*" (Skt. *Dharmabhāṇaka*) designated proselytizers, and specifically lay householders, as opposed to monks who recited and explained *The Prajñāpāramitā Sūtra*.[57] This is why, at this early stage in the Daoist use of the term "*fashi*," I have translated it as "preceptor" rather than "ritual master."

Be that as it may, by the Tang, when the various Daoist traditions had become organized hierarchically into a single ordination system, the title "*fashi*" became the appellation conferred upon a "disciple of pure faith" (*qingxin dizi*) who had mastered, and then formally received, a particular group of texts along with their corresponding registers and regulations, all of which corresponded, in turn, to a particular tradition and/or section of the Daoist canon.[58]

None of this really prepares us for the Song-dynasty use of the term "*fashi*" to designate a class of lay Daoist practitioners—or even a group of clerical exorcists who looked very much like them. There are, however, antecedents for, if not direct ancestors of, such exorcists. There is, for example, the ancient "Master of [Demonic] Projection" (*fang-xiang shi*), who served, and even transformed himself into, a fierce martial deity in order to expel demons from tombs and the imperial court. In the Tang, we also find a group of practitioners known as "Master Demon Seers" (*jiangui shi*), and of course there is the perennial spirit-medium (*wu*), whose influence on the therapeutic practices of the Song Ritual Master may have been more profound than is commonly thought. All of these were exclusively or primarily exorcists, as will be acknowledged in the following chapters. The influence of Esoteric Buddhist exorcisms on Daoist Ritual Masters must also be considered. Mantras, mudrās, and Tantric iconography and paraphernalia figure prominently in the texts of the new Daoist therapeutic movements of the Song. Many lay Daoist exorcists of the twelfth century, moreover, counted themselves as devotees of Tantric cults, and some of their distinctive ritual practices have antecedents in a set of popular Tantric scriptures composed in China during the eighth and ninth centuries. Exploring the complex relationship between the Daoist Ritual Master and Tantric exorcists, both past and present, will occupy most of Chapters 6 and 7.[59]

However many antecedents we may find for the Daoist Ritual Master, however far back we may trace the origins of the new therapeutic lineages of the Song, both the new ritual traditions and their clerical and lay practitioners come into sharper focus only in the twelfth century. This higher profile may be explained in part by the attention paid to these practitioners and traditions by the emperor Huizong and by the Daoist religious organization, especially the Celestial Master sect. We must assess their contributions very carefully.

In the early part of Huizong's reign, the emperor continued to support the traditional Daoist lineages, their temples, and their current leaders—the twenty-fifth patriarch of Maoshan, Liu Hunkang, and the thirtieth Celestial Master, Zhang Jixian.[60] A shift in Huizong's interests, however, is already suggested in the sixth month of 1106, when he issued an edict proclaiming an empire-wide search for provincial magicians (*fangshi*) and recluses (*yinshi*). This search continued for more than ten years, judging from a similar edict proclaimed in the eighth month of 1116. A passage in the *Xu Zizhi tongjian changbian jishi benmo* (*Narratives from Beginning to End from the "Collected Data for a Continuation of the Comprehensive Mirror to Aid in Government"*) reveals the precise manner in which these "accomplished literati" (*gaoshi*) were identified by local village servicemen, and the not inconsiderable pressure, including thinly disguised bribery, that was brought to bear to convince them to follow local officials to court.[61]

Among the so-called *fangshi* who came to Kaifeng were Wang Laozhi, Wang Zixi, and Lin Lingsu.[62] To varying degrees all sought to protect, and especially to exalt, the imperial person, his consorts and favored courtiers, yet the claims made on behalf of the emperor by Lin Lingsu were the most grandiose and, from the point of view of the traditional Daoist orders, the most presumptuous. As we have already seen, Lin was preoccupied with a portion of the cosmos called the Divine Empyrean (*Shenxiao*), one of nine such empyreans (*jiuxiao*) and the most sublime of all Daoist heavens. The Divine Empyrean was ruled by the Emperor of Jade Purity of Shenxiao, also called the "Great Lord of Everlasting Life," who was the eldest son of the Jade Emperor (Yuhuang dadi). The political implications of this creative cosmology were worked out soon enough. In the fourth month of 1117, following the subordination of all previous Daoist lineages to the new Shenxiao order, Emperor Huizong announced that he was none other than the Sovereign of the Grand Empyrean (Taixiao dijun), the eldest son of the Jade Emperor, who had descended to Earth. The celestial administration of the Divine Empyrean, meanwhile, had been handed over to the younger brother of the Sovereign, Qinghua dijun, while many of Huizong's courtiers, including the minister Cai Jing, were identified with transcendents in the region of Shenxiao.

The search for nontraditional practitioners like Lin Lingsu is often presented in the context of Huizong's call for the reconstitution and publication of a new Daoist canon.[63] The submission of Daoist texts and the preparation for a printed edition began in earnest in 1114, two years before Lin's arrival at court. However, our most learned student of Song bibliography, Piet van der Loon, has concluded that "there is hardly any evidence that [the] new movements or cults were represented" in the canon, which was printed sometime after 1119 with blocks cut at the Tianning Temple in Fuzhou.[64] The texts inspired by Lin's revelation of the Divine Empyrean were clearly composed or edited much later, and van der Loon doubts that the canon would have contained any books on Thunder Magic, including those ostensibly revealed to Lin Lingsu.[65] He is even skeptical of an account claiming that a work attributed to Yang Xizhen (1101–1124), revealer of the "Rites of Youth's Incipience," was included in the canon. Van der Loon does think it possible "that works deriving from the *T'ien-hsin cheng-fa* tradition were included in the *Daozang*, since it had been officially recognized by 1122 at the latest."[66] Yuan Miaozong, the author of a major compendium of Tianxin rites, was assigned to the "scripture office" in 1115 and submitted his work to the throne in the following year.

At best, then, Huizong's call for the submission of Daoist texts in 1114 provided only a limited inspiration to the new Daoist movements of the Song, and the canon reflected only a partial affirmation and recognition of these new trends in the provinces. Even Huizong's interest in representatives of these new trends, such as Lin Lingsu, seems to have been prompted more by their greater willingness to serve his inflated ideological needs; as we have seen in passing, later Daoist exegetes even found it necessary to cut Huizong down to size by recasting the cosmology of the Divine Empyrean.[67]

From a more general point of view, however, Huizong's patronage of Daoism was part of a larger and coherent religious policy that, I believe, set the tone for the rest of the century. In the first decade of the twelfth century, the emperor undertook a large-scale reformation of court ritual and music. This had been attempted before, but never with such comprehensiveness or success. A guiding principle of the undertaking was the abolition of the ritual order established in the Qin and Han, and the restoration and adaptation to present circumstances of the rites and music of the Three Periods (i.e., the Xia, Shang, and Zhou dynasties). In the first month of 1107, a special Ritual Service (Yili ju) was created within the Department of State Affairs (Shangshu sheng). Over the next six years, the Ritual Service produced several massive compilations of classical liturgy.[68] Even then, the project was thought to have remained incomplete, and the *Jishi benmo* attributes this to Huizong's shift to Daoism during the Zhenghe reign period (1111–1118). Yet even this seems to be overstated. Already in 1108, Huizong called for the emendation of Daoist liturgy, which resulted in the production of the *Jinlu lingbao daochang yifan*. This collection of more than four hundred rituals was to be sent to all Daoist temples in the empire: "Prefects and county administrators," according to Piet van der Loon, "were entrusted to select *daoshi* who would perform the new liturgy according to the law."[69]

The reformations of classical and of Daoist ritual, therefore, were the warp and woof of a single weave, bound ever more tightly by Huizong's suppression of Buddhism. In 1110, the emperor instructed the Ritual Service to put a stop to the invasion of Buddhist tendencies in court rituals, and in 1117 Huizong's identification as the Great Sovereign of the Divine Empyrean was explicitly announced "to rectify the fact that the Central Kingdom had become blanketed by the teachings of the Jin barbarians"—as a counterweight, in other words, to the Buddhist claims of the Liao emperors. "The buttressing of Daoism against its foreign rival," in the more emphatic proposition of Michel Strickmann, "was tantamount to a move in the interests of national security."[70] Huizong's anti-Buddhism, however, did not lead to a suppression in the Tang sense of this word. In 1107 Huizong merely placed Daoist monks and nuns above their Buddhist counterparts in the religious hierarchy, and in 1119 he Daoicized the titles of Buddhist priests and the terms for Buddhist monasteries and temples. The Daoicization of Buddhism was an attempt to sinify it, and an attempt to force it to submit to Huizong in the same way that Huizong thought the Liao should submit to a Chinese emperor.

Huizong's anti-Buddhism was a base upon which he erected the twin pillars of the Song dynasty: classical and Daoist ritual. And it is clear that these pillars were mined, at least in the eyes of Huizong, from exactly the same quarry. In an edict of 1118, Huizong expressed his view that the Dao of the Yellow Emperor and Laozi and the Dao of Yao, Shun, and the Rites of Zhou derived from the same Dao that was equally present in the classicist's governing of the country and in the gentleman's cultivation of himself. Since the Han, unfortunately, the Dao of classicism and the Dao of Daoism had been unnaturally distinguished and separated, and it was the purpose of Huizong's religious policies to restore this ancient and happy unity.[71] This sentiment was widely shared. The major effect of Huizong's religious policy was, I believe, to create the atmosphere in which classical and Daoist ritual could be performed enthusiastically, and without a sense of contradiction, by members of the bureaucratic elite. As we shall see, Daoist ritual, and especially Daoist exorcisms, were an expression of the legalistic and penal arm of Confucian administration, while the Daoist exorcist was conceived of and represented in precisely the same terms as a Confucian magistrate.

If the effect of Huizong's religious policies on the new Daoist therapeutic movements was both more and less than is commonly represented, the same can be said for the Celestial Master sect. Longhushan, site of the Celestial Master organization, was located in the southern

corner of Jiangxi and at the center of the region that produced many
of the new Daoist lineages. Some of these lineages claimed that their
exorcistic traditions derived directly from Celestial Master, or Orthodox Unity, Daoism. As we have seen, Lu You noted that Tan Zixiao
"obtained the Rectifying Rites of the Celestial Heart of Zhang Daoling," while the texts of the rites are replete with references and attributions to Zhang Daoling and his tradition.[72] In addition to the
Shangqing Tianxin zhengfa (HY 566), several major texts of the Leifa,
or Thunder Magic, tradition recommend that the practitioner entrust
himself to the tutelage of an Orthodox Unity priest (*Zhengyi daoshi*),[73]
while still other exorcistic texts representing other traditions, such as
The Rites of the Earth-Spirits and *The Rites of General Chu*, to name just
two, are attributed specifically to the thirtieth Celestial Master, Zhang
Jixian.[74]

In general, we can read these attributions as grants of legitimacy
and of the imprimatur of orthodoxy. Yet this still begs the question of
the precise relation between each of these new exorcistic traditions
and the Celestial Master priests. Although we may accept Poul Andersen's characterization of the *Tianxin zhengfa* as "a form of Orthodox Unity Daoism," we as yet know little of the nature of post-Tang
Celestial Master Daoism of which the Rites of Tianxin were supposedly a form.

What we do know, however, is that during the reign of Emperor Li-
zong (r. 1225–1264), the thirty-fifth Celestial Master, Zhang Keda, was
granted undisputed control over the "talismanic registers of the Three
Mountains" (*Sanshan fulu*), which is to say, control over the ordination of priests in the Zhengyi, Lingbao, and Maoshan traditions.[75] This
control was enhanced in the Yuan, when the thirty-sixth Celestial Master and his descendants were recognized as the "masters of Daoism
south of the Yangzi" (*ming zhuling Jiangnan daojiao*).[76] Could it be that
the climb of the Orthodox Unity priests to the top of the Daoist hierarchy and their ultimate recognition as the leaders of southern Daoism were made possible in part by their ability to stay slightly ahead of
the curve of local trends and claim many of the new therapeutic lineages as their own, whether or not they had anything to do with their
development?[77] Be that as it may, already by the early thirteenth century, the great Daoist exegete Jin Yunzhong thought that the Rites of
Tianxin formed the core of the Orthodox Unity tradition,[78] and that
"all the miscellaneous registers below the Covenant Authority Regis-

ter [of the Celestial Masters] had been unified in the altars of Orthodox Unity and that the rites of *Tianxin*, the various rites of the Five Thunder [Gods], the writings on [the rites of] summoning and investigating [demons], and the art of writing spells, had [all] been subordinated to the same."[79]

Meanwhile, as the new therapeutic movements were being subsumed by the Orthodox Unity tradition, the Celestial Masters themselves were being portrayed, increasingly and even exclusively, as exorcists. In the anecdotes of the *Yijian zhi*, the Celestial Masters of the twelfth century appear as Ritual Masters writ large.[80] Moreover, the event which now captures the imagination of Song and Yuan hagiographers of Zhang Daoling is a great cosmic battle on Mount Qingcheng (Sichuan) between Zhang and eight classes of demons.[81] Each of these classes of demons is identified with a particular illness. What is so interesting about them is that many, if not all, appear as the spirit-generals (*shenjiang*) in the texts of the new exorcistic lineages of the Song! Such are the ways of Daoist orthodoxy.

The assimilation of the new Daoist movements by the Orthodox Unity tradition, and of the Celestial Masters themselves to the Daoist Ritual Master, was not simply an accident of history. It has, I believe, a more profound explanation. In a very real sense, the concerns of the new Daoist movements represented a return to the concerns of the Celestial Masters of the Han—namely, therapeutic ritual—and therefore a return to the origin of religious Daoism itself. Like Huizong's call for a restoration of the rituals of the classical period, these new movements shared in the general fundamentalism of the age, with its return to antiquity (*fugu*), which until recently has only been viewed as a defining characteristic of Song Confucianism. Like all fundamentalisms, moreover, this one was not an accurate gauge of the time to which it hoped to return. A brief review of the place of therapeutic ritual among the early Celestial Masters will allow us to calibrate exactly how much had changed in the intervening millennium.

The centrality of illness and its cure to the early Celestial Masters is made eminently clear in the biography of Zhang Lu in the *Wei History* and its commentary. These passages have been translated many times; here I follow the felicitous rendition of Michel Strickmann:

> They [the Celestial Masters] taught people to have wholehearted faith, and not to cheat or deceive others. If someone fell ill, he had to con-

fess his misdeeds. . . . The priests constructed "houses of justice," [placed at regular intervals] like the post stations of the present day. Inside, they put grain and meat, and travelers might take as much as they needed. But if someone took too much, the spirits would inevitably afflict him with illness. . . . In addition, they had "chambers of quietness," where they made such people stay to meditate on their transgressions. . . . A priest ["director of spirits"] would pray on behalf of the sick person. The method of the prayer was to write out the family name and given name of the sufferer, and words explaining that he admitted his misdeeds. Then copies of the document were to be made. One was sent up to Heaven, and placed on a mountaintop. One was buried in the earth, and one was sunk in water. These were called "the documents of the Three Officers."[82]

What these passages reveal, above all, is the link that was forged at the heart of early Daoist ritual between illness and morality. Illness was the result of moral transgression, and its cure was effected by confession overseen by a Daoist priest in an oratory. These ideas are underscored in a fifth-century text of the Celestial Masters: "Any sick person must only recollect and repent all the sins and misdemeanors he or she committed from first reaching consciousness at about age seven. One must then perform the proper observances and submit a petition and talisman to the spirits. This will invariably cure even longstanding ailments and severe illnesses."[83] The "proper observances" followed a set pattern. After a purification of the oratory and invocations to Lord Lao and the Four Directions, the priest prepared a written memorial stating the facts of the case. The memorial was then consumed in the incense burner and carried to the celestial officials by divine emissaries that had been generated from the priest's own body. Finally, the priest prepared a written talisman addressed to specific disease-demons, commanding them to desist. The talisman was also burned, but then ingested by the patient in a mixture of ashes and water.[84]

For knowledge of these disease-demons, the priest would turn to a distinct genre of religious literature known as "Demon Codes" or "Demon Statutes" (guilü). The earliest extant example of such a text is *The Demon Statutes of Nüqing*, which was produced by the Celestial Masters in the fourth century.[85] Page after page of this code is given over to an enumeration of demons and the specific diseases identified with each. Yet while demons may be said to be the proximate cause of disease, in the sense that all disease was conceived of in terms of internal or external pathogenic agents, demons are not the ultimate or even real cause of disease: the real cause is moral transgression. Chapter 3 and parts of chapter 5 of *The Demon Statutes* enumerate, respectively, twenty-two and fourteen rules and prohibitions the infringement of which would inevitably invite demonic attack and shorten one's life span. The entire work, in fact, is addressed to "the faithful," and we soon realize that the "statutes" of the title apply not to the demons but to the Daoist adept or lay believer.[86]

Demon Statutes, and the related "Writings on Law" (*fawen*), continued to be produced by the Orthodox Unity tradition. They were also produced, however, by some of the new therapeutic movements of the Song. As we have seen, Rao Dongtian, one of the founders of the Rectifying Rites of Tianxin, was responsible for *The Demon Code of the "Spinal Numinous Writ" of Highest Purity*, edited by Deng Yougong.[87] This code, in a slightly abridged form, was reproduced as chapter 6 of *The Secret Essentials of Unified Perfection* by Yuan Miaozong. In the *Daofa huiyuan*, moreover, we find such examples as *The Celestial Statutes and Edicts of Nüqing: Red Writs of the Primordial Cavern of the Most High* and *The Ritual Models and Black Statutes of the Great Darkness Fengdu*.[88] If the presence of such Demon Statutes among the new movements speaks to their continuity with the Orthodox Unity tradition, and in some cases provides further evidence for its direct influence, an analysis of the content of these Song codes reveals the extent to which we have entered an entirely different world.

The most obvious change is that the "Demon Statutes" of the Song are no longer addressed to the faithful. Rather, they are addressed to the demons, and not simply to the demons. All the spirits, but especially those that constitute the lower and sub-bureaucracies, and even the Daoist Ritual Master himself, are the object of the statutes, which now apply only to them and no longer to the Daoist adept or lay believer. These statutes essentially specify the punishments to be suffered by demons who consort with humans, by earth-spirits (*tudi shen*), by City Gods (*Chenghuang*), by spirit-generals who consort with demons or who allow demons to consort with humans from negligence or corruption, and, finally, by "the officers who practice the rites" (*xingfa guan*; i.e., the Ritual Masters) who either willfully pervert or unwittingly fail to exercise those rites in the proper manner. The fault for illness, therefore, has been placed entirely at the feet of the demons and of the lesser spirits whose job it is to keep these demons away. The medieval link between illness and morality has been severed, and the implications of this are profound.

By the Song, we are no longer dealing with self-conscious religious communities held together by rules, regulations, and prohibitions and by a parish priest who uses illness as a means to bind the individual ever more closely to the community. Illness here was transparent to group morality. In the Song, the faithful are absent from the Demon Statutes because, I believe, there are no faithful in the sense that there once were. In the Song, we are dealing with a society that was relatively—I hesitate to use the term—secularized. We are dealing, that is, with households highly differentiated by geography, by economic and social status, and by the nature and strength of their ideological commitments. These households now invite to their home a lay or clerical Daoist exorcist who may, in fact, have been preceded by a doctor or a spirit-medium or a Buddhist monk. The Daoist exorcist, whether lay or clerical, has become, quite simply, a ritual expert who must share the field with many others. He is differentiated from these others, however, by the fact that he is an outsider who may have traveled great distances and by the fact of a reputation that is based not only on therapeutic success but on a moral probity derived from a long and demanding personal ascesis. All this held out the promise of objectivity and impartiality among villagers and urban neighbors weighed down with competition and envy. In this the Daoist exorcist was highly preferable to the spirit-medium, who might see in someone's illness an opportunity to make some personal hay, or to the monk, who appeared to many as just another neighbor always asking for something.

The approach of the Daoist exorcist to a particular case was not unlike that taken in criminal proceedings by another outsider, the magistrate, whose office had been gained after years of study and moral paideia. From the de-moralized view of the Demon Statutes, a case of illness was simply a case of breaking and entering. The point was to round up the usual suspects and submit them to questioning. It is not surprising, then, that the suspects might turn out to include those sub-bureaucratic "servicemen" (the earth-spirits) who had remained on too good terms with the local population (the demons), or that, if the proceedings went badly or produced no result, the presiding judge (the Ritual Master) would now be held accountable for administrative misfeasance.

There is another, equally significant implication of the de-linking of illness and morality in the Demon Statutes of the Song period—namely, that if illness is no longer the result of sin, then the demons have been liberated as the agents of punishment to become free agents of the imagination. The anecdotes of the *Yijian zhi* reveal that the men and women afflicted by demonic illness now manipulate the demons as representations of their inner states. Analysis of the exorcistic rituals in the texts of the Daoist canon confirms that this manipulation was precisely what the rituals were meant to encourage. The descriptive and prescriptive accounts of exorcism complement each other perfectly in this respect. The man or woman who is suffering from various symptoms is first made to understand that these symptoms reflect an illness caused by one or another *category* of demon. He or she is then induced to become possessed by the afflicting demon, which is to say that he or she now identifies in trance with a *particular* demon with a particular name that is irreducible to any known demon. He or she then proceeds to provide a narrative account of its history and why it has come to harass him or her.[89] What is remarkable is that these demons and their narratives are unique, and reveal an uncanny relationship to the structure or characteristics of what we learn in the anecdote of the patient's family situation. The exorcist finally proceeds to negotiate with these "inner objects" in a way that satisfies them, and thereby brings a satisfying resolution to the family crisis by which they were produced. Thus we have moved from morality to psychology.[90]

A paradox of the absence of the patient from the Demon Statutes of the Song period is that the patient is now included more forcefully in his or her own cure. This point is best made by comparison with medieval exorcisms once again. We have already seen how, except for the initial confession of sin, the afflicted remained a passive bystander to ritual actions taken by the priest. One of the more peculiar ramifications of the transparency of individual illness to group morality was that the transgressions that left an individual vulnerable to demonic illness were not necessarily committed by that individual. Rather, in many instances, these sins or crimes or transgressions might be imputed to a dead member of the patient's family. The mechanism that set the illness in motion was a "lawsuit from beyond the tomb," or "sepulchral plaint" (*zhongsong*), filed with the celestial prosecutors by those (also dead human beings) who had suffered at the hands of their ancestors. The cure required not that the suffering individual dispute the truth of these ancient crimes, which were in fact acknowledged, but that the priest himself file a vigorous countersuit, which, by the very fact of its having been filed and by the forcefulness of its counter-charges, would itself block the demonic process.[91] Therapy, therefore, was merely a matter of the priest's opposing one lawsuit against another, of charge and counter-charge. Except perhaps for the sufferer's initial help in recalling family history—though this information could be gotten from others, or even from the celestial spirits—he or she was noticeably absent from the cure.

The contrast could not be greater with the Song. By then, illness had become a matter entirely of and for the individual; and therapy had become a process of negotiation between an exorcist and a patient, speaking in the voice of another whom he or she had colonized symbolically. We now investigate more closely this world of exorcists and their patients.

3
New Therapeutic Movements
in the Song: Practitioners

The importance of the new therapeutic rites in the social life of the Song upper and lower strata is confirmed by the secular, anecdotal literature of the twelfth century. In Hong Mai's *Yijian zhi*, those addressed in the canonical text as "Ritual Masters" or "Ritual Officers" emerge as an identifiable class of exorcists distinct, on the one hand, from both the Daoist priest and spirit-medium, yet associated, on the other, with a broader group of lay religious experts and healers. If these exorcists can be said to constitute a class, they do so precisely as a function of these distinctions and associations. In terms of social origins, the *fashi* were as diverse as the clientele they served.

The Ritual Master as Exorcist

The term "*fashi*" might best be translated as "Master of Rites," suggesting the diversity of noncommunal "lesser rites" (*xiaofa*) that define the repertoire of his modern-day descendant. Even the *fashi* in the Song, as we shall see, performed simple versions of Daoist "offerings." I will refer to the *fashi* as an exorcist, however, because that was his most important function. For example:

> Somewhere in Jiangxi, after the failure of various treatments, medical and otherwise, a father invited a certain Long *fashi* to his home to cure his son (who was also a doctor). The son's feverish illness had progressed from

bouts of inspired and sonorous poetry to loud chanting
of scriptures, songs, and even medical prescriptions.
When the *fashi* arrived, the son was on the verge of
demonic possession. The *fashi* put an end to all this
by placing an exorcistic seal (*fayin*) in his hand—his
writing hand, no doubt—which was then bound tightly
with rope.[1]

In the subprefecture of Changshu, a retired magistrate invited a *fashi* named Chen Guoqian, who assembled his various spirit-soldiers (*jiangli*) to identify the
demon afflicting the son of a deceased minister (*shangshu*). It transpired that the son's illness was in fact a
punishment sought by the spirit of the minister for
his son's unfilial behavior.[2]

In 1193, in the canton of Xiangdun (Dexing, Jiangxi),
the younger of two unmarried brothers who were living
together after their parents' death took up with a female
apparition that tried to separate them. The elder brother
conferred with a certain Zhang *fashi*, who advised the
younger one to stop by his ritual sanctuary (*fayuan*) at
night, at which time he would be given some talismanic
water to drink and another talisman to hold in his hand
while sleeping.[3]

In Mingzhou, the Vice Censor-in-Chief (*zhongcheng*),
Shu Xindao, became so obsessed with a female apparition in the very hall where he lectured his disciples that
his family summoned the *fashi* Zhu Yancheng, who went
on to perform a most extraordinary exorcism.[4]

In 1135, in Pingjiang, the elder of a monastery summoned Dao *fashi* to cure one of his monks who had
transformed himself into a "hungry ghost," refusing all
food because he believed it to be made of iron. The *fashi*
appealed to the monk's Buddhist values, recommending
a confession of past sins, which, with a little sacralized
water again, seemed to do the trick.[5]

A doctor, a magistrate, a commoner, a vice-censor, a monk—all required
and sought the exorcistic services of *fashi*. But who were these *fashi*?
In a number of anecdotes in the *Yijian zhi*, the *fashi* is explicitly dis-

tinguished from the Daoist priest (*daoshi*). One such anecdote describes an exorcism of a fox-demon, performed at the patient's home in Haikou xian (Dexing, Jiangxi), by a certain Tan *fashi*. Tan was a village practitioner of something called the "Rites of Maoshan" (*Maoshan fa*). He is identified as a layman, or "*suren*," a term that also suggests a lack of the refinement that necessarily accompanied clerical (or official) status. Most importantly, the text states that "although Tan was not a Daoist priest, he nonetheless acquired this appellation [i.e., *fashi*]" (*Sui fei daoshi, er de ci cheng*).[6] The implication of the Chinese passage is clearly that, in the Song, the appellation "*fashi*" was understood to be a title of a Daoist priest, and that it was being usurped by a group of lay practitioners who were not priests at all.

Such passages should alert us to the possibility that in certain social contexts someone who was called a Daoist priest may not, in fact, have been one. In Yihuang, on the occasion of a multi-village festival known as "*xiangshe*," a man named Hu Wu performed the functions of a Daoist priest (*daoshi*) and was so addressed or regarded by the people.[7] Yet it is unlikely that this commoner (*ximin*), who made his living by hawking boiled mollusks, was actually a Daoist priest. One would be hard-pressed to find a priest residing in a village. The village was the province of the spirit-medium and, now perhaps, of exorcists like Tan *fashi*.

The Rites of Maoshan, Tan's speciality, were probably unrelated to the august Daoist lineage identified with Mount Mao in Jiangsu.[8] Another anecdote gives us some idea of both the content of these rites and the nature of those who practiced them:

> Cheng *fashi*, from Zhang village [Wuyuan, Jiangxi], practiced the "Rectifying Rites of Maoshan" (*Maoshan zhengfa*). Many commoners in the vicinity went to his altar to entreat [his aid], and none was not completely cured. Chan Cong, a man from the neighboring village of Xinding, suddenly fell ill and summoned Cheng to save him. Cheng complied and promptly restored him to health. The time was already dusk, and Cheng desired to return home. Cong's father begged him to remain until morning, but Cheng declined and went on his way. As soon as he reached the Sun Family Hill, when the moon's color revealed a weak luminescence, a black, bell-shaped prodigy (*wu*) emerged directly out of the trees in

front of him. It circled and turned, producing a noise as if it
intended to attack him. Cheng anxiously recited a spell and
walked the [Celestial] Outline (*bugang*). The prodigy showed
not the slightest fear and gradually pressed in upon his body.
Cheng realized that this was a "rock sprite." Consequently, he
recited the "Spell of Nezha's Fireball" (*Nezha huoqiu zhou*)
and, forming a mudra (*jieyin*), recited, "Do you think that
my spirit-general would permit a *wangliang*-demon to obstruct my forward progress! Quickly stop and pull back!"
And suddenly a fireball emerged from behind his body and
struggled with the black lump. After a while a noise burst
out, like clashing metal, and the black lump disappeared.
The fireball made several revolutions around Cheng's body
and also vanished. At the time, the resident at the foot of the
Sun Family Hill, Xiang Dun, as well as his entire household,
had heard the clamor of metal drums atop the mountain,
like the sound of a hundred thousand men at war. With his
sons and nephews, Xiang Dun watched from a distance, yet
they saw only Cheng, standing absolutely rigid, in stillness
and in darkness. Then they called out to him, and Cheng
became aware (*jue*). Immediately they took him back home,
and his heart and intention stabilized. From that time he
didn't dare travel at night.[9]

Evidently, Ritual Masters Cheng and Tan belonged to a group of lay
exorcists and to a tradition of exorcism peculiar to the villages of two
neighboring subprefectures in Jiangxi—Wuyuan and Dexing. These
exorcists visited the homes of their clients, though in the case of Ritual Master Cheng, clients might apparently make the trip to his private altar as well. Central to this episode, and perhaps to the Rites of
Maoshan, is the reference to a particular Tantric deity, Nezha (Skt.
Naṭa), who was also the spirit-general invoked by Cheng.

Nezha was the third son of the Devarāja of the North, Vaiśravaṇa,
one of the four *lokapālas* (guardian deities) of Buddhism. The cult to
Vaiśravaṇa and to his sons entered China from Khotan in the eighth
century and inspired a series of apocryphal Buddhist scriptures that were
attributed to the Tantric monk Amoghavajra but that probably date
some generations after his death. Nonetheless, these scriptures accurately reflect the courtly activities of Tantric monks during the reign of

the emperor Xuanzong (r. 712–756), and the role of Nezha and his father as defenders of both the imperial person and the Tang empire.[10]

Nezha, in fact, appears in the pantheon of an identifiable group of Tantric exorcists active at precisely the same time and in precisely the same place (Jiangxi) as Ritual Master Cheng. The use of mantras (spells) and mudrās (hand-seals), characteristic of Tantric practice, had long been assimilated by Daoist exorcists, and Nezha plays a significant role in a number of exorcistic texts in the *Daofa huiyuan*.[11]

One of the defining features of the rituals described in the exorcistic texts of the *Daofa huiyuan* is the transformation of the Daoist Ritual Master into his spirit-general. During the recitation of a spell and the formation of a particular seal, the practitioner evoked and visualized his tutelary deity and then visualized himself as that deity. This identification subsequently empowered the practitioner to manipulate his spirit-general's lethal accoutrements and military subordinates. All this is implied in what I read as Cheng *fashi*'s ability to generate Nezha's characteristic weapon, the fireball, and then recall it into his own body. And the sights and sounds of battle I take to be the externalized effects of an internal meditative process that left Cheng *fashi* in a distinctive state of concentration and self-absorption, and from which he emerged only after Xiang Dun called out his name. I will return to the nature of this state shortly.

Fashi who were explicitly distinguished from Daoist priests were to be found in urban as well as rural environments. They were not exclusively "country priests," as Lagerwey calls them:

> Within the Yongjin Gate in Lin'an [i.e., Hangzhou], a *fashi* named Wang daily practiced the Rites of the Celestial Heart and performed "offerings of petition" (*changjiao*) on behalf of people. He wore a star hat and ritual vestments, yet he was not a Daoist priest (*fei daoshi*). Commoners (*minsu*) considered that he charged as much as thirty percent less than real Yellow Cappers (*huangguan*) [i.e., Daoist priests], and so many employed him. Wang always used his neighbor Li Sheng to write the petitions and to memorialize with green writs (*qingci*).[12]

The relative cheapness of Wang's services does not appear to have limited his clientele to the underprivileged, however. On the occasion of a New Year's celebration in 1132, Wang was invited by a wealthy family to conduct a private "offering to secure peace" (*bao'an jiao*). Unfortunately, Wang's neighbor and secretarial aide, Li Sheng, could not contain his holiday enthusiasm. On the way to the offering, Li feasted with friends and composed his petitions in a state of inebriation. Toward the end of the ceremony, Wang *fashi* had a vision in which he was brought before a celestial official only to find that his amanuensis had already been taken prisoner and tortured. The judge criticized Li Sheng for his sloppy calligraphy and for his inability to abstain from meat and alcohol. Wang protested that it was his responsibility only to take charge of the ceremonial feast (*jiaoxi*), which he had done with great merit, and that he knew nothing of Li's transgressions. These excuses did not particularly impress the celestial court. Wang was rebuked and sent on his way with a blow to the chest, an event that punctured his vision and brought it to an end. Within a matter of days, Li passed away, and Wang followed three months later.[13]

The point is that there were lay practitioners who looked and performed very much like Daoist priests but who were not priests, and that the rules of purity and correct procedure applied to the *fashi* just as they did to the Daoist priest.[14] Priests were also punished for their inattention to such rules or details, and it might equally well be a particularly unimpeachable *fashi* who would find himself in a position to point out these clerical shortcomings:

> The *fashi* Li Mingwei was a native of Fuzhou [Fujian] who observed the precepts of the Dao with exceptional care. He sent petitions and submitted writs (*baizhang fuci*) on behalf of the people, and the response was immediate. In 1135, the Controller-General (*tongpan*) of Jianzhou, Yuan Fuyi, had him perform an "offering" (*jiao*) together with Ye, a Daoist priest of the Tianqing Abbey. After the completion of the ceremony, Li addressed Ye: "When I was sending up the petition, I arrived before the Gate of the Three Heavens and saw the Daoist priest of the commandary, named Zhang, also memorializing green writs on someone's behalf. The envelope of the memorial had been prepared very clumsily, and it was damaged a bit as well. The Celestial Master [i.e., Laozi] said, 'This cannot be offered to me (the imperial person),' and Zhang threw it away." Ye responded:

"Zhang is a Daoist colleague in my abbey. However, I do not
know in whose home he is spending the evening." On the
following day Zhang returned from outside, and Ye asked
him where he had been. Zhang said, "Last night I performed an offering at the home of the Ye family twenty
miles away. The village households were crude and careless,
and the paper for the green writs was not good at all.
Moreover, at the point of burning the memorial, the
[wooden] envelope turned over, and the writ fell upon the
ground. I quickly used a calling-card (*shouban*) to prop it
up, so it was not seriously damaged. However, my feathered
outer-garment (*hechang*) was burned." Ye told Zhang what
Mingwei had seen. Zhang became very frightened and
immediately prepared an offering (*jiao*) to confess his
transgressions.[15]

The presentation of the memorial, accompanied by the visualization of one's presence in Heaven at the time of its submission, was and
still is the climax of the *jiao*, or offering, performed by the Daoist
priest.[16] Here someone called a "*fashi*" specializes in this aspect of
Daoist liturgy for individuals, much like Wang *fashi* in the preceding
andecdote. Yet he also performs at the request of a vice-prefect (i.e.,
controller-general) and in conjunction with a Daoist priest and resident of a Daoist abbey. We find, moreover, that the priests of the same
abbey made excursions into the surrounding villages to perform private ceremonies with paraphernalia, unfortunately of low quality, provided by the local family itself. These two comments spawn two questions. Is the designation "*fashi*" sufficient to associate Li Mingwei with
that group of lay exorcists and practitioners whom we have explicitly
contrasted with the Daoist priest? How do we distinguish between *fashi*
and *daoshi* in those situations where the first performs with the second, and the latter acts like the former?

Perhaps we can approach an answer to these questions from another
direction. Just as we have found certain lay practitioners who adopted,
presumptuously, the title of Daoist priest (like Hu Wu, mentioned
above), so we will find many Daoist priests adopting the title "*fashi*."
There appear to be two explanations for this—one formal, the other
functional.

As mentioned in Chapter 2, by Tang times the term "*fashi*" appeared as a title conferred upon a disciple who had mastered a particular text or group of texts that corresponded to a particular Daoist tradition and/or section of the Daoist canon. Mastery of the *Daode jing* and its various commentaries included in the Taixuan section of the canon conferred the title "*Taishang daode fashi*"; the titles "*Wushang tongxuan fashi*" and "*Wushang santong fashi*" corresponded to the Lingbao and Maoshan corpuses, respectively.[17] One might easily imagine, theoretically, how the term "*fashi*" could have been extended to new traditions as they evolved and were taken up by the Daoist establishment. Thus, on the one hand, someone referred to as a "*fashi*" may have been a Daoist priest;[18] on the other hand, he may not have been. In the *Yijian zhi*, the term "*fashi*" is sufficiently flexible and overdetermined that it should be understood to refer to a master (*shi*) or practitioner of a particular exorcistic technique (*fa*), and such a person may not have been a priest at all.

It is precisely in the context of exorcisms that we find Daoist priests (*daoshi*) referred to as "*fashi*." In 1166, for instance, during the course of an exorcism performed at the patient's home in Poyang (Jiangxi) by a Daoist priest of the Tianqing Abbey, the demon, who had been pursued and arrested by the priest's spirit-general, refers to the priest, Xu Zhongshi, as a "*fashi*."[19] Without slighting demons or their testimonial veracity, other examples could be cited where the narrator or a participant employs the term "*fashi*" in reference to someone initially identified as a Daoist priest.[20] The point is that in these and other instances, the term "*fashi*" is best understood as denoting an exorcist, and that priests were so called when they were fulfilling this function. Here we are presented with an anticipation of the modern situation in which the Daoist priest literally exchanges his black hat for the red one of the *fashi* when performing exorcisms and other vernacular rites associated with the latter role.

The role or appellation of "*fashi*" was not limited to Daoist priests or lay exorcists, however. We also find the term applied to some spirit-mediums (*wu*). For example, an elderly spirit-medium who specialized in the exorcism or eradication of snakes (*jinshe*) was addressed as "Cheng *fashi*" by villagers in Xiangdun (Dexing, Jiangxi). The anecdote concerns the fatal result of Cheng's encounter with a snake at a time late in life, when his powers had abated considerably. In his prime, however, his method (*fa*) was evidently so effective that it had been coveted by and passed on to the Commercial-Tax Official of Nankang.[21]

In another case, in the subprefecture of Houguan (Fujian), the magistrate Zhang Delong summoned a village medium (*liwu*) named Wen *fashi* to cure one of his five maidservants who was possessed and harassed by a demon. Apparently, exorcism was not Ritual Master Wen's only talent. Recently he had opened his own wine shop, though economic diversification clearly undermined his exorcistic authority. When Wen appeared before the maidservant, she commented, doing her best to hide her laughter, "How could someone whose body is pervaded with the pneuma of distilled sediment and yeast possibly get hold of me?!" Wen *fashi* retreated, and after another failed attempt by Zhang Delong's brother-in-law, the magistrate enlisted the services of two lay exorcists—also called *"fashi"*—one of whom served and employed as his spirit-general the Tantric deity Ucchuṣma.[22]

The most spectacular example is the case of Shen Anzhi, a spirit-medium in Wenzhou (Zhejiang) who used his mother's illness to impress his neighbor's child and two nephews with his therapeutic abilities. Anzhi was then summoned to the home of the child's father, Xue Jixuan (1104–1171), a student of the Neo-Confucian Cheng Yi and a scholar of practical learning (*jingshi zhi xue*). Anzhi proceeded to make use of these impressionable children in a nearly successful attempt to convert the entire household into dependents and patrons of his cult to the "Nine Saints of the Five Penetrations" (Wutong jiushen). But in the rites he practiced and the divine powers he called upon, this spirit-medium was indistinguishable from the Daoist practitioner of Thunder Magic, and it took another Daoist Ritual Master to discredit him.[23]

The class of lay exorcists called *"fashi"* were clearly finding recruits among village spirit-mediums, though some spirit-mediums may have attained this title simply in their capacity as exorcists or as a result of their proficiency in such activities: in Linchuan (Jiangxi), for instance, a medium of the cult of Third Master Muping (Muping sanlang) who specialized in exorcisms was addressed as *"fashi"* by two clients appearing at his door.[24]

I should point out that all these examples derive from provinces—Jiangxi, Fujian, and Zhejiang—characterized by the strong presence of lay Daoist exorcists called *"fashi,"* and that we might well ask what manner of social or ritual interaction existed between the Ritual Master and village spirit-medium. Their relationship was, in fact, profound.

The Ritual Master and the Bureaucratic Elite

In the preceding pages, I have sought to identify the existence in the Song period of a class of exorcists who were distinguished from Daoist priests and spirit-mediums but who also mediated between these other practitioners. The religious practice and experience of the Ritual Master combined elements of Daoist meditation and the trances of possession associated with spirit-mediums; his martial, humanized deities linked the ethical order of the absolute with the raw power of the conditioned realm; his mobility took him from villages to towns and to all points in between. I have shown that some Ritual Masters might work together, as assistants, with Daoist priests, while others became officiants of spirit-mediums. Conversely, we have seen that some Daoist priests and some spirit-mediums might become, or play the role of, *fashi*.[25]

The class of Ritual Masters was a kind of "fuzzy set" that also tended to bifurcate into two social groups, depending on whether it leaned toward one or the other of two poles defined by the Daoist priest and the spirit-medium. One group consisted of relatively uneducated, unsophisticated, and localized practitioners whose clients looked much like themselves, and who themselves looked much like the spirit-mediums with whom they frequently interacted. Ritual Masters Tan, Cheng, and Wang all belonged to this group, which I examine more extensively in Chapters 4 and 5. The other group consisted of highly literate, worldly, and mobile practitioners who found their clientele almost exclusively among the bureaucratic and economic elite. This group also consisted of members of these elites, who themselves became lay practitioners of the new therapeutic rites of the Song.

Examples of lay exorcists who began their careers outside the Daoist religious organization yet came to serve an elite clientele include Wang Wenqing and Lu Shizhong. As we have seen, Wang Wenqing ultimately found himself in the atelier of Lin Lingsu at court and was responsible for several theoretical texts now preserved in the Daoist canon. Initially, however, he established his reputation moving along the Southeast Coast, first as a physiognomist (*xiangshi*) and then as a popular practitioner of Thunder Magic.[26]

If we follow Wang's career in the anecdotes of the *Yijian zhi*, establishing this reputation was not without its difficulties. From Wenzhou, Wang moved to Fujian, where he was as yet an unknown quantity. His shoddy appearance and behavior immediately brought him into conflict with the monks of the Qingcheng Monastery in Fuzhou, where he was lodging. Wang then sought out and antagonized yet another monk, who was revered by the urban community as a thaumaturge and director of "offerings" (*jiao*). Eventually, Wang found his opportunity in a Daoist "offering" established by the yamen to bring rain. Holding a sword, Wang danced "the steps of Yu" (*Yubu*), and a rainstorm followed immediately upon his submission of a writ (*ci*) to Heaven. From this point, the text says, both Daoists and laymen (*daosu*) began to revere him. Hong Mai, however—or perhaps the transmitter of this anecdote, a Fuzhou resident named Liu Cunli—remained skeptical: "Wang employed [the Rites of the Five Thunder Gods] to deceive and cheat people."[27]

Even after Wang Wenqing was well established in the Baozhen Palace in Kaifeng, his therapeutic practice did not always run smoothly. After a difficult but ultimately successful cure of a literatus who had been bewitched by a woman he met while taking a stroll on the eve of the Lantern Festival, Wang was incarcerated temporarily in the city jail because of a lawsuit filed with the sheriff by the family of the girl. A temple sinecure in the capital obviously did not immunize Wang from accusations of sorcery or from the hasty workings of the judicial system.[28]

Even before Wang's arrival in Kaifeng, students were evidently coming so fast that Wang could have had little control over their behavior. Such was the case with Zheng *daoshi*, who was struck down for making idle use of his powers,[29] and with Fu Xuan, the governor-general of Jiangxi, who had demanded instruction in Thunder Magic and summoned Wang from Linchuan. Wang took an immediate dislike to the man and, fearing his temper, chose to instruct him as little as possible. This tactic proved prescient, for this high provincial official went on to abuse his unknowingly insufficient powers by attempting to burn down a Buddhist pagoda that he thought was too high. When he then complained to Wang, Wang offered a stern reprimand.[30] Here and elsewhere, Wang reveals himself to have been an astute judge of character, which belies Hong Mai's early and critical remarks. Perhaps it was this very quality that recommended Wang to the retired minister Cai Jing. Making use of his earlier talents as a physiognomist, Wang was asked to assess the future fortunes of Cai's family. On this occasion he predicted the importance to Daoism of Cai's nephew (named

Chen), who in fact went on to become a master of the Rites of Tianxin.[31]

Lu Shizhong, one of the premier Daoist exorcists of the twelfth century, also found himself ministering to the needs of another Cai, Cai Juhou (?–1125), who ended his career as a Vice-Minister of Revenue. In 1125, Lu was invited by Cai's widow to perform a Yellow Register Retreat for the salvation of his soul.[32] Cai's soul evidently needed saving. According to the anecdote, Cai's death was attributed to divine retribution for his merciless execution of five hundred rebels who had surrendered to Cai in Yun prefecture. This fact, revealed during a Daoist "offering" performed at Cai's request when still ill, is of great historical interest.

Lu Shizhong (Dangke) was either the son or grandnephew of Lu Guan (Junbao), magistrate of the subprefecture of Shangshui (Chenzhou, Henan).[33] Sometime during the Zhenghe reign period (1111–1117), when Lu was seventeen years old, still unmarried, and studying in the yamen, he had one of those close and fortuitous encounters with an unnamed Daoist holy man (or divinity) that presaged a career outside the Daoist establishment. The Daoist instructed Lu in "the art of talismans so that he could control all the demons and spirits under Heaven."[34] Information provided to Hong Mai by a nephew of Shizhong himself suggests that he actually obtained his Daoist instruction in Sichuan.

However obscure the facts of Lu's early life, he went on to establish a new Daoist tradition. In 1120, Zhao Sheng, a disciple of Zhang Daoling, descended into Lu's room and directed him to a scroll of "secret writings" (bishu) on Maoshan. This scroll formed a large part of what would become The Great Method of the Jade Hall of the Three Heavens of the Supreme Mysterious Origin (HY 220) in thirty chapters.[35] Several late chapters of this work were apparently revealed by spirit-writing in the decade before 1120, but only copied in 1158. Poul Andersen, whose analysis I am relying on here, has demontrated a deep connection between the Rites of the Jade Hall and the Rites of Tianxin.[36] The major differences, he points out, are an emphasis on meditational practice in The Great Method of the Jade Hall and its inclusion of the funeral rites of the Lingbao tradition. We have seen above that Lu Shizhong was invited to perform a Yellow Register Retreat for Cai Juhou. Andersen, in fact, cites Jin Yunzhong's early thirteenth-century criticism of the practitioners of the Rites of the Jade Hall for performing such Lingbao funeral rites "while having only Zhengyi titles and registers," as well as his criticism of Lingbao priests themselves for incorporating elements of the Rites of the Jade Hall.[37] The fluid situation revealed in these criticisms will form the basis for an examination in Chapter 8 of the deep structural continuities between rituals of exorcism and rituals for the dead.

In any event, Lu Shizhong built a career primarily by performing exorcisms for an elite clientele. As one anecdote explains, "Lu . . . made a reputation by exorcising demons with talismans and registers. Among high officials (*shidaifu*) he was known as 'Lu the Perfected Official' (Lu Zhenguan), and he was constantly pursued by suits brought against demons."[38] Throughout the 1120s and 1130s, Lu seems to have been always on the move. While traveling in Xinjiang, he was asked by a ferryman to explore the mysterious and demonic deaths of his two sons;[39] in Chen prefecture (Henan), he was invited by a magistrate to bring an end to a six-month drought;[40] in Lingbi subprefecture, the magistrate asked Lu to cure his daughter, who was haunted and then possessed by the spirit of her younger sister;[41] in Yan prefecture, he cured another daughter of a rural magnate who had become possessed on the eve of her marriage;[42] and in Nanjing, Lu was summoned by a high official to exorcise his son.[43]

Not only did many *fashi* come to specialize in ministering to the therapeutic needs of the sons and daughters of official or wealthy families, but many of those sons and some of their fathers became lay practitioners of the new exorcistic traditions associated with the Daoist Ritual Master. Lu Shizhong, in fact, represents both trends simultaneously, for he was the scion of an official family who went on to become a full-time exorcist catering to an elite clientele. There are many other examples from the twelfth century, a few of which follow:

> Xu Shisan, son of Xu Chaofeng from the prefectural
> city of Huzhou, is described as a member of an official
> family (*guanren*). After relatives became prone to de-
> monic afflictions, Shisan dedicated himself to the Dao
> and practiced the "Rites of the Celestial Heart for
> Summoning and Investigating" on behalf of the resi-
> dents of his urban community, rich and poor alike.
> During the Dunxi reign period (1174–1189), he cured

the possessed daughter of a merchant after numerous
Daoist priests had failed.[44]

In Fuzhou, Ren Daoyuan, the eldest son of a vice-
chamberlain, became a disciple of the Daoist master
Ouyang Wenbin, from whom he received instruction
in "Rites of Salvation by Refinement" (*liandu*). He also
practiced the Rites of the Celestial Heart and went on
to perform exorcisms even when he himself assumed
office after his father's death.[45]

Li Henglao, the eldest son of the Grand Minister Li
Shimei, studied the Rectifying Rites of the Celestial Heart
as a youth, during which time he learned some painful
lessons about not taking those studies seriously enough.[46]

Yan Fu practiced the "Rites of the Five Thunder Gods"
(*wulei shu*) just after his father passed away in the yamen
of Poyang, where his grandfather had moved the family
from Kaifeng in order to take up an official post. The
members of this official family, we learn later, were enthusiastic devotees of the Four Saints (i.e., Tianpeng,
Tianyou, Zhenwu, and Heisha), whose effigies adorned
their residence.[47]

As a youth, the son of Hong Mai's own sister-in-law
received instruction in "ritual registers" from a Daoist
priest and practiced the Rites of the Celestial Heart.[48]

Interest in Daoist therapeutic rituals even extended to younger
members of the imperial family. In Mingzhou, one such member, who
goes unnamed (as is sometimes the case when Hong Mai passes on
sensitive gossip), practiced the Rites of Tianxin and was summoned to
exorcise a demon afflicting the members of a study society made up
of the sons of the city's great families.[49] Another descendant of the
imperial family, Zhao Ziju, studied the Rites of Tianxin with a holy man
(*daoren*) and became a devotee of the Six Jia and Six Ding spirits (*liujia liuding*). Zhao went on to treat his relatives and friends.[50] His son,
as we learn from another anecdote, attempted unsuccessfully to carry
on his father's practice of the Rites of the Celestial Heart, underscoring Schipper's remark that the role of the Ritual Master, unlike that
of many Daoist priests (and some spirit-mediums, I might add), was
and is vocational, not hereditary.

Officials, as well as their sons, became lay devotees of the Rites of Tianxin in particular. In Nanjing, an Attendant Censor (*shiyushi*) "practiced the Rites of the Celestial Heart to cure people's illnesses," and on one occasion summoned a Daoist priest to assist him.[51] In Changzhou, Yao Jiangshi, who had acquired his official post by purchase, practiced the "Rites of the Five Thunder Gods of the Celestial Heart" and was invited to cure a relative of Hong Mai.[52] In the subprefecture of Tianchang (Zhizhou), a Commercial-Tax Official (*shuiguan*), Sun Gu, who had received the Register of Highest Purity (*Shangqing lu*) and practiced the Rites of Tianxin, was invited to cure a Military Inspector (*Dayizhen xunjian*).[53] And in Fujian, the Edict Attendant (*Daiji*) and a member of the Hanlin Academy, Zhen Yuancheng, gave up meat and alcohol after a vision of the immortal Lü Dongbin, studied and practiced the Rectifying Rites of the Celestial Heart, and went on to perform "retreats" (*zhai*) and "offerings" (*jiao*) for others.[54]

Devotees of the new therapeutic rituals of the Song were also to be found among students and literati of nonofficial status.[55] And among the many literati or members of the bureaucratic elite who were curing friends and relatives, some were actually performing the new therapeutic rituals in the course of their official duties. Song Anguo, the Intendant of Zhexi, practiced the Rites of the Celestial Heart and regularly performed exorcisms for the people of Deqing, a subprefecture that has been made famous recently by Philip Kuhn as a center of the sorcery scare in the eighteenth century. One failure led Song Anguo to a temporary but intense ascesis in a local Daoist abbey. Returning to the home of the patient, Anguo adopted the characteristic guise of spirit-mediums and now exorcists—he loosened his hair and held a sword, and then defeated the demon with Thunder Magic.[56] In Jiankang, a military grandee (*wugong daifu*) named Cheng Chun also "loosened his hair and bared his feet," after which he actually donned Daoist robes and summoned his spirit-general while performing an exorcism of snakes at the behest of the magistrate.[57]

A motif related to the emerging theme of the Song official as Daoist exorcist is introduced by the case of Yang Zhonggong, a high official (*youcong zhenglang*) who practiced the Rites of the Celestial Heart and who could determine the nature of someone's illness simply by looking at him. During the Qiandao reign period (1165–1173), Yang became the Managing Prefectural Adjutant (*Lushi canjun*) in Daozhou.

With a Daoist priest looking on, he performed an exorcistic rite of "summoning and investigation" for a local clerk, which resulted in the destruction of a medium temple dedicated to the Four Maidens (Siniang miao).[58] Many of these "official exorcists," in fact, employed the new Daoist exorcistic rituals not simply to cure their subjects of demonic obsession but to rid them of their demonic cults and practices. During the Zhaoxing reign period (1131–1162), the magistrate of Nanling county (Xuanzhou) employed the Rites of the Celestial Heart to destroy the rural cynosure of the subprefecture, a temple dedicated to the Bee King (Fengwang ci), which was supported by spirit-mediums (*wuzhu*), clerks (*limin*), and the village commoners (*lisu*).[59] In 1194, the incoming magistrate of Jingxian, Tang Xianzu, the grandson of a vice-minister of war, practiced the Rites of the Five Thunder Gods and refused to debase himself by prostrating himself before the god of the local temple, to the consternation of the clerks and residents. Tang ultimately rebuilt and became an enthusiastic devotee of the temple, though only after adorning it with effigies of his Daoist spirit-generals.[60] This local cult was therefore Daoicized rather than destroyed (more on this later).[61]

Occasionally, the diffusion of the new Daoist ritual traditions throughout local society presented the magistrate with difficulties in his attempt to undermine village cults and their representatives. In one case described in the *Yijian zhi*, a spirit-medium and a local literatus (*shiren*) combined their talents to terrorize a rural community. After accusations of sorcery, the medium was imprisoned by the magistrate. The medium claimed to practice the "Rites of the Celestial Heart," a claim that we must take seriously. The text refers to the medium's use of talismans, to his control over spirit-generals, to a "ritual sanctuary," and to an entourage of thirty disciples. Usurping the power and the persona of a Daoist Ritual Master, the medium raised the stakes, so to speak, and was met by a magistrate employing an even higher power, the "Demon-Suppressing Seal of the Celestial Master."[62]

The conflict between officials on one side and local cults, spirit-mediums, and sub-bureaucratic functionaries and commoners on the other had existed in a more primitive form in earlier centuries.[63] By the Song we are no longer dealing simply with a literary trope; the Confucian magistrate actually could become a Daoist exorcist. A magistrate wielding Thunder Magic was a powerful combination of an office conferred from above and a supernatural authority deeply rooted in the local culture of his subjects. He was now a formidable competitor of local spirit-mediums.

And if the Song official had become, in some instances, a Daoist Ritual Master, the Daoist Ritual Master was almost always portrayed as an official. Throughout the new ritual compendia of the twelfth and thirteenth centuries, we find that one overriding mandate has been conferred on the Daoist Ritual Master: everywhere, irrespective of a particular tradition or lineage, he is charged with "civilizing and transforming on behalf of (or, as the representative of) Heaven, by destroying temples and rooting out the demonic" (*xinghua daitian famiao quxie*).[64] The same compendia are replete with special ritual instructions for carrying out this charter.[65] In doing so, the Ritual Master also oversaw the behavior of spirits and ghosts in a way that was modeled on the legal and administrative law of the Song magistrate. Moreover, as we shall see in Chapter 5, his exorcisms captured the precise rhythms of the judicial proceedings with which the magistrate dealt with criminal suspects.

The confrontation between exorcists ("official" as well as Daoist) and local cults was a unique episode in a more global strategy to suppress spirit-mediums by the Song state and its representatives. It is important to recall that the Tang court continued to employ at least fifteen master spirit-mediums (*shiwu*) in the Imperial Divination Office (Taibu shu) of the Court of Imperial Sacrifices (Taichang si), plus a number of related exorcists known as "Spellbinding Erudites" (*Zhoujin boshi, Zhoujin shi,* or *Zhoujin gong*). A thorough review of the *Taiping guangji* reveals, moreover, that Tang courtiers, aristocrats, and officials consistently sought the services of spirit-mediums for private and community purposes.[66]

Intimations of a real change only occur in the north, beginning in the middle of the tenth century, when spirit-mediums were not only excluded from the bureaucracy of the Later Zhou dynasty but were actively targeted, along with Buddhists, in the countryside. Rulers of the northern kingdoms, in fact, generally appear to have personally turned to Daoists, doctors, and other ritual experts to perform functions once demanded of spirit-mediums.[67] A precious account, written in 956, of a magistrate's reasoning behind his attempt to eradicate a local cult in Shandong indicates the extent of a spirit-medium's following in the Five Dynasties period. During each of the four seasons of the year, a female medium residing in the administrative city of Qizhou, He Niang, would direct a major celebration at an altar on Mount Changbai in the county of Zhangqiu. These festivals attracted the residents of four prefectures (Zhizhou, Zizhou, Dezhou, and Dizhou), while the medium's entourage included not only a team of lesser mediums, who would impersonate the gods, but another team of actors and actresses, who would put on plays at the same time.[68]

A policy of active suppression targeted spirit-mediums with even greater force and specificity under the Song. At the time, the policy was extended throughout the South, where spirit-mediums had been enthusiastically patronized by the rulers of many of the southern kingdoms in the tenth century.[69] The evidence of their suppression by enterprising magistrates is extensive and has been documented, reign by reign, by Nakamura Jihei.[70] From these memorials and edicts we can actually deduce the number of spirit-mediums per capita in several areas. These numbers are not small. In Hongzhou (Nanchang, Jiangxi), for example, nineteen hundred spirit-mediums were rounded up in the early eleventh century, which produces a ratio of one spirit-medium household for every 135 families;[71] in Chuzhou (Zhejiang), there were thirty-seven hundred spirit-medium households in the prefecture in the late eleventh century, and therefore one medium household for every 24 families;[72] and in Fujian, Kanai Noriyuki has used similar evidence to calculate that there were four or five spirit-medium households for every village![73]

From the same evidence we can learn much about the nomenclature, attire, allies, practices, and altars and temples of spirit-mediums in the Song. We can also learn about the nature and techniques of official suppression (which included corporal punishment, tattooing, exile, and particularly conversion to the agricultural or medical professions), as well as something about the limitations, contradictions, failures, and unanticipated consequences of suppression. I make use of this evidence from time to time in later chapters. A full treatment of official attempts to suppress spirit-mediums would, I believe, also have to take into account heightened concerns about (1) sorcery (*yaoshu*; *nanfa*), both real and imagined, with which the spirit-medium was identified, for better or for worse;[74] (2) witchcraft (*gudu*), especially the phenomenon of ritual murder (*sharen jigui*), reports of which, significantly, do not precede the Song;[75] and even (3) heresies (*zuodao*) in the twelfth century, especially the Vegetarian Devil-Worshipping

Sects.[76] Exploring all of these would, however, take us too far afield at the present time.

The suppression of spirit-mediums and of the practices with which they were associated (sorcery, witchcraft, and so forth) was the dark side of a marginally more benign and long-standing strategy on the part of officials to penetrate and control local society through its cults and religious institutions. The destruction of the altars of spirit-mediums was only one element of this strategy in the Song, and not necessarily the most significant or effective one. A famous edict from Huizong's reign, dated to the first year of Zhenghe (1111), called for the abolition of approximately thirteen hundred "spirit-altars" (*shenci*) in Kaifeng. This so-called abolition, however, actually entailed the removal of the spirits of those altars—or, rather, their images—into Buddhist monasteries, Daoist abbeys, and community temples (*ben miao*). Images of Zhenwu, for instance, were moved into Daoist abbeys, while images of earth-spirits (*tudi shen*) were transferred to City God temples (*chenghuang miao*).[77] Here we find not so much suppression as the integration of cults and spirits into a hierarchy of temples and gods. Integration rather than suppression also informed Huizong's so-called anti-Buddhist policy, as we have seen.

The same memorial did single out three classes of spirits as "perverse cults" (*yinci*) to be extinguished completely. These are the *Wutong, Ziyi,* and *Shi Jiangjun* spirits. I can find little information about the latter two, but the *wutong* spirits were the characteristic divinities of village spirit-medium cults in the South during the twelfth century. These quasi-natural and highly sexed spirits were worshipped at "*congci,*" which both Nakamura Jihei and Kanai Noriyuki have shown to be a technical term for the religious foci of new villages since the late Tang. These "rustic altars," and their spirits, continued to spring up in the eleventh and twelfth centuries wherever new land was brought under cultivation, especially in Jiangnan and Fujian. Huizong's edict called for their eradication, yet even these cults were not really destroyed, as we shall see. Rather, they were transformed, and their spirits worshipped under other names.[78]

The effects of Huizong's edict, or the trends that it merely codified, can be traced throughout the twelfth century. Everywhere in the South, we find examples of an altar or small temple dedicated to one or another spirit being handed over to a Buddhist monk or Daoist priest to administer, or being moved into the precincts of a Buddhist monastery.[79] Occasionally the themes of suppression and integration are brought together, as in Changzhou, where, in 1195, the prefect replaced the spirit-mediums attached to an Auxiliary Temple of the Eastern Peak with Buddhist monks, who then oversaw worship for the community besieged by an epidemic.[80] Other attempts to control local cults, however, often met with considerable and successful resistance. In the canton of Changtian (Poyang, Jiangxi), in 1196, more than one hundred spirit-mediums and artisans intervened to prevent the destruction of a rural temple, the Mingshan miao.[81] The spirits of the medium, moreover, enjoyed external control no more than the medium himself. In 1162, in Hong Prefecture, an Earth God resisted the destruction of his temple and removal to the City God temple by an Army Commander (*shuaishou*).[82]

If the spirit-medium had to contend with the pressures of external control, he had also to fend off various internal challenges to his or her position. In Nankang, during the Zhaoxing reign period (1131–1162), a spirit-medium backed by local literati confronted a villager attempting to destroy a local temple in order to expand his living quarters.[83] Even in villages where the power of the medium and the economic development of the village itself had been so closely linked, a spirit-medium might find unexpected challenges. Sometime during the twelfth century in Jiangdong (Eastern Zhejiang), the leading men in a village rallied behind the female medium of their *congci* who had been threatened at the altar by a skeptical, abusive, and desecrating youth. Fearing that all their work over the years might be lost in this one moment, the village leaders conspired to neutralize the youth, unwittingly transforming him into a sacrificial substitute. With the entire village looking on, the boy was bribed to repeat his blasphemous performance and recklessly consumed the offerings, which had been poisoned; his death was widely seen to have been caused by the god. Here the village elders closed ranks around "the medium" through which their power over the community had been sustained, even to the extent of murder and a judicial investigation![84]

Outside of such a village, however, a medium was normally left to his or her own devices. In the city of Yi, a medium of a *congci* successfully conspired with his clique to neutralize yet another blaspheming youth in order to demonstrate his spirit's power, and thereby win contributions to renovate his altar from the urban residents (*yimin*) who had thus far been unaccommodating.[85] In the city, therefore, a spirit-medium confronted challenges similar to those he faced in the village, but exploited them to secure patrons he had never before had. Along the same lines, another medium in Tongzhou used complex duplicity to gain a permanent sinecure in a temple patronized by literati (*shiren*).[86]

The position of the spirit-medium was inherently unstable. The medium was often one power broker among many, dependent on alliances with landlords, functionaries, local literati, and his band of acolytes. Sometimes, however, even the goodwill of the community was unable to guarantee a spirit-medium control over his destiny:

> In the subprefecture of Chong'an [Fujian], there was a spirit-medium (*wu*) named Weng Chishi who served the spirits with great efficacy. The villagers (*cunmin*) flocked to him eagerly. On the first of the ninth month of 1161, just as he was petitioning on behalf of the people, he spoke all of a sudden in the voice of his spirit: "I must go far away and will be temporarily unable to respond to people's requests and cure their illnesses." The members of Weng's household angrily complained: "For generations we have held on to the power of you, the spirit, for our livelihood. We have burned incense and reverentially served you without any disrespect. We do not understand why we have been rejected." Three times they came forward and kowtowed. But the spirit responded, "The barbarian bandits are coming south. The Lord on High (*shangtian*) has given a general order that all cavalry soldiers that belong to each general of the Community Temples of the City God (*chenghuang shemiao*) under Heaven should defend the River. Therefore I must go." They asked, "How long before you return?" and he said, "I cannot yet determine. I suspect it may be before the winter solstice." From this moment, communication was cut off. Meanwhile there was an illness in a rich family, and they beseeched Weng to come to their home. Though he exhaustively prayed, the spirit would not descend. [Yet,] when the first of the twelfth month arrived, he assumed once more the voice of the spirit, saying, "We have already killed the desired barbarian king. Worship of the earth deities (*shenqi*)

in all the circuits has been liberated and continues." From
that day, Weng's spiritual power was like it had been.[87]

Here a hereditary medium temporarily loses his power because his
tutelary divinity is called away by the Emperor on High for the defense
of the realm. The significance of this anecdote lies in its demonstration of the extent to which even the spirits of the medium had become
integrated in, and on occasion subordinated to, a spiritual hierarchy
that placed limits on their autonomy. The tutelary divinity of this spirit-
medium is identified as one of an army of mounted soldiers, the minions of various generals (i.e., the deities of the Daoist Ritual Master)
who are, in turn, the subordinates of the City Gods. This is but a segment of a much larger and complex bureaucracy of souls of the dead
that crystallized in the tenth century and became an integral part of
the pantheon of Daoist Ritual Masters in the twelfth. The bureaucratization of the medium's tutelary divinity reflects a process of accommodation on which we have yet to touch—between Daoist exorcists
and spirit-mediums at the level of ritual practice. The entire conflict,
in fact, between exorcists (Daoist or "official") and spirit-medium cults
was held in check by a profound and lasting ritual relationship that
emerged in the twelfth century among these same practitioners.

Exposing this relationship is the subject of the next five chapters.
Chapter 4 examines the relationship between Ritual Masters and
spirit-mediums in the context of Daoist revelation and, in particular,
the divine revelations of the talismans, rituals, and texts associated
with the new therapeutic lineages of the Song. Chapter 4 juxtaposes
two seemingly unrelated episodes: one associated with the court and
the founding of the Song dynasty in the late tenth century, the other
emanating from the countryside, from the ritual crisis of a Daoist exorcist in the twelfth century. The link between these two episodes will
expose the profound relationship between court and countryside, between imperial legitimization and popular religion. Chapters 5, 6, and
7 offer a precise genealogy and delineation of the working relationship between Ritual Masters and spirit-mediums in the twelfth century.

4

The Cult of the Black Killer

By the Northern Song, the Mandate of Heaven had moved squarely within the fold of Daoist interpretation. It became clear, moreover, that even with the consolidation of the South, this mandate was in serious need of shoring up. After 1005, the emperor Zhenzong (r. 998–1022) woke up to the defeat of his armies, the loss of territory, and the humiliating treaty with the Liao. In 1006, the architect of this treaty, Kou Zhun, was dismissed, and the emperor turned increasingly to Wang Qinruo. Wang would be excoriated by Song historians for allowing the emperor to fiddle away his time in Daoist pavilions while the capital, Kaifeng, was threatened. It is true that, as a southerner in a courtly and bureaucratic milieu still dominated by northerners, Wang's views on defense seemed callous. Yet in the Daoist Wang Qinruo, the emperor found a minister who let the emperor be himself.[1]

The Supporter of Sageliness and Protector of Virtue

Wang suggested that the emperor might best overcome the shameful treaty by performing the *feng* and *shan* sacrifices and by searching for celestial omens. In the first month of 1008, the first of four "heavenly texts" (*tianshu*) was "discovered" on the palace grounds. In several cases their discovery was indicated directly to the emperor by a spirit dressed in Daoist costume. All these texts were "dynastic treasures," celestial talismans that explicitly confirmed the Zhaos' possession of the mandate, thereby guaranteeing, incidentally, the emperor's right to perform the sacrifices recommended by Wang. Amidst an outpouring of support, but also much criticism, the emperor went to Mount Tai in the ninth month of 1008 and performed the *feng* and *shan* sacrifices. And in the second month of 1011, he performed the great sacrifice to the Earth at Fengyin.

Meanwhile, the identity of the spirit who had appeared to the emperor was taking shape. In the tenth month of 1012, the emperor had a vision in which a spirit-being descended and conveyed to him a command from the Jade Emperor (Yuhuang) which said, "In the past I ordered your ancestor Zhao [Yuanlang] to confer upon you the 'heavenly texts.' Honor him as the Tang honored Laozi!" Several days later, during the course of what appears to have been a Daoist "offering" (*jiao*) in the Abbey of Extended Mercy, the "holy ancestor" appeared again to the emperor and declared that he was in fact the Yellow Emperor (Xuanyuan huangdi) who, in one last incarnation, had descended during the Later Tang (923–935) as the first ancestor of the Zhao clan. In 1017, Zhenzong visited the Palace of Reflection and Response of Jade Purity (Yuqing zhaoying gong), built three years previously to house the "heavenly texts," and set up tablets for the Jade Emperor, the Holy Ancestor (i.e., the Yellow Emperor), and all subsequent ancestors of the Zhao clan. The claim of descent from the primordial Yellow Emperor, patron of Daoism, was a quite self-conscious attempt not only to imitate but to surpass the divine genealogy of the Tang.

Already, from 1007, much of this had been prepared behind the scenes. Through a eunuch intermediary, a certain Wang Jie had been lodged in a building in the Capital Security Office (Huangcheng si), the bureau that controlled access to the imperial city. Wang was from Fujian and claimed to have met there, in the closing years of the tenth century, a magician named Zhao. Zhao taught Wang his techniques and entrusted him to perform them in the service of the emperor. When Wang Jie finally arrived in Kaifeng, he identified his master Zhao as none other than the Perfected Lord "Controller of Destiny" (Siming zhenjun) and the original ancestor of the ruling family. From 1007 on, the Controller of Destiny descended and transmitted to Wang a series of revelations and predictions that were passed on to the emperor.[2] We can agree with Michel Soymié that the imperial visions that began in 1008 probably originated through the offices of this medium from Fujian.[3]

The years between 1007 and 1022, when the emperor died, were a period, therefore, of intense Daoist activity. All this is well known. What is perhaps less well known is Zhenzong's devotion to a god known as the Perfected Lord "Protector of Sageliness" (Yisheng zhenjun):

> The emperor received the "primordial talismans" [i.e., the heavenly texts] and [as a consequence] performed the *feng* sacrifice on Mount Tai. He built the Palace of Reflection and Response of Jade Purity. Within the Palace grounds, to the northwest of the Tower of the Precious Talismans (Baofu ge), he constructed a Pavilion for Extending the Mandate (Ningming dian). And behind this was the Tower for Extending the Mandate (Ningming lou) in which he honored the Perfected Lord.[4]

In 1014, Zhenzong issued an edict granting the Perfected Lord a new title, "Supporter of Sageliness and Protector of Virtue" (Yisheng baode). "In the generation and execution of the precious mandate," he wrote, "we have relied on this greatest of gods to bear the burden; as a luminous reward for the extraordinary evidence of his power, we reverentially add to his fine title."[5] Indeed, after reviewing the support this god had provided to his predecessor, Emperor Taizong, Zhenzong took this opportunity to announce "the completion of the mandate." In 1016, none other than Wang Qinruo presented to the emperor *The Transmissions of the Supporter of Sageliness and Protector of Virtue*, the source of the previous quotations.[6] The process of discovering the identity of the Perfected Lord "Supporter of Sageliness" will take us from the lofty world of imperial legitimation to the daily routine of Daoist exorcists.

The Ritual Master Zhang Shouzhen

The Transmissions open with an account of the god's first epiphany:

> At the beginning of the Jianlong reign period [960–963], a commoner from Zhouzhi subprefecture in Fenghuang [Shanxi], Zhang Shouzhen, was wandering on Mount Zhongnan. Suddenly he heard someone calling him from above in a pure and sonorous voice. Shouzhen was startled and looked around, but saw nothing. He picked up the pace, listening intently for several miles. Again he heard a voice, saying, "If you walk ahead, I'll be right behind you."

This went on for several days. Shouzhen could not figure it out. Thereupon he returned home. Inside his house, he again heard the voice: "I have received an order to send down my spirit. Why have you been so obstinate in this way, refusing to listen to my words?! If I am not able to perform great deeds for the Song dynasty, then you will surely be ground to powder!" At this moment Shouzhen knew that he had encountered something extraordinary, but at the same time was terrified. Therefore he said, "I am unclear what star has descended in this manner. I am ignorant and cloudy by nature. I only wish that you do not intimidate me. I have nothing with which to worship you." Therefore the god said, "I am an Assisting Minister of the Jade Emperor and a Great Sage of the Highest Heaven. I have received a mandate to protect these times and have descended among men, riding on a dragon. However, there are no upright and true gentlemen who revere my teaching. You have exceptional bones which are completely out of the ordinary. You will be able to receive, with a reverent heart, my holy instructions." Shouzhen replied, "Your servant has heard that in the case of men such people are called *wu* and in the case of women, *xi* [sic]." Although Shouzhen was of mediocre intelligence, his sense of humility was of the benevolent sort. Again the god spoke: "I am a god of the Highest Heaven, not a ghost or demon. I can cause the spirits of the Five Peaks and Four Rivers to serve me. If you turn your heart and enter the Way and respectfully offer me incense, I will have you respond to the sought-after mandate of the Great Dynasty [i.e., the Song] and receive the kindness of the True Ruler [i.e., the emperor]. What has this to do with the vocation of a *wu* or *xi*?" Shouzhen replied, "If you intend to teach and instruct me like this, I have indeed dared to serve you with disrespect. Therefore, I will lay out offerings of wine and meat as a sacrifice to you." Again Shouzhen heard the words, "I am a spiritual being. How can you pollute me with offerings of meat? Since, however, you do not understand, I will not punish you. From now on, only use incense, vegetables, and fruit as tribute. Although I

do not consume these, still I will appreciate the thought."
Shouzhen kneeled and thanked him.[7]

Following the advice of the god, Zhang Shouzhen became a disciple of the Daoist master Liang Quan of the Tower Abbey (Louguan).[8] After Shouzhen was ordained as a Daoist priest, he built a hermitage on some empty land next to his home and entered the religious life (*chujia*). He also set aside a pavilion within the Palace of the Northern Emperor (Beidi gong) where he worshipped the god and received from him a series of revelations. The first involved three sets of "Sword Rituals" (*jianfa*) to use in performing exorcisms on behalf of the dynastic family, villages, and individuals, respectively; the second involved three sets of "Rituals for the Construction of Altars" (*jiantan fa*) to secure blessings for the dynasty, officials, and literati and commoners, respectively.[9]

All this transpired during the three years after the founding of the dynasty in 960. Subsequently, the divine revelations became more intertwined with imperial politics. At some point during the Qiande reign period (963–967), the Prince of Jin (Jinwang, who was Lord of Kaifeng and the future emperor Taizong) commissioned the performance of a Daoist offering (*jiao*) in the Temple of the Northern Emperor during which a representative conveyed the Prince of Jin's vow to enlarge the temple. In response to this commitment, the god—probably through the mediation of Zhang Shouzhen—prophesied that he would make the Prince of Jin the second ruler of the Song dynasty.[10] The Prince of Jin's brother, the current emperor Taizu, grew alarmed when he heard about this and summoned Shouzhen to the palace. Shouzhen warned the emperor that the god would only respond to a proper memorial and would not descend in the face of insincerity. The emperor, however, went ahead and had a small child in the domestic service—a eunuch—stand to the side and whistle (*changxiao*). Taizu asked whether this was how the god conveyed his words, only insulting the god further while incidentally proving his own unworthiness.[11]

Later, during an offering performed by Zhang Shouzhen in the Jianlong Abbey in Kaifeng, the god descended again and claimed to be a supporting minister of the Jade Emperor who had been given a mandate to protect the Song dynasty and its altars. The god also renewed his praise for the "benevolent heart" of the Prince of Jin. All this apparently transpired on the evening of the nineteenth day of the tenth month of the ninth year of Kaibao (976)—the eve of Taizu's death.[12] Thus these prophecies and claims amounted to nothing less than a divine justification for the Prince of Jin's usurpation of the throne, made more problematic by persistent rumors of fratricide.[13]

After Taizong's accession, he had Shouzhen perform a "Great Offering of the Entire Heaven" (*Zhoutian dajiao*) in the Qionglin yuan, a park in the western suburbs of Kaifeng where the emperor entertained the newly graduated examination candidates for the *jinshi* degree.[14] In verse, the god confirmed his support for the founding and continued stability of the Song dynasty. In response, the emperor commissioned two officials to oversee the construction of a major temple dedicated to the god. The "Palace of Great Peace of [the Heaven of] Highest Purity" (Shangqing taiping gong) was built in the northern foothills of Zhongnanshan, home of Zhang Shouzhen. The temple complex included (a) four pavilions in the center dedicated to the Jade Emperor, Purple Tenuity (Ziwei), the Seven Primordials (Qiyuan), and the Perfected Lord, respectively; (b) four pavilions to the east, the first of which was dedicated to the divinity Tianpeng; (c) four pavilions to the west, the first of which was dedicated to the divinity Zhenwu; (d) special halls dedicated to divinities known as "spiritual officers" (*lingguan*), among others; (e) a Bell Tower and a Scripture Tower; and, finally, (f) a tablet (*bei*) that recorded the history of the temple and its god.[15]

The Bell Tower and the Scripture Tower had been defining features of the Tang-dynasty Tower Abbey. According to a temple inscription engraved in 988, the Bell Tower of this abbey, which had since been moved to another place, was installed in the Palace of Great Peace at the request of Zhang Shouzhen.[16] It seems quite probable that the Palace of Great Peace not only came within the jurisdiction of the Daoist lineage of the Tower Abbey but was its successor. Given that our text, as we have seen, identifies Liang Quan, the ordination master of Zhang Shouzhen, as a priest of the Tower Abbey, we can hypothesize that the link between the cult of the Perfected Lord "Protector of Sageliness" and the emperor Taizong had been engineered by this particular Daoist faction well-versed in the ways of imperial legitimization.[17]

Even if this hypothesis is too conspiratorial, *The Transmissions of the Supporter of Sageliness and Protector of Virtue* remains an ideologizing document. This is particularly true with respect to the identity of the god himself. Throughout *The Transmissions*, the god who descends is referred to as the "Perfected Lord" (*zhenjun*), a rather general and common term for Daoist divinities that forms part of the title conferred upon the god by Emperor Zhenzong. Twice we have seen that the Perfected Lord introduces himself as a "supporting minister of the Jade Emperor," yet this is clearly a functional description and was probably meant to impress a later audience, for the Jade Emperor became recognized as a tutelary divinity of the Song dynasty only during the reign of Zhenzong.[18]

In 983, Taizong granted the Perfected Lord his first title: "General Who Supports the Sage" (Yisheng jiangjun). This investiture (*feng*), normally *pro forma*, created an amusing difficulty. After the title was reported to the god by Zhang Shouzhen, the god asked him which sage he was supposed to be supporting. The implication that the god may have been subordinated to the emperor was not lost on Shouzhen, who became terrified as the messenger of a potential insult. The god, however, told Shouzhen that it was not his fault, and he was relieved to learn, after further inquiries, that the sage whom the god supported was the Emperor on High (Shangdi).[19]

That the god himself is not quite sure exactly who he is supposed to be I take as just one more indication that the authors of this text found his identity to be a problem. The text seems intent on dancing around the issue in a studied attempt at avoidance, even effacement. The title "General" (*jiangjun*), however—a title that the god does not dispute—is a trace, and the only indication here, of his true nature. The god's identity in fact emerges with great clarity in other, non-Daoist, accounts of Zhang Shouzhen's relation to the Song court. A passage in the *Xu Zizhi tongjian changbian* (*Collected Data for a Continuation of the "Comprehensive Mirror to Aid in Government"*) opens with the following:

> In the beginning, a spirit descended before Zhang Shouzhen, a commoner in Zhouzhi subprefecture, and said, "I am a venerable god of Heaven. My title is 'General Black Killer' (Heisha jiangjun). I support the Jade Emperor." Each time Shouzhen purified himself and invited the god with prayer, the spirit would always descend into the room. The wind would whistle, and his voice was like that of a small child; only Shouzhen was able to understand it.[20]

And a section devoted to the General Black Killer in the Southern Song *Huangchao shishi leiyuan* offers a significant variant of this account:

During the Kaibao reign period [968–976], a spirit descended before
Zhang Shouzhen, a Daoist priest on Zhongnanshan, and said, "I am a
venerable spirit of Heaven. My title is 'General Black Killer.' Together
with Xuanwu, Tianpeng, and their retinue, we are the Three Great Generals of Heaven." [Henceforth] the god spoke about matters of fortune
and misfortune with great efficacy. Each time Shouzhen purified himself and invited the god, he would descend into the room. The wind
would whistle, and his voice was like that of a small child; only Shouzhen
could understand it.[21]

The General Black Killer appeared to Zhang Shouzhen as one member of a divine trio that included Xuanwu and Tianpeng. Like his companions, Black Killer was a god of the north—hence his black color—
and a lieutenant of the Emperor of the North (Beidi). It is not
insignificant in this respect that after Zhang Shouzhen took up the religious life, he worshipped his god and was the beneficiary of his revelations in the Palace of the Northern Emperor (Beidi gong). Moreover, the trio of deities subordinated to Beidi was represented spatially
in the Temple of Great Peace of Highest Purity, the temple complex
built by Taizong on Zhongnanshan, where there was a central hall dedicated to the Perfected Lord (i.e., Black Killer) that sat along a vertical axis headed by halls to the Jade Emperor and to Purple Tenuity,
both emperors of the north, and that was flanked by halls to Zhenwu
(i.e., Xuanwu) and to Tianpeng. The important point, however, is that
Heisha, Zhenwu, and Tianpeng were the central cultic divinities of
many of the most significant and innovative Daoist exorcistic lineages
of the Song. These three were the source both of their revelations and
of the powers that were embodied in, and made effective by, their therapeutic practices.

The Four Saints

The General Black Killer was appropriately named. He was, above all,
a demonifuge, a destroyer of demons. The *Huangchao shishi leiyuan* provides a graphic description of his appearance. After construction began on the Palace of Great Peace on Mount Zhongnan, artisans set
about creating the all-important effigy of the god. To this end, they
first invited the Black Killer to descend. Perhaps through the intermediary of Zhang Shouzhen, he told them: "I am of human form and
I have angry eyes and disheveled hair. I ride on a dragon and hold a

sword. In front I point to a star."[22] The god's self-description is
confirmed in a poem by Su Shi on the occasion of a visit to the temple in the second month of 1062: "The secret pavilion opens by a
golden lock, the god is riding on a golden dragon; dressed in black,
he grasps a massive sword; his hair is disheveled, and his two eyes cause
one to shiver with fear."[23] A Qing-dynasty commentary adds that images of the "Protector of Sageliness" all represent the god with "disheveled hair and bare feet, grasping a sword and riding a dragon."

The human body, military implements, and aggressive and wild demeanor are also characteristic of Heisha's divine comrades-in-arms,
and of the entire class of divinities venerated by the Daoist exorcistic
lineages of the Song. According to one text, Tianpeng was armed to
the teeth—of which he also had, apparently, several sets. He had three
heads and six arms, which held a hatchet, rope, bow, arrow, lance, and
spear. He was dressed in black clothes and a dark hat, and led an army
of three hundred thousand soldiers.[24] Tianpeng was the first of the
"Divine Ennead of the Occultated Jia" (*dunjia jiushen*), the nine stars
of the esoteric Dipper; these are described in the sixth-century book
of divination, the *Wuxing dayi*,[25] where Tianpeng is assigned the function of security and protection.[26] In the sixth century, he was already
venerated as an exorcistic divinity and lieutenant of the Northern Emperor. An entry in Tao Hongjing's *Zhengao* describes the "Rites of the
Northern Emperor for Killing Demons" (*Beidi shagui zhi fa*), which en-
tail, for the most part, the recitation of a rather dramatic spell to Tianpeng.[27] By the ninth century, his cult had spread west to Sichuan, where
a Daoist exorcist who worshipped the Northern Emperor engraved a
Seal of Tianpeng to protect families from the period's civil wars.[28] The
cult to Tianpeng remained popular among military circles into the
Southern Song, when he aided various generals in their battles with
the Jin.[29]

Since the Warring States period, Xuanwu, or the Dark Warrior, had
been one of the theriomorphic spirits identified with the four directions. He governed the northern quadrant and, in another scheme,
the seven stellar mansions (*xingxiu*) associated with this direction. His
body was a composite, part tortoise and part snake; he was dark like
Tianpeng and Heisha; and his martial spirit was represented not only
by his name but by the protective armor of the turtle shell.[30]

The development of an independent cult to Xuanwu can be traced
in the *Xuantian shangdi qishenglu* (*Record of Revelations to the Sages by the*

Supreme Sovereign of the Dark Heaven, HY 957). The purpose of this Ming-dynasty hagiography was to establish the god's association, both legendary and historical, with Mount Wudang, a major pilgrimage site closely identified with the fortunes of the Ming emperors.[31] Although several passages testify to the god's appearance in the Tang[32]—on Mount Wudang but also in Jiangxi—the popularity of his cult becomes significant only with the founding of the Song in the tenth century. Renamed the "Perfected Warrior" (Zhenwu), the god was honored prodigiously by the first emperors of the Song, not least for his contribution to the dynasty's consolidation of the South and to its continuing defense of the frontiers.

In this regard, one of the more astonishing revelations of the Ming hagiography is the link between the Perfected Warrior and Zhang Shouzhen. Toward the end of the tenth century, Zhang took under his wing a "presented scholar" (*jinshi*) named Zhuan Hong from Yangzhou. Zhuan Hong was a lifelong devotee of the Perfected Warrior and had made a pilgrimage to the Palace of Great Peace of (the Heaven of) Highest Purity in the Zhongnan mountains. There, at the altar of the Western Pavilion dedicated to the Perfected Warrior, this literatus entered into a trance and was possessed by the god under the watchful eyes of the temple administrator (*zhigong*), who was none other than Zhang Shouzhen. In four allusive lines, the Perfected Warrior prophesied the birth of a son to the childless emperor, as well as the renewal of the Song mandate in the son's accession to the throne. Zhang wrote down the verse and presented it, through military intermediaries, to the throne. The emperor was both astonished and delighted. Many years later, after Zhang had died and the thirteen-year-old Renzong (r. 1023–1063) had succeeded his father, the possessed scholar was worshipped as a transcendent, and a small altar was dedicated to him in the Western Pavilion of the Perfected Warrior. Here we see not only Zhang's role as a mediator of divine revelation and imperial legitimization, but his role as an officiant (and interpreter) of possession trance—a role characteristic of Daoist Ritual Masters in the twelfth century.[33]

The main focus of imperial attention, however, was neither Mount Zhongnan nor Mount Wudang, for that matter, but the Abbey of the Four Saints of the Northern Pole (Beiji sisheng guan) constructed by the emperors Taizu and Taizong in Kaifeng.[34] The abbey was dedicated to Purple Tenuity, Emperor of the North, and to the Four Saints:

Heisha, Zhenwu, and Tianpeng—the Three Great Generals of Zhang Shouzhen's Temple of Great Peace—and a fourth, Tianyou, who had been invoked along with Tianpeng in the sixth-century Rites of the Northern Emperor for Killing Demons. This divine quartet, moreover, formed the central pantheon of an important Daoist exorcistic tradition indigenous to the lower Yangzi in the early twelfth century, the "Great Rites of Youth's Incipience" (*Tongchu dafa*).[35]

In response to the imperial patronage of Zhenwu, pavilions to him were established in many Daoist abbeys.[36] Imperial patronage, however, does not account for the popularity of this god, who was worshipped quite independently, and privately, in the homes of officials, soldiers, and merchants.[37] By the twelfth century he was the focus of many large-scale community festivals.[38] Zhenwu was the god par excellence of village spirit-mediums (*wu*); in a very concrete sense, he was their alter ego.[39] The legendary portion of the *Xuantian shangdi qishenglu* can be read as a mythogenesis of Zhenwu's iconographic representation. In each and every epiphany of the god, he appears with "disheveled hair and bare feet" (*pifa xianzu*), armed with a "precious sword" (*baojian*), and accompanied by a turtle and snake—animal transformations of the Demon King (Mowang) whom Zhenwu defeated in a great cosmic battle on Wudangshan.[40] "Disheveled hair and bare feet" are precisely the terms used to describe possessed spirit-mediums. Put more strongly, to describe someone in this way was either to describe a spirit-medium in trance or someone imitating such a person. Examples of this are legion in the anecdotal literature of the Song and before.[41] Any photograph of a modern "divination youth" with his unkempt hair, half-naked body, and handheld weapon shows that not much has changed at this level of village religion.

As we have seen, the Black Killer was described in precisely the same terms—with disheveled hair and bare feet, holding a sword. The origin of Heisha is somewhat obscure, though perhaps no more obscure than the origin of any god. What we do know is that during the third decade of the tenth century, in Fujian, a Daoist priest named Tan Zixiao came to possess a set of talismans "discovered" by a spirit-medium.[42] These talismans formed the basis for his creation of the Rectifying Rites of Tianxin (*Tianxin zhengfa*), which would become the most widely practiced therapeutic rituals of the twelfth century. According to one source, the divine object of Tan's personal cult was none other than the Black Killer, and indeed, we find that the "Talisman of the Black

Killer" (*Heisha fu*) is of fundamental importance in the texts of the Rites of Tianxin and their derivatives.[43] These texts, moreover, identify the Black Killer as the "Talismanic Envoy of the Dark Warrior" (Xuanwu fushi);[44] he is, therefore, closely linked—and in a sense even subordinated—to Xuanwu, who may be invoked separately in the Tianxin rituals. Filling out the triad is the "Great Prime Marshal Tianpeng" (Tianpeng da yuanshuai), supreme commander of thirty-six generals.[45] Heisha, Xuanwu, and Tianpeng are the three principal agents of the Emperor of the North (Beidi), who presides over the Department of Exorcism (Chuxie yuan) and who is both the "patriarchal master" (*zushi*) and the central divinity of the Rites of Tianxin.[46]

Therefore, at the core of the imperial cult to the Perfected Lord "Supporter of Sageliness and Protector of Virtue" was a precise set of fierce martial deities who would become the principal agents of the rituals practiced by a number of Daoist exorcists active mainly in the South during the late Northern and Southern Song. And however we read Zhang Shouzhen's relation to the court, both as a prophet of imperial succession and as an officiant of large-scale Daoist "offerings," he was, above all, originally if not exclusively an exorcist.

The initial set of divine revelations in the Palace of the Northern Emperor were "Sword Rituals," and the last third of *The Transmissions* is given over entirely to an account of exorcisms performed by Zhang Shouzhen for commoner and official residents in the vicinity of Chang'an.[47] The text of a biographical inscription, the first part of which was composed by twenty-one disciples of Zhang Shouzhen and engraved in 999, three years after his death, explains that, following the revelations in the Palace of the Northern Emperor, Zhang pacified the local area by exorcising demons and became known by the title, "Gentleman Who Penetrates the Numinous, Zhang the Black Killer" (Tongling xiansheng Zhang Heisha).[48] This appellation suggests that Zhang was so identified with his divinity that he was named after him. (In the Song, if not before, it was common for village spirit-mediums to adopt as personal names the very name of the god who possessed them.)[49]

The temple tablet, moreover, opens by referring to Zhang Shouzhen as a "Ritual Master" (*fashi*) and by identifying him as a descendant of the immortal Zhang Zifang, the sixth-generation ancestor of Zhang Daoling, the founder of the Celestial Master sect and religious Daoism.[50] This identification is, of course, a complete contrivance based on the similarity of their family names. It is not, however, gratuitous. The defining concern of Zhang Daoling and the Celestial Master tradition was therapeutic ritual. And many of the Daoist exorcistic lineages of the Song found their inspiration in, or claimed a direct relation to, the "Orthodox Unity" (Zhengyi) tradition of the Celestial Masters, who had, since the late Tang, relocated on Mount Longhu in Jiangxi.[51]

Spirit-Mediums and Daoist Revelation

By now, the nature of the Perfected Lord and of Zhang Shouzhen himself have become fairly transparent. What is less clear is the relationship between this dark, murderous spirit and his demon-quelling devotee. How, precisely, did the Black Killer reveal himself to Zhang Shouzhen? *The Transmissions* state merely that the god "descended" (*jiang*), or that he "sent down his words" (*jiangyan*), statements that are then followed in every case by a direct quotation from the spirit. Are we dealing here with auditory hallucinations or with descriptive terms that are willfully imprecise so as to obscure some other means of divine revelation?

Recall that, when the Perfected Lord first made known his intention of conferring upon Zhang Shouzhen his holy instructions, Zhang naturally thought that he himself was being put in the position of a spirit-medium (*wu/xi*), the time-honored representative of village religion who offered blood sacrifices and who either transmitted messages from, or became possessed by, a guardian spirit. The Perfected Lord protested this quite vigorously, as he did again when Zhang tried to honor him with meat offerings: the Perfected Lord is a heavenly deity who does not require provisions of food. Yet could it be that, just as this text is at pains to efface the true nature of its divinity, so it is at pains to hide or transform the true manner of his revelation?

Recall, further, that the Perfected Lord was absolutely beside himself with anger when the emperor Taizu had a small child (*xiao'er*) whistle in order "to imitate" the voice of the Perfected Lord. Here, I think, we have a clear case of textual, if not also psychological, displacement. The accounts in the *Xu Zizhi tongjian changpian* and *Huangchao shishi leiyuan* agree that when Zhang Shouzhen summoned the Black Killer, "the wind would whistle, his voice was like that of a small child, and only Zhang Shouzhen could understand it." Could it be that the voice of the Black Killer manifested itself as the voice of a small child precisely because it was a small child—a child-medium—who embodied him? We know, for example, that large portions of *The Great Rites of the Jade Hall* (*Yudang dafa*)—the ritual manual compiled in the early twelfth century by Lu Shizhong—were transmitted from a divinity by "spirit-writing" (*jiangbi*). And there we read that "when the Celestial Lord descended, *his voice sounded like a small child,* and only [Lu] Shizhong and his disciple, Zhai Duwen, could hear it."[52] As we shall see immediately below and in subsequent chapters, real children played precisely this role in the new revelations, as well as the therapeutic rituals, of twelfth-century Daoist exorcists like Lu Shizhong.

In the preceding pages, we have found the revelations of the Black Killer to be at the center of imperial legitimization, succession, and the Mandate of Heaven in the early Song. The transformation of the dark, militaristic god of a tenth-century cult into the Perfected Lord of an eleventh-century text—into a supporting minister of the Jade Emperor and defender of the Song dynasty—seems to me entirely homologous with the transformation of the military elite of tenth-century kingdoms into bureaucratic servants of eleventh-century emperors.[53] The cult to the Black Killer, moreover, seems to me equally paradigmatic of the new Daoist movements of the twelfth century: these movements were built upon the revelation of therapeutic ritual; they invoked fierce martial deities, such as the Black Killer or the Perfected Warrior; and they involved a special class of exorcists who, like Zhang Shouzhen, were referred to by the term "Ritual Master." It is to one of these that I now turn:

> Zhao Zujian, a Daoist priest (*daoshi*) from Heng prefecture, once practiced the Rites of the Celestial Heart (*Tianxin fa*) and would cure demonic illness for rural folk (*xiangren*). Suddenly he could no longer perform. Unable to control his anger, he summoned a spirit to take possession of someone so that he could interrogate him. The spirit responded, "It is unlawful to dare come without authorization. Yet because a spirit-general in the law courts (*fayuan shenjiang*) received a certain bribe, this was allowed to happen." Zhao silently thought to himself: "In suppressing *chimei*-demons by upholding the Rectifying Rites to make a living, I have put my trust in the spirits and employed them.

Now this spirit[54] has received a commission by bribery; in what way have I presumed upon my authority?" And Zhao intended to report this transgression to the Eastern Peak (Dongyue).

That night, Zhao dreamed that an armored knight with a particularly fierce demeanor came before him with clasped hands and said, "I, your disciple, am the spirit-general under you, the Ritual Master. When alive, I was a soldier with awesome power, and people called me 'Chen the Iron Whip' (Chen Tiebian). In death I became a god and was attached to a sacrificial altar. I was unable to control myself to such an extent that I offered a demonic bribe. Now I hear that the Ritual Master intends to inform Mount Tai, whereby I will fall into the eternal prison of Fengdu, forever without salvation. I hope you will condescend to pity and forgive me, and I beseech you to purify your heart and reform yourself." Zhao replied, "I cannot bear to report your transgression and will only mention that I am no longer willing to practice these rites and that I have caused you yourself to return." The soldier then bowed in gratitude and retreated. In the end, Zhao sent up a memorial to nullify his practices. He considered changing to practice the Rites of the Five Thunder [Gods], and without his spirit-general, he burned incense before an effigy of Tan the Perfected (Tan Zhenren) and anticipated receiving admonishment.

After several years, Zhao again practiced "rites of summoning and investigating [demons]" (*kaozhao*) for people. At the time he compelled a boy to investigate by illumination (*shi tongzi zhaoshi*). Suddenly the youth jumped up, and with his hair disheveled and his feet bare, he shouted angrily, "I am Tan the Perfected. I have taken pity on your diligence and industry. Therefore I will instruct you in ritual. Have you heretofore obtained anything?" Zhao responded, "Only four talismans that were transmitted to this world by the Perfected Warrior (Zhenwu)." The spirit said, "My talismans of the Five Thunders have seventy-two manifestations. Those that you have already received are only one-eighteenth of them, so how can you possibly

control demonic malignancies?! It would benefit you to take
one hundred sheets of paper and place them upon the
table, and I will transmit them to you." Then, planting his
sword in the ground, the spirit said, "I have welcomed a
Judicial Officer of the Five Thunders to quickly transmit the
seventy-two talismans, and I specified that they only be
completed now." From the beginning Zhao did not see what
was being done, but after a mealtime had passed, the spirit
said, "The talismans have already been completed," and he
ordered Zhao to take them in his hands. Raising them up,
Zhao examined the paper. Altogether there were sixty-eight
sheets. On each was drawn a talisman, and the celestial seals
(*tianyin*) were resplendent. They were not written in an
earthly style. Zhao was ecstatically happy and he held them
up in supplication. The youth also became conscious. From
this time Zhao used the talismans with spiritual efficacy.[55]

Zhao Zujian is described as a Daoist priest and a practitioner of the
Rectifying Rites of the Celestial Heart. Yet at one and the same time,
he was what Lagerwey means by a "country priest," a priest who resided
not in a Daoist abbey or ordination center, but one who, in the words
of the text, "made a living" by exorcising demons "for rural folk." It is
hard to distinguish this clerical Ritual Master from lay exorcists like
Tan or Zheng *fashi*, and Zhao's therapeutic practice is paradigmatic
of the way in which the new exorcistic rites of the twelfth century were
embedded in local cults.

Zhao's spirit-general, Chen the Iron Whip, was a soldier who received blood sacrifices at a local altar or temple and who undoubtedly
manifested his power through village spirit-mediums, perhaps even
through those whom Zhao himself employed. Indeed, the implication
is that, in exorcising local demons, the Daoist Ritual Master had no
choice but to trust in the local spirits. Just as the Song state sought to
solve its personnel and fiscal problems by creating a range of village
service positions, so the Daoist exorcist sought to maintain local order and spiritual well-being by creating an entire sub-bureaucracy from
the gods of local cults. Yet by absorbing these unreconstructed spirits,
the Ritual Master left himself open to the consequences of their volatile
nature, which neither he nor apparently they could control.[56]

The most remarkable aspect of this episode is its adumbration of what we will discover to be the binding links that were being formed in the twelfth century between Ritual Masters and spirit-mediums. On the one hand, spirit-mediums were employed by Zhao Zujian as surrogates in a therapeutic rite known as "summoning for investigation" (*kaozhao*), which we examine in Chapter 5. On the other hand, spirit-mediums functioned as this Daoist exorcist's principal means of communication with the other world, and even as the source of his esoteric knowledge. Initially, Zhao employed a spirit-medium—"someone whose body was possessed"—to question a spirit belonging to the celestial hierarchy about the interruption in his ability to perform. This interview led Zhao to abandon his practice of the Rectifying Rites of the Celestial Heart. He then placed his hopes in the Rites of the Five Thunder Gods and, in the meantime, focused his devotion on Tan the Perfected. Several years later, Zhao resumed his practice of the exorcistic "rituals of summoning for investigation," which, as we shall see, commonly employed spirit-mediums. On one of these occasions, the young boy (*tongzi*) became spontaneously possessed by the object of Zhao's devotion, Tan the Perfected, in the wild manner of village spirit-mediums—"with loosened hair and bare feet" and holding a sword—precisely the terms used to describe the divinities of the Rites of the Celestial Heart, namely, the Black Killer and the Perfected Warrior. Tan the Perfected, in fact, was none other than Tan Zixiao, the "Patriarchal Master" and tenth-century founder of the Rites of the Celestial Heart. Tan the divinity now decided to transmit to Zhao talismans of Thunder Magic to supplement those already in his possession. Apparently Zhao had been making do with a handful of common and perhaps locally distributed talismans revealed by the Perfected Warrior.

What is so fascinating here is that the means of the transmission from Tan Zixiao was nothing less than the automatic writing of a possessed spirit-medium! The spirit-medium, in other words, was the source of continuing Daoist revelation, and this fact forces us to entertain the possibility that the so-called original talismans and revelations of the Rectifying Rites of the Celestial Heart, of Thunder Magic, and of other exorcistic rites were transmitted in precisely the same manner. Recall that the first set of revelations (talismans and seals) of the Celestial Heart lineage were supposedly discovered, buried in the ground, by a Daoist/medium who passed them on to Tan Zixiao to decipher; the second set was also discovered, buried in the ground, by the clerk Rao Dongtian, who because of their unintelligible, oth-

erworldly nature was instructed by a spirit to seek out Tan Zixiao—
the man or the spirit?—for their interpretation (see Chapter 2, "The
Rites of the Celestial Heart"). But who is to say that these stories were
not elaborate attempts to make the origin of rituals conform to the
traditional Daoist ideology of "textual" discovery, even though that origin was to be found among those (spirit-mediums) who would actually form the cynosure of those same rituals? Put another way, it was
precisely because the spirit-medium was at the center of the Ritual Master's exorcistic rituals from the outset that Daoists felt compelled to
displace him.

This is obviously an *a fortiori* argument, one that tries to prove a
weaker and chronologically earlier point by a stronger and chronologically later one; one may do with it what one wants. What needs to
be taken seriously, however, is the fact that the generation of Daoist
talismans by a spirit-medium possessed by Tan Zixiao is very similar to
the ritual operations of a Daoist Ritual Master. If we turn to the texts
of the Rites of the Celestial Heart, we find that when the Ritual Master writes the talismans to be used in subsequent exorcisms, he must
first transform himself into the divinity (the Perfected Warrior, for example) whose power is embodied in these talismans![57]

The Daoist exorcist as well as the spirit-medium identify themselves
with a particular divinity. Now, possession has been defined, quite simply and accurately, as a trance of identification. Yet the exorcist is
definitely not possessed by his deity. If anything, the exorcist takes possession of the deity that has first been generated by a hyperconscious
process of visualization (*xiang*) and actualization (*cun*). The Ritual Master's identification with his divinity enhances his ego rather than erases
it; his self has been enlarged rather than diminished. The issue of control is fundamental here, as is the question of consciousness, for the
Ritual Master is not entranced any more than he is possessed. His experience, in fact, approaches what has been called "ecstasy," a term
that is often taken, mistakenly, for "trance."

Gilbert Rouget has demonstrated convincingly that the experiences
represented by these two terms oppose and contradict each other at
every level of comparison. Trance, whether that of the shaman or possessed spirit-medium, is always associated with convulsions, movement
(dance), noise (music), amnesia, and the company of others (an audience), whereas ecstasy is characterized by immobility, silence, and
solitude.[58] Phenomenological descriptions of the Ritual Master's psy-

chophysical state are hard to come by. Yet when we recall the episode involving Ritual Master Cheng translated in Chapter 3, we find that the values of immobility, silence, and solitude were precisely those that were attributed to the exorcist. After the residents of the Sun Family Hill were drawn to the sounds of a great battle between Cheng's armies and the demon's, they saw nothing but the Ritual Master "alone, standing absolutely rigid, in stillness and in darkness." This, in fact, is as he has been all along. The observers, moreover, discover what we will learn from the ritual texts: that the anecdotal account of the clash between the exorcist's armies and the demons is a narrative trope and a reification of visualizations that were entirely internal to the exorcist. Rouget has also demonstrated that visualizations of any kind, whether visions or hallucinations, are not to be found in possession trances. Like the spirit-medium, therefore, the Ritual Master identifies with his divinity; yet like the Daoist priest, he does so through a controlled process of meditation and visualization.

In contrast to the Daoist priest, however, both the lay Daoist exorcist and the spirit-medium found their institutional base in local cults to particular divinities. This was what brought them together and encouraged these exorcists to employ spirit-mediums in their therapeutic rituals on a regular basis. The control that the lay exorcist had over his given deity extended to those who were defined by their transparency to the divine. Yet unlike the spirit-medium, the Daoist Ritual Master might transcend the geographical and ideological limitations of cult. As we have seen, a growing reputation for successful exorcisms would take many Ritual Masters through the market towns and urban centers of South and East China and into the homes of landed magnates, magistrates, high officials, and courtiers, whereas the spirit-medium rarely strayed from his village or urban neighborhood.

Thus the spirit-medium was, literally, the child of his god and the local community, whose presence was required to confirm his identification with the god. Moreover, like the unpredictable terrestrial divinities whom he embodied, the spirit-medium was either benevolent or malevolent depending on how he was treated. If one spirit-medium might open a wine shop, as we have seen, another might poison all the produce of a group of taverners he was trying to extort.[59] The spirit-medium was an involved, competitive, and thoroughly interested member of his local community, no better than anyone else and occasionally far worse. He was considered "wild" in part because he and his gods were unrestrained by the ethical concerns of organized religion.

The behavior of the Ritual Master, in contrast, was restrained by laws of purity, morality, and correct bureaucratic procedure. His humanized, historicized, and mythologized deities were either fierce manifestations or lieutenants of cosmological powers or they were transformations of dangerous terrestrial divinities now sworn to uphold and defend the religious law. The Ritual Master tamed or civilized the dangerous forces present in uncontrolled form in spirit-mediums and harnessed the power of their divinities in the service of the ethical concerns of Daoist teaching. In the ritual texts, some of these gods might be presented as fierce subordinates of the high gods of Daoism, while others appeared as wrathful forms of the high gods themselves, in much the same way that the Black Killer, who manifested himself in the wild demeanor of spirit-mediums, was presented as an all-powerful minister of the Jade Emperor, a protector of virtue and a high god himself who had nothing to do with sacrificial offerings.

5

The Daoist Ritual Master
and Child-Mediums

In a recent essay on vernacular and classical traditions of contemporary Daoist ritual, Kristofer Schipper offers a modern perspective on the notion of the Daoist Ritual Master's mediating function in the Song, just outlined in Chapter 4. Following J. J. M. de Groot's observations in nineteenth-century Amoy, Schipper states that Ritual Masters (*fashi*) were, and for that matter still are, recruited from two sources: from among "the junior, non-ordained members of *daoshi* families," and from among the local initiation groups of "gong-beating lads," or young spirit-mediums.[1] This "double direction of recruitment" obtained in the Song period, though with respect to the *daoshi*, or clerical, provenance of the *fashi*, the evidence is more oblique. In Chapter 2 I considered elite relations with the *fashi* and their extensive involvement in exorcism. Here I am concerned with the other side of the *fashi*'s mediating function—his relation with spirit-mediums.

In the modern period, the relationship between the Daoist Ritual Master and spirit-mediums is not defined simply by recruitment. The two actually perform together in varying religious contexts in which the Ritual Master officiates and directs the trance of the spirit-medium. Schipper makes the following general comments in reference to one complex of rituals that concern journeys to the other world:

> The transaction between the living and the dead is the favorite field of action for mediumistic practices, and in these cases the *fashi* may yield his place of officiant to a spirit-medium (*dangki*; Mandarin: *tongji* or

tongzi). While the latter takes the leading role in the dancing and miming, the *fashi* remains at his side as his assistant, directing the trance. When the ritual has progressed to the point that the emissary stands before the judges of the Inferno, the singing is interrupted, and the seance takes over. Speaking in different voices, now the plaintiff's, then the judge's, the medium transmits the voices of these spirits of the nether world to the accused persons. In some cases, a speaking medium may be replaced by experts in spirit writing. The *fashi* acts as the interpreter of the medium's utterances or the scribbled signs of the writing stick.[2]

We must look, I believe, to the Song dynasty for the formation of the special relationship between Ritual Masters and spirit-mediums. In the twelfth century, Daoist *fashi* and spirit-mediums were brought together for the first time, primarily in the performance of therapeutic ritual. Ritualized spirit-possession became an enduring feature of the exorcisms of the Daoist *fashi*, and these exorcisms can be seen as a momentous episode in the process whereby Daoism entered into a lasting and complex accommodation with those representatives of village religion and their practices to which it had previously stood in firm opposition.[3]

Let us begin, then, with an anecdote from Hong Mai's *Yijian Zhi* as a way to introduce this characteristic practice of the lay Daoist Ritual Master:

> In the summer of 1192—twenty-two years since I recorded [the anecdote entitled] "The Retribution of Qingxi's Cat" (*Qingxi maobao*)—Qingxi's mistress became ill from water vermin and daily her condition became increasingly dangerous. The woman's hired servant, Wang Fu, said, "I have heard Mr. Qianyong Erlang of the teashop in Tianjing alley remark that a Mr. Pan, who resides outside the gate of Mount Gen, is good at matters that concern the other world. People call him 'Pan the Demon Seer' (Pan Jiangui). I will beg him to go with me and pay my respects." Wang consequently dragged Qian to Pan's residence.
>
> Pan burned mulberry paper money and with his hands offered up a handkerchief before the effigy of the spirit he served. At the top of a lantern, he saw a woman and a cat standing opposite each other. Pan said, "Both of you have grievances, yet I do not understand the cause." Wang and

Qian took the handkerchief, returned home, and explained to the mistress what had transpired. The mistress was astonished and said, "Years ago, I was in fact angry and blamed this servant. However, her death was from injuries. It was not I who caused her death. For what reason does she cause demonic visitations like this?" And she sent them back to see Pan.

Pan [performed a rite of] summoning for investigation by compelling a boy to become possessed. The boy said, in the voice of a woman, "My name is Qingxi. I died before my allotted time. Up to now, I have not yet been reborn. Originally it was not my mistress who killed me; yet it was because of her that I died. Hitherto her good fortune has not declined, and therefore I have waited and held on these many years." Pan promised to perform a fast (*zhai*) and an offering (*jiao*), but there was absolutely no response. Moreover, the boy cried out several times in a cat's voice and then fell asleep. When he awakened he was unable to recall anything. Pan sent an official dispatch [a warrant] to the City God, who ordered that her spirit be placed in the Palace of Fengdu. Moreover, Pan sacralized some jujube and water, and gave it to the woman to drink. She seemed to improve somewhat, but within several days her condition became grave, and she could not get up at all. Qian went to mourn her death. That night, Qian dreamed that Qingxi arrived, saying, "I myself will avenge the injustice. Why did you interfere in this matter, hiring and ordering the Ritual Master Pan to imprison me in purgatory? It is an injustice for which you will go to purgatory to bear witness!" And she caused him to come down with a fever, and he died within a day.[4]

I begin with this anecdote because of the exemplary way in which it reveals the process of exorcism employing a child-medium and the very palpable manner in which that medium was possessed. Yet the anecdote also presents a difficult interpretive problem that calls into question the entire therapeutic process, for even after a single reading one cannot avoid the conclusion that this exorcism was a tragic failure. Not only one but two people died, and one might well ask if the patient's hired servant might have better served his mistress had he called in a doctor. This query is not entirely rhetorical, however. It would be wrong to second-guess Wang Fu, whose familiarity with his employer's history and temperament may have suggested a psychological treatment. More importantly, the Chinese understanding of the illness from which his mistress suffered was pervaded by a central ambiguity that explains, if it does not justify, the treatment she in fact received.

Gu illness resulted from a contamination by *gu* poison, which a recent analyst has characterized as "an alien evil spirit which entered [the] body and developed into worms or some similar animal that gnawed away at the intestines or genitalia."[5] This poison was thought to be picked up in damp and humid wetlands, and after a considerable incubation period, it would cause severe symptoms, including derangement and debauchery, ending in death. The parasitical, grubby, and toxic character of *gu* has led, inevitably, to speculations about various diseases to which the illness might actually correspond—Japanese encephalitis B, for instance. Yet the search for a medical etiology is frustrated by the metaphorical nature of the evidence that inspires these speculations. As it turns out, the *gu* itself was produced from the sexual secretions of men and women engaged in lascivious and incestuous intercourse, or from the similar secretions of various insects and animals purposely cultivated by a person with the intention of poisoning another.[6] These and other accounts point to an origin of *gu* in an abnormal and degenerate intensification of the emotions, and N. H. van Straten has persuasively argued for a connection with the transgression of taboos on sexuality and aggression:

> This *gu* poison and various related aspects can be considered to represent an intensified materialization of the various notions which centered on fear of the instincts as causes of disorder. In theory this disorder was believed to be the natural concomitant of disturbed sexual relationships and the overt expression of aggression that had been dormant for a long time. In practice this meant the repression of the instincts in order to cut out potential sexual and social conflicts; and the psychological problems that arose from this demand are concreted in the concepts of *gu* poison.[7]

It seems to me that a very similar view emerges in the course of the exorcism of Wang Fu's employer. Indeed, the exorcist and his informants had good reason to suppose that her illness was a result of "the overt expression of aggression that had been dormant for a long time." Fortunately, we have access to these long-repressed feelings of hostility, or at least to those that were assumed by the exorcist to have been repressed. In its first sentence, the anecdote refers to another case that occurred twenty-two years before the events we are considering. This other story was told to Hong Mai by a relative of Wang Fu's employer and is preserved in the *Yijian zhi*:

> In the household of Lü Deqing's relations by marriage, a female slave named Qingxi brought a mouse into the kitchen to feed her cat surreptitiously. She met with a scolding from her mistress and could not overcome her resentment. Qingxi caught the cat and threw it atop a pile of firewood. There happened to be a forked branch which caught its abdomen. Bamboo thorns penetrated right through the cat's stomach and bowels; cries and screams filled one day and night before they ceased. A year passed, and, because of some exposed clothing, this slave tripped and fell upon the ground and was injured by a sharp piece of bamboo. Her dainty abdomen was split open, her body covered in flowing blood; by the following day she was already dead.[8]

This episode, I suspect, would have been brought to the attention of the exorcist and his medium, perhaps through the servant Wang Fu and his friend. Yet can it really be said that the exorcist had good reason to believe that her illness was the result of hostility too long repressed? Would there not be more reason to suppose, in this case, that the exorcist's particular understanding of *gu* illness predisposed him to focus exclusively on a certain kind of information? Apparently the patient herself was none too impressed with this bit of ancient history. She readily admitted to past anger, yet refused any suggestion of guilt. The slave Qingxi, for her part, readily admitted the accidental nature of her death, yet refused any satisfaction. Thus each woman refused to acknowledge the other, severing the abiding link between demon and demoniac, which is both the premise of any exorcism and the *sine qua non* of its success. The application of a potion was too little too late.

Precedents, Daoist and Otherwise

Despite the probability of misdiagnosis, exorcisms of the kind just described might be highly successful. Pan is called a "*fashi,*" and he clearly belonged to that group of lay exorcists whom we have distinguished from the Daoist priest. Yet he was also called a "Demon Seer," an appellation that locates Pan within a long tradition of religious practitioners, beginning perhaps with spirit-mediums in the Han, who boasted an ability to see ghosts or to cause them to manifest their true forms. In 434, for example, the magistrate of Wuning consulted a spirit-medium after a hallucinatory encounter and conversation with his recently deceased wife. To the trained eye of the medium, however, there appeared two domestic animals, and the medium revealed that it was one of these—a chicken—that had in fact impersonated the magistrate's wife. The identification of the chicken was by no means fortuitous. We are meant to understand this chicken as the very same one that the wife had once butchered as a youth, or so we learn from that earlier conversation between the magistrate and what he thought was his wife. Apparently the wife paid for this crime by spending three days in purgatory before she bribed her way out with a pair of golden rings. The hapless chicken, however, was doubly unlucky. The magistrate then summoned a Buddhist holy man, styled Huilan Daoren, who recited various *dhāraṇīs* to ward off the demon fowl.[9]

From the Tang dynasty on, spirit-mediums who were "expert in seeing ghosts" were joined first by Daoist priests and Buddhist monks and then by a group of Master Demon Seers, lay practitioners who were obvious forerunners of *fashi* such as Pan Jiangui.[10] Already by the third century, however, the ability to perceive demons was considered a necessary, if only defensive, strategy for the Daoist priest. In a famous passage in *The Master Who Embraces Simplicity* (*Baopuzi*), Ge Hong mentions that the Daoist practitioner who plans to enter the mountains should carry with him a mirror with which to reflect the true forms of the various demons trying to obstruct his path.[11] Reflective materials of all kinds quickly became a frequent staple of Daoist exorcisms.[12] Quoting the *Laozi zhongjin*, an eleventh-century compendium of the medieval Daoist tradition advises the practicant to suspend a talisman and sword over a basin of water, or to use the light of celestial bodies when confronted by illusory prodigies on the road.[13] Detection of the demon is then followed by the exorcism proper (here designated by the term "*zhi*")—the second part of a two-stage process already evident in the division of labor between the spirit-medium and Buddhist monk in the anecdote above.

A variety of terms were used before the Song to describe what we have conveniently called "exorcism." These included *bi* (to get rid of), *qianhe* (to reproach and accuse), *zhaohe* (to summon and accuse), *shiyi* (to compel and dispatch), and so forth.[14] An analysis of the contexts in which these terms occur would bear out what is implied by many of the terms themselves: a general mastery and control over spirits and demons, of which the ability to expel or ward them off was merely a logical corollary. The demon, in other words, might just as easily be summoned to a particular place as driven away, a possibility clearly exploited in the rite that defines the second stage of the therapeutic procedure of Pan *fashi*.

In the first stage of that process—that which I have called "detection" (*jiangui* or *shigui*)—Pan perceived a woman and a cat facing each other within the reflective glow of a lantern. This took place, interestingly enough, before the altar of his spirit-general, whose aid he had enlisted with a sacrifice of paper money and clothing. The mere illumination of two revenants was, by definition, sufficient to have deduced a grievance, but Pan sent Wang Fu and his friend home to discover the basis for their unhappiness. Having heard from the afflicted, Pan proceeded to hear from the afflictors, to embody them and thereby give them voice. In the second stage of the process, which also appears to have taken place before the *fashi*'s domestic altar, Pan performed a rite of "summoning for investigation by compelling the possession of a young boy," which is to say, he summoned the offending demons to take possession of a young spirit-medium so that he might interrogate them. And there is no doubt that the boy was possessed: he identified with the two demons, speaking first as the slave girl and then as the cat, and he also remembered nothing of what transpired, amnesia being a necessary aspect and ready indicator of all possession trances.

The "Rite of Summoning for Investigation" (*kaozhao fa*) formed the centerpiece of the *fashi*'s therapeutic repertoire in the twelfth century. It deserves and will receive a full analysis. Explicit references to *kaozhao fa* before the Song are sporadic and generally frustrating. Some of these references, moreover, designate ritual performances that bear only a superficial resemblance to what we will come to expect from performances similarly designated in the Song period.[15] And a Tang-dynasty account of what appears to be a true antecedent of the Song "Rite of Summoning for Investigation" is neither described as such nor occurs within a Daoist context. A consideration of this account, however, will be put off until we can better appreciate its contents.[16]

Here it seems more appropriate to follow a lead in one of the founding texts of the Tianxin lineage. The text is *Secret Essentials of the Most High for Assembling the Perfected Ones for Relief of the State and Deliverance of the People* (*Taishang zhuguo jiumin zongzhen biyao*, HY 1217) and dates from 1116. The preface to a chapter devoted to *kaozhao* procedures cites as one of its authorities a work entitled *Flowing Pearls of the Golden Lock* (*Jinsuo liuzhu*).[17] The Daoist canon, in fact, preserves a *Guide to the Flowing Pearls of the Golden Lock* (*Jinsuo liuzhu yin*, HY 1009), which is an abridgment of and commentary on a now-lost scripture of the same name (*Jinsuo liuzhu jing*).[18] It is unclear whether the *Taishang zhuguo jiumin zongzhen biyao* is referring to the *Scripture* or the *Guide*, or perhaps even to both. The *Guide* is attributed to the seventh-century Grand Astrologer Li Chunfeng (602–670).[19] Some scholars have readily accepted this attribution, whereas others have opted for a Song date for the text.[20] Based on internal evidence, however, both Poul Andersen and Timothy Barrett have separately and convincingly concluded that the attribution to Li Chunfeng is false and that the *Guide* should be placed somewhere between the late eighth and early tenth century.[21] The *Guide*, and presumably the *Scripture* on which it is based, were ostensibly transmitted by the Latter Saint (Housheng), a manifestation of Taishang laojun, to Zhang Daoling. Internal evidence, again, does appear to place the book within the late Zhengyi, or Celestial Master, tradition.

Much of the *Guide* is taken up with the choreography and visualizations for "walking the [celestial] outline" (*bugang*). Several chapters, however, include instructions for the performance of *kaozhao fa*, instructions that were supposedly transmitted to future generations by Zhao Rui, a disciple of Zhang Daoling, in the Later Han.[22] The *kaozhao fa* is glossed here as a ritual for "investigating demons and summoning spirits" (*kaogui zhaoshen*).[23] The initial instructions fall neatly into three parts. The first concerns the creation and purification of the ritual area, which includes an altar, a prison, and various gates.[24]

The second constitutes "the rites of investigating and summoning" proper.[25] And the third identifies six categories of demonic illness against which the ritual will prove effective.[26] A large part of the instructions for the rites proper is taken up with the visualizations necessary to actualize various spirit-generals, spirit-armies, and the divinized masters of the practitioner. From the perspective of the Song procedures, the most interesting sequence, rather hastily enumerated, involves: (1) the summoning of the demons and spirits into the ritual area; (2) an interrogation to ascertain the personal and family name of "one who has caused demonic illness" (*kaowen zuosui zhi zhe mingzi*); (3) the consignment of the demon to a period of incarceration in the prison; and (4) the submission of a "red petition" (*chizhang*) requesting that the "celestial soldiers" carry out the execution of the demon. None of this is elaborated upon.

Several later chapters in the *Guide* include further instructions addressed to a Daoist priest or practitioner identified as the "Ritual Master of Investigating and Summoning." On the tenth of every month, this Ritual Master is expected to visualize himself at the head of large armies of spirit-generals and spirit-soldiers, patrolling the cosmos for demons that bring disease and disaster.[27] In the event of individual illness, the Master is first told to visualize himself patrolling outside the patient's house, and then to visualize himself actually entering the home and examining the patient lying in bed. Finally, the Master summons and actualizes (*cun*) a host of ferocious theriomorphic spirits who seize, devour, or trample to death the afflicting demon.[28]

All three of these sets of ritual procedures, and especially the first, include elements that anticipate the Song-dynasty rituals of *kaozhao*—in particular, the visualization of the spirit-generals and soldiers, the summoning of the demon, and the interrogation of his identity.[29] All these procedures, however, and even the first, seem oddly isolated from the person of the patient; and the last two procedures appear to occur entirely within the priestly realm of mental projection. Yet it is the engagement of the patient directly in his own cure that will characterize the *kaozhao* rites of the Song. There is, moreover, no mention whatsoever of the use or possession of a spirit-medium. Yet again, it is possession—and not just the possession of a spirit-medium, but of the patient as well—that will come to define the Rites of Summoning for Investigation in the twelfth and thirteenth centuries.[30]

The Daoist Rite of Summoning for Investigation

It has been suggested by some commentators that the Rite of Summoning for Investigation was employed in the Song as a cure for demonic possession. This view, however, is misleading. In almost all accounts of psychosomatic illness and its cure in the *Yijian zhi*, the subject is engaged, at least initially, in behavior that we can justifiably call symptomatic. These symptoms include highly erratic and demonstrative behavior, extreme mood swings, loss of appetite, lassitude, self-imposed isolation, auditory and visual hallucinations, conversations with imaginary people, fixation on inanimate objects such as trees, uncontrolled laughter and insulting speech, dressing up and putting on cosmetics, and so forth.[31] The parents or relatives of the subject interpret this symptomatic behavior as sign of demonic harassment. They interpret it, in other words, in a manner very similar to what in a Christian and Renaissance context was meant by the term "obsession," "the state of a person thought to be disturbed, besieged by the devil, which is different from possession, which signifies actual habitation by the devil within the body."[32]

On the recommendation of a friend, neighbor, or local spirit-medium, the parents or relatives of the subject then invite an exorcist—often a Daoist priest or Ritual Master. Yet he is thereby misnamed by us, for what he does has little to do with exorcism. What he does in most cases is perform various ritual actions the purpose of which is first to control or stabilize the afflicted and then to compel him or her to become possessed, just as if he or she were a spirit-medium employed by the Master. This view of what has been traditionally called "exorcism" as a process of induced possession—as a cult of possession, in other words—is confirmed by a patient analysis of the large corpus of Rites of Summoning for Investigation described in the Daoist canonical texts from the twelfth through fourteenth centuries, and by the fact that the possession of the subject is then followed by complex negotiations and an additional set of rites the purpose of which is, in turn, to reach an accommodation with, rather than an exorcism of, the demon. To demonstrate that the *kaozhao* ritual really is a process of inducing a possession trance in the patient, I present here a representative ritual sequence, extracted from several dozen sources referred to in the notes to this chapter, and divided into four essential movements:

A. *The Metamorphosis of the Master.* The *fashi* transforms or
metamorphosizes himself into either his spirit-general
or one of several cosmic powers through a complex process of external and internal visualization. The Master
first visualizes both the deity within his own body and
an external environment that forms the cosmic background for this internal representation. He then actualizes himself (*cunwei*) as the deity.[33] In other words, the
Master empowers this deity as much as he is empowered
by it. The point of the metamorphosis is that the Master
can now manipulate or command the various subordinate spirit-soldiers under the spirit-general's control, and
employ the various instruments and weapons associated
with him. Yet there is also, I believe, a hidden agenda.
The identification through visualization of the Master
with his deity is meant to encourage a kind of mimetic
role-playing on the part of the patient that will result in
the identification, through possession this time, of the
patient with his demon.

B. *Rites of Detection* (corresponding to *jiangui* or *shigui*).
These rites are characterized by a double action. On
the one hand, the Master—with the aid of various hand-
seals, talismans, and Chinese or pseudo-Sanskrit spells—
bids his subordinate deities bring the afflicting demon
into a mirror, basin of water, or some other object or
bounded space. On the other hand, the patient, who is
standing before the Master with his eyes closed, is asked
to exhale into this object; the implication for the patient,
as the subsequent materialization makes clear, is that he
has been contaminated or infiltrated by a demon that is
causing his illness. The patient is then asked to open his
eyes and describe what he sees. In one case the Master
asks whether the patient sees a demon of nature or a soul
of the dead.[34] In contrast to earlier accounts of detection, the burden of identifying the afflicting demon has
shifted from the practitioner to the patient, introducing
the patient into a process that will lead to his identification of himself with the demon. The patient, we

should recall, is suffering from various symptoms of a
hysterical nature. The rites of detection are first a means
of focusing the patient's attention. (To say that he or she
is distracted would be an understatement.) Second, they
involve a process of externalization and objectification
whereby the patient is led to convert a surplus of affect
into an economy of symbols, to express a private subjective state in terms of a public and cultural idiom of
demonology. Yet it is important to recognize that the
demon the patient identifies in the reflecting object is a
category of demon (a *hun* or a *jing*) and not a particular
demonic being. It will be the function of the patient's
possession to allow him or her to select a specific being
with a particular name and history—to invest, in other
words, these public, cultural symbols with personal
meaning and to manipulate them to express his or
her psychological needs.[35] Through possession, the
kaozhao rituals offer the patient access to the symbolic,
in contrast to Renaissance exorcisms in which the
patient leaves all responsibility for interpretation to
the exorcist, and the exorcist in turn aims not to save
the patient but to use the patient's possession to save
a particular theology.[36]

C. *Rites of Seizure.* Following the externalization and objectification of the patient's symptoms, the Master
   prepares for the ritual re-introduction of the demon
   into the patient. In the simplest form of these rites, the
   Master merely invokes one or more subordinate deities,
   commanding them to pursue, seize, yoke, or bind the
   demon and to force it to take possession of the body of
   the afflicted.[37] The Master may attempt to "substantiate"
   the command to seize and bring down the demon into
   the patient: in one sequence where the spirits of the
   Four Directions are enlisted to arrest the avenging soul
   of a deceased, the Master inhales the pneumas of the
   Four Directions, mixes them with a mouthful of water,
   and finally spits out the water on to the head of the
   patient at the very moment when he commands these

spirit-generals to seize the demon and force it to possess the patient.[38] This unsettling assault was expected to produce a violent shaking or trembling in the patient— a "fit" that signifies the onset of trance.[39] It is also, I believe, appropriate to inducing a particular kind of trance, what we call "identificatory" trance or possession: "spitting," here, has been assimilated to "seizing," and the patient was being encouraged to conclude, at a cognitive if subconscious level, that the demon who was seized was none other than the one who was spat upon: in other words, himself. Other variations of these rites of seizure are discussed below. Their complexity is in direct proportion to the resistance of the patient.

D. *The Possession of the Afflicted or a Surrogate.* Following the rites of seizure and the onset of trance, the patient submits to the Master's interrogation in which he (the demon) relates his name and provides an account of himself. The patient, in other words, identifies with a particular demon, and it is only now that we can speak of actual possession. For the content of this possessed speech and for the continuing dialogue and negotiations between the Master and the demon/patient, we must turn to the anecdotal accounts in the *Yijian zhi,* which essentially pick up where the ritual texts leave off. Before we leave these texts ourselves, however, it is essential to point out that many of them offer an alternative to the possession of the afflicted, though one that only slightly alters the process we have been examining. In cases where the patient is either too weak to withstand the rigors of trance or too young to articulate himself or herself verbally, the Master might employ a surrogate (*dairen; lizhe ren*) to be possessed by the demon afflicting the patient. In the Tianxin tradition, the possession of the surrogate was brought about by a transfer of breath from the patient to the surrogate.[40] When the afflicted was an infant, the transfer was made to a wet-nurse who held the baby in her arms, indicating perhaps that, in other cases as well, the surrogate might be a family

member or someone near at hand.[41] In other traditions,
however, particularly those that evolved around the local
cult to a particular deity, the *fashi* employed, on a permanent or ad hoc basis, one or more adolescent boys
or spirit-mediums (*tongzi*) otherwise referred to as "the
possessed" (*furen*)."[42] These spirit-mediums were not,
strictly speaking, surrogates, for their use in *kaozhao*
rituals was a corollary or subset of their more encom-
passing function as possessed oracles. A fragmentary
but important text representing one of these local cultic
traditions indicates that the spirit-mediums—in this case
three were employed—might be possessed by the *fashi*'s
spirit-general as well as by the demon.[43] Be that as it may,
the full range of rites of seizure would precede the possession and interrogation of the spirit-medium. These,
however, might also be encased within or even subsumed
by another rite, what we may call a "rite of dispossession,"
in which the three *hun*-souls representing the conscious
self of the medium were themselves "seized" and removed
through an opening in his head.[44] This rite, and similar
ones, seems to me to be particularly appropriate for those
subjects for whom trance was a voluntary rather than involuntary matter, and for whom resistance was minimal.
The ritual texts, in fact, give more space to the difficulties
presented in getting the medium out of trance than to
those of getting him into it.

This analysis gives a somewhat idealized representation of the Rites
of Summoning for Investigation. Both the sequence as a whole and
its individual movements were subject to great variation. Some sequences, for instance, lack the rites of seizure (A-B-D),[45] while others
drop the rites of detection (A-C-D).[46] In some, the rites of seizure are
greatly expanded, subjecting the demon/patient to a succession of
seizures, yokings, pummelings, beatings, and so forth;[47] in others, they
are significantly contracted, being subordinated to or even replaced
by a rite of dispossession. Finally, we encounter sequences in which
rites of detection also expand and contract, even within a single text.
The Great Rites of Shangqing for the Subjugation of Evil by Tianpeng is obsessed throughout its several hundred pages with the physical con-

struction and visualization of "fiery detention houses," which can, among other permutations, take the form of vessels of oil placed under the patient's bed or a demarcated area assimilated to the household hearth.[48] These detention houses become the focus for elaborate rites of detection and exorcism in which the demon is confined, identified, and incinerated, and in which the patient returns to the passive role he occupied in the more traditional performances of earlier Demon Seers. These rituals are called "Rites of Investigation by Illumination" to distinguish them from "Rites of Investigation by Possession," which are now branded "unorthodox" and unacceptable.[49]

What appears to be a rigid stance and an exclusive opposition, however, turns out not to be, and the text rather unwittingly undercuts itself: at one point, the use of detention houses is reserved for severe illness, specifying the Rites of Investigation by Possession for less serious cases; at another point, their use actually follows these Rites of Investigation by Possession;[50] and at still other points, the use of detention houses is fully integrated in a *kaozhao* rite employing a child-medium.[51] The *kaozhao* rites involving spirit-possession may be unorthodox because innovative, but they are now the dominant mode, exerting considerable pressure on more traditional conceptions of therapy.

What strikes me as particularly compelling about these rituals is the way in which they captured the rhythms of Song-dynasty criminal proceedings. The analogy is, indeed, more profound than the ritual use, in some instances, of a version of Song prisons or detention houses, where the accused was confined pending trial, sentencing, and execution.[52] The Rites of Summoning for Investigation were introduced in almost all traditions by a "rite of entrapment" (*zhaofa*), a rite I have mentioned only in passing, but one that corresponds to Song methods of initial search and arrest, including a general blockade and the saturation of the area within the blockade by a large-scale mobilization of police and military personnel. Like criminal proceedings, moreover, the *kaozhao* rites concluded with an "application of the law," the rendering of a judgment based on elaborate Daoist codes (*lü*), statutes (*ling*), and regulations (*ke*) that specified punishments for the infractions and crimes committed by demons, as well as by spirits and the Master himself.

Both the actual case histories in the *Yijian zhi* and the religious codes reveal that these judgments were highly open and discretionary and

that they were based on Chinese notions of equity. The afflicting demon might have been beaten, exiled, or executed, but it might just as
easily have been granted amnesty, restored to its spiritual community,
or even rehabilitated and promoted in the celestial hierarchy—all depending on the nature of the demon, the circumstances that led it to
attack the patient, and its blood relationship to the patient. The *fashi*
was a judge rather than an exorcist, and his title "Master of the Law,"
whatever its Buddhist origins as such, resonated less with the monk-
ish propagation of the Dharma (*fa*) than with the legalistic and judicial functions of the Song magistrate. The most profound link between
therapy and law, however, emerges from an analysis of the second and
central stage of Song criminal proceedings: the trial.

Ritual and Judicial Trials

Research on Chinese procedural law is still somewhat unsystematic,
and we are far from a comprehensive, historical treatment of the subject that would allow us to identify significant shifts in trial practice
over long periods of time. Unlike earlier dynasties, for example, the
Song excluded the police from participation in the interrogation and
thereby guaranteed the magistrate a degree of control that the *fashi*
appears to have attained as well. And unlike the trials of later dynasties, the Song trial was closed to the public (a corollary of the first
innovation), which accords with comments made over and over
again in the ritual texts advising the Master to seal off the home of
the afflicted from visitors as well as intruders. Such parallels will remain superficial and less than convincing, however, until we expose
the essential structure shared by both the Song trial and the *kaozhao*
ritual. To this end we can hardly do better than to quote Miyazaki
Ichisada on the importance of torture and confession in the criminal interrogation:

> In major cases the actual fact of a completed offense was established by
> the criminal's confession, and not by the material evidence or the tes-
> timony of witnesses. Even when material evidence existed, if the accused
> did not acknowledge it, guilt could not be legally established. However,
> when despite a substantial showing of evidence the accused refused to
> confess, the magistrate could have him tortured. All that was required
> procedurally was the consent of the assistant magistrate and the record
> keeper. The magistrate would issue a writ ordering a certain number of

blows, obtain the signature of his colleagues signifying their assent, and show the writ to the chief clerk and the runners on duty. The runner then carried out the beating in the presence of the officials and clerks.[53]

Xu Daoling, in contrast, argues from statutory evidence that obtaining a confession was not always necessary for conviction.[54] I prefer to follow Miyazaki here because his conclusions are based on an early twelfth-century record of a magistrate's own judicial practice and administrative experience.[55] Ideally, perhaps, a confession was not necessary. Yet I suspect that it was precisely because the burden of evidentiary proof and testimonial veracity became so onerous in the Song that confession became indispensable, not simply as one kind of proof but as the *regina probationum*—the queen of proofs. And as confession came to constitute the only full proof, torture also became indispensable. Among the dozens of criminal trials represented in *Outlaws of the Marsh* (*Shuihu zhuan*), the popular novel that reflects Song as well as Ming social conditions, all but one attain their verdict, even if a false one, through the accused's confession under torture.[56]

However we choose to view the mechanism that propelled confession up the hierarchy of proofs and that reinvigorated the use of torture in the Song, it should be less difficult to see that judicial torture and confession served as a model, or one of the models, for the essential events of the *kaozhao* ritual—the rites of seizure and the possession of the afflicted (C-D). The link is even made explicit in a description of a proto-*kaozhao* ritual performed by a Tang-dynasty spirit-medium in the subprefecture of Baitian in Chuzhou.[57] The medium, named Xue Erniang, served the cult of the Great King of the Golden Heaven and specialized in exorcisms that were evidently highly esteemed by the residents of the subprefectural city. In this case, however, she had been invited to the home of a villager to attend to his daughter. The girl had been afflicted by an incubus (*mei*), though at this stage her parents merely thought her mad. Occasionally she would walk through fire and water or do physical harm to her body. However mad she may have appeared, the girl's obliviousness to physical pain strikes me as not too dissimilar from the kind of trance entered into by the medium:

> When [the medium] had arrived, [the family of the
> afflicted] set up an altar in a room and laid the patient
> down beside it. Then they constructed a large fire pit next

to [the altar] and heated a large iron pan over it until it
was red. Thereupon the medium donned her ritual attire
and, dancing to music and drums, called her spirit. In a few
moments the spirit descended [into her?]. The onlookers
made repeated obeisances, and [then] the medium respectfully invoked [the spirit], saying, "In haste summon the *mei*-
demon to come!" As she concluded, the medium entered
the fire pit and sat down inside; her expression remained
completely unperturbed. After a long while she shook her
clothes and stood up, and, placing the burning pan upside-
down on her head, danced to the beating of drums. When
the song concluded, she got rid of the pan and then cried
out in barbarian fashion, commanding the patient to bind
herself. The girl placed her hands together behind her
back, as if they were tied up. [Then the medium] commanded [the afflicted] to confess. At first the girl merely
cried and did not speak. The medium became enraged,
and drawing her sword, struck her so that the sword passed
through her, though her body remained unharmed. The
afflicted, however, said, "I surrender," and made the following confession. . . .[58]

We need not quote the entire confession here, but merely point out
that the "I" under which it is made refers to someone—or, rather,
something—other than the girl: an incubus that has assumed the form
of an old otter. The girl, in other words, has become possessed, and
the story that this seemingly benign demon tells (= *tongzhuan*) refers
to the girl, as one might expect, in the third person. Possession and
confession intersect here, and both are preceded by a rite of seizure
(a ritual binding, specifically), which, in turn, intersects with or slips
into torture. The confession is made, quite literally, under the knife.

This text presents the most stimulating and coherent description
of the actual performance of a *kaozhao* ritual before the Song. It is extraordinary that we should find it performed not by a Daoist priest
but by a spirit-medium, a fact which suggests to me that it may very
well have been the interaction of the visualizing techniques of the
Daoist (as represented in the Tang *Guide to the Flowing Pearls of the Golden
Lock*) with the more demonstrative ritual behavior of spirit-mediums
that produced the *kaozhao* rites of the Song-dynasty *fashi*. Such a hy-

pothesis, if true, would give a certain historical dimension to the *fashi*'s mediating function, analyzed in Chapter 4, and would provide yet another perspective on his emergence from the encounter of Daoism with local cults. The contribution of spirit-mediums to the practices of Ritual Masters, Buddhist as well as Daoist, is explored in great detail in Chapter 6.

In the meantime, the performance of this Tang-dynasty medium anticipates all the significant elements of the *kaozhao* rites of the Song. She identifies with her divinity and commands it to bring down the afflicting demon; the patient, in turn, is seized (bound) and possessed (A-C1; C2-D). Other elements are characteristic not only of this medium but of all possession cults. First, there is the role of dance and music. Possession trances, as we have said, are trances of identification, and in possession cults the means par excellence of representing this identification is through dance to the accompaniment of instrumental (percussive) and/or vocal music provided by a group of individuals other than the possessed.

Following Gilbert Rouget, we might say that spirit-possession is a socialization of trance behavior and a domestication of the divine whereby the possessed and the group make a simultaneous identification of the possessed as the divinity. The music of the acolytes and the dance of the possessed are the auditory and choreographic signifiers corresponding to a single signified, which is the divinity. In the *kaozhao* rites of the Daoist *fashi*, all such identificatory trances through dance and music will be dispensed with and replaced by the Daoist/Tantric metamorphosis of the Master. Another element characteristic of possession cults will also be dropped. Trances of possession are often the occasion for fakiristic displays of bravura,[59] and it is clear that the medium's descent into the fire pit was meant to impress and overwhelm the patient and demon with her own physical power and even greater imperviousness to pain. The aggression that the medium directs toward herself is then turned outward; anger and violence now assume the role of intimidating the patient.[60]

The fact that the body of the girl remained untouched by the violent assault upon her should not be taken primarily as a test of our credulity, but as a sign either that the girl is in trance or that it is the demon who is being tortured, not the girl. This leads to a more general point about the relation of the *kaozhao* ritual to criminal proceedings. The relation of torture and confession to ritual seizure and pos-

session, though isomorphic in the biological sense of the formal convergence of two organisms of different origin, is not strictly analogous—
or, rather, is analogous only when viewed from the perspective of the
demon, for it is the demon who confesses, not the patient, and the demon confesses because it is only the demon who has something to
confess. By disrupting the link between illness and morality in the
patient, the new Daoist codes, regulations, and protocols of the *fashi*
locate guilt solely on the side of demons, identifying their transgression essentially with their refusal to remain where they belong.[61] And
therefore we find, in the ritual texts, that it is only the demon who is
tortured. The Master invokes his spirit-soldiers to seize, bind, flog, pum-
mel, yoke, burn, freeze, or crush the demon. The afflicted, in contrast,
is possessed, nothing more or less, and the rites of seizure are intended
not to inflict pain on the patient but to encourage him or her to identify with the demon. Therefore, the medium commands the patient
to bind herself, and the patient places her hands together as if they
were tied.

In the ritual texts of the Song, there is the expectation that the patient, face to face with the Master, will respond directly to the latter's
invocation to the demon by becoming possessed or, alternatively, by
acting out the content of the invocation. Thus it is said that if the Master calls for the demon to be struck or pounded, the patient will strike
or pound himself or herself.[62] If the patient does not identify so easily with the demon, the Master may perform certain actions to drive
the point home. Hence we find that if the patient does not become
possessed when the Master commands his spirit-soldiers to yoke the
demon in cangues and force it down, the Master actually borrows a
cangue from the City God temple and places it around the neck of
the patient;[63] similarly, if the patient is unresponsive to an invocation
to seize and flog the demon, the Master will place several thorned
branches across the patient's back and legs.[64] In all these situations,
the Master is clearly not torturing the patient but attempting to induce a possession trance by encouraging the patient to identify with
the object of his invocation, or by encouraging certain mimetic, rep-
resentational action in the patient that will lead to this identification.
The model here is not judicial but theatrical. The ritual area has now
become a stage where the Master, who is playing the role of one spirit,
induces the patient to play the role of another.

The Rites of Summoning for Investigation resided at the overlap of two cultural spaces—the judicial and the theatrical—and existed within a constant state of negotiation and vacillation between them. To a certain extent, this vacillation was a function of shifting perspectives—that of the demon and that of the patient—yet both perspectives, and therefore both models, were held in a persistent tension by the central ambiguity of the *kaozhao* rite, namely, the identification and potential confusion of the demon with the patient. One of the consequences of this ambiguity was that, in practice, the patient might be so demonized that the *kaozhao* rites threatened to devolve into pure torture; another was that the demon might become so humanized that the same rites were reduced to pure theater.

Ritual and Therapy

We can explore these alternative possibilities in two anecdotes from the twelfth century. Both offer fascinating portraits of the lay exorcist:

> During the Qiandao reign period [1165–1173], Yu Ronggu of Leping [Jiangxi], because of famine, sailed along the Huai River. By chance he obtained the Method of the Five Thunders (*Wulei fa*) and practiced it after a little study. At the time, many of the field oxen in the villages had become ill, and Yu went about curing them, each time with success. After procuring small remunerations, he could make a living and subsequently established his residence there [i.e., around the Huai].
>
> In 1185, Yu returned to his native area for a while. The wife of his brother's son, Zhiquan, was named Lu; her father and mother had just then gone to the land around the Huai River, and Zhiquan and his wife had seen them off. When his wife returned home she felt ill, talked recklessly and nonsensically as if she were mad, and no longer understood human matters. Therefore they invited Ronggu to examine her condition.
>
> Thereupon, Ronggu practiced his method for summoning and investigating [the demon]: it was a deceased ancestor of Lu. Ronggu looked at her and said, "We can bind it up." The afflicted at that moment lay down inside her room and extended her hands in front of her as if to receive

shackles; and he continued, having her beaten and interrogated, whereupon she cried out and admitted her crimes.
Yu chastised [the demon], saying, "You are an ancestor of
this Lu household who attaches yourself to the residence
of your descendant to receive incense—how can you dare
to wantonly enter the domicile of humans and, moreover,
cause such misfortune?! I have kept in mind that you are
a relative by marriage and am not yet about to extend my
method. It would benefit you to make a hasty retreat." Then
she confessed her transgressions and begged for liberation.
He granted it, and shortly thereafter the afflicted became
as calm as normal.[65]

As mentioned in Chapter 3, the class of lay exorcists, or *fashi*, that
emerged in the twelfth century was comprised of two social groups.
One was highly literate, more urban than not, and served an elite clientele. This group was probably responsible for a good proportion of
the ritual and theoretical texts of the new therapeutic lineages. It approached, if some of its members did not actually merge with, the person and the social and intellectual environment of the Daoist priest.
Members of the other group were in every way less literate and less sophisticated, and attended to the needs of rural or suburban people
more like themselves. This second group, to which Yu Ronggu clearly
belonged, was not any less mobile than the first, yet its mobility was
certainly more circumscribed and defined by economic circumstances.
Yu Ronggu was perhaps himself a casualty of the famine mentioned
in the text, and I do not think it too farfetched to infer that Thunder Magic held out the promise of, and provided the opportunity for,
some badly needed employment. Certainly Yu wasted little time in
making use of his magical windfall, and the continuing economic
tragedy of the region guaranteed a stream of rural clients that
financed his wanderings.

What concerns me here is the Rite of Summoning for Investigation
that Yu Ronggu performed on his return home after several years in
the Huai area. One suspects that even if Ronggu had found the leisure
time, he would have had neither the economic nor intellectual resources, perhaps not even the inclination, to master the complex visualizations and correlative cosmologies that characterized the Thunder Magic of the ritual texts. Ronggu's performance, at least, places

him in a world closer to that of spirit-mediums than Daoist priests. As in the account of the Tang medium Xue Erniang, Ronggu commanded the binding of the demon, and the patient extended her hands in front of her as if to receive shackles. The *fashi*, however, does not wait for the patient to become possessed before he interrogates the demon. Histrionics give way to torture, to an interrogation accompanied by the infliction of pain. The distinction between patient and demon collapses, as does that between the resulting confession and possession.

Yet if the patient has become demonized, the demon ultimately becomes humanized. The *fashi* treats the possessing spirit not as something to be exorcised, but very much as someone whose special relationship to the patient needs to be acknowledged. In so doing, the *fashi* is acknowledging the issues raised by the patient's illness, for there can be little doubt of the intensity of the patient's symptoms or of the fact that they followed immediately upon her parents' departure. Clearly, her symptoms were related to problems of separation and, more specifically, to feelings of abandonment and estrangement. The departure of her parents may have brought home to her with some finality the reality of the ritual, as well as familial disenfranchisement that came with marriage. Thus it seems appropriate that she should objectify her symptoms in terms of an unrecognized and wandering spirit of a deceased but ill-defined ancestor who is seeking ritual attention. And if, in fact, she sees her situation as that of an abandoned spirit, the desire of this spirit to attach itself to a descendant is representative of her own desire to maintain those links to her natal family at a moment when those links seemed most threatened. One can only conclude that the young woman's symptoms disappeared (she was cured) precisely because the *fashi* allowed her to give voice to a demonomorphic representation that was symbolically meaningful to her. If the patient was demonized in torture, the purpose was only to rehumanize her. In the end, therapy reclaimed its territory from the judicial.

Another anecdote reveals how this territory might be lost to the theatrical:

> The youngest son of Lü Chunnian was three years old when, in the summer of the year 1193, he became ill, coughing up phlegm. His mother and father worried over him, and medical attention and prayers were exhaustively employed.

Someone said that there was a certain Ritual Master
Wu whose talismanicized water was extremely efficacious
and that they had better get him to bring the illness under
control. Thereupon Lü hastened to invite him, and he
advanced Wu one hundred cash to hire a small boy in the
marketplace whom Wu would compel to become possessed
[by the demon] and speak.

Wu scolded the demon vituperatively and angrily demanded an explanation. He ordered his spirit-general to
bind its hands, whereupon the boy deliberately raised his
hands in the manner of receiving shackles. Continuing, Wu
ordered the spirit-general to bind both its feet, and once
again the boy acted in a similar fashion. Wu then scolded
it, saying, "You are such and such a demon, correct?" The
boy hung his head and said, "Yes." Striking him with several
lashes, all were met with murmured assent. Again Wu said,
"I cannot bear to punish you. You want some 'ritual of
merit' [performed on your behalf], right?" The boy raised
his head and said, in gratitude, "That would be very fortunate," and in a moment Wu reviled the demon and caused
it to go away. The boy fell upon the ground in a daze and
after a little while stood up. The Ritual Master retreated,
and Lü asked of the little boy, "What I have just witnessed,
are you still able to recall it?" To which he answered, "Hoping for a profit of one hundred cash, I therefore complied
with everything he said. Its binding and responding, that
was all my doing." All the spectators laughed and went away.
The young child got well on his own.[66]

The therapy here takes place not in the privacy of the patient's home
or of the exorcist's sanctuary, but outdoors, in the marketplace, before a crowd of spectators who had come, perhaps, for other purposes.
The one who is to be possessed, moreover, is neither the patient nor
one of his kin acting as a surrogate, but a complete stranger to the
fashi as well as to the patient's family, a boy selected at random and
secured temporarily by a monetary transaction. One can imagine that
these two factors alone might well work to transform, and even undermine, the serious goal of therapy that was kept on track by familial concern and commitment in an environment of domestic seclusion.

Released from these pressures, the ritual now had to submit to new ones—to the expectations of a different audience accustomed to other kinds of spectacles—for the market was a place, and often a periodic one at that, for more than the exchange of goods and services. Here the state or its representatives executed in public those it condemned in private trials; here, too, roving actors paused to put on plays formed from bits of pantomime, music, and dialogue, as well as more kinetic performances in the tradition of the "One Hundred Entertainments." These actors were called "*luji*" or "*sanyue.*"As itinerant and unregistered troupes or individuals, they stood in much the same relation to the established actors of the court and permanent urban theaters as the class of *fashi* did to the Daoist hierarchy and urban temples.[67] And if the Rites of Summoning for Investigation owed something to both judicial proceedings and the theater, it would seem that a therapeutic ritual ran something of a risk in returning to the venue where these other spectacles converged.

Despite the focus on the boy rather than the patient, the ritual just described opens on a familiar note. As in the previous anecdote, the *fashi* orders his spirit-general to bind the hands and feet of the demon; the young boy then responds, mimetically, by extending his own hands and feet, as if he were the demon being bound. The process of identification is complete when the boy admits under questioning to being "such and such a demon." At this point one expects some elaboration on the identity of the demon and its circumstances, some articulation of the demonic with the illness of the patient. Instead, therapy immediately gives way to a spectacle of punishment and mercy—a public demonstration, through the body of the surrogate, of the *fashi*'s power over the demonic, not unlike the political ceremonial of execution, in which the power of the state was felt just as much in the suspension as in the extraction of vengeance.

One spectacle, however, gives way to another. The entire ritual performance, from bindings to beatings, turns out to have been scripted and choreographed beforehand. Even the trance was faked. A question from the patient's father, a question that demonstrates how well he understood the necessary relation between possession and amnesia, forced the confession of fraudulence. Therapy has become theater, a kind of "demon play" in which the *fashi* directs a cast of one. The audience appears to have been appropriately surprised by the deception, if not entertained. Several decades earlier, however, a court official was not at all amused when he realized too late that the priest he had hired to perform a Daoist sacrifice, as well as all the transcendents whom he witnessed descending during the service, were roving actors intent on pilfering his valuable sacrificial vessels.[68] If the *fashi* could become an itinerant dramaturge, roving actors could also play the Daoist priest.

Ritual and Theatrical Performances

To greater and lesser degrees, both trances of possession and exorcisms normally involve an element of theatricalization. It is this element that has recently led the Shakespearean scholar Stephen Greenblatt to argue that possession is in fact theater that cannot "confess its own theatricality."[69] Greenblatt's understanding of possession as theater that must hide this fact from itself is a felicitous formulation in the context of early Stuart England, a time when possession and exorcism had to defend themselves against the charge of being theater—against the charge, in other words, of falsity, counterfeit, and illusion. In Song China, however, possession and the theater did not lean up against each other in quite the same way—and this despite the fact that the Song tolerated a full-blown secular stage that, like its English counterpart, stood at the margins of urban society but also enjoyed the support and encouragement of the court.

This is not to say that the question of inauthentic possession did not arise (we have seen that it has), but only that possession itself did not have to defend itself against the charge of fraudulence. At worst, possession was rejected by some groups in the society as an undisciplined intrusion of the divine into human affairs, or as an unwelcome assault on the integrity of the body. At best, it was something to be actively encouraged in controlled situations, such as *kaozhao* rituals, as a means of overcoming and giving form to an outburst of inarticulate and chaotic symptoms. I would argue that, in Song China, possession was decidedly not theater, and that for this very reason it had no problem whatsoever in revealing its theatricality. Possession was distinguished from the theater by the feature that defined it—a trance of identification—and the presence or absence of this feature determined its authenticity or fraudulence. Conversely, theater was not possession, though it, too, was not unwilling to stage such an event. Thus, in the Song, we find rites of spirit-possession followed by theatrical performances, and theatrical performances that represent spirit-possession without the actor or spectators becoming possessed.

The relationship between ritual and theater in the Song is a large and still largely unexplored subject. Fortunately, our focus on therapeutic ritual circumscribes one piece of relevant evidence—the *Great Exorcism (danuo)*, as described in the *Liji, Zhouli*, dynastic histories of the Han, and poetic enumerations (*fu*) of the Tang.[70] Despite a general impression to the contrary, the *Great Exorcism* continued to be performed at the Song court and flourished in the countryside. The significant feature of the court performance is the fact that the spirits of the classical *nuo* (the twelve beasts and the ten demoniform pestilences) were replaced by the civil, and especially the martial, gods of Song popular religion, and that these roles were assumed by actors with painted faces rather than by masked priests.[71] This aestheticization and theatricalization of the *Great Exorcism* was mirrored by the ritualization of court theater. One cycle of "farce" (*yuanben*) performed in the Southern Song focused on the tragic fate of dead emperors or heroes (e.g., Huizong, Xiang Yu). Three extant scripts in this genre from the Yuan dynasty reveal that their structure derived from ritual "offerings" (*jiao*) for the dead. The actors represented the descent of the wandering soul into the ritual area; the possessed speech of the medium, in which the wandering soul described its "grievance" and related its sad fate; and, finally, the performance of a ritual of salvation (within the play) by a Daoist priest or Buddhist monk.[72]

In contrast to the *Great Exorcism* at court, *nuo*-exorcisms in the countryside (*xiangnuo*) were performed by troupes of village spirit-mediums (*liwu*), who are alternatively referred to as "children" (*xiao'er* or *ernü*) or barefoot lads.[73] On occasion, such village exorcisms were performed in homes (*tangnuo*), for which we have a superb thirteenth-century account from Nanfeng, Jiangxi. In this commemorative poem—clearly written by a literatus for a friend among the local elite—the spirit-mediums invoke the gods to liberate the soul of a deceased family member from the chains of purgatory, and they assume many of the divine roles that will be central to the *nuo*-exorcisms and *nuo*-plays of late-imperial and modern villages—*Chongkui, Leigong, Wufang bingma, Jinhua nu/Yinhua nu, Tudishen, Yama*, and so forth.[74]

Although the choreography of the village *nuo* may have derived from both Daoist ritual and *juedixi*-style entertainments, the crucial factor in the precipitation of *nuo*-plays out of *nuo*-exorcisms was the transformation of the object of the exorcism from the "miasma" or "pestilence" of the classical ritual to the souls of the dead by the time of the Song period.[75] During the *nuo*-exorcism, spirits of the dead would take possession of a medium and tell its story, just as in the Rites of Summoning for Investigation. Some of these stories became paradigmatic and developed into elaborate narratives that would be dramatically rendered and that came to form a distinct segment of the larger ritual.

The quantity and quality of the evidence for the ritualization of theater increases exponentially in the Ming and Qing periods. The relative paucity of the evidence from the Song should not, however, be understood as an indication of the importance of ritualized theater in the twelfth and thirteenth centuries. In the Song dynasty, writing on theater in general was not yet a form of elite discourse suitable for either public consumption or preservation. This situation changes significantly after the Yuan, when in several areas of China the theater comes to rival Confucian discourse in the cultural self-definition of the local elite. The later evidence, even that of the twentieth century, must be considered relevant as well, if handled judiciously.[76] Be that as it may, the evidence we do have is sufficient to demonstrate the mutual appropriation of ritual and theater, and highlights the activities of village youths, who will become ready recruits for the Buddhist, Daoist, and other exorcists examined in the next two chapters.

6

Tantric Exorcists
and Child-Mediums

Our analysis will now move freely across the boundaries that distinguish China's religious traditions, for at the very same time, in many of the same areas, there were Buddhist monks who were using child-mediums in exorcisms. Buddhism, in fact, had its own, very specialized tradition of the ritualized possession of children, a tradition we consider below. By the Song, however, we have moved so far beyond the rather restricted milieu of the Tang court, where this tradition was first elaborated, that it becomes difficult to know when and where we are justified in speaking of continuity. By the Song, we have entered the vastly different world of rural or suburban monks whose practices were already in an advanced stage of convergence with those of their competitors, namely, the Daoist exorcists and village spirit-mediums. Thus it is fitting that we begin in an area of Jiangxi where all these practitioners were very active.

Tantric Monks and Child-Mediums

The Rites of the Three Altars

> Xu Yuquan was a native of the village of Hukou in the subprefecture of Leping [Jiangxi]. The front of his house looked on a large stream, and there he constructed a tower and vegetable garden. On a spring day, the members of the

household made an excursion there, and they returned
after sundown. His young daughter suddenly became ill.
She seemed completely bewildered and confused. Only
occasionally would she talk and laugh to herself. Xu knew
that she had been bewitched by a demon. A band of spirit-
mediums was unable to cure her. Xu had heard that a monk
named Master Dong Shen, from the nearby village of Baishi,
practiced the "Rite of the Three Altars" (*santan fa*) with
great efficacy, and he summoned him immediately. Shen
said, "This one, being a water spook, is easy to cure. However, the house of a commoner is not clean or pure; we must
perform [the rite] in the temple at the boundary of your
house, and then can it be accomplished." Thereupon, Dong
Shen went to the Cloister for Assisting the Nation (Zhuguo
yuan), fasted, set up an altar, and recited incantations. He
called upon three boys to investigate by illumination. And
afterward, he set up a sacrifice to welcome the spirit[s]. The
boys subsequently collapsed upon the ground and, after a
short while, rose and hastened into the sitting hall. They
addressed Xu Baowen, saying, "Do you still have implements
and knives? If you do, it would be beneficial to lend them to
us." The Xu household originally had implements to protect
itself against bandits, but Xu, fearing that they would cause
injury, deceivingly said that he had none. The boys went
straight to another room. The outside lock opened by itself, and the boys reappeared, each grasping a knife. They
skipped and jumped into the middle of the stream. With
the utmost sincerity Shen approached the water and recited
incantations incessantly. After two nights he became silent.
The parents of the three boys complained to Xu, but Shen
said, "The spirit is going to possess them. Certainly there
will be no harm." Then, unexpectedly, three different
possessed boys ran into the stream. After a while, one
of them came out and proclaimed, "The evil demon has
already descended into my hand. It would be convenient
to boil thirty catties of sesame oil in order to dispose of the
demon completely." With these words he again entered the
water. When the oil pot was boiling, the six boys together
grasped a tortoise as large as a mat and weighing over one

hundred catties. The boys zealously wielded their knives, cut it up, and put it in the oil to cook until ready. Then they discarded it deep in the mountains. The girl's illness immediately subsided, and within another ten days she was pacified. Shen has disciples who learn this art. They neither eat meat nor marry. They considerably exorcize malignancies for people. But their self-cultivation cannot last, and they break all the regulations and die within a short while. Shen survived until the end of the Junxi reign period [1174–1190], and then his long life ended.[1]

The Rite of the Three Altars, at least as it is described here, reveals the influence of Daoist *fashi* and even of the local cult of spirit-mediums. For reasons of purity, the ritual takes place in part of a temple borrowed temporarily because of its proximity to the patient's home. The Master marks off a ritual space, recites incantations, and commands three young boys to identify the true form of the water demon in a rite of "investigation by illumination." Identification is then followed by possession, though at this point the rite swerves from the Daoist pattern, for the boys are possessed by divinities rather than demons. The Master brings down the divinity (or divinities) into the ritual area with a sacrifice, and the boys enter into a trance indicated by their collapse on the ground. Armed with knives, the boys then jump into the stream that runs in front of the patient's home. (The god or demon of this stream has evidently been offended by Xu Yuchan's additions to his home.) The boys apparently remain in the river for two days, while the Master recites incantations over it. The three boys are then joined, mysteriously, by three others, also in trance, and together they finally emerge from the river holding a tortoise, which is cut up, boiled in sesame oil, and discarded in the mountains.

The social content of this account is equally impressive. The (Ritual) Master Dong Shen is a monk, yet it is not at all certain that he is attached to a monastery. Hong Mai is quite careful—indeed, he is thoroughly consistent—about identifying the institutional affiliations and ordinational names of Buddhist monks and Daoist priests. Dong Shen may have been a monk who resided in the village of Baishi and who was more involved with villagers than with the members of a monastic community. In the first place, Master Dong devoted himself to a group of disciples who were instructed in the Rite of the Three Altars

and who practiced it on condition that they adhere strictly to vege-
tarianism, refuse to marry, and carefully attend to their own moral cultivation. In other words, he was the leader of a local sect of lay exorcists modeled on Buddhist laws of purity, a sect that may be seen as a
distant ancestor of those groups and traditions of red-head Daoists still
to be found today on Taiwan and Southeast China (i.e., Lüshan jiao,
Puan jiao, and so forth).[2]

In addition to instructing villagers in ritual and the rigors of a Buddhist lifestyle, Master Dong maintained enduring links with village
households through their children. As we might infer from the anxiety and concern voiced by the parents of the three boys who had entered into trance, these children were not professional, or at least habitual, spirit-mediums. Rather, they can best be compared to those
known on modern Taiwan as *shengtong* ("raw youths"), who become
spontaneously entranced, most often during the festivals of the local
tutelary spirit.[3] This "seizure" (*lüe shengtong*) is viewed as a sign of their
election, and one or more of these youths are then chosen to become
"divination youths" (*tongji* or *tongzi*), or oracles of the god. They pass
through an elaborate intitiation overseen by a *fashi*, which includes an
incubation period in the god's temple.[4] The techniques subsequently
used by the *fashi* for compelling the god to descend into the *tongji* are
known as "*guan*," and at this stage the boys are known as "*guantong*"
or "*guan tongji*"[5]—precisely the words used in our text to describe the
three other boys who joined the first set of three. It is impossible to
confirm, however, whether the first group, like the second, were actually village "divination youths." Nonetheless, whether the Buddhist
master employed them on an ad hoc or consistent basis, we can be
fairly confident that the first three might become, had already become,
or were at least representative of those who did become recruits for
the local bands of spirit-mediums like the one that initially tried to cure
the young girl in question.[6]

In the last two decades, the village tradition of initiating boys as
spirit-mediums has been revived in Fujian under the rubric "*guanjie*"—
meaning the rules or prescriptions (*jie*) received by those who are en-
closed (*guan*) within the temple. It has been observed and documented by Kenneth Dean and Zheng Zhenman of Xiamen University.[7]
In the village of Liangcuo, for example, near the township of Jiangkou
(Putian), the initiation is the culmination of an elaborate process extending over several months, or even years, and overseen by Ritual Mas-

ters of the Lüshan Daoist tradition. Boys are selected and instructed in the arts of trance, the recitation of spells, and the performance of *nuo*-exorcisms. The initiation ceremony itself follows a Daoist "offering" (*jiao*). Inside the temple, before three altars, three Daoist priests perform a ritual of announcement that includes the "opening of light and dotting the eyes" to animate the effigies of the divinities and a black paper crow. Then, led by a "group of eight" (*baban*), who are the temple security guards, the priest conducts about thirty-five of the "altar lads" across the courtyard to an altar set up on the theatrical stage facing the temple. The "altar lads" are divided into three groups: six initiates, who face the priest, and the rest equally distributed to their right and left:

> The ritual lasted about an hour. The priest read from the liturgy, summoned the black crow, gave it a message, and then had it burnt to send the message to the gods. The ashes were placed in a bowl of talisman-water. At that time, he read in a loud, clear voice, the various prescriptions the lads were to adopt. Then he animated the various ritual objects by blowing his long curved buffalo horn at them . . . [then] he climbed up a footstool so that he stood at the top of the altar . . . holding his Thunder Seal before his face while the altar lads, in pairs, moved up to the altar, put their heads under a pair of crossed swords held by elder initiates, and drank from the bowl of talisman-water. When everyone had completed the rite, he came forward, stood before the mediums and twirled back and forth. Then he sprayed the mediums with sacred water. They immediately went into trance. The priest moved back, and the support lads came forward to hold up the six mediums. The elder initiates assisted them with the ritual clothing and headdresses. When everyone was ready, the support lads led the mediums, now fully dressed in god's clothes and holding a sword between their arms, back into the temple. The door of the temple was fastened tight. Altar-tables were piled up in front of it, and the doors of the temple were sealed with paper that read *Lüshan dafayuan* (The Great Ritual Institute of Mt. Lü).[8]

The initiates remained in the temple for nine days. On three of these days, representatives, or the entire population, of more than two hundred neighboring villages came to pay their respects. At 3 a.m. on the ninth day, the doors of the temple were opened, flames flared, and the six initiates burst out, chanting and shouting, and made a procession around the village. Later that day, after they had been feasted at home, they would make another procession around the village and then perform a *nuo*-exorcism in front of the temple. The initiation ceremony would conclude, as it had begun, with another Daoist ritual.

It is, of course, difficult to determine the significance of the fact that the number of initiates in the modern rite and the number of spirit-mediums in the Buddhist exorcism is the same—six. Nonetheless, there is a profound link between these two events separated by almost eight hundred years, and it is fascinating that we first encounter these village boys in a Buddhist, rather than Daoist, context, which perhaps begins to explain some of the Buddhist elements found in the Lüshan Daoist tradition.

The popularity of the Buddhist practitioners of the Rites of the Three Altars is attested to in an unlikely source. During the twelfth and thirteenth centuries, in the Southeast, there were a number of Daoist therapeutic lineages that had evolved from the cultic devotion to various specifically chthonic deities, including the ancient hero Xiang Yu. One of these lineages is represented by three texts in the *Daofa huiyuan*—"The Rites of the Earth-Spirits,"[9] "The Secret Rites for Summoning and Investigation of Grand Protector Wen of the Eastern Peak,"[10] and "The Great Rites of the Earth-Spirit, Prime Marshal Wen."[11] The *fashi* of this lineage once again performed "rituals of summoning for investigation," during which the patient would become possessed by the afflicting demon.[12] Like their spirit-general, Prime Marshal Wen, they also specialized in individual and communal exorcisms of epidemics. A partial genealogy of the lineage was recorded by Huang Gongjin,[13] a native of Jiangxi, who was also responsible for composing, in 1274, the hagiography of its central divinity, *The Biography of Grand Protector Wen, Supreme Commander of the Earth-Spirits*.[14]

The most fascinating and relevant aspect of this hagiography is its presentation of "Grand Protector's Wen's Secret Rites" as an instrument in the religious conversion of the Southeast. The Daoist Wang Zongjing sends his disciple Wu Daoxian on a missionary expedition into Fujian, a trip that takes him as far as Quanzhou. Daoxian's travels reveal a religious topography drawn entirely with a Buddhist brush. This is significant. Buddhism has now come to occupy the space once reserved for the popular cults by which Daoism differentiated itself. In contrast, the gods of the popular cults (i.e., Wen Qiong) are looking better and better, wanting nothing more than to be integrated into the hierarchy of the Dao—an indication of the extent to which Daoism was willing to integrate them.

The description of the Buddhist cults of the region occupies the largest part of the biography of Grand Protector Wen. Everywhere, for example, Daoxian encounters worship of a certain Kālayakṣa (Jialuo wang), a spirit linked here with the practice of sorcery (*gudu*) and the cultivation of "golden caterpillars" used to poison strangers, steal their property, and enslave their souls.[15] Outside of Fuzhou, on a mountain named after the Buddhist monk Sengjia, Daoxian confronts an entire congregation reciting *The Diamond Sūtra* (*Jin'gang jing*) in a temple dedicated to what is perhaps another *yakṣa*, Jialu wang.[16] The most remarkable and drawn-out confrontation, however, is with a "heterodox" Buddhist sect led by two non-clerics, Xu Wen and Hao Bian. The "perverse teachings" of these two individuals are identified as the "Way of the Saṇgha-Households of the Three Altars" (*Santan sengjia zhi dao*), which includes adherence to something called the "Diamond (or Vajra) Dhyāna" (*Jin'gang chan*).[17]

Between 1163 and 1166, the scholar-official Lu You (1125–1210) submitted a memorial on a number of lay religious associations, including the Diamond Dhyāna, and the threat they posed to public order. "In Huainan," Lu You writes, "they are called 'People of the Two Knots'; in the two Zhe they are called [followers of] 'the doctrine of Muni'; in Jiangdong, they are called the 'Four Fruits' and in Jiangxi they are called the 'Diamond Dhyāna' (*Jin'gang chan*); in Fujian they are called followers of the 'Religion of Light' or [those who observe] the 'Gati Fast' and by various other titles."[18] Lu You makes no attempt to distinguish between these sects. He views them all as potentially seditious successors of the late Han rebel Zhang Jue, and, more recently, of Fang La. The enumeration, in any case, immediately gives way to an extended discussion of Manichaeism, the "Religion of Light." Lu You's association of the Diamond Dhyāna with Jiangxi, however, is confirmed in the writings of a late twelfth-century official, Wang Zhi. Wang was an eyewitness to a sect of "vegetarian demon-worshippers" in Jiangxi that identified itself in part by the term "Diamond Dhyāna."[19] Wang Zhi gives a list of the various scriptures employed by the sect, a list almost identical to one found in an exposition and denunciation of Manichaeism by the Buddhist historian Zongjian.[20]

We now know, however, thanks to the research of Chikusa Masa'aki, that the Diamond Dhyāna was not a subsect of Manichaeism at all, but a lay Buddhist sect founded by a monk in Liangzhou during the tenth century.[21] The popularity of this group continued into the twelfth century, in Zhejiang as well as Jiangxi, though little else is known except that its followers based their devotion on *The Diamond Sūtra*. Unfortunately, the laconic accounts of the Diamond Dhyāna are so negative that the term itself may also have become one of reproach, much like "vegetarian devil-worshippers," and therefore unreliable as a signifier of the nature of the Way of the Saṇgha-Households of the Three Altars.

Although Dong Shen, master of the Rites of the Three Altars in Jiangxi, also appears to have been at the center of a lay Buddhist association, I would like to suggest that we pursue the rites themselves within the context of the popularization of Tantric Buddhism after the Tang.[22] This much is suggested by the opening passage of another anecdote from the *Yijian zhi*, one which confirms, by the way, that, as the biography of Wen Qiong indicated, Buddhist practitioners of the Rites of the Three Altars were found in Fujian as well as in Jiangxi:

Ye Dao, styled Faguang, was a native of [the subprefecture of] Jianning [Fujian]. He neither drank alcohol nor ate meat. He transmitted and practiced the "Rites of the Five Divisions of the Three Altars" (*Santan wubu fa*) in order to exorcise malignancy and cure illness.[23]

The qualification of the Rites of the Three Altars as "Rites of the Five Divisions (or Classes)" clearly locates these rites in the Tantric Buddhist tradition. In the dictionaries and encyclopedias of Esoteric Buddhism, the term "*wubu*" is normally taken to refer to the five Buddha families, or, by extension, to a fivefold classification of presiding Tantric divinities, sections of the mandala, ritual genres, and altars. Yet I suspect that, several centuries earlier, "*wubu*" had become a kind of synecdoche for Esoteric Buddhism in general, and the "Rites of the Five Divisions" a kind of shorthand for Tantric exorcisms of a particular kind. In the Tang dynasty, for example, a monk named Zhuan Qing was summoned to the home of a "man of the market" to cure his wife who had been bewitched by a demon for several years. Zhuan Qing was an expert in *wubu fa*. He made a straw puppet, eight inches high, and dressed it in clothing made from five-colored threads. The monk then constructed an altar and, standing the puppet up, recited incantations over it until the image became animated by the demon and cried out for help. Zhuan Qing interrogated (*jiewen*) the demon and threatened it with beatings if it reported falsely. The demon, in turn, confessed that he had spied on the young woman in the Temple of Yu (Yu miao) in Guiji and had caused her to lose her mind. Zhuan did not believe this story, and he used a whip to chase the puppet into a jar, which he then sealed with a red talisman, encased in mud, and finally buried in a mulberry grove. The wife was cured.[24]

This anecdote suggests that, in the Tang, the term "*wubu fa*" did imply exorcisms, and that these exorcisms included the possession of a surrogate, albeit a nonhuman one. However, at the end of the biography of the Tantric monk Vajrabodhi in the *Gaoseng zhuan*, the editor Zanning (919–1001) comments:

> According to the "Rites of the Maṇḍala of the Five Divisions," young boys or virgins must be used as mediums to summon spirits, and it was once extremely easy to cure illness or exorcise evil. People in modern times, [however,] use this [method] to profit their body or mouth; therefore little result is obtained. Generally [this method] is held in contempt by the world. Alas, that the deterioration of the Correct Law has gone so far as this![25]

Zanning's comments were no doubt prompted by the central episode in Vajrabodhi's biography, an exorcism he performed for one of the daughters of the emperor Xuanzong in which two seven-year-old female mediums were employed to embody the souls of the sick daughter and her dead nurse.[26] It is also in the Tang, in the texts of Tantric Buddhism, that we find ritual instructions not only for the animation of images but for the possession of child-mediums as well.

Tang-Dynasty Precedents

These rituals for the possession of child-mediums were referred to by the term "*aweishe*," a transliteration of the Sanskrit *āveśa* ("to take hold of" and, by extension, "to possess"). They are described in a number of texts, dating from the seventh and eighth centuries, that were translated by, attributed to, or generally reflective of the practices of a number of Esoteric Buddhist masters at the courts of the emperors Xuanzong and Taizong. For our purposes it is not necessary to analyze each of these texts separately. They reveal a set of practices of considerable coherence in both form and function.[27]

Basically, the Tantric master recites various incantations to summon one or more Buddhist deities, sometimes identified, sometimes not, into either a luminous, reflective object (water, mirror, jewel, pearl), the image or icon of the divinity, or the body of a child. In the case of children, considerable attention is given to their number (anywhere from two to ten boys or girls, in some cases) and to their age (between eight and fourteen). The texts describe an elaborate process of purification and the physical appearance of the children both before and during the trance. It is said that when the divinity has descended into the children, they will speak of "all matters past, present, and future," of "things yet to come," or of "good or evil fortune," or that they will be able to answer any question asked of the god.[28]

The divinity, as we have said, could also be compelled to enter a reflective object or hollow icon, whereupon it apparently revealed itself directly to an audience through visual or auditory hallucinations. Yet even in these cases, children were given a prominent, if not preferred, part to play as mediators. In two of the texts, children were asked to gaze into a mirror, which had either been purified with the ash of the *homa* offering or otherwise empowered by the divinity, and then to answer all manner of questions based on what they saw. This was a variation on the art of catoptromancy, or divination by mirrors, which would play an important role in the Song period in Daoist as well as Buddhist rites employing child-mediums.[29]

Whatever the form taken by the "*āveśa* rites," the function of the children was clearly mediumistic and oracular. Because of the therapeutic nature of some parts of the texts in which descriptions of *āveśa* were embedded, we cannot rule out the possibility that diagnosis was indeed part of prognosis. There is no reason to suppose that a question posed to the divinity possessing the child might not have concerned the nature of a demon causing illness. Yet therapy and exorcism are hardly mentioned, much less emphasized, in the ritual accounts per se. The boys do not appear to have been acting as vehicles for demonic possession or as surrogates for a demoniac. One text does mention that in the course of the ritual of divine possession, the children might become possessed by a *yakṣa*, but this eventuality was not encouraged, and the Master is advised to send the demon away immediately.[30]

All in all, the *āveśa* rituals seem to have been not too distant from the most popular kind of seance performed by the Tang-dynasty spirit-medium for officials and members of the aristocracy. In these seances the spirit-medium summoned a divinity either into himself or into some other localized place. Then he either answered himself, or communicated the divinity's responses to, specific questions posed by the supplicant about "good and evil fortune," "matters past, present, and future," or "things yet to come."[31] What has changed in the *āveśa* rites is the fact that the spirit-medium's trance was officiated by a Tantric master and resulted from the power conferred on the master by his own identification with a Buddhist deity. In *The Rites of Āveśa as Explained by the Deva Maheśvara*, a text in one short scroll submitted to the throne by Amoghavajra, the officiant or "practicant," as he is called, must first transform himself into the eponymous Maheśvara,[32] thereby empowering the mantras and mudrās he then employs to compel an "emissary of Maheśvara" to possess the children.[33] The text notes that after the appropriate spell has been recited seven times, "the boys and girls will tremble violently, causing one to realize that the 'Holy One' (*shengzhe*) had entered their bodies."[34]

The unity of practitioner and divinity is a defining feature of Esoteric Buddhism and a mark of the extent to which even Daoist therapeutic rituals had become "tantricized" in the Song. In the canonical "Rite of Summoning for Investigation," the metamorphosis of the Ritual Master was just as necessary to effect the possession of the patient or his surrogate, though the purpose of these Daoist rites, as I have argued, was to listen to the demonic voice rather than to impart divine knowledge. Of course, it is precisely as an officiant of spirit-mediums that the Tang masters of *āveśa* may be seen to have anticipated not only the Daoist practitioners of *kaozhao* but also the Buddhist practitioners of the Rites of the Three Altars. Yet the social context for the performance of these and other Buddhist rites employing child-mediums had changed so significantly by the twelfth century that I find it difficult to see as much continuity in substance as I do in form. The monks who were practicing these rituals were no longer associated with the court. They were operating out of provincial monasteries with close ties to the surrounding villages and to their inhabitants. The changed milieu seriously affected the content of these rites, to the extent that they owed as much, if not more, to the wild theatrics of the spirit-mediums whom the monks employed as to the Tantric patrimony of the monks themselves. This will become increasingly evident as we reconsider this patrimony within the context of the exorcisms of another group of Tantric monks in the Song dynasty.

The Rites of Ucchuṣma

The people of Zhang and Quan prefectures [in Fujian] enjoy practicing the "Rites of the Vajra-Being of Impure Traces [i.e., Ucchuṣma]" (*Huiji jin'gang fa*) to cure sickness and to perform exorcisms. The deity descends and possesses a young boy in order to speak. In 1152 the monk Ruochong was residing in the Guang Fu Cloister on Mount Xi in Quan prefecture. In the middle of the night a monk sought him out, and Chong was surprised at the improper hour. The monk said, "I am very poor. My almsbowl, which contained several taels of silver, was stolen by someone. I just now entreated the 'Holy One' (*daozhe*) to employ his method. The spirit said to me, 'I will wait for the Elder to come and then speak,' and fortunately you came for alms." Chong accompanied the monk to a room where a village youth was standing on a table holding a sword. The youth looked at Chong and greeted him, saying, "The monk should sit for a while; in the middle of the night it is not fitting that we humble ourselves to each other." Chong said, "I didn't realize that the Venerable Spirit had descended here; I have been deficient in offerings. Can I ask you to reveal yourself to me?" The spirit said, "I am a high-ranking spirit of Heaven. It is not difficult to certify the owner of something lost in the temple. I am afraid, however, that a litigious suit might arise which would harm my purity (*benxin*). If you do not make a report to the officials, then I will help you." Chong bowed many times in gratitude and said, "We will diligently respect your warning." The spirit said, "Then the rite will be performed." The youth went out of the room clasping his sword, jumping at one moment, walking at another. Suddenly he threw himself into a large well. After a long time he came jumping out and passed through the temple gate until he reached a pile of cow dung. He flung himself about, circling it as he went. Then he struck the pile three times with his sword, and all of a sudden collapsed on the ground. After a spell, the youth came to. They asked about this, but he wasn't aware of anything. Then they noticed that there was a mud brick

that was uneven, under the dung. Picking it up, the silver
was underneath. They said it was what the thief had
concealed.[35]

The most interesting social fact we can glean from this anecdote
concerns the nature of the boy. He is referred to by the poor mendi-
cant monk as the "Holy One" (*daozhe*), either because he was considered to have dedicated himself to a religious life as a follower of "the
Way," and/or because he was transparent to the divine, the "Venerable Spirit," who in this case we may assume to have been either the
"Vajra-Being of Impure Traces" or perhaps one of several subordinate
deities we will see to have been associated with his cult.

The presence of this possessed oracle in the monastery elicits no
surprise from the temple elder or from his unfortunate visitor. We can
infer from this that he was a regular and accustomed feature of the
monastic environment, to such an extent that he and his divinity were
occasionally taken too much for granted: the elder apologizes for having been negligent in sacrifices. According to another anecdote in the
Yijian zhi, a young medium was also present in the "Dharma hall" (*fatang*) of a remote temple in Wuyuan, Jiangxi, when, in 1165, an unnamed fierce deity descended twice to criticize and condemn the
monks for various transgressions.[36]

The medium of Guang Fu Cloister exemplifies, both in his person
and in his actions, the porosity of the membrane that separated the
monastery from the surrounding environment. This can be seen in
the worries of the god himself about the consequences of being
dragged into a matter normally left to the secular authorities. In addition, like the group of boys employed by Dong Shen, the Ritual Master of the Three Altars, the monastic medium here was a village youth,
drawn, I suspect, from that fund of local boys who would have become
possessed during village festivals. The medium, in fact, brings to his
monastic service of the Bodhisattva Ucchuṣma all the autonomous
characteristics of that other role. First, he appears to be—and to always have been, even while in the monastery—the master of his own
trance, spontaneously possessed by the god. Second, he even appears
to be the initiator, if not master himself, of the "rites" he performs;
knowledge of these rites, in any case, is claimed by the divinity with
whom he has identified, rather than residing in a Buddhist master who
mediates this identification. Finally, his entranced performance ex-

hibits all the frenzy and theatricality of village mediums. The young boy works himself up in fits and starts, throws himself into a well, and then, leaving the monastery, circumambulates a pile of excrement that he slashes repeatedly with his sword. The intensity of the trance finally overcomes him, and he collapses on the ground. Once again, amnesia is taken as a necessary mark of authenticity by the spectators.

Here we are far from the highly controlled, rarefied, and even claustrophobic atmosphere of the Buddhist *āveśa* rites, in which two or more virginal and purified children stood passively before the master amidst lighted incense and strewn flowers; in which the descent of the divinity and the onset of trance were distinguishable only by the most subtle of signs—the cessation of breathing, unblinking eyes, and a slight reddish tint around the pupils; and in which the children had in essence become living icons, as luminescent, but also as confined, as the pearl or crystal for which they were substitutes.[37] In the Song, Buddhist rites employing possessed children had become invaded by the sound and fury of village spirit-mediums, while part of the temple had, in a sense, been commandeered as an outpost of village culture.

Though it is unclear to whom Hong Mai is referring when he says that it was "the people of Zhang and Quan prefectures" who practiced the "Rites of Ucchuṣma," they were obviously not limited to monks. Indeed, we will find that, in addition to clerics, both laymen and village spirit-mediums claimed these rites for themselves, and at that point we will be in a better position to judge what they brought with them. Meanwhile, it is necessary to examine the Rites of Ucchuṣma within the context of the history of Tantric Buddhism, if only to discover that the monks who practiced these rituals in the Song were not cut from exactly the same cloth as those who frequented the court of the Tang emperors.

Ucchuṣma's Cult in the Tang and Song

The deity Ucchuṣma (Wuchusema) is described by Marie-Thérèse de Mallmann in her study of Tantric iconography as "Le Crepitant," or "the One Who Crackles," an attribute of the Hindu god Agni with whom Ucchuṣma is also closely identified as a "devouring" divinity.[38] Ucchuṣma is frequently represented within a garland of flames, the fire that transforms and purifies all impurities. Many of his popular names, in fact, take into account his contact with the impure, including the above-mentioned "Vajra[-Being] of Impure Traces." Iyanaga

Nobumi suggests, more convincingly, that the name Ucchuṣma derives from the Sanskrit "*ucchista*," for "rejected [from the mouth]," an evocation of the alimentary remains of the meal or sacrifice that are enthusiastically consumed and transformed by him.[39]

In the Buddhist canon, there are at least five texts especially devoted to Ucchuṣma, three of which date from the early eighth century, and several other scriptures in which he figures to a greater or lesser degree.[40] We shall return to these momentarily. What is remarkable with respect to the exorcistic rites performed in the name of Ucchuṣma is that the cult to this relatively minor bodhisattva was considered by some observers to have attained a position of central significance in the devotion and practice of Esoteric Buddhism in the Song. Evidence for this is found in *The Recorded Conversations* of the great thirteenth-century Fujianese Daoist Bo Yuchan. At one point in these discussions, a disciple asks about the current state of Buddhist yogic (i.e., Tantric) teaching. Bo Yuchan answers that contemporary practice derived from the posthumous teaching of the Buddha Śākyamuni—from the teaching, that is, of a future incarnation of the Buddha, whom he identifies with none other than Ucchuṣma. He goes on to explain that "Śākyamuni transformed himself into the Vajra[-Being] of Impure Traces in order to suppress the Brahma King Śikhin"; as a consequence, the "teaching" (*jiao*) associated with this event was disseminated widely and applied broadly against all evil beings (Māra) and heterodox ways (*waidao*). Its comprehensive efficacy, in fact, seems to have been in inverse proportion to the complexity of the teaching itself, which was condensed into a thirty-three syllable mantra called the "Spell of [the Vajra-Being] of the Golden Disc and Impure Traces" (*Jinlun huiji zhou*).[41]

The Daoist master Bo Yuchan was evidently intimately familiar with a group of Tantric Buddhist practitioners in Fujian who still maintained traditions associated with the eighth-century texts devoted to Ucchuṣma. The story of the Brahma King Śikhin is found in *The Scripture of the Essential Ritual Techniques as Explained by the Vajra[-Being] of Impure Traces*,[42] an apocryphal scripture attributed to the North Indian monk Ajitasena, working in the Western Protectorate (Khotan) of the Tang empire. I include here Iyanaga Nobumi's translation of the scriptural narrative:

> The scene is Kusinagara at the time when the Buddha is preparing himself to enter *paranirvāṇa*. All the Beings have assembled except the

Brahma king Śikhin . . . who remains in his heaven out of pride, surrounded by thousands of celestial maidens. Upset, the Beings send
vidyadhāna [transcendents] to escort Śikhin to assist in the Buddha's
extinction, but they are prevented from approaching the god by a wall
of refuse that surrounds his palace. Then, out of pity for the Beings,
the Buddha causes a divinity called Adamantine Diamond to appear
from the "Heart of the Right Hand." The divinity points to the wall of
refuse with his finger and it collapses to the ground. Adamantine Diamond then points to the Brahma king, who is converted to Buddhism.
The king produces the "Spirit of Awakening" and joins the Assembly of
Beings. Adamantine Diamond makes a vow whereby he promises that
after the Buddha's extinction, those Beings who pronounce his mantra
will invariably be helped, and he explained the mantra which was called
the "Mantra of Impure Traces."43

The motifs mentioned in this eighth-century text—the transformation of the Buddha into Ucchuṣma ("Diamant indestructible"), the
conversion of Śikhin, the provision of a mantra for general use—and
perhaps even the text itself were very much alive among the thirteenth-
century devotees of Ucchuṣma as they were described by Bo Yuchan.
Nonetheless, it would be wrong to assume an easy continuity between
these Song practitioners and those who wrote the Tang scripture. Bo
Yuchan continues his discussion of the Rites of Ucchuṣma with the
word "however," and indeed, he believed that current practice, which
he goes on to describe, was a gross deviation from the original intent.
Still, we do not have to accept this judgment, and might very well come
to accept the opposite view—namely, that the so-called deviations he
describes were very much part of the original, or at least an earlier,
situation.

In any case, Bo Yuchan proceeds to show not only that, by the thirteenth century, the cult to Ucchuṣma had moved to center stage in
the ongoing Tantric drama, but that Ucchuṣma himself had come to
occupy the pinnacle of a large and most interesting pantheon of divinities as well. Ucchuṣma is paired here with the Medicine King
Dragon Tree.44 Long Shu ("Dragon Tree") is the Chinese name for
Nāgārjuna, the great Indian philosopher and patriarch of Mahāyāna
Buddhism, who lived anywhere from the second through fourth centuries C.E. According to a biography translated by Kumārajīva in the
first decade of the fifth century, Nāgārjuna owed his name to two leg-

endary facts: his birth under a tree (Skt. *arjuna*), and his instruction in the Mahāyāna scriptures by serpents (Skt. *nāga*).[45]

All the so-called biographies, however, in Tibetan as well as in Chinese, are so steeped in legend that it is impossible to say anything significant about Nāgārjuna as a historical person. What we have in these accounts are really different Nāgārjunas—or, rather, different versions of a single uncommon intelligence revered not just for his philosophical disputation but for his mastery of astronomy, clairvoyance, and even sorcery. At least one, and perhaps two, Tantric Buddhist texts composed in China were attributed to this mythic and deified Nāgārjuna, a personality not unlike Hermes Trismegistus or one of the venerable Old Testament figures (Enoch, for example) claimed as the source of esoteric wisdom by Jewish apocrypha. We will return to these texts and their possible association with devotion to Ucchuṣma later in this chapter.

Ucchuṣma and the Medicine King Dragon Tree (Longshu yiwang) apparently formed a divine pair at the center of the cult. Bo Yuchan then mentions a series of ten subordinate deities:[46] the Two Great Lords Incense Mountain and Snowy Mountain (Xiang shan xueshan er dasheng);[47] the Two Great Lords Swine Head and Elephant Trunk (Zhutou xiangbi er dasheng);[48] the Two Great Lords Heroic Authority and Flower Radiance (Xiongwei Huaguang er dasheng);[49] Prince Nezha and the Lordly King Dinglun (Nezha taizi Dinglun shengwang);[50] and the God of Deep Sands and the Jiedi God (Shensha shen, Jiedi shen).[51] These ten divinities, in turn, are assisted by the Adjutant Emissary (Yushi) Jin'gang lishi, who commands four military hirelings (*jiangli*)—Hu jialuo, Ma jialuo, Niutou luo, and Jintou luo.

As far as I have been able to determine, this pantheon is without textual precedent. It represents, I believe, the distillation of several independent cults into a unique configuration of fierce bodhisattvas, guardian deities, and converted demons. The origin of many of these divinities in the region where China meets Tibet and Central Asia lends the pantheon a distinct air of exoticism. On the surface, it would appear to divide itself neatly and hierarchically into three distinct tiers, much like a Chinese temple mural: Ucchuṣma and Nāgārjuna sit at the top, with the ten Great Lords and other divinities stretched out along the middle, and the Adamantine Stalwart and his lackeys at the bottom.

Another arrangement, however, is suggested by the maṇḍala-like configuration of the five pairs of divinities of the middle tier and by certain associations between the divinities of the top and bottom: the Adamantine Stalwart (Jin'gang lishi; Skt.: Vajramalla) is to be identified with the Bodhisattva Vajrapāṇi (Jin'gang shou), also known as the "Vajra[-Being] of the Traces of the Mysteries" (Miji jin'gang) or the "Vajra[-Being], Master of the Mysteries" (Mizhu jin'gang).[52] Vajrapāṇi, however, is closely associated with Ucchuṣma,[53] with whom he shared, among other characteristics, the task of vanquishing the recalcitrant Hindu deity, Maheśvara (i.e., Śiva). Vajrapāṇi also shared with other deities (Vaiśravaṇa, for example) the role of king of the yakṣas, demonic beings which, I believe, are represented here by Vajrapāṇi's four military subordinates, Hu jialuo, Ma jialuo, Niutou luo, and Jintou luo. The names of these demons suggest that they were conceived as two pairs, a fact that perhaps results from the bifurcated appearance of Vajrapāṇi himself as a pair of fierce divinities (Jin'gang and Lishi) guarding the gates of Buddhist monasteries in China and Japan.

We learn from Rolf Stein's study of Buddhist door gods that in Chinese monasteries these guardian deities were placed back to back, one in the north, facing the temple, the other in the south, facing the entrance gate. In the northern position one usually finds the fierce and ascetic figure of Weituo (Skt. Skanda), and, in the southern position, the rather benign and glutinous figure of Miluo (Skt. Maitreya), or, perhaps, the equally comic and hungry monk Budai heshang. Depending on the particular Buddhist tradition, cultural area, and historical period, this initial pair gives way to an extensive range of substitutes (of doubles and of partitioned deities) based on the oppositions north/south, fierce/benign, ascetic/glutinous, and so forth.[54] About the Esoteric Buddhist tradition in particular, Stein writes:

> We find here, in both association and opposition, two principal characters in a variety of partitioned forms. On one side is Vajrapāṇi (in China divided into Jin'gang and Lishi, guardians of the temple gate) and his Tibetan variations (Heruka or Vajrakūmara); on the other side is Gaṇeśa (in China doubled as male and female elephants who embrace and are called Huanxitian, a name corresponding to the epithet Hehe). Despite contingency and the many possible reasons for arbitrary transformation (personal or local convention, economic reasons, confusion, lack of information, etc.), the play of the imagination that results in the

transformation of the central characters is not made freely, arbitrarily, or by chance, but is a response to a bipartitioned structure which subtends a coherent meaning formulated by a limited number of forms.[55]

Ucchuṣma, Gaṇeśa, and Vajrapāṇi each appear in our thirteenth-century Chinese Tantric pantheon as the Vajra-Being of Impure Traces, the Two Great Lords Swine Head and Elephant Trunk, and the Adamantine Stalwart, respectively. Given their prominence in and their representation at all levels of this pantheon, I would like to suggest that all the divinities might be submitted to the same bipartite logic that Stein has applied in his analysis of the door gods—and, further, that the hierarchy implicit in Bo's description of the pantheon might collapse, under further analysis, into a series of divine pairs drawn along a north/south axis.[56] This, however, will remain hypothetical until we can identify the attributes of all the divinities in the pantheon.

As already noted,[57] many of the Buddhist deities in the pantheon of Ucchuṣma had already penetrated the cults and discourse of the Daoist Ritual Master. Yet, as even Bo Yuchan noticed, the thirteenth-century Tantric devotees of Ucchuṣma were equally influenced by the Daoists. Continuing his discussion of contemporary practitioners of the Rites of Ucchuṣma, Bo remarks,

> The wayward masters (*xieshi*) of today mix [their practices] with prescriptions of Daoist rites. And, in addition, they trace the steps of the Celestial Outline and pinch their fingers to form secret signs (*bugang nianjue*); they cry out in loud voices; they jump about like barbarians and dance like Chinese (*hutiao hanwu*); they shake small bells and rattle clappered ones; they whip with hempen stalks and strike with peach staves. In doing so, the truth of the ancient teachings has been lost entirely, and [their behavior] seems completely contrary to that of Buddhism. Nonetheless, yoga is still one method of the Buddhists for subjugating evil[-beings] (*mo*).[58]

Bo Yuchan was a man forever on the lookout for breaches of orthodoxy, even within traditions other than his own. In this respect he was much like his near contemporary Zhu Xi, with whom his efforts to establish a true line of transmission in Daoism, a *daotong*, ought to be compared. To Bo, the Tantric practitioners of his day were essentially a class of popular exorcists who had more in common with Daoist *fashi*, and even with spirit-mediums, than with Buddhists of the past.

Indeed, the phraseology he employs to describe the singing, dancing, shaking of bells, and wielding of sticks is almost proverbial in Song accounts of spirit-mediums. We may accept Bo Yuchan's characterization of these Buddhist exorcists, without, however, accepting his judgment that they either were alienated from or had seriously corrupted their tradition. Long before the Song, Daoism had been fraying the edges of Esoteric Buddhism; in some cases, it had actually altered its content. And no better example of Daoist influence on Tantric Buddhism can be found than in the texts of the early devotees of Ucchuṣma.

The Scripture on the Rites of the Vajra[-Being] of Impure Traces for Exorcising the One Hundred [Demonic] Transformations,[59] one of the pseudo-epigraphical and apochryphal scriptures attributed to the eighth-century Ajitasena, is largely devoted to illustrations and instructions for engraving Chinese-style wooden seals and writing Daoist-style talismans. The talismans were to be written on paper with vermilion ink and then swallowed to ward off various disease-demons or to protect against the elements, to prolong life, and even to cause the spontaneous appearance of all kinds of precious treasure.[60]

Several scholars have recognized the similarities between this scripture and another inspired by the deified Nāgārjuna, *Nāgārjuna's Treatise on the Five Sciences.*[61] Our present, canonical version of this other work is based on a late Heian manuscript preserved in the Japanese monastery, Sekizanji.[62] Parts of it evidently date back to the Six Dynasties period. In his monumental study of Tantric Buddhism, Ōmura Seigai mentions a now-lost *Treatise on the Five Sciences* (*Wuming lun*) that was translated in the second year of Emperor Ming of the Northern Zhou (558).[63] The *Treatise*, as we have it, is a sprawling, eclectic work in which the Chinese and Daoist elements sit side by side with, if they do not actually overwhelm, the Indian and Tantric ones.

The first part of the *Treatise* opens with a Daoist-style spell in the bureaucratic language of Chinese edicts ("Quickly, quickly, do as the law commands"),[64] and closes with a stream of Sanskrit *dhāraṇīs*.[65] In between we find a list of eighteen talismans to be written on silk,[66] and a catalogue of twelve apotropaic talismans whose application is correlated with an astronomical matrix of time and space that goes back at least as far as Ge Hong's *Baopuzi*.[67] In the second part, we find illustrated instructions for engraving ten wooden seals composed of linked stars and pseudo-constellations, Chinese characters, and various geometric patterns, all as they appear in Daoist texts.[68] In some cases these seals were to be impressed upon the body of a patient or some other object that needed protection;[69] on other occasions they were to be used to print paper talismans that were ingested or similarly worn by a person or object.[70]

The claims made for these seals and talismans are comprehensive. In addition to curing disease and securing one's person against all forms of environmental and human assault, one talisman printed from a wooden seal allows you how to enter the home of a great minister unseen and subject him to such a barrage of incurable demonic visitations and nightmares that, in the end, he will be forced to summon you and listen to a sermon on the Dharma. As a result, the minister will be cured and converted to Buddhism, and in the name of this high purpose, there will be nothing you cannot extract from him.[71] One understands how Daoists encountering such lack of human fellowship might link certain popular Buddhist devotions with sorcery.

Toward the end of the *Treatise*, it becomes clear that the efficacious use of all these seals and talismans depends on a rigorous devotionalism carried out in a precise cultic context. The "practitioner" (*xingzhe*) is advised to place effigies of the bodhisattvas Nāgārjuna and Aśvaghoṣa (Maming),[72] Vajrapāṇi (Jin'gang miji) and the Spirit Kings of the Eight Powers (Bali shenwang) in a carefully constructed room—actually a Daoist-style oratory—cluttered with canopies, banners, and seven incense burners.[73] Amidst all the smoke and many rounds of recitations, the two bodhisattvas will finally send down various spirits who will do anything the practicant commands. And it is these subordinate deities, along with Nāgārjuna and Aśvaghoṣa, who actually empower the seals and talismans subsequently employed by the practicant.[74]

All the religious activity described in the *Treatise* is to take place in rooms—ordinary rooms, apparently—that have been purified and outfitted for the particular purpose at hand. There is no reason to suppose that these rooms did not exist in monasteries, though it is just as likely that they belonged to the patient or practicant. Similarly, it is just as probable that the practicant was a Buddhist layman as it is that he was a monk. Osabe Kazuo has demonstrated how the texts of mature and systematic Tantrism, translated or composed during the middle of the Tang dynasty by monks affiliated with the court, insist on the absolute secrecy of their content and warn in no uncertain terms about the necessity for nonproliferation. The strictures against trans-

mission, however, become significantly softened in *Nāgārjuna's Treatise on the Five Sciences*, as well as in many scriptures of a similar nature
composed in China in the eighth and ninth centuries.[75] The *Treatise*,
for example, warns only against the reckless transmission of its contents;
it is perfectly acceptable, even encouraged, to pass it on to anyone who
sincerely professes the Buddhist faith.[76] A popular, nonclerical profile
of the practicants and beneficiaries of this text is supported by the mun-
dane and materialistic objectives of the rites, by the suggestion of class
tension that characterizes some of these objectives, and by the fact that
the rites themselves are said to have been offered originally to King
Aśoka in response to the king's concern for the suffering and poverty
of his people. Among the rites offered to King Aśoka were a set of Daoist
talismans, spells, and rites brought by a Buddhist nun and former
heretic from southern India.[77] The heterodox origin of her ritual practices is symbolic of the non-Buddhist nature of much of the text itself.

As we have said, scholars have already asked us to compare *Nāgārjuna's Treatise* with *The Scripture of the Vajra[-Being] of Impure Traces for
Exorcising the One Hundred [Demonic] Transformations*. We may perhaps
go farther and surmise that these two texts, among others, represent
and anticipate a distinct social and Buddho-Daoist milieu that becomes
visible only in the twelfth and thirteenth centuries, crystallizing in a class
of Buddhist-style Ritual Masters and devotees of a cult to the two divine
patrons of those earlier texts. When we focus once again on this class
of twelfth-century monks, moreover, we find that ritual practices of such
similarity were being performed, in the name first of Ucchuṣma and
then of Nāgārjuna, that we are already justified in referring these practices to a group or sect of Tantric practitioners who, according to the
testimony of Bo Yuchan, actually honored these divinities together.

Ucchuṣma, Nāgārjuna, and Village Spirit-Mediums

To the exclusion of almost everything else, the twelfth-century devotees of Ucchuṣma and Nāgārjuna specialized in exorcisms employing
child-mediums. The style of these exorcisms appears to reflect many
things at once—the late Tang rituals of *āveśa*, the Daoist rites of *kaozhao*,
and especially the characteristic practices of village spirit-mediums in
the Song.

> The resident of Leping [Jiangxi], Xu Jixian, had his home
> in Jiudun; later he bought the house of the great monk

Cheng to live in. He lived there for several years while a demon spied on the dwelling. Occasionally it would take form and speak on its own: "I am [the spirit] of one of the three Yellow Rivers. We [i.e., you and I] were both traveling merchants selling silk and cloth and died there together. Now I should share this dwelling with you." At first it had not yet spooked them, but after a while it would enter the room of their son. Originally the husband and wife would sleep [together] without incident, but by morning their hair became so tangled together that they moved into another room. Just when they were eating cooked rice, it suddenly transformed into barley. When they were eating morning gruel, it transformed into evening rice. When, on occasion, guests shared a meal with them, the food would transform as they ate, and the guests would all become frightened and flee.

Xu Jixian summoned magicians (*shushi*) to exorcise it and invited Daoists (*daoliu*) to hold offerings (*jiao*) to beg for the forgiveness of the spirits and for their long life [i.e., rebirth], all without the slightest efficacy.

The monk, [Ritual] Master Quan of the Fenglin Temple next to their residence, could practice the "Incantations of [the Vajra-Being of] Impure Traces" (*Huiji zhou*), and Jixian intended to summon him. At the time, his son's wife had become ill. The demon proclaimed to her, saying, "I have heard that your household is about to have Master Zhuan exorcise (*zhi*) me. Although the Vajra[-Being] of Impure Traces has a thousand hands and eyes, yet during the liberation through the offerings of a Great Retreat (*dazhai*), he often only seizes spoiled dumplings. How can he harm me?" When the monk received the invitation, he first marked off a ritual space in the temple and recited spells for seven day and nights. When this was completed, the demon spoke to the wife, saying, "Baldhead comes after all, but I will prudently avoid him. However, before several months have passed I will return. How can he be worth fearing?! I have not yet caused your household any misfortune. If I had known it would come to this, how I regret not having devised strategies earlier!" The monk arrived and ordered

a boy to stand in the middle of the room and gaze
and examine. He then called for him to be infused by
the spirit. The boy saw great spirits holding halberds and
pennants run quickly into the room. One spirit held up a
large streamer with a title above that said "Spirit-Soldiers
of Impure Traces" (*Huiji shenbing*), and it circumambulated
one hundred times. The demon proceeded to hide under
the wife's bed. The spirit left, and only then did the demon
come out. Its head was now several hundred times larger
than before. Soon he was arrested by someone and taken
away. The monk said, "You should again see two figures
appear from behind the bed of the afflicted; for the first
time they will be truly extirpated." The following day, a pair
of ox horns sprang out from the side of a large cabinet
behind the wife's bed and, after a long time, disappeared.
From that point on, the demon was cut off and didn't
return. All those who caused evil were lodged in the spring
and autumn [sacrifices], and the Xu household became
pacified because of this.[78]

The manner in which the monk, (Ritual) Master Quan, is addressed
in this anecdote suggests a certain familiarity both with him and with
his role as exorcist. He may very well have resided in the temple, the
Fenglin si, which in any case was the venue for a week of intense prepa-
rations for the exorcism—that is, of devotion and ceaseless spell
recitation, as described in the Tang ritual texts.

The monk, as we see, was actually the third person summoned to
the home of Xu Jixian. Over and over again in Hong Mai's accounts
of healing, we find that the local reputation and charisma of the practitioner counted more in determining the choice of a therapist than
the particular devotion, class, or ideology of the client. In matters of
healing and, increasingly, in matters of liturgy in general, Buddhists
and Daoists, spirit-mediums and lay religious practitioners were viewed
primarily as ritual experts and were judged accordingly. Moreover, the
choice of a healer, or rather the succession of choices, was often determined by what we might call "hierarchies of proximity and expense." Afflicted families often turned first to a spirit-medium or even
to a knowledgeable household member, and then, if treatment failed,
to a lay Daoist exorcist, Buddhist monk, or Daoist priest.

It is unclear in the present case why the first two kinds of therapists—the magicians and the Daoists—failed, especially given that the general assumption underlying the Daoist approach ultimately resolved the issue satisfactorily, as we will see. Perhaps it is the fact that the demon and his affliction remained too amorphous, too unlocalized, until the monk was summoned. The invitation to the monk coincided, more or less, with the daughter-in-law's illness, creating a concrete focus of attack as well as an embodied point of resistance. The demon (or the patient with whom he communicated) initially dismissed his spirit-opponent, making fun of Ucchuṣma's well-known association with the impure remains of the sacrifice. After the monk's period of ascesis, the demon then directed his sarcasm to the monk himself, although, feeling the pressure, he now adopted a tone as evasive as it was threatening.

In an earlier anecdote, Hong Mai commented that the people of Fujian who performed the Rites of Ucchuṣma in exorcisms caused the spirit "to descend and possess a boy in order to speak." The rite as performed by this monk in Jiangxi offers an interesting variation on this pattern (a variation also taken up by Daoist priests, as we shall see). At the patient's home, Master Zhuan asked a young boy to stand in the middle of a room and literally gaze out into space and examine what he sees (*guanci*). The monk then called for "the opening of light" or "the commencement of illumination" (*kaiguang*). In contemporary religious usage, the term "*kaiguang*" has a very precise ritual meaning. It refers to the opening—actually, the painting—of the eyes of a religious idol, which is understood to animate and vitalize the effigy with the spirit of the god it represents. In the early thirteenth century, Bo Yuchan speaks of *kaiguang* and *futi* ("bodily possession") in the same breath.[79] I do not think it is too farfetched to infer that the young spirit-medium here, like an effigy, was infused and animated by a deity, which empowered him not simply to see but actually to visualize and describe in material terms the exorcistic action effected by the spells and recitations of the master.

The action involves the pursuit and arrest of the demon by the armies of Ucchuṣma all around the bed of the patient, who was no doubt lying there and taking it all in. This kind of symbolic narrative was evidently convincing to the daughter-in-law but insufficient to resolve the issue for the household at large. The demon was the spirit of an itinerant merchant who had drowned while peddling his wares and who was now seeking some sort of ritual recognition. This is why he is granted a position in the biannual village festivals, where his soul, along with the other unknown, unburied dead, would be invited to take part in the sacrifice.

At the same time, the festival allowed the household of Xu Jixian to overcome publicly the social alienation accompanying its long demonic ordeal, to integrate itself within the community, and, in its patronage of the sacrifice, actually to redistribute food to those guests whose meals at the Xu home had been disrupted and the cause of so much distress. One sorely wishes for more information about Xu Jixian so that we could accurately assess the extent to which the demonic visitation may have been a mark of the anxiety and apprehension posed by the recent arrival of a large and nouveau-riche family; the extent to which the wandering ghost of an itinerant merchant who claims Xu as his former colleague may have been an actual representation of both their own occupation and their status as outsiders; and, finally, the extent to which giving the wandering ghost a place in the biannual festival marked Xu's acknowledgment by the community.

The Rites of Ucchuṣma practiced by Master Quan appear to have retained the basic structure of the Tang rituals of *āveśa*—namely, the controlled possession of a boy by a cultic divinity and his subsequent clairvoyance. The context, however, has become more explicitly therapeutic and exorcistic, while the child-medium offers a running commentary on the action rather than responding to questions or making oracular pronouncements. The following short anecdote describing an exorcism performed by a devotee of Nāgārjuna seems to me even more characteristic of the Song:

> The Hu family of Bilong subprefecture [Changzhou, Jiangsu] wanted to expand the halls and rooms [of their house], and they cut down a large tree in the central courtyard that they considered to be in the way. They sliced the tree through the middle, exposing a ceramic jar large enough to hold three pecks of rice and with a surface and gradient that were just so. That day, they became spooked by a mountain sprite (*shanxiao*). There was a [Buddhist] acolyte (*xingzhe*) who was proficient in the recitation of the "Spells of Nāgārjuna" (*Longshu zhou*). They summoned him to exorcise (*zhi*) the demon. He ordered a boy to visualize it

(*ming tongzi guan yan*). The boy saw a figure several inches
tall being pursued by Nāgārjuna onto the wife's bed. Subsequently the demon possessed him, so as to speak. Moreover,
the acolyte marked off the altar and, examining the demon,
bound and expelled it. In all, the disturbance lasted half a
year before being settled.[80]

This exorcism, performed in the name of Nāgārjuna, begins in
much the same way as the previous one. The Buddhist acolyte places
a young boy in the master bedroom of the Hu household and compels him to gaze at the demon. The boy envisions Nāgārjuna himself
pursuing the demon into the wife's bed. But then events take an unexpected turn. The demon itself takes possession of the boy, and almost imperceptibly we have slipped into the Daoist-style Rite of Summoning for Investigation (*kaozhao fa*). The acolyte examines, binds,
and expels the demon, which we may understand to mean that the
acolyte first interrogates the boy—who has been possessed by the demon specifically, it is said, in order that it can speak—and then has
the demon bound, perhaps by one of Nāgārjuna's spirit-generals, and
taken away.

We may well imagine that the spirit-medium is also bound or binds
himself, though the narrative is much too parsimonious here for us
to do anything but speculate on this point. Also unclear is the extent
to which the demonic possession of the spirit-medium was anticipated
by the acolyte, although he was clearly prepared for this eventuality
and had brought to his Buddhist apprenticeship a familiarity with the
simple rites of lay Daoist Ritual Masters. Indeed, we must pay close attention to the way in which young acolytes may have been particularly
well placed as conduits for the penetration of the monastery by the
rites of Daoist and other village practitioners. One acolyte, for example, in the Cloister of Dizang (Dizang yuan), in Poyang, actually became a spirit-medium when called upon.[81]

Tantric Cults and Daoist Ritual Masters

If the rites of the Daoist *fashi* were reflected, on occasion, in the performances of Buddhist exorcists, then the practices of the Tantric devotees of Ucchuṣma and Nāgārjuna had clearly penetrated Daoist circles as well. No better example can be found than the case of Liang

Hun, a young man from Fujian who was a nephew by marriage of Ren Daoyuan, a lay Daoist exorcist and the son of an official. Liang Hun was apparently pursuing on his own a religious career similar to that of his uncle, and he often assisted him and another sought-after Daoist *fashi*, Shang Rixuan, in Fujian. On one of these occasions, Liang Hun accompanied Shang Rixuan to the home of the magistrate of Houguan subprefecture in Fuzhou. Shang Rixuan had been summoned to cure one of the magistrate's maidservants of a demonic illness. Liang Hun was actually invited to perform first, and it transpired in the course of his confrontation with the demon that the evil spirit had already tried to bring misfortune upon Liang Hun's own household, but had been rebuffed by an array of Ucchuṣma's spirit-soldiers (*Huiji shenbing*). Hong Mai comments that Ucchuṣma was in fact the object of Liang Hun's private cult, so we can assume that he was also the basis for Liang's exorcistic practices, though these are not described in any detail.[82] Ren Daoyuan and Shang Rixuan, however, both employed child-mediums—in very innovative ways, as we shall see—and it seems reasonable to infer that their young disciple did the same.

At the very end of *The Biography of Grand Protector Wen, Supreme Commander of the Earth-Spirits*, the author Huang Gongjin narrates an episode in the itinerant career of Lu Yanghao,[83] a Daoist priest who played a significant role in the transmission of the "Secret Rites of the Earth-Spirits."[84] The episode concerns an exorcism that Lu performed on behalf of a family named Xiao in the commandary of Linchiang, again in Jiangxi. Given what we know about the attitude of these Daoists to Buddhism, it is surprising to find that Lu Yanghao performs his therapeutic rite—an "investigation by possession" (*kaofu*)—not at the patient's home but in front of a Buddhist temple, the Huili si. Lu evidently knew where he might draw a crowd, but perhaps he was trying to make another point as well, for as the text continues, with little explanatory preparation, each of the three boys whom he has caused to become possessed jumps into the river, where they apparently remain for quite a while. Meanwhile, the spectators are growing rather skeptical—until, that is, Lu Yanghao causes yet another youth to become possessed. This youth grabs the sword that the Ritual Officer (*faguan*) has been holding and also jumps into the river. Finally, after another long period of time, all three (!) of the young boys emerge from the water lifting the head of a fish and climb back onto the riverbank.

The exorcism performed by Lu Yanghao and his three entranced youths, one wielding a weapon, is hardly distinguishable from the Rite of the Three Altars as it was practiced by the Buddhist Master Dong Shen. Despite the ideology and rhetoric of the biography of Grand Protector Wen, despite its hereticization of the Way of the Three Altars, Daoist practitioners of the Secret Rites of the Earth-Spirits were in some cases doing exactly the same thing as the Buddhist *fashi*, and it was perhaps precisely because of mutual influence and competition that the Daoists felt compelled to anathematize them. In fact, in the *Yijian zhi* we actually encounter a lay Daoist exorcist named Peng *fashi* who was an expert in what are now termed the "Rectifying [!] Rites of the Three Altars" (*Santan zhengfa*). Peng was a resident of Village No. 20 in Leping, Jiangxi.[85] Moreover, a fragmentary Daoist ritual text, *The Secret Rites of Prime Marshal Wang, Spiritual Officer of the Fiery Thunder of the Southern Pole Star*, expressly calls for the possession of three boys during a "ritual of summoning for investigation."[86] And it transpires, in the course of the ritual instructions, that the three boys, in addition to becoming possessed by demons, might become possessed by the *fashi*'s "Celestial Officers" (*tianguan*), of which there were also three: Prime Marshal Wang Shan and two Assistant Commanders (*fujiang*), Chen Wei and Qiu Xian.[87]

By the Song period, it becomes very difficult to resolve the problem of exactly who was influencing whom, which is perhaps symptomatic of the extent to which the practices of Daoist and Buddhist *fashi* were already in an advanced stage of convergence. If the Rites of the Three Altars, as practiced by Master Dong Shen, revealed a Daoist component in the "investigation by illumination," or at least in the use of Daoist terminology to describe a component of that rite, then there were also Daoist *fashi* who practiced either the Rite of the Three Altars or rites that were very similar in form and content. Barring the discovery of new evidence about the meaning of the term "Three Altars" outside a Buddhist context, one might appeal to the mechanism of convergence as a means for understanding how the "Three Altars" ultimately became, in Schipper's words, "a name for the traditions of the *fashi* in Taiwan and among the *daoshi* from Quanzhou in Singapore."

Tantric Cults and Village Spirit-Mediums

The Chinese spirit-medium (*wu*) was even more influenced by the Tantric cults of Ucchuṣma and Nāgārjuna than was the Daoist Ritual

Master. This, at least, is how the evidence appears on the surface. When we submit the relevant texts to serious questioning, however, we find that the spirit-medium was not simply a passive recipient of outside influence, nor, for that matter, a perennial village presence whom we can presume easily to understand. In the Song, the spirit-medium was just as much a historical player in the cultural field as was the Daoist Ritual Master or Tantric exorcist. His role in the village and beyond was becoming increasingly segmented and complex, and with respect to matters of religious influence, he gave as much as he took.

In Fuzhou, there was a spirit-medium (*wu*) who was able to practice the "Rites of [the Vajra-Being of] Impure Traces" (*Huiji fa*) and who was extremely efficacious in exorcizing the demonic for the benefit of people. The uneducated (*su*) called him "the Great Compassionate" (*dabei*). A virgin girl of a village family suddenly became pregnant. Her mother and father pressed her for the cause. At first, not knowing how it could be, they summoned the spirit-medium to investigate and exorcise (*kaozhi*) it. At the moment when he had just arrived, a small child dallied and then opened and entered the gate to their home. For a long time he danced and jumped about and, without further ado, threw himself into a pond in front of their house. The child was, in fact, the son of the rich family that lived next door. At sundown, the child had still not come out. On the following day, another child did exactly the same thing. The fathers of the two households assembled to revile and attack the spirit-medium. They intended to seize and send him to the magistrate. The spirit-medium said, "If you grant me a slight reprieve and allow me to complete my rite, your sons will come out [of the pond] on their own, unharmed." Onlookers rushed to the scene, surrounded the pond on all four sides, and waited. After a while, a sound as if made by hundreds of thousands of people rose out of the pond, and the bystanders recoiled in fear. The two children emerged from the water on their own—one holding a carp bound with rope, the other following behind and flogging it with a whip. They were dragged up onto the bank; the carp was already dead. The two children looked as spritely as ever,

but they were not aware in the slightest of what had transpired. The spirit-medium ordered that pitcher tiles be tied
to the girl's stomach and smashed to pieces with a wooden
rod. It was done, and [the tiles] crashed to the ground. The
pregnancy was miscarried. They say it was the carp that had
been the cause of her demonic suffering.[88]

In Fuzhou, the cult of Ucchuṣma and its associated rites had found
devotees among spirit-mediums as well as Daoist Ritual Masters. The
spirit-medium in the anecdote above was described as "the Great Compassionate," an epithet widely applied to the Buddhist deity Avalokiteśvara (Guanyin). The common people of this area viewed the
spirit-medium's successful application of the Rites of Ucchuṣma for
their benefit in light of the universal pity and concern that defined
the bodhisattva's nature and motivation.

Evidently, not all members of the village looked at him in this way,
however. The fathers of the two children saw an example not of generalized compassion but of particularized self-interest and a less-than-
perfect guardianship of their sons' welfare. To a certain extent, they
were right. A spirit-medium could never get out from under the vigi-
lant eye that villagers trained on any of their neighbors on the make.
He could never be that comfortable and well-received bearer of objectivity that moral discipline and outside status permitted the Daoist
priest to be. Yet we should not exaggerate the fathers' distrust, despite
the harshness of their reproach. In the first place, the fathers were
spurred to action only when it appeared to them, justifiably, that their
sons were in physical danger. In any case, they allowed the spirit-
medium to continue after he promised the safety of their children.
Second, it would be naive of us to assume that these heads of households were not fully aware of what had been going on all along. Their
two young sons were apprentices to the village spirit-medium, "divination youths" (tongji) who embodied either Ucchuṣma himself or
one of the deities associated with him.

These divination youths were hardly passive transmitters of divine
messages. What is so compelling about their performance is that it recalls nothing so much as the Rite of the Three Altars officiated by
Tantric Master Dong Shen in Leping, Jiangxi. Recall that Dong Shen
employed six village youths rather than two, and that the first set of
three was initially asked to identify the demon in a Daoist-style "rite of

investigation by illumination" that took place in a Buddhist cloister. But from that point on, and in every other respect, the rite imitates the one officiated by the spirit-medium in Fuzhou. Possessed by the gods, the three youths threw themselves into a body of water. After the Master calmed the fears of their anxious parents, the submerged boys were joined by a second set of entranced children, and finally all six emerged from the water carrying a turtle, which was identified with the demon afflicting the patient.

I mentioned earlier how this scenario was taken up as well by Daoist practitioners of the Rites of Grand Protector Wen. We must now entertain seriously the hypothesis that the mechanism for this convergence was that Buddhist and Daoist *fashi* were both imitating an exorcistic scenario that originated with spirit-mediums, and that spirit-mediums, in turn, having accommodated themselves to the devotional cults and spells of the Tantric Buddhists, were now bringing their characteristic exorcisms within the fold of the Rites of Ucchuṣma. The second part of this hypothesis is even more evident in the case of a female spirit-medium in Yangzhou.

Following the fall of the Northern Song, Yangzhou had become a temporary refuge for important officials fleeing the North. There they waited for new appointments and for the families they had been forced to leave behind. One such official was Jiang Yanyan, who had yet to receive a letter from his mother and younger brother, who were traveling from Shandong. Jiang's anxiety occupied him day and night and ultimately led him to consult a female spirit-medium named Sheng Qiniang, whom Hong Mai tells us was highly regarded by the local people. She practiced the Rites of the Vajra-being of Impure Traces, which empowered her to communicate with spirits (*xing Huiji fa tongling*) and to predict the future, "making known matters which had yet to take place." (It is this that undoubtedly had recommended her to Jiang.) When Jiang arrived at her house, he was surprised to find the spirit-medium to be a woman in her prime who was already in the midst of a deep trance, stepping on red-hot tiles and balancing a burning iron cooking plate on her head. Then the spirit-general (*shenjiang*) descended into the medium and declared himself to be the "Master of Merit and the Path of Righteousness in charge of the Temple of the Southern Peak that lies within the stream." Jiang knelt before her and inquired after the fate of his mother and brother. The spirit-general answered that Jiang would learn of this in ten days and, after another three days, would actually see them—a prediction that was corroborated by subsequent events.[89]

The confirmation of this spirit-medium's talent for prognostication is less interesting to us than the fact that the traditional scenario of the mediumistic seance—the trance (of dispossession) and fakiristic display, followed by the possession trance and the direct consultation of the divinity by the suppliant—is now performed under the rubric of "the Rites of Ucchuṣma." The medium was simply doing what spirit-mediums had always done, here in the service of a local temple god and perhaps Ucchuṣma himself. Even the use of young boys by spirit-mediums, as in the exorcism officiated by the Fujianese medium influenced by the Rites of Ucchuṣma, was a practice that had developed independently in the Song, in the context of the traditional consultative seance of the spirit-medium:

> In the village of Shili in the canton of Fanshang, Wujiang subprefecture, there was a farmer named You Da. In front of his entrance stood a tall poplar tree whose drooping shade obscured his house. On a summer day in the year 1166, for no reason, he unwittingly ascended the tree and fell asleep on a branch. The members of his household gazed at him, perspiring with trepidation. His son climbed a tall ladder to retrieve him, but he would not come down. Three days passed, and, seeming to regain some awareness, he returned after a while to the house. From this moment he was able to know [the time of] people's life and death. In his sixty-seventh year, he addressed his wife, saying, "My allotted years are already exhausted. You may prepare a dowry." After he had bathed, they set down wine and invited his marriage relations and neighbors to discuss his parting. He inquired, "Has the noon hour passed?" His wife responded, "It is still morning." Then You said, "As soon as I have died, there will be a scar, made by a rod, on my back. This will be the result of the struggle between the spirits and myself." When the day had reached the noon hour precisely, he died. They examined his back, and there turned out to be a scar from a wound. After they buried him, the rural folk often saw him wandering as if alive, followed by a band of demons. When someone would become ill, they would

engage a spirit-medium (*wuzhe*) to invite [his presence],
and he would always come. The medium would compel him
to possess the body of a young boy (*ming tongzi futi*) in order
to determine good and ill fortune. Sometimes he would
recommend the consumption of medicine; other times he
would recommend the establishment of Daoist retreats and
offerings (*zhai* and *jiao*). All were immediately efficacious.
Those who attained well-being were many. This is still going
on today.[90]

This anecdote is precious in several respects. First, it describes the
origin of a village cult served by spirit-mediums—a celebration, in a
sense, of the spirit's powers of prognostication in life. Second, it emphasizes the often limited, diagnostic function of the spirit-medium.
In the Song, depending on the nature of the illness, the gods of spirit-
mediums found no difficulty in recommending that the client consult
a pharmacist or Daoist priest. Third, and most importantly, the anecdote demonstrates that, in contrast to some spirit-mediums like Sheng
Qiniang, others were handing over their traditional function as possessed mediums to young boys—true ancestors of the modern "divination youths" (*tongji* or *tangki*), though these last are not necessarily young. The spirit-medium, for his or her part, was becoming an
officiant, much like the Daoist or Buddhist *fashi*, and in Chapter 3 we
saw that some spirit-mediums were actually called "*fashi*."

As officiants, however, spirit-mediums were not simply imitating
their functional counterparts among the Daoists and Buddhists. In
early medieval China, one invariably finds the spirit-medium working
alone. (At least I have yet to find a single description of a medium's
performance where this is not so, which is, of course, not to say that
it was always in fact the case.) After the late Tang and Five Dynasties
period, however, we begin to make out the outlines of a functionally
differentiated entourage. Some sources speak of musicians and actors.[91] Others describe a band of youths who number as many as twelve
and accompany the spirit-medium everywhere.[92] Poems composed in
commemoration of rain rituals or of spring and autumn festivals further distinguish the spirit-medium and his band of acolytes as the "great
medium" (*dawu*), sometimes also referred to as the "master medium"
(*shiwu* or *wushi*), and the "little mediums" (*xiaowu*), who dance and
become possessed.[93]

All this suggests that the spirit-medium's use of young boys—in exorcisms as well as in divination seances and village festivals—was a parallel but independent development. By the twelfth century, spirit-mediums, Daoist Ritual Masters, and Buddhist exorcists were all competing for the same group of village boys, and in the process they came to assimilate one another's therapeutic styles and cultic traditions. On occasion, the convergence of role, style, and substance was so absolute as to actually create a new tradition in which the spirit-medium was hardly distinguishable from the Daoist or Tantric Ritual Master. Witness Hong Mai's account of his own younger brother's activities:

> In my village there are many mediums (*liwu*). Reciting
> spells, they can enter boiling water and fire (*dao tanghuo*).
> Yuanzhong, my younger brother, received their instructions
> (*jue*). He cures illness for people without any mistakes. The
> spell (*zhou*) he employs goes as follows: "Nāgārjuna (Long-
> shu wang) authorized me to practice and maintain 'the
> Great Method for Exorcizing Fire of Beifang Rengui'
> (*Beifang Rengui jinhuo dafa*). Nāgārjuna, I am Beifang
> Rengui! With water I execute all the fire stars under
> Heaven! The fire stars within a thousand miles must surren-
> der! Hastily, do as the law decrees!" When the spell is fin-
> ished, he grasps in his hand the Seal of Zhenwu (*Zhenwu
> yin*) and blows on it. He uses a little water to wash them. All
> those with blisters on their hands and feet can be cured.[94]

It may surprise the reader that such an illustrious family as Hong Mai's should have a son who was not only on familiar terms with the mediums of their village (near Poyang, Jiangxi), but was actually a practicing apprentice as well. This fact alone should warn us against drawing too fast a distinction between elite and popular culture in the Song. Other distinctions similarly collapse in this anecdote.

The mediums of Hong Mai's village walked through boiling water and fire, which is to say, again, that they did what Chinese mediums have always done and still do: they subjected themselves to harsh physical trials to demonstrate the authenticity of their trance, their imperviousness to pain, and the power of their divinities. Apparently, however, they did not do so in the characteristic manner of mediums, by entering into a trance state. Rather, they entered fire and boiling

water—and cured burns and blisters—by reciting a spell and performing the operations of the "Rites for Exorcizing Fire of Beifang Rengui," which are referred to in this spell.[95] Both the spell and the ritual operations, moreover, are completely Daoist.

First, the spirit-medium transforms himself into the divinity Zhenwu
by the kind of ego-exchange that characterized the Daoist Ritual Master (*bianshen*). Zhenwu was a "Daoist" divinity of the north, a personified and martialized asterism and an embodiment of water with
power over the southern asterisms and fire. After commanding these
fire stars to surrender, the medium, alias Zhenwu, infuses his exorcistic
seal with his own spirit. One suspects that he continues to hold this
seal when he throws himself into boiling water or across burning coals,
and that the water with which he washes burn victims was similarly
sacralized, either by his breath once again or by the seal itself.

While all this is going on, the spirit-medium is indistinguishable
from the Daoist Ritual Master. But there is evidently still another cultural layer to apply, for the patron of these mediums—and the patron
of the Daoist rites of Zhenwu that the mediums practice—is none other
than Nāgārjuna, aide-de-camp of Ucchuṣma and the source of the
Tantric/Daoist wisdom represented in *The Treatise on the Five Sciences*.
The spirit-mediums of Hong Mai's village engage in their characteristic exhibitionism in the role of Daoist *fashi*, all within the devotional
context of the cult to a Tantric deity and to a Daoist god who serves
as this deity's subordinate and spirit-general.

The convergence of so many cultural traditions here provides a rare
opportunity to assess the influence of these tantricized and Daoicized
spirit-mediums on the as yet unwritten history of the so-called Daoist
red-head sects on Taiwan. In the complex pantheon of contemporary
practitioners of the Lüshan jiao, we find, amazingly, that Nāgārjuna
and Zhenwu occupy the left and right altars, respectively, and that they
are consistently treated as a divine pair in the hymns that invite their
descent into the ritual area. Moreover, the pantheon and hymns give
particular prominence to many of the divinities associated with the
cult to Ucchuṣma as described by Bo Yuchan in the thirteenth century. In addition to Nāgārjuna, who assisted Ucchuṣma himself and
who is now paired with Zhenwu, we find the Two Great Lords Incense
Mountain and Snowy Mountain; Prince Nezha, Prime Marshal Li, of
the Central Altar; the Dragon Officer of the Five Saints, Ma Huaguang,
a fusion of the Daoist divinity Ma Sheng and the Bodhisattva Flower

Radiance; and the *yakṣas* Ma jialuo and Hu jialuo.[96] This array of divinities cuts across too wide a spectrum of the early thirteenth-century pantheon of Ucchuṣma to be coincidental. I believe we must seriously consider the hypothesis that the Lüshan jiao, Puan jiao, Santan jiao, and other so-called Daoist sects are a product of Tantric as well as Daoist traditions as they were filtered through spirit-mediums like those in Poyang, Jiangxi, in the Song.[97]

Thus, in the Song period, spirit-mediums cannot simply be taken for granted as timeless relics to be unearthed from the religious soil of China's "shamanic substrate." Rather, they were active players in the historical work of cultural negotiation between China's written and martial religious traditions—a negotiation that produced, in the Song, a distinctive milieu that I initially identified with the Daoist Ritual Master. In this chapter this milieu has been widened to include Buddhists and even spirit-mediums. We have found, in Southeast China during the twelfth century, a group of Tantric monks and acolytes who were hardly distinguishable from the Daoist Ritual Master. These Buddhists specialized in exorcisms, and though many clearly resided in temples or monasteries, they performed for the most part in the homes of their clients. Some, like Master Dong Shen, clearly found not only their clientele but their disciples among lay villagers. Villagers also supplied their sons to be used in the Buddhist rituals.

As with the Daoist Rites of Summoning for Investigation, the exorcisms of the monks invariably came to center on the possession of one or more boys. The convergence of Buddhist and Daoist exorcisms around the possession of spirit-mediums was probably both cause and effect of a process of competitive mimesis that occurred as Buddhists and Daoists came to terms with village religion. This process, in turn, was the occasion for a great deal of cultural exchange between Buddhist and Daoist exorcists: in the case of the Rites of Ucchuṣma, the exchange took place at the levels of cult and textual discourse, as well as of ritual practice; some Daoist Ritual Masters, moreover, became devotees of the Buddhist Rites of the Three Altars and Rites of Ucchuṣma, while Buddhist performances of these rites often included elements borrowed directly from Daoist Rites of Summoning for Investigation.

Unlike their Daoist counterparts, the Buddhist Ritual Masters did have a well-defined if somewhat socially circumscribed tradition of using young boys and girls as possessed mediums. In the tenth century,

Zanning wrote that people in his day did so for profit. It would be un-
wise to discount the influence of the *āveśa* rituals of the Tang on the
Tantric exorcisms of the Song and, in particular, on the seeming preference for the divine possession of a divinatory medium over the demonic possession of a surrogate for the patient. Yet the tradition developed by the Tantric masters of the Tang weighed lightly on their
Song successors. As Chinese Tantrism's center of gravity shifted from
court to country, the style and content of its exorcisms came to reflect
the exuberance, unpredictability, and variation of the village culture
of the mediums. As we saw in Chapter 5, for example, much of the
"plot" of the Daoist Rite of Summoning for Investigation in the Song
was anticipated by the exorcism of a Tang-dynasty spirit-medium.

In the twelfth century, spirit-mediums, in turn, became masters of
the Buddhist rites of Ucchuṣma and Nāgārjuna. Thus they became Ritual Masters, although their experience as officiants of possessed
acolytes had already prepared them for this role and the style of their
"Buddhist" exorcisms remained very much their own. Some even managed to combine Tantric cult, the operations of the Daoist Ritual Master, and manifestations of their own trance behavior to produce hy-
brid practices that would gain the force of tradition. From whatever
perspective we examine the question of influence in the context of
therapeutic ritual, the spirit-medium was a player as well as a pole of
attraction that would now prove irresistible even to Daoist priests.

7

Daoist Priests, Confucian
Literati, and Child-Mediums

In the previous pages, I have purposely restricted my analysis to the rural and suburban world of lay Daoist Ritual Masters, Tantric exorcists, and spirit-mediums. To this picture of village and vernacular life we must now apply a more classical and highborn veneer, for just as spirit-mediums became *fashi*, so members of the religious and bureaucratic elite did, and these Daoist priests and upper-class laymen also performed exorcisms in which they employed child-mediums. Moreover, they did so in ways that particularly engaged their moral anxieties and moralizing sensibilities. Before we come to these and other concerns that reflect the distinct expectations of elite practitioners and their clients, I present three episodes in which upper-class spirit-mediums were central to the therapeutic process.

Daoist Priests and Child-Mediums

On Maoshan, Pilgrimage Site
of Aristocratic Daoism just South of Nanjing

On a New Year's evening in 1137, two literati from Nanjing set out on an excursion and encountered two beautiful women—immortals, in fact—who invite them to join their retinue and associates in the garden belonging to a certain Du household.[1] In our source there now follows a detailed description of the kind of fairy banquet well known to us

from the religious literature and *belles lettres* associated
with the medieval Daoism of Maoshan. Before leaving
the next morning, the two literati are given elixirs to allow
them to avoid cereal foods and extend their lives. They
are asked, however, not to seek another meeting through
divination. From that moment they subsist only on fruit
and are absolutely ecstatic about the prospect of becoming
transcendents.

To hasten this eventuality, the two gentlemen proceed
to Maoshan, where they stay with the resident Daoist priest,
Liu *fashi*. At this point, however, their hopes are deflated,
and the narrative swerves significantly from our expectations about the generic nature of what we are reading. The
priest remarks that his two new disciples appear to him to
have become increasingly listless and disaffected (*suomo*),
something that should not occur had they encountered
"true immortals" (*zhenxian*). Liu suspects that they have
been weakened by some "perverse pneuma" (*yaochi*) and
sets out to get rid of it.

Initially, things do not go well, and after a disquisition
on the vagaries of life and death, Liu *fashi* changes course.
The priest has an incense table prepared and selects three
or four spirit-mediums (*tongzi*) to stand next to it. Forming
mudrās and reciting spells, he orders the boys to face the
incense burner, in which they envision a luminous reflection in the circular shape of the sun and moon. The priest
remarks that this is exactly what they should see, and then
has the boys look into the light more closely. This time they
notice an emissary. The priest then orders this soldier to
pursue the local Earth God and have the god capture and
escort into the ritual area the "evil-causing agents of the
Du family garden."

After half an hour or so, one of the spirit-mediums
confirms their arrival: "Two ladies have taken off their hats
and are prostrating themselves on the ground and confess-
ing their crimes. In addition, there are several maidservants
by their sides." The priest then commands the ladies to
convey their names (*tong xingming*). One declares herself
to be Zhang Lihua, the other, Kong Guipin; both follow up

with an exhaustive account of their involvement with the
two gentlemen.

[All this may have been transmitted directly through
the mouths of the spirit-mediums. In the texts of the "Rites
of Summoning for Investigation," the communication of
the spirit's name and story (*tong xingming* and *tongzhuan*)
are semantic markers of possession. In contrast, these
spirit-mediums may only have been repeating what they
alone heard in conversation. As we shall see throughout
this chapter, in the more refined atmosphere of upper-
class exorcisms, the visual and auditory powers of the
spirit-medium are emphasized at the expense of the
identificatory.]

In the final moment, the priest turns to the two gentlemen and takes up the matter of punishment. He asks them
to recall the ladies-in-waiting who had actively encouraged
their aspirations of immortality. These women, Liu argues,
had actually endured punishment in life (for reasons that
are not specified), and in any case they had not caused the
gentlemen serious injury. It therefore seems sufficient to
Liu that, having stood accused, they should be released. The
literati accept this resolution, take their leave, and resume
a normal diet.

This episode seems to mark the end of a historical era. It is not that
the immortals were really demonic beings. The fairy feast, the elixirs,
the names of the transcendents, the reluctance of the priest to impose
any punishment, and even the reason he gives for this reluctance all
suggest that they were very much immortals, even "true immortals."
Rather, it is the effects of their intercourse with men that are now being interpreted as demonic. Elixirs that aid in the avoidance of cereal
consumption and in the extension of life—once thought, and evidently still thought by the two literati, to be signs of election—are now
viewed by the priest in terms of the immediate ill-effects on their mor-
tal constitutions.

The time when men should aspire to become transcendents has evidently passed. Moreover, in a stunning reversal, this message is conveyed by ritual means—by the ritualized use of spirit-mediums—to
which the ideology of transcendents and the revelations of Highest

Purity (*Shangqing*) had always stood in firm opposition. The priest of Maoshan has become a Ritual Master, engaging the transcendents through spirit-mediums and treating them just like any other spirit summoned for investigation, whether god, ghost, or ancestor, whose primary transgression is an inability to stay in its place. At the end, the priest stands before the two literati plaintiffs as an attorney for the defense, pleading mitigating circumstances. It is as if the immortals are the ones who require pity from men and are visitors from another time who have not yet heard that the world has changed.

In an Official Compound in Jiangsu

> In Changzhou [Jiangsu], Hong Jinggao, the magistrate
> of Qinling and Hong Mai's cousin, summoned a local man,
> Yao Jiangshi, to examine his ten-year-old nephew. The
> nephew had become delirious and irrational after return-
> ing from a family pilgrimage to an Auxiliary Temple of the
> Eastern Peak (Dongyue xingmiao).[2]
> Yao Jiangshi was an expert in the Five Thunder Rites of
> the Celestial Heart (*Wulei tianxin fa*). Though not a Daoist
> priest, he must be considered to have belonged to the same
> social class as his client, having purchased an office. When
> this lay exorcist arrived at the magistrate's home, he or-
> dered his spirit-general to bring down the local Earth God
> (*tudi*) for questioning. The descent of the Earth God was
> witnessed by a small boy (*xiaotong*), a spirit-medium to
> whom the spirit communicated directly: "An official resi-
> dence (*guanfu*) is serious and upright. How can some
> polluting and evil-causing agent get inside? I fear it is the
> doing of a cabal of maidservants and concubines from
> another family; how can you accuse me? In fact, there is
> no demon to be arrested!" Yao Jiangshi apologized and
> went home. There he continued his ritual applications.
> After two weeks, the afflicting spirit was finally brought
> before him and identified (again by the spirit-medium?)
> as the mother of a certain Xun.
> How this woman came to be identified as the culprit
> is explained by information given at the beginning of the
> anecdote. Xun was a younger brother of Wen Huigong, the

posthumous name of Hong Gua (1117–1184), a brother
of Hong Mai (Xun and Hong Mai were probably half-
brothers). Hong Xun had accompanied Wen Huigong when
the latter became Overseer-General of Huaidong (*Huaidong
zongling*). Xun's "birth mother" (*shengmu*), who had accompanied them as well, became ill. Because of a lack of good
medical doctors, she was moved to Changzhou and came
under the care of Wen Huigong's paternal cousin, the
aforementioned magistrate of Qinling. The magistrate, in
turn, eventually moved Xun's mother to the nearby home
of a certain Fan An because he feared that she might be
suffering from some contagious disease. (Evidence later in
the anecdote suggests that Fan's residence was outside the
walls of the county seat.) Medical mediums (*yiwu*) were then
summoned, but to no avail. Xun's mother died, and her
coffin was placed in the sanctuary of a Buddhist monk
(*sengshe*).

As it turns out, Fan An's residence was contiguous to the
Auxiliary Temple of the Eastern Peak that the magistrate's
nephew would visit, in the company of his relatives, several
months later. On the way home, this party would stop off
at Fan An's for some refreshment, and it was precisely then
that the nephew became ill. Still later, when the exorcist
Yao Jiangshi was interrogating the spirit of Xun's mother,
she was unwilling to say anything about why she had come
before him, and Yao memorialized the City God (*chenghuang*) to keep her. On another day, Yao summoned her
again for questioning, and finally she admitted: "It was
because the young master (*xiao guanren*, i.e., the nephew)
had come to the Fan household that I followed him back to
his residence in the subprefectural seat (*xianshe*)." At that
point, Yao prepared a variety of sacrificial offerings and
appealed to the Prefectural Office of Taishan to secure her
rebirth. Her coffin, and the body in it, were burned, and the
nephew recovered at long last.

Two aspects of this anecdote require comment and emphasis. The first
is the wide array of religious practitioners operating within this official
milieu. Doctors, spirit-mediums, and a lay Daoist exorcist were sum-

moned at various stages in the therapeutic process; Buddhist monks were engaged to keep and then cremate the coffined body of Xun's mother. The second aspect is the appearance, both here and in the previous anecdote, of the local earth-spirit (*tudi shen*) in Daoist exorcisms. In both cases, and in striking contrast to those examined in Chapter 5, the Earth God is called on to identify the afflicting demon and then bring it within the ritual area. His insinuation into the Rites of Summoning for Investigation, and the involvement later on of the City God and Lord of Taishan, represent a reliance on bureaucratic hierarchy, procedure, and responsibility that becomes more pronounced in circles of clerical and literati exorcists.

As we saw in Chapter 2, the various "Demon Codes" of the Daoist Ritual Master in the Song held these local Earth Gods and City Gods ultimately responsible for permitting demons to attack the residents within their respective jurisdictions. These territorial spirits of the dead, moreover, were not to be trusted any more than a magistrate, in the midst of a criminal trial, could depend on the local people who served as clerks, policemen, and in other village service positions. It is therefore not surprising that in this and in other Rites of Summoning for Investigation considered below, it is the local Earth God who is "summoned" into the ritual area under restraint and who is "investigated," sometimes under torture. Determining which is more guilty, the Earth God or the demon, becomes increasingly difficult in these elite and bureaucratic versions of the Rites of Summoning for Investigation.

In the anecdote under consideration, the Earth God's anxiety and defensiveness are therefore understandable. He argues that the moral standing of an official household ought to leave it immune to the depredations of demons and that, in any event, the demons in his area have all been accounted for. Moreover, his surmise that the source of the illness must, by default, be the domestics or concubines of another family (i.e., ancestral spirits over which he had no control) proves to be essentially correct. Xun's "birth mother" is so designated, it seems to me, because she was not the mother of Xun's elder brother, Wen Huigong, and was therefore their father's concubine.

Once the afflicting spirit had been identified, its disposition continued to be a matter for the purgatorial bureaucracy. The exorcist entrusted the soul of Xun's mother to the City God and then to the Lord of Taishan. The various Temples of the Eastern Peak were in fact branch offices of the central bureau on Taishan, and one wonders whether the Auxiliary Temple visited by the magistrate's nephew did not now become the venue for Daoist rites for the dead that would have guaranteed the rebirth of Xun's mother referred to in the text.[3]

At the Home of an Extended Confucian Family in Zhejiang

In 1181, in the subprefecture of Fenghua, [Zhejiang,] a literatus named Dong Song summoned an exorcist to cure his wife, Lady Wang. Lady Wang had become possessed by an incubus. The exorcist, Zhao Shandao, was related to the imperial clan, bore an official title, and was also a resident of Fenghua. His Daoist career began in his youth when he received the "Great Rites of Numinous Treasure" (*Lingbao dafa*) from a certain Mr. Zhou of Mount Jiuhua [Anhui].[4] I include here only the central events of Zhao's exorcism, which took place at Dong Song's home.[5]

On the first day, Zhao Shandao pressed a ritual seal (*fayin*) against the chest of Lady Wang. Suddenly, she acted as if she were drunk and related that, in fact, she had been drinking with a young man. At that point a sword-bearing, red-clothed emissary appeared and took away the youth.

Three days later, Zhao returned. He constructed an altar and began the ritual. First, he burned incense and danced "the steps of Yu" (*Yubu*). Then he ordered the "young boys of the Dong household" (*Dongjia zidi*) to search for demonic images (*wuxiang*) in the incense burner. Hong Mai comments here that Zhao's technique enabled light to be retained in the incense smoke like a mirror and to gradually expand until ghosts, spirits, and the demonic forms of inanimate things all manifested themselves, and a person could converse with these directly.

Dong Song's eleven-year-old nephew, Dun, saw a fierce spirit of barbarian appearance descend in a garland of flames and take a seat at the altar, surrounded by his bodyguards. Humbling himself, Dun approached the god, who declared himself to be "Commander Deng of the Celestial Prime Who Summons for Investigation" (Tianyuan kaozhao Deng jiangjun). In the ensuing conversation with the nephew, Commander Deng identified the incubus as the transformation of the pollution associated with a canine corpse buried long ago behind the house by some of Dong's relatives. The corpse was located, exhumed, and brought before the altar, whereupon Commander Deng expressed his surprise that a family with pretensions to classical learning would not have been more familiar with the principles of natural transformation embodied in the *Yijing*.

Dong Song then asked Zhao to get rid of the pollution. If this were an exorcism performed by one of the Daoist or Buddhist Ritual Masters examined in Chapter 6 and in previous sections of this chapter, the remains of the dog would simply have been boiled in oil or disposed of somewhere in the hills. But here, among the members of a literati family with official aspirations, everything must first follow bureaucratic procedure. On the following morning, the nephew witnessed the descent of a band of martial youths whom Commander Deng ordered to restore the corpse to its original canine form. Then the Commander had the nephew ask the Ritual Master to memorialize the Emperor on High. On the following evening, the nephew again witnessed the descent of a yellow-robed Daoist priest holding the Ritual Master's memorial, with four characters now written on the back: "*Chaotiao juzhan*" (Certification for Decapitation). In parallel actions, the Commander's spirit-soldiers then cut up the restored dog into three pieces while Dong Song sliced what remained of the corpse with a steel saw and threw it in the river. His wife subsequently recovered.

It is remarkable that the children of this extended literati family were being encouraged to serve as spirit-mediums. That this caused the father none of the anxiety that resulted from the use of household children by the "tantricized" medium in Fuzhou (see Chapter 6) may have something to do with the nature of their role in the exorcism. The children function here not as possessed and frenzied mediums, but as hypnotized and highly suggestible visionaries whose perceptions served to complement and "realize" for an audience the results of the internal operations of the Ritual Master. The children, however, are not simply ancillary to these operations. It is the nephew who sees and communicates directly with the spirit-general, who relates the spirit-general's commands to the Ritual Master, and who conveys the imperial response to his memorial. The Ritual Master is very much dependent on this boy who, while not possessed, is not any less a spirit-medium.

Confucian Literati and Child-Mediums

At several points in this and earlier chapters, we have had occasion to discuss the de-linking of illness and morality in Song Daoist exorcisms. Guilt was transferred from the patient to the spirits, whether demons or the deities that had jurisdiction over them, and the spirits, in turn, were transformed into personal symbols that could be manipulated as demonomorphic representations of the patient's inner states. Illness now became open to psychological as well as moral interpretation.

There were special circumstances, however, in which the medieval understanding of illness as a consequence of moral transgression remained compelling. In those groups defined by a strong sense of religious or cultic community, the individual was somehow transparent to the group, and his illness was viewed in terms of either a particular or a more generalized failure to meet the group's moral expectations, religious rules, or ritual protocol. These communities might just as well have been Confucian as Daoist or Buddhist. Yet even when Confucian, as we shall now see, Daoist priests and spirit-mediums were entrusted with the task of articulating the precise relationship between individual illness and group morality:

> The Assistant Secretary Li Zhongyong resided within the
> boundary-fields (*jietian*) of the subprefecture of Fouliang
> [Raozhou, Jiangxi], where he had retired in seclusion
> during his later years. Within 3 *li* east of his residence he
> built for himself a "charitable school." In addition, he con-
> structed a Temple to Confucius with a clay effigy that
> he worshipped reverently. The craftsmanship was elabo-
> rately ornate to the point where sandalwood had been used
> for the tongue. At the sacrificial periods of the spring and
> autumn, he invited teachers and classicists and summoned
> the entire lineage (*zongtang*) to gather. More than thirty
> persons received instruction. He also endowed [the tem-

ple/school] with 200 *mu* of fertile land to support its
operation. Moreover, each day during his free time, he
personally went to lecture on the *Changes of Zhou* (*Zhou Yi*).
Among the disciples in his lineage there were those who
neglected [their studies] for pleasure and considered the
repetitions and discipline of study to be painful. They would
return home under the cover of darkness, and would take
the wooden boards of the bridges they passed and overturn
and throw them aside. Li could not have them stopped. In
the year 1160, Li died. His descendants barely prospered
and were unable to carry on their ancestor's aspirations;
gradually, studies became overgrown and uncultivated, and
teachers and students swept away all rules. Some broke up
the buildings, others took away the wood and stone, and still
others used the place as their residence. The sandalwood
incense was stolen and sold. One grandchild was extremely
brash and consequently erected a room on the school's
foundation. In the year 1197, this grandchild was struck
with a feverish illness. Doctors prayed for his recovery,
working incessantly for a month, but were completely unsuccessful. There was a Daoist priest (*daoshi*) who could
investigate and illuminate demonic misfortune (*kaozhao
suihuo*), and he was summoned to examine the grandchild.
The priest commanded a small boy (*xiaotong*) to stand on
top of a table. While looking into the distance, the boy saw
a man wearing a bejeweled crown, of lofty and ancient
demeanor, and followed by ten men. The man said, "I am
Wenxuan wang, and those who follow me are ten wise men
(*shi zhe*)." The priest inquired, "Why have you come here?"
and he explained, "I received incense from Li and he was
extremely conscientious and sincere. Since the death of
the Assistant Secretary, all his descendants no longer pay
attention to this and have already destroyed the temple and
knocked down my effigy. Now, forty years later, not the
slightest trace remains. I will call up an eminent and awesome spirit (*xianwei ling*) to warn them." Then the small
boy saw a man who had had the Assistant Secretary Li
summoned and who was about to punish Li for not being
able to instruct his descendants. After a little while the man

returned and said, "I have just had an audience with
the City God of Ezhou. Today he has an official obligation
and is unable to follow the order." Then the man addressed
the group, saying, "If you again renew the old matter, I will
secure blessings." The group said, "We all respectfully
comply." The small boy then awakened, and the illness
of the brash one abated.[6]

This episode provides a unique perspective on that repertory of institutions developed in the eleventh and twelfth centuries by certain
enterprising officials to sustain their lineages and agnates. The most
famous of these, and the one most relevant here, was the "charitable
estate" (*yitian* or *yiquan*) founded by Fan Zhongyan and his son near
Suzhou during the latter half of the eleventh century. In addition to
the estate proper, which included large tracts of fertile land, the income from which was used to cover marriage and funeral expenses,
there were "sacrificial fields" (*yitian*) to provide for the ancestral rites
performed by Buddhist monks in a private chantry, or "merit-cloister"
(*gongde si*); "incense lands" (*xianghuo tian*) that guaranteed a stream
of Buddhist prayers for the dead; a "charitable residence" (*yizhai*) that
served as a kind of hostel; various assembly halls; and provisions for
the hiring of teachers and the education of agnates that may be seen
as a kind of proto-lineage school.[7] All these endowments remained
distinct from household property, thereby allowing those wealthy
households to meet their obligations to their less fortunate kin without a significant redistribution of income.

Reviewing the work of Shimizu Morimutsu, Patricia Ebrey finds few
imitators of the charitable estate proper and "even more references
to unsuccessful attempts to found estates than to estates that survived
for over a century." She goes on to say, however, that "if anything, Fan's
example may have had a greater influence in areas outside kinship.
Endowments for charitable purposes became extremely common in
the Song, but if surviving references are any indication of their prevalence at the time, most were community-based activities. These included charitable schools, charitable granaries, and estates to help de-
fray labor costs. . . . Sometimes these community services were seen
as particularly aiding the donor's agnates, presumably because the
community was largely composed of agnates."[8]

The "charitable school" founded by Li Zhongyong is just such an

example of an institution serving a community that was largely composed of agnates. In any case, the school seems to have been restricted
to Li's kin, whom he lectured each day on *The Book of Changes.* The
pedagogy of Li's charitable school was carried out in an atmosphere
of religious cult. A temple to Confucius was built on the school
grounds and included an effigy of Confucius himself (Wenxuan
wang), the object of Li's enthusiastic devotion. Daily instruction at the
school was supplemented by guest lectureships presented to the entire lineage when its members gathered for the spring and autumn
sacrifices. Since the Five Dynasties period (i.e., tenth century), these
agricultural and ancestral sacrifices had become occasions for the expression of Confucian notions of family hierarchy and morality among
landowning families.[9]

Before Li Zhongyong's death in 1160, his charitable school, Confucian temple, and supporting lands were already suffering serious
depredation. The account of the students' lack of enthusiasm and ra-
pacious activities is probably neither proverbial not hyperbolic. The
rules of Fan Zhongyan's charitable estate, as they were amended in
the early thirteenth century, suggest that the managers of even a successful lineage enterprise had to struggle with the less than respectful
activities of many of their kin.[10] It is no wonder that estates that were
not as well-endowed, vigilantly managed, or protected by local officials
as Fan Zhongyan's did not survive for more than a generation or two.
Obscurity, I suspect, was also the fate of Li Zhongyong's school and
estate, despite the somewhat hopeful note struck at the end of the anecdote. The dismantlement of property began almost immediately with
Li's endowment, and forty years later, hardly anything remained. It
was in this context that a particularly delinquent grandchild became
sick, although initially his illness was viewed and treated as a medical
matter. After the doctors proved unsuccessful, new interpretations of
the boy's illness became inevitable, and as in so many other cases, a
Daoist priest was summoned to examine him.

The priest has a "small boy"—a spirit-medium—stand on top of a
table and gaze into space.[11] We would like to know where this boy came
from and what means were used to induce his trance. That he was in
trance is indicated by the fact that he "awakens" or "becomes conscious" at the end. In any case, the boy envisions the arrival of Confucius and his ten worthy disciples.[12] Confucius, in turn, criticizes Li's
descendants for their lack of devotion and for the destruction of his

effigy. In this view, cultic observance and reverence emerge as the foundation of Li's educational enterprise, while the grandchild's illness is interpreted as a residual aspect of a collective contempt. Guilt, in fact, is so generalized that even Li Zhongyong comes to share in it, for failing to instruct his descendants in a sufficient manner.

Moreover, although it may appear that Li is being singled out for censure, the temporary absence of the City God strikes me as a convenient trope for an unwillingness on the part of the Daoist priest and/or spirit-medium either to impose punishment or to limit guilt to a single individual. Rather, the vision of Li's otherworldly fate is being dangled before his descendants as a poignant example of the consequences of their actions. The priest, here, is working on their latent feelings of filial remorse, and Li's sons and grandsons now respond eagerly to a call to renew their cultic devotions in exchange for continued beneficence. The group rededication results, almost incidentally, in the grandchild's recovery and the spirit-medium's return to consciousness; the two boys are, in a sense, alter egos.

The spirit-medium functions here as an embodiment of the voice of moral criticism. In the name of restoring an individual to health, he has been employed as the agent in the restoration of a moral and cultic community. In the twelfth century, the use of spirit-mediums in this way became indispensable in cases where the transgressions belonged to the Daoist priest himself. These mediums provided objective access to a clerical conscience too muddied for self-reflection.

One such priest was Ren Daoyuan, the uncle of Liang Hun, the Daoist devotee of Ucchuṣma (on whom see the discussion in Chapter 6). Ren Daoyuan was the eldest son of Ren Wenjian, an Assistant Chamberlain of Ceremonials (*Taichang xiaoqing*).[13] Daoyuan belonged to that significant group of sons of official households who were attracted by Daoist ritual, and we might speculate that his father's work in the Court of Imperial Sacrifices contributed to his interest. Daoyuan studied with a Daoist master, Ouyang Wenbin, from whom he received instruction in the rites of "salvation by smelting" (*liandu*), the climax of the Retreat of the Yellow Register (*Huanglu zhai*) in which the souls of the dead are purified in an alchemical holocaust.[14] The text I am following adds that Ren Daoyuan also practiced the exorcistic Rites of the Celestial Heart, a fact that should advise us again against drawing too hard a distinction between practitioners of funerary and therapeutic ritual.

At some point during or soon after the Qiandao reign period (1165–1173), Daoyuan's father passed away, and Daoyuan himself received an official position. While in office, Daoyuan is said to have become careless with respect to his religious devotion; each day he would pass a spirit-hall (*shentang*)—the hall dedicated to his own spirit-generals, perhaps—and send a small boy inside to take care of the incense rather than doing it himself. Several members of his own household thought this was serious enough to merit attention, but Daoyuan ignored their warnings.

Lest we think that an official appointment was an obstacle to the continuation of clerical functions in the Song period, Ren Daoyuan was invited by the residents of the northern quarter of Fuzhou to serve as the "Inspector of Merits" (*gaogong*)—the head priest—in a "Great Offering of the Yellow Register" (*Huanglu dajiao*) sponsored by these same residents. The offering was held on a New Year's evening in 1186 at the Temple of Lord Zhang (Zhangjun an). The ceremony went smoothly, but throughout it Daoyuan persisted in directing a stream of lewd remarks and sexual puns, in dialect, to a pair of female servants among the spectators. At the end of the offering, a painful cyst appeared on the back of his neck, and Daoyuan returned home in misery.

> After several days had passed, Daoyuan said to his nephew Liang Hun, "I have been having extremely bad dreams. Already I have secretly written the Ritual Master Shang Rixuan, inviting him to come here and [perform a rite of] examination and illumination (*kaozhao*)." Shang arrived and said, "This is something I am unable to make out. I must have a Holy Boy (*shengtong*) come so that it can be solved. After a while, a village youth (*cuntong*) appeared outside the gate and, jumping on top of a bridge, spoke in a spirit's voice: "Ren Daoyuan, all the gods have protected you for a long time, yet you do not burn incense diligently and have performed while acting licentiously—offenses that are unpardonable." Ren was deeply ashamed of his earlier crimes and, knocking his head on the ground, confessed his sins. Again the spirit said, "It is fitting that you explicate the general outline by the fifteenth night." Ren bowed one hundred times. Begging for his life, he vowed to reform his

misconduct and renew himself. The spirit said, "If by now you had responded to what I said, I would not deny you a single service. You should receive the punishment of a disciple who has received a ritual method. However, I will grant you a leniency period of twenty days." When the spirit had finished speaking, the boy collapsed on the ground and awakened. Muddle-headed, he was not at all aware of what had transpired.

When a Daoist priest became ill, it is only to be expected that he would consult a trusted colleague. That the colleague should require a spirit-medium, however, is a reflection of the extent to which these time-worn representatives of village religion now proved indispensable even in matters of a most personal nature to Daoist priests. We may recall the case of Zhao Zujian, the Daoist priest who practiced the Rites of the Celestial Heart in Heng prefecture.[15] When, mysteriously, Zhao was no longer able to perform his rites, he immediately turned to a possessed medium and thereby discovered that his access to the divine realm had been blocked because of the venality of his own spirit-general.

Here, in contrast, the priest is entirely to blame. Ren Daoyuan's colleague, the Ritual Master Shang Rixuan, was the teacher of Daoyuan's nephew Liang Hun, who had accompanied Rixuan on a therapeutic visit to the Fuzhou magistrate.[16] Baffled by Daoyuan's illness, the Ritual Master resorts to a "holy youth," a designation that brings to mind that divine oracle of the *āveśa* rites called the "Holy One" (see Chapter 6). While also a divine oracle, this particular "holy youth" has more in common with the rustic boys employed by the various practitioners of the Rites of the Three Altars and of Ucchuṣma. Like them, he is a village boy who appears seemingly out of nowhere and who goes into a frenzied trance outside the patient's home. There is little to add to the ensuing exchange between the medium and Ren Daoyuan, except to point out, once again, that the purpose of this confrontation appears to be the guilty party's reformation rather than punishment.

In the twelfth century, the critique of a priest's moral or ritual transgression was not always a welcome event. When the criticism was unsolicited, those who voiced it might even find themselves to be the object of an exorcistic investigation:

In the spring of the year 1197, Liu Zhuhui of Leping subprefecture in Nanyuan [Jiangxi] set up a Daoist offering
within his household. When it was completed, his small son
Mingge suddenly began talking like a lunatic, as if he were
possessed by a demon (*ru wu pingfu*). He said, "The Jade
Emperor has ordered Zhenwu, Spirit-Lord of the North,
to bring down into our household an imperial edict [such
that] today's offering-feast and memorials were completely
without sincerity, and we must again choose an auspicious
day for the entire household to purify themselves, construct
another 120 places for the spirits, increase the contributions
of gold coins, confess our sins, and pray for blessings. If it is
not done like this, then he will visit upon us a great misfortune." Liu was frightened and thought that this had been
brought on by the irreverence and contempt of the Yellow
Cappers [i.e., Daoist priests]. Bitterly, Liu blamed and
scolded them. The priests addressed the group, saying,
"How could we dare not be completely sincere and reverent?! Moreover, the Lord on High is lofty and luminous;
would he be willing to manipulate fortune and misfortune
in order to intimidate and mislead the people below and
receive sacrifices by extortion? It must be a demonic sprite
(*guaimei*) of trees and stones who has done this by bringing
a false charge (*jiatuo*)." The priests elected their disciple,
Master Wang (Wang shi), to employ the rectifying rite to
summon [the demon] for investigation (*kaozhao*). A spirit-
medium (*tongzi*) saw within the glow of a light the Earth
God, Lord of the *She* (Tudi sheling), being brought there.
They investigated him under restraint, and he responded,
"Three noncanonical spirits have caused this in a deceitful
fashion." And then they chased the Earth God out of the
boundary. Moreover, they cut down a grove of trees near
the place. From a small hole under a large tree that had
been set on fire, three large pythons slithered out and died.
Liu took this tree and gave it to the monk of the Xingfu
monastery. That day, a Daoist priest (*daoshi*) of the Chongxian abbey, Xie Shiting, was at a retreat-altar [i.e., was performing a purification ceremony]. He went out to buy some
dog meat to eat. Mingge also said, "The [Jade] Emperor is

aware that Xie Shiting has wantonly eaten a loathsome
animal. Tomorrow at noon he must die." And when his
words were finished, the mad boy abruptly calmed down.
Shiting died at the designated time. Liu was even more
frightened and consequently set up another offering-feast.
However, during the first week of the fourth month, Liu
became slightly ill and died.[17]

With this anecdote we come up against the limits of the clerical relationship with possessed juveniles. When trance was spontaneous and
was the vehicle for a direct and unsolicited assault on the moral basis
of clerical authority, the tolerance of the priest was necessarily strained.
Moreover, it is a matter of Daoist ideology that true gods, including
the Jade Emperor, do not receive offerings by threatening some future misfortune. (Daoist "offerings" are not "sacrifices" with the expectation of a return.) The priests, therefore, interpret the exorbitant
demands of Mingge as pure extortion, perpetrated by a cabal of
demons that conspire to seek cultic recognition by possessing the child
and having him speak in the name of Daoist divinities.

For the priests, it is just a matter of uncovering the plot. They entrust this task to their disciple, Ritual Master Wang, who makes use of
the clarifying visionary capacities of a spirit-medium (a kind of counterweight to the reckless and deluded trance of Liu's son). As in previous examples of "rites of summoning for investigation" performed
by Daoist priests, it is the Earth God who is summoned, investigated
under torture, and unceremoniously expelled from the ritual area as
if he were an unsavory police informant. The tree that housed the three
demonic pythons is entrusted to the monk of a local monastery—an
acknowledgment, I suspect, of the Buddhist willingness to deal directly
with all forms of pollution.

Although this identification and disposal of the demonic serpents
may have satisfied the Daoist priests, it is hardly an adequate explanation of the boy's behavior. The entire exorcism seems less a serious
attempt at therapy than a political spectacle intent on shoring up the
shaken confidence and damaged reputations of the Daoist priests. The
boy, for his part, goes on much as before. On the very same day that
the matter is brought to a supposed resolution, Liu Mingge attacks another Daoist priest, with dire consequences not only for the priest but
for Mingge's father as well. The cycle of death certainly stretches the

narrative's credibility, yet has the uncanny effect of restoring the boy's. We can only speculate about the deep motivation that led this child on such a relentless moral crusade, abetted by an evidently neurotic father intimidated by his son. The child and the priests are on a collision course, and the former's direct attack on the latter precluded any symbolic communication between them.

The example here of a child's involuntary trance during the performance of a Daoist offering opens up an entirely new field of inquiry. In the twelfth century, the most popular kinds of offerings sponsored by individual households, as well as by larger communities, were Daoist and Buddhist offerings for the dead. The compelling climax of many of these ritual performances turns out to have been nothing less than the possession of a child-medium. These mediums were not normally brought along by the priest but were the sons and grandsons of the deceased; they were possessed, moreover, not by gods or demons but by ancestors or, more correctly, ghosts waiting to become ancestors. Chapter 8 is devoted to exploring the complex ways in which rituals of exorcism and of the ancestral cult were converging around the experience of possession in the twelfth century. Not only did possession emerge as the central drama in descriptions of exorcism and mortuary ritual, but Daoist and Buddhist rites for the dead were actually being annexed to exorcisms—or being performed as forms of exorcism in themselves.

8

Spirit-Possession
and the Grateful Dead:
Daoist and Buddhist
Mortuary Ritual in the Song

In the Song, Buddhism had a monopoly on death, although Daoist priests increasingly demanded a share in this lucrative market. In the twelfth century, both began to be challenged by the small but articulate group of Neo-Confucians so exhaustively studied by historians. Though methodical and impassioned, these critics were not very convincing. Yu Wenbao (fl. 1250), the Zhejiangese Confucian, tells the following story with a palpable resignation:

> Jiangxi tended toward Neo-Confucianism [lit., "the school of principle"]. When the Vice-Minister Huang Lao of Linchuan died, his son Huang E did not want to use the Buddhist or Daoist priests. His relatives both inside and outside the lineage collectively rose up and opposed this. He [Huang E] consequently decided to follow methods that conformed partly to the past and partly to the present. They used an omnivorous [nonvegetarian] feast for the sacrificial offerings and Daoist and Buddhist priests for the liturgy.
>
> Now, these are filial sons and obedient grandsons who remember and keep in mind [their ancestor] with great sincerity; they call out in tears to Heaven. They have no other way to express their grief. [These procedures,] though conforming to common rituals and barbarian religion [i.e., though they were not ideal], did nevertheless express their intent.[1]

This anecdote speaks volumes about ritual practice among the Song-dynasty elite and about the isolation that greeted Confucian fundamentalists even within their own families.[2] Moreover, by identifying the use of Daoist priests and Buddhist monks as the "contemporary" part of the ritual compromise reached by the Huang household, this anecdote confirms the perception that the pervasive use of Daoist and Buddhist practitioners was a "modern" phenomenon.

Indeed, since the beginning of the Song dynasty, the use of Buddhist "merit-cloisters" (*gongde si/yuan*) had become a necessary staple of filial expression, and a much sought-after privilege of China's super-elite, just as Buddhist monasteries had become the vehicle for the cult to the Song emperor. In the eleventh century, as we have seen in the case of Fan Zhongyan, these merit-cloisters also became the medium for new experiments in the formation of descent groups, and continued to so function well into the fourteenth century, especially in the Southeast, where Buddhist monasteries claimed up to a third of the land and had been, since the tenth century, central to the creation of an agricultural infrastructure (i.e., the reclamation of land, the creation of irrigation systems, and the construction of roads and bridges).

The most popular rites for the dead in the Song dynasty were the Buddhist "Retreat of Water and Land" (*Shuilu zhai*) and the Daoist "Retreat of the Yellow Register" (*Huanglu zhai*). Both liturgies had their origin in the tenth century, but their textual elaboration and social diffusion must be seen as a product of the twelfth and thirteenth. I include a detailed historical and structural analysis of these ritual complexes in the Appendix. Among other things, this analysis reveals that the Retreats of Water and Land and of the Yellow Register were converging during this period of textual elaboration and social diffusion. Both liturgies had come to share a similar tripartite structure that included (1) the construction and purification of a ritual space; (2) the summoning of the gods, saints, and souls of the dead, including ancestors and hungry ghosts, into the ritual area; and (3) rites for their deliverance. In the all-important central panel of this liturgical triptych—the panel that forms the implicit frame for much of the analysis in this chapter—the convergence of the two liturgies was even more exact: both included rites for destroying the earth-prisons; for opening the roads from purgatory; for releasing souls from sin or ignorance; for bringing souls into the ritual area; for washing, dressing, and feeding them; and, finally, for subjecting the souls of the dead to transformation and/or conversion.

Some of these rites were understood differently in the Buddhist and in the Daoist context, while others found different relative positions with respect to the larger liturgy. All these rites, moreover, might occasion long discussions as to whether they were originally Buddhist or Daoist contributions.[3] The important point at present is the convergence of both ritual complexes around the summoning of the soul and the fact that this convergence appears to have been anticipated by another convergence—namely, the focus of noncanonical accounts of the performance of Buddhist and Daoist death ritual on the epiphany of the dead. More precisely, it is the argument of this chapter that the summoning of the soul, visible in the liturgical discourse of the thirteenth century, and the appearance of the dead, visible in the anecdotal discourse of the twelfth, were not unrelated events.

Daoist and Buddhist Mortuary Ritual in Song Society

If the Retreat of the Yellow Register and the Retreat of Water and Land had both achieved a certain textual maturity by the thirteenth century, this literary accomplishment came after several decades of immense popularity. Not only were these Daoist and Buddhist mortuary rites the most frequently mentioned in Hong Mai's *Yijian zhi* but, as these anecdotes (discussed below) reveal, by the twelfth century they had achieved as wide a social diffusion and distribution as the exorcisms treated in previous chapters.

There are several ways we can gauge this social distribution. One, obviously, is geographical. The anecdotal evidence shows that these death rituals were performed in rural villages, market towns, and large metropolitan neighborhoods.[4] The actual sites of performances outside the home were normally Buddhist monasteries and Daoist abbeys, or community temples dedicated to one or more divinities with a nominally Buddhist or Daoist affiliation. Gold Mountain Monastery near Nanjing, site of the original, pseudo-historical performance of the *Shuilu zhai* in the reign of Liang Wudi, remained an important producer of the ritual in the twelfth century,[5] while the *Huanglu zhai* came to be a fixture of the liturgy of Gezaoshan, the medieval pilgrimage center of the Lingbao tradition of communal Daoism.[6]

Another social measure of Buddhist and Daoist death ritual involves the degree of participation. Briefly, there were public rituals for the dead and private rituals for the dead. But there were also private performances that permitted the participation of non-kin,[7] and public performances in which there were designated special places for the private dead.[8] Whether there was a historical evolution from public to private masses for the dead, as in medieval Europe, is questionable. The variety of venues and nature of participation will continue to be revealed in the course of a more detailed examination of the patrons and beneficiaries of death-ritual performances.

Granted that Hong Mai's *Yijian zhi* does not represent a random sample of social practices, but it does seem to me significant that although all social classes are represented among the sponsors and beneficiaries of Buddhist and Daoist death ritual, officials and literati are by far the most numerous. A number of anecdotes, for example, refer to *shuilu* sponsored by *shidaifu*, or high officials: in one instance, a group of *shidaifu* in Hangzhou invited a monk who was a specialist in the *shuilu* rite to perform their ancestral sacrifices;[9] in another, a single *shidaifu* household sponsored a *Shuilu zhai* that was apparently open to the participation of "commoners,"[10] an eventuality we return to below. At the other end of the social register, Chen Mao, a "cultivated talent" from Jianyang, habitually brought his several dozen students to the Dizang Cloister in the Kai Fu Monastery, where its monk would recite *The Peacock Sūtra* and officiate at *shuilu* feasts.[11] Experiences such as this might last a lifetime as fellow students sponsored *shuilu* rites for each other at death.[12] After passing the examinations, Liu Yanshi returned home and sponsored, with his brother, a *Shuilu zhai* in the Xizhou Cloister of Yongning Monastery,[13] an act of filial piety equal to a visit to the ancestral shrine.

Between circles of local students and teachers and circles of the pseudo-aristocrats of the Southern Song capital lay the entire range of provincial officials. In 1167, the magistrate of Wujiang, Zhao Boxu, gathered all the Daoist priests and had them perform a Nine Obscurities Offering (*Jiuyu jiao*) in the county seat to save the souls of the community that were languishing unaided in purgatory. And just as a private retreat might be open to the public, so a public retreat might come to include a private aspect, for the magistrate reserved two special seats in the ritual for the deceased friends of his current house guest.[14] The Daoist priests of the Tianqing Abbey were often called upon to perform rites for the dead by magistrates, vice prefects, and officials.[15] At an unknown date in the twelfth century, the controller-general (*tongpan*) of Dexing, Ren Boxian, chose a Buddhist monastery on Zishan, north of the county seat, in which to have a *shuilu* performed for his deceased son, bringing out the nearby villagers in the middle of the night. Cemeteries are said to have covered the two slopes of the mountain, while the corridors of the monastery were piled high with coffins.[16] Another magistrate sponsored a *shuilu* in a pagoda cloister of a temple where his servant's son was a monk.[17]

Sponsoring a *shuilu* could also function to mediate and mitigate the tense relationship between officials and local cults. In Fuzhou, for example, a chief minister and his household performed a *shuilu* to guarantee the return of treasure that had been buried on land under the jurisdiction of a local Earth God.[18] They did so upon the recommendation of a spirit-medium who, we may infer, served the Earth God, but who spoke for the resentment of the entire community about the encroachment of private wealth upon public land. It is unclear in this case whether the *shuilu* was meant to benefit the dead of the community or the Earth God, who may have been a dead soul as well.

In another case, in the district of Haimen (Tongzhou), the Salt Superintendent promised to summon monks to perform a *shuilu* for the otherworldly benefit of the gods of a small temple whom he accused of bringing bizarre visitations upon his young son. The superintendent also threatened to destroy their effigies if they didn't respond to the *shuilu* by leaving his child alone. Yet we should not take this as a representation of ideological rigidity: the superintendent had been making offerings to these local deities since he had taken office.[19]

In addition to officials and literati, "the people" often undertook to sponsor these ceremonies on their own initiative. In 1174, for example, a commoner named Xiao Chunli and a clerk named Ouyang Xuan, among others, circulated throughout the villages and towns of Ningyuan (Daozhou) collecting contributions for a "Yellow Register Offering" that was to be performed in the Jiuyi Abbey.[20] Every year it was customary for the people of Poyang in Jiangxi to perform a Daoist exorcistic ritual, but on the fourth night of the ceremony they would go to a Buddhist temple and have the monks perform a Water and Land Retreat.[21] And the people of Xiangzhou actually sponsored a "Retreat of the One Thousand Paths [of Rebirth]" (*Qiandao zhai*) in which

Buddhist monks and Daoist priests would participate together.[22] In Jiangxi, the monk of a small cloister undertook to perform a Water and Land Retreat for the people of Leping and Mingxi subprefectures,[23] while the people of Yingcheng subprefecture in Dean fu were the beneficiaries of a Great Yellow Register Retreat sponsored by a particularly enterprising priest in the Abbey of Gathering Transcendents (Zhixian guan).[24]

Buddhist and Daoist rites for the dead might also be sponsored single-handedly by wealthy individuals, as when a commoner named Zou paid for a *shuilu* in a Buddhist temple in Xinchang county.[25] This "commoner" was most probably a rich peasant, for when the person in question was a merchant, Hong Mai designated him as such: in Huating county, a merchant sponsored a Water and Land Retreat in the Monastery of Universal Enlightenment (Puzhao si) in gratitude for a monk who had saved his boats;[26] in Quanzhou (Fujian), a merchant would call on the gods when anticipating a storm at sea and direct an oath to Heaven, promising that he would adorn a pagoda temple (*tamiao*) and sponsor a Water and Land Retreat in gratitude for his safety;[27] and finally, in Wuzhou, two merchant families sponsored and bankrolled a general Yellow Register Retreat on the birthday of the god Zhenwu.[28]

We could continue giving examples at some length, though it seems to me that the popularity of these death rituals has been sufficiently suggested, if not yet definitively established, by the preceding enumeration. The following account of a conversation between the Daoist priest Bo Yuchan and his disciple Peng Xiang will lead us to a consideration of what was judged to be central in the performance of Daoist and Buddhist mortuary ritual in the twelfth and thirteenth centuries:

> On the day of Upper Prime in the *renwu* year of the Jiading reign period [1222], the Patriarchal Master Haiqiong [i.e., Bo Yuchan], carrying a letter received from Helin Peng, was traveling from Zhe to Min to officiate at a Yellow Register Retreat for Gentleman Jue Fei, formerly of the Board of Personnel and a friend of the Ordination Master Helin Peng; he arrived early in the morning of that day [i.e., Upper Prime.]
>
> The Ordination Master, with incense in his sleeve, came forward, touched his forehead to the ground [as one does with those who attend the funeral of a parent], and then bowed deeply. He spoke the follow-

ing: "I, [Peng] Xiang, have remained in Min. Since Honored Teacher (*xiansheng*) went away, I have been 'Practicing the Way' (*xingdao*) from morning until evening and have not dared at all to engage in reckless pleasure. How can Heaven have dictated that the one that I depend on be taken away?! The letter that I submitted to you recently, offering my regards and sending greetings, also touched on the one on whom I rely [i.e., my friend the deceased], exhaustively begging Honored Teacher to pity him. The fact is, at the moment when he [Jue Fei] collapsed, the wind swirled and howled, and the entire room was filled with a fragrant aroma. But outside the room, it was clear and bright, and no one heard anything. Doesn't this seem strange? When other people die, until the time when they are buried, rain will fall for several days. A Retreat is hastily performed for them, and when the burial is finished, the rain continues. Local people also are aware of this and think it strange. I, [Peng] Xiang, have presumptuously [sought to] bother you with performing a Yellow Register [Retreat]. But now Honored Teacher has arrived here and the matter of the Yellow Register may be carried out! How great is the fortune of the Three Worlds and the joy of the Ten Thousand Spirits!"

The Patriarchal Master responded, "There is no need for my disciple to be so excessively polite! Today happens to be the day of Upper Prime. Hastily have a Peaceful Parish established, a Jade Hall constructed, and the Office of the *Yu Kui* set in place. Then, mark off the location for the Yellow Register Retreat. Between the hours of 7:00 a.m. and 5:00 p.m., compose the written documents. Announce the oath [of alliance] with Heaven and Earth and plant the giant pennants at the gates. Make the *xuyi* Zhao Juhui act as the 'Priest of High Merit' (*gaogong*) . . . [and so forth, listing other individuals and assignments]. I will perform the role of the Emissary of the Yellow Register Retreat of [the Heaven of] Highest Purity and Supervisor-General [of the Liturgy]. On the last day of the first month [of the New Year], we will all assume our official appointments. On the first day of the second month, we will begin the liturgy. On the fourth day, we will perform an Offering (*jiao*) that is in gratitude for divine mercy (*xie'en*). On the fifth day, we will worship thunder. With respect to the entire performance of the Retreat and the Offering, the ancient style will be employed; the ordered libations of the Nine Audiences will follow the Eternal Protocol."

The Ordination Master said, "Agreed."

At dawn on the day of *genchen*, the first day of the second month, a great rain poured down. From this first through the third day, wind and rain darkened the sky. For these three days and nights, all Nine Audi-

ences followed one upon the other continuously. At the moment when
they took their seats and had an audience [with the Emperor on High],
the rain stopped, and when the audience came to an end, the rain continued. All Nine Audiences were like this.

Between 5:00 p.m. and 7:00 p.m. on the day of *xinsi*, the second day
of the second month, [when they came to] the submission and presentation of the written memorial, everyone was anxious about the rain.
But just when they were about to submit the memorial, the rain stopped
all of the sudden. Clouds formed around the perimeter [of the ritual
area]. Only the Northern Dipper shone above the altar, while outside
the altar the rain came down in sheets. After a while, when the performance was finished, the rain once again also poured down upon the altar. The spectators were joyful.

The Patriarchal Master said, "Whether it is cloudy or clear is of concern only to astronomers [i.e., is a meteorological matter]; it is purely
a matter of chance. Why be anxious or happy?"

In the evening of the day of *renwu*, the third day of the second month,
something was made visible within the family temple (*jiamiao*); they
knew that the ancestral spirit had come. The Ordination Master was ecstatic and went in to report [to the Patriarchal Master].

The Patriarchal Master abruptly stopped him and said, "Allow this to
be naturally so [i.e., leave the matter alone]. The Great Dao has no form
and does not esteem [i.e., put stock in] images. Ritual (*fa*), as the practical effect of the Dao (*dao zhi yong*), can cause the dark to become luminous. Although today there was a vision, what is strange about
that?"[29]

I have included this entire passage from Bo Yuchan's *Recorded Conversations* for two reasons: first, for the universal appeal of the contrast between the fawning, hyperbolic student attracted to mystical
explanations and the skeptical, even blasé teacher more impressed
by coincidence; and second, to suggest that it is Bo Yuchan's very
matter-of-factness that makes all the more startling what we are led
to take as the ineluctable climax and terminus of the entire ritual
performance—the appearance of the dead! This appearance was not
like other events that so impressed the young Ordination Master; it
was, as the Patriarchal Master pointed out, a direct result of ritual practice and hardly deserving of comment (and certainly not of a report).
We, however, will spend the remainder of this chapter exploring the
nature of this integral relationship between the appearance of, and
rituals for, the dead.

Rites for the Dead and Child-Mediums

In the *Yijian zhi,* almost all the accounts of Buddhist and Daoist mortuary ritual concern, in one way or another, the appearance of the dead. Their appearance, normally but not exclusively in visions and in dreams, captured the imagination of Hong Mai's informants more than any other aspect of these rituals, and it can be surmised that it did so precisely because this aspect, again more than any other, best expressed for them what the rituals were all about. The dead were wont to appear as often at a Buddhist Retreat for the Spirits of Water and Land as at a Daoist Yellow Register Retreat. In the case of the Buddhist ceremony, however—befitting Buddhism's universalist claims—the dead would appear as a group as often as they would appear individually, whereas in the Daoist ceremony, even if it were open to all, the dead would appear only individually. The following anecdote may be taken as representative of the Yellow Register Retreat, on which I will now focus:[30]

On the sixteenth day of the second month of 1198, a Yellow Register Offering was held in the Tianqing Abbey in Rao prefecture. It was offered for people who wanted to summon the dead. For each person it cost 1,200 copper cash. Almost a thousand people participated in the ceremony.

Just at the end of the ceremony, the merchant Fu San saw his mother, who had recently died. She was wearing the clothes that she wore when alive. She was drenched from top to bottom and had come from afar. She entered the ritual area. Watching this was so painful that Fu couldn't bear it; he cried bitterly and immediately returned home. His mother gradually followed him home. Their conversation was just as in earlier days. She said, "Because of the effort of your paying the money at the sacrifice, my voice is the same as when I was alive." Fu wanted to ask in detail about what had happened to her, but she disappeared suddenly.

The daughter of the eye doctor, Wei Sheng, was married to Zhou Si. In the first month she had died because of something related to producing milk. She also participated on the altar. When the priest summoned her, Zhou saw her

distinctly. Her body was covered in white clothes. She
walked through water in bare feet. He could still hear the
sound of the water. After she appeared before him, both her
feet were still wet. Suddenly fear came over him. He hur-
riedly left his wife and returned home. His wife also chased
after him. Zhou hid in the bathroom, and his wife entered
the kitchen. Zhou observed that his wife's facial expression
was just like when she was alive. He became even more
frightened. He ran to his room and immediately took off
his clothes and went to bed. His wife also slept by his side.
She left at dawn.[31]

Anecdotes such as this evidently made compelling reading because
of the pathetic testimony they gave to the conflicting emotions with
which the living greeted the souls of their dead relatives. In the end,
the living usually attempted to flee the dead, not least because the uncanny lifelikeness of the dead made their presence too difficult to bear.
This is not a moot point, for the anecdote's emphasis on how similar
the deceased appears to when he or she was alive suggests that we are
dealing here not with "appearances"—with visions or hallucinations
on the part of the living—but, rather, with the ability of these rituals
to bring back and actually raise the dead. This much is suggested by
the fact that the "realness" of the dead, the degree of their materialization, is admitted to be in direct proportion to the amount of money
paid out by the surviving relative—in direct proportion, that is, to the
number of prayers and the elaborateness of the rite performed for
the deceased.

The "realness" of the dead is also suggested by the fact that the dead
are actually "summoned." Not only do the priests summon the dead,
at designated times and for specific individuals, but the entire ritual
was apparently "offered for those who wanted to summon the dead."
Whether this means that there was a special class of Yellow Register
Retreats especially dedicated to this end or that the summoning of the
dead was a characteristic of all Yellow Register Retreats, it does not seem
necessary to decide; indeed, I hope to show that, to the extent that
some Yellow Register Retreats emphasized the summoning of the dead,
this was the case because all Yellow Register Retreats included it. In
the meantime, this anecdote is indispensable for demonstrating beyond a doubt the integral relationship between the appearance of, and

rituals for, the dead. The dead were purposefully summoned during Yellow Register Retreats, and these Retreats were defined, more often than not, by this purpose. More often than not as well, the dead were summoned not just anywhere, but into a very particular place:

> Xu Dake, the "Gentleman for Fostering Temperance" (*Zheng jielang*) from Lin'an, was keeping track of the inventory in the Department of Trade and Business. He died in 1178, and his brother Bolu, who had loved him as a friend, mourned him excessively.
>
> Bolu invited to his home a Daoist priest from Mount Gezao in Linjiang named Tan Shiyi, who performed a Yellow Register Offering (*Huanglu jiao*). After the middle of the night, Xu Dake possessed his small son, who got hold of paper and brush and wrote on three sheets under a lantern: the first said, "In life I, Dake, drank wine to the point of delirium. . . . Availing myself of this merit-making service, I return to my family to pay them a visit. The mercy of the Emperor is so heavy one cannot contemplate it"; the second said, "I have received the mercy of Heaven"; and the third said, "In life I, Dake, had no regrets." The Daoist priests all looked upon his writings, while Bolu and the members of his household tearfully held them up, noticing that the characters were all in his handwriting. They had them engraved on a block and shown to the people so that they would know that the moving power of the Offering was like this.[32]

The central event of this Yellow Register Retreat was the possession of a child by the deceased and the child's transformation into a spirit-medium who transmitted messages from his father in writing. If the text does not say explicitly that the priest actually summoned the soul of the deceased into the body of the child, this does not mean that it was not the case; indeed, the cumulative evidence of this chapter will lead us to conclude that possession occurred at the precise moment toward the end of the Retreat when the soul was summoned into the ritual area, and that possession was a result of this summoning. In any event, the son's possession in this instance was most definitely seen as a direct result of ritual action—"the moving power of the *jiao*."

Unlike the case of the Fujianese children co-opted by and as spirit-mediums (whom we examined in Chapter 6), the possession of this child was not something that particularly worried family members. Quite the contrary: it was a boon that glorified the family as well as the efficacy of Daoist ritual, and that needed to be proclaimed before the entire community. The eagerness with which upper-class families greeted the possessed during funerary rites is made even more plain in the following account:

> In 1148, Zhang Xun, who styled himself Zigong, became
> a Consulting Official to the Pacification Commission in
> Zhedong (*Zhedong Anwusi canyi guan*). He lodged in the
> Monastery of Great Delight (Daxi si). He rose early in the
> morning and hastened to the prefectural office. [Once,]
> when he had not yet gone halfway, some who were urgently
> pursuing him compelled him to return; when they arrived
> at his home, he was already dead.
>   After a hundred days, they had a Daoist priest (*daoshi*)
> perform a Yellow Register Offering (*Huanglu jiao*). Sud-
> denly, and without further consideration, his son took a
> bath, changed his clothing, and donned a hat; his voice was
> [exactly that of] Xun. His wife and children surrounded
> him, in tears, and exclaimed, "In life you had many hidden
> virtues. How is it that you died in your prime? Moreover, as
> the end neared, there was not a word of parting, leaving us
> to nurture a limitless sense of regret." Xun said, "Summon
> for me the Governor of the Abbey (*zhiguan*)." The Governor
> of the Abbey was presiding over the performance of the
> Offering; hearing about this, he came in haste. Xun said
> to him, "I was in the Palace of Taiqing when I received your
> summons and invitation. I am therefore visiting you for a
> short time face to face. While traveling in the early morn-
> ing, I received an urgent decree from the Emperor on High
> and had no time to say goodbye to my family. It was not that
> I died before my time." Turning to his wife, Xun said, "You
> only should exert yourself to do good. Do not engage at all
> in the business of deceiving people. In the event that a
> single good deed can be recorded, then straightaway you
> may be entered onto the rolls of the transcendents. For the

moment, do not inquire into the departments of famous mountain-caverns. Even the Mansion of Penglai itself has three thousand vacancies, which is not to say that it is difficult to ascend [as an immortal], but rather to regret that mortals who commit evil are legion!"

A moment later, Xun ordered that a bench and table, a brush and inkstone be brought in. He wrote several hundred characters, all "family words of spirits and transcendents" (*shenxian jiayu*). The Daoist priest asked, "At present, which office among the transcendents are you occupying?" to which Xun responded, "I am in charge of the four seasons and the wind and the rain. Anything more you do not need to know." Xun remained seated throughout the night, observing the performance of the liturgy. When he asked what time it was, and the response was that it was already the fourth watch, he was about to leave. The Daoist priest invited him to stay a little longer and set out some sacrificial food. Angrily Xun said, "I am not a ghost. How can you act in such a way?" [Xun] grabbed a brush, outlined a circle on top of the table, and, making a hole in the front[?], he wrote the four characters "*Da zhen zhi lu*" ["the Path for Contacting the Perfected"]. He also wrote the characters "*Longche fengnian*" ["Dragon Cart and Phoenix Carriage"], and with his hands folded in front, he bowed and said, "Make an effort to do good. This spring we will see each other again." Xun's son subsequently took a nap. When he awakened, they asked him about what had transpired, but he wasn't aware of having said anything. From this time, the household placed a plaque in front of the table which read, "Hall for Contacting the Perfected" (*Dazhentang*).[33]

This anecdote conveys the extent to which possession by the deceased came to be institutionalized in the Yellow Register Retreat during the twelfth century. At some point during this particular performance, the deceased was "invited and summoned" by the presiding priest. It was then that the son bathed and changed his clothing as preparation for becoming possessed by his father. Although the child's behavior is described as "sudden," it can hardly be described as spontaneous. The bath and change of clothing are highly deliberate and ritualized actions that recall nothing so much as the purificatory bath and change of clothing described in the liturgical texts—actions (described in the Appendix) that the soul was made to undergo immediately after it was summoned to join the ritual assembly. The bathing and clothing of the boy and the bathing and clothing of the soul were, I would argue, not merely homologous events but alternative representations of the same event. I return to this point below.

Zhang Xun, as incarnated by his son, now remains throughout the performance of the liturgy as an observer and participant. His son's embodiment of his father, which is given pride of place within the liturgy, also takes on a life of its own outside it. The area (inside the home?) to which Zhang Xun descends is designated the "Hall for Contacting the Perfected" and threatens to become the venue for a permanent possession cult within the family. Indeed, Zhang Xun returns to possess his son twice more, the first time to engage his wife in further discussions about morality and to produce more written testaments.

The second time, however, Zhang Xun's voice has noticeably altered, and he explains that this is because he is no longer the "Consulting Official" (*canyi*) but a "Perfected One" (*zhenren*). During the autumn, apparently, Zhang Xun had participated in an oral examination given by the deified Laozi within the Palace of Great Purity—a debate on the thesis that "there is substance within the vacuous" (*xu zhong yu shi*). Having received high marks, Zhang Xun had been promoted and could no longer descend among human beings. In the end, therefore, the distinction between the cult of transcendents and cult of possession is maintained: possession is terminated precisely at the moment when Zhang Xun becomes an immortal.

The institutionalization of the possession of the deceased during Daoist funerary rituals in the Song requires explanation. What needs to be explained—and what can in fact be explained—is not so much why possession by the deceased appeared in funerary ritual in the Song period as how its appearance in this context and at this time made sense to the men and women of the twelfth century. The possession of the children of the deceased, I would argue, was a particularly compelling event to contemporaries precisely because of how it intersected with—that is, resonated with, usurped, or encroached upon—other religious forms and ritual spaces. Each of the forms or spaces I have in mind has its own age and history, and each intersected with a different aspect of the liturgical moment we have been describing.

From one point of view, this liturgical episode marks the incorporation, even co-optation, of the traditional mediumistic seance by Daoist ritual. Before the Song, the function of communicating with the dead was left entirely to those who were described as spirit-mediums (*wu*).[34] Even religious persons such as Buddhist monks or laymen would not hesitate to go to a spirit-medium when they wanted to hear directly from a beloved and recently deceased relative:

Xindu Yuanfang was from the subprefecture of Fuyang in Xiangzhou. As a youth he was noted for his rectitude and especially esteemed Buddhist books. In the first month of 674, in the spring, when Yuanfang was twenty-nine, he died.

For more than a month after his death, his brother Daojie, a monk of the Faguan Monastery, mourned him continuously. Daojie therefore led a spirit-medium (*wu*) to his house and asked him to communicate with Yuanfang. Daojie knew some magical techniques (*fashu*) as well, and he made a talisman (*fu*) to assist Yuanfang. He ordered the medium to ask Yuanfang where he had been sent. The medium did not understand characters, so he sent for a scribe to hold the brush. The medium transmitted Yuanfang's verbal instuctions (*koujue*). He produced a page of writing [consisting of] a statement about his life's ambitions, along with those of his fellow student Feng Xingji, together with two poems.

Also within the house his letters were preserved. Their reasoning and arrangement were very logical, and their words and phrases melancholy. For the most part these letters were concerned with ascetic merit, the recitation of the Buddha's name, and the copying of sūtras. He considered the karma associated with the killing of living things to be the greatest crime, and that nothing surpassed this [in evil].

In addition, the medium said, "Yuanfang has not entered an earth-prison, nor has he fallen among the *pretas*. [Rather,] he relies entirely on the administrative divisions of the officers of the underworld. Presently he is a male

servant in the household of Li Renshi of Shizhou. However,
there is a certain Shi Mingyuan of Wushan in Longzhou
who is praying for a son at Hua Yu. Yuanfang will be transformed into a male of the Shi family. The day of his rebirth
is approaching. He is being compelled to quickly change his
residence. From the second month, when he enters the
womb, to the twelfth month, when he will be born, he
wishes that his brother and others will travel there and
visit him." His words ended, and Daojie wept and left.[35]

A tag indicates that this anecdote was passed on to the editors of the
Taiping guangji by two monks of the Zhili Monastery, Huiyong and
Fazhen—associates, I imagine, of the deceased or his circle. The
rather haphazard, even awkward, description of what transpired during the seance suggests a certain authenticity and absence of literary
embellishment.

Be that as it may, there seems to be little doubt that, by the Song
period, what had been a discrete and distinctive space of the Chinese
spirit-medium had moved within the precincts of Daoist death ritual.
This space was defined not simply by possession by the deceased, but
by the written as well as verbal transmission of pronouncements about
his moral status and otherworldly location, and by a suggestion as to
the relation between the two. To see the incorporation of the mediumistic seance within the Daoist Retreat of the Yellow Register is not,
however, to say that spirit-mediums ceased to perform their traditional
functions in the Song.[36] Nor is it to ignore the fact that, in making a
place for these functions, Daoist rites were not necessarily or coincidentally making a place for the person of the spirit-medium, even
though this appears to be the case in modern times and perhaps even
in the Song (for which see below). In the Song Retreat of the Yellow
Register, the one who took on the role of the spirit-medium was a young
child, a son of the deceased.[37] From the perspective of exactly who
was allowed to incarnate the deceased, the possession of a young son
in the Daoist rites for the dead seems to represent the assimilation of
an entirely different religious space—namely, the space occupied by
the long-forgotten character known as the "*shi.*"

The *shi,* or "corpse," actually designated the person who represented
the deceased during the "sacrifice of repose" performed in the an-

cestral temple by the Zhou aristocracy. Some scholars refer to him as "the Personator." The nature of his representation of the deceased is a matter of interpretation, and has been since the early imperial period. The point we need to emphasize from the outset is that the role of the Personator, who had to be a child or adolescent, was invariably played by a younger son or grandson of the deceased. (The eldest son assumed the role of the Sacrificer, who had to be an adult.) Formal music and poetic recitatives described and marked the Personator's entrance to and exit from the ancestral temple. Some of these songs are preserved in the ancient *Book of Poetry*.[38]

Once inside the temple, the Personator took a seat, and it was at this moment that he was actually addressed as the ancestor.[39] The Personator remained seated throughout the liturgy, as a recipient of sacrificial food and wine and as an observer of theatrical performances.[40] Recall the anecdote above in which the son of Zhang Xun, as an incarnation of his father, took a seat during a Yellow Register Retreat and remained seated throughout the evening, receiving sacrifice and enjoying the spectacle. It is difficult not to see in this child's incarnation of the deceased a reenactment of the role of the ancient Personator. But was the Personator also possessed?

> The climax of the Sacrifice of Repose came with the ancestral blessing: . . . The spirit-protectors (*shenbao*) will surely come and requite us with great blessings. . . . The rites have been accomplished, the bells and drums are ready. The pious son (*xiaosun*) goes to his seat, and the skillful recitant (*gongzhu*) conveys the message, goes and gives it to the pious son. "The spirits are drunk." The August Dead One (*shi*) then rises and is seen off (*songshi*) with drums and bells: The spirit-protectors have gone home.[41]

As I interpret this episode, a priestly figure called "the Invoker" (= Skillful Recitant) transmitted a message from the Ancestor (= Spirit-Protector) through the Personator (= August Dead One) to the Sacrificer (= Pious Son), who has finally taken a seat himself.[42] This is a strong reading of this poem, and one that sees the relationship between Personator and Invoker as paradigmatic of all future historical relationships between kinds of spirit-mediums and their officiants, whether Ritual Masters, Buddhist monks, or Daoist priests. The interesting question is the nature of the child's impersonation of the de-

ceased. Was he possessed, as Arthur Waley suggests, or did he merely
represent the dead? To the first-century author of *The Debate in the White
Tiger Hall* (*Bohutong*), it was definitely a matter of theater, not trance:

> The Personator is found in the ceremony wherein sacrifice is offered
> to ancestors, because the soul emitting no perceptible sounds and hav-
> ing no visible form, the loving sentiment of filial piety finds no means
> of displaying itself. Hence, a Personator has been chosen to whom meats
> are offered, after which he breaks the bowls, as if his own father had
> eaten plenty. The Personator, drinking abundantly, imparts the illusion
> that it is the soul which is satiated (*Shi xiao ruo shen zhi zui*).[43]

Here the Personator "was an image of the soul" (*shi shen xiang ye*),
a representation but not a vessel that it inhabited. By the Tang, the institution of the Personator was not merely little remembered but was
vilified so that it would remain that way. In the ninth century, Du You
(735–812) wrote in *The Continuing Canon* (*Tongdian*):

> The ancients employed a Personator. This rite deserves censure and has
> been abolished by our great worthies. One vied with the other in prac-
> ticing it. Now that an era of progress has set in and these silly customs
> have disappeared, it is important not to revive them, common sense bids
> to refrain from them. Some half-baked literati of our days would fain
> reestablish this ceremony of the Personator. This is quite absurd.[44]

It is almost heartwarming to see the familiar appeal to "common
sense" and an "era of progress" in a medieval Chinese attack on superstition. Such an appeal, however, destabilizes the distinction that
many Neo-Confucians and modern scholars make between custom
(*su*) and ritual (*li*), between what people ordinarily do and what the
classics have determined that they should do, for the Personator was
considered absolutely indispensable by the ritual classics; moreover,
to offer a sacrifice to the dead adult without a Personator representing it—in a remark attributed to Confucius by the *Liji*—is like mis-
treating an adult as an adolescent.[45] The point is that this ritual sanc-
tioned by the classics has become a "silly custom," which is a symptom,
perhaps, of the fact that it had long ceased to be customary.

Given the disappearance of, and eventual disdain for, the institution of the Personator, it is startling that he should receive such a sensitive reevaluation by Song Confucians. In the eleventh century, Cheng
Yi (1033–1107) offered the following:

> When sacrificing to the dead the ancients employed the Personator, because the soul and the vital force of the dead person, after being separated from the body, seek an agent of the same nature (*bi qiu qi lei er yi*). Now, men being all the same kind, the father and mother and the children being all of one family and the same stock, the soul of the departed person is requested to come and establish its seat in one of them as an agent.[46]

And less than a century later, Zhu Xi (1130–1200) echoed Cheng Yi's interpretation even more emphatically:

> In ancient times all employed a Personator when sacrificing to the dead. Since the descendents continue the life of their ancestors, the Personator shares, therefore, in the life of the departed person, and the ancestor's soul descends necessarily into his descendent and reposes therein to enjoy the sacrifice offered.[47]

Since neither Zheng Yi nor Zhu Xi actually revived the role of the Personator in his own liturgical program, both would probably manage to avoid Du You's list of "half-baked literati," but they probably wouldn't qualify as "great worthies" either. Both men presented a serious and positive reevaluation of the institution of the Personator. Unlike the author of the *Bohutong*, who saw in the Personator a mere representation on which the survivors could focus their feelings of loss, Zheng Yi and Zhu Xi defended his presence in terms of metaphysical necessity: the Personator was the seat or agent for the soul that willfully seeks out one of its own kind to inhabit. Their argument binds biological continuity to religious identification so tightly as to make the Personator's possession by the soul of the deceased not only a logical interpretation but an ontological inevitability. It seems to me significant that these scholars should advance such an original interpretation of the Personator at the very moment when such an interpretation was essentially being played out regularly within the context of Daoist mortuary ritual. Classical Confucian scholarship and Daoist ritual enactment were converging around the eagerness with which they greeted the return and embodiment of the dead.

But the link between Daoist mortuary ritual and the ancient institution of the Personator was more conscious than has been suggested thus far. In a Daoist text from the Southern Song, the *Daoshu yuanshen qi* (HY 1221), the author includes a short essay on the notion of *futi*, or "reliance on the body," a technical term used in Daoist liturgical manuals for the ritualized possession of a surrogate:

> In the ritual sacrifice, which has come down to us since ancient times, it is necessary to employ a Personator. And for the Personator, one employed a grandson who wore the clothing of the ancestor and was seated on a mat before the spirit-tablet. The Personator was also called the "felicitous one." *The Book of Rites* says that the Invoker makes an announcement with words of filiality while the "felicitous one" makes an announcement with words of compassion. Today's practice of having the dead borrow a body and tell its story originated in this ancient practice.[48]

Through his choice of vocabulary, specifically "borrowing a body to tell its story" (*jieti tongzhuan*), this Daoist priest designates the classical ritual as the basis not only of Daoist mortuary ritual but of the exorcistic "rite of summoning for investigation" as well.

The implications of this passage, and of the text generally, go far beyond our immediate concern. In his preface to the text, the author argues that what is referred to in the Song as the "teaching of Laozi" (i.e., Daoism) had its origins among the "classicists" (*ju*) of ancient times and was not understood as a "teaching" distinct from the "eternal Dao," which had been transmitted from the legendary sage-kings (Yao, Shun, Yu, and Tang) to the founders of the Zhou (Wen, Wu, and the Duke of Zhou) and, ultimately, to Confucius himself. Both Confucius and Laozi, the author maintains, were equally concerned with hierarchy and ritual; the former just happened to direct his inquiries to ritual, while the latter devoted them to the Way. And what caused this classical tradition to be understood as two separate "teachings" was a problem of historical contingency rather than logical necessity. As the "Way of the Zhou" collapsed in the Warring States period and classical ritual and music disappeared, the laity mistakenly came to see the "Way of Confucius" as distinct from the times in which they lived. The Way of Confucius became, therefore, something to be taught and transmitted by a succession of masters and students. These disciples, moreover, adapted their dress to the changing fashions of the laity. The disciples of Laozi, however, refused to conform to the taste or practices of commoners, and therefore even the Daoist priests of the Song dynasty wear the ancient vestments of the "classicists" as described in *The Rituals of Zhou*. Unfortunately, in the Southern Song, Daoism is not only understood as a distinct teaching but is fraudulently classified as belonging to the tradition of spirit-mediums. So claims the author of our text.[49]

The thirty-four essays that make up the body of this text are meant to demonstrate that the liturgies, spirits, altars, clothing, and clerical paraphernalia of the Daoist religion all descend directly from what is described in the various ritual canons and protocols of the Zhou dynasty.[50] This demonstration is compelling and makes a strong argument for viewing the Daoist priests of the Song dynasty as the priests of the Chinese classical tradition. And it may be our modern prejudicial identification with the Neo-Confucians of the Song that prevents us from seeing this.

Daoist Liturgy and Possession

In the preceding pages, I suggested that the possession by the deceased during Daoist mortuary ritual derived much of its energy from the way it appropriated the postmortem seance of the medieval Chinese spirit-medium and the role and interpretation of the ancient Chinese Personator. The argument here is not unlike that made in Chapter 5, where I suggested that what made the Rite of Summoning for Investigation particularly compelling was the way it intersected with the theater and the Song judicial process. Here, however, I have been talking about the diachronic reoccupation of religious layers, whereas there I was talking about a synchronic intersection of separate cultural domains (religion, play, and the law). In the rest of this chapter, I bring the argument full circle by suggesting that in the twelfth century there was a convergence of the Daoist rites for the dead and the Rite of Summoning for Investigation. We can demonstrate this convergence by locating the possession of the deceased more emphatically within the structure of the Yellow Register Retreat.[51]

In connection with the Yellow Register Retreat performed for the official Zhang Xun, described earlier in this chapter, I suggested that the bathing and clothing of Xun's son actually substituted for actions to which the soul was subject in the canonical versions of the liturgy. If this inference is correct, then we might expect to place the possession by the deceased somewhere during the second act of the Daoist "rites of deliverance"—that is, somewhere between "The Destruction of the Earth-Prison," which ends the first act, and "The Refinement of the Soul," which begins the third. When we turn once again to the Song liturgical texts, we find that this expectation is not unwarranted.

In Jiang Shuyu's *Protocols for Establishing the Great Purificatory Fast of the Supreme Yellow Register* (*Wushang huanglu dazhai licheng yi*, HY 508, late twelfth-early thirteenth century), the central scene of the second act is the summoning of the soul(s) of the deceased into the ritual area[52] and, more precisely, into a "Soul Banner" (*lingfan*) that is held by two young boys before a small altar strewn with flowers and incense and situated at the "Gate of Demons" (*guimen*) in the northeast corner of the ritual area.[53] Several priests invoke the Divine Tiger, two spirit-generals, and a host of soul-catchers, compelling them to bring down the soul of the deceased. The commentary indicates that while the soul is being summoned, the Ritual Master tranforms himself (*bianshen*) into the Celestial Venerable "Great Unity" (Taiyi tianzun). Moving through a succession of significant mudrās, he finally punches in the celestial stem and branch corresponding to the birth year of the deceased, inhales the pneuma from the Gate of Demons, and blows it onto the Soul Banner.[54]

Later versions of the Yellow Register Retreat seem to pick up where Jiang Shuyu's rite leaves off. In the corresponding chapter of Jin Yunzhong's *Grand Lingbao Methods of [the Heaven of] Highest Purity* (*Shangqing lingbao dafa*, HY 1213, early thirteenth century), there is a long description of something called the "Rites of Ascent and Deliverance of the Grass Body." The opening includes the following instructions:

> First take some fresh grass and, following the form of either a man or woman, create the former living body [of the deceased]. Dress it in its former clothes. Around its waist secure "Secret Words of the Great Brahma" (*Dafan yinyu*), while on its head it wears a "Great Contract for Ascending to Heaven" (*Shengtian dazhuan*). Employ a balance and frame and attach the "grass body" to the weighted hook so that it is suspended in air and does not touch the ground. Proceed to take the balance and place it in the midst of the "Altar Where the *Hun*[-Soul] Resides" (*zhuhun tan*) outside the gate. Then have a small boy hold the "Banner for Summoning the *Hun*[-Soul]" made out of white silk. The Master sings the "Dipper Stanzas" (*douzhang*) and summons the *hun* [soul] to come. The "grass body" falls down while the weighted hook becomes heavier than normal; the Soul Banner also falls down while the pole also gets somewhat heavier. One therefore knows that the soul has already arrived![55]

Here the Soul Banner plays a complementary but subordinate role to a straw puppet. The puppet is not merely a representation of the deceased but a "substitute body" (*tishen*) into which his soul has been summoned. We are but a short step from the possession of a human body, whether that of a relative of the deceased or that of a spirit-medium. The textual evidence strongly suggests, in fact, that both these human figures played important roles at this point in the liturgy.

The same chapter of Jin Yunzhong's text includes variant instructions for causing the *hun*-soul of the deceased to "immediately reveal its true form and carry on a conversation with the living."[56] All these instructions involve, in one way or another, the ingestion by the priest of water mixed with the ashes of burned talismans and the projection of this charged fluid into some corner, or onto some wall, of the ritual area. On one occasion this area is hidden from the public by a screen, and the relatives are admitted one at a time to see and communicate with the dead.[57] A corresponding moment can be identified in Wang Qizhen's *Shangqing lingbao dafa*. Again a curtain is drawn around the ritual area to prevent "people from coming and going." Behind the partition, however, the talismanic water is rubbed on the body of a young spirit-medium (*tongzi*) who is ordered by the Master to point out the beginning of any manifestation of the deceased. For a long time it appears that the medium concentrates on its traces. The text adds that "if there is a pious son who is loyal and filial and compassionate and sincere in intent, he will definitely be able to see the form of the deceased and converse with him, and every detail can be taken in."[58]

An alternative and more revealing ritual involving a spirit-medium is found in Wang Qizhen's work in the explanation that follows instructions for creating a "Talisman for Apprehending the Celestial Eye" (*tong tianmu fu*).[59] This talisman is burned in a basin of water and subsequently sprinkled around the altar. In front of the altar stands a "Flag for Summoning the Soul" and the body of a young spirit-medium (*tongzi shen*) of roughly the same height. The Master closes his eyes and actualizes a spirit. Holding the "Seal of Ziwei" in his left hand and forming the "Sword Mudrā" with his right, he transforms his body into the god Tai Yi. He also actualizes an array of Heavenly Soldiers to his left and right and imagines the transformation of the remaining Daoist priests or acolytes into "Perfected [Ones] Who Save from Distress."

Next, the Master invokes various civil and military officials and the local earth-spirits, and compels them "to bring the soul of the deceased forward so that it will take possession of the banner and manifest its form" (*fufan xianxing.*). Forming the "Mudrā of Shangdi," the Master inhales the pneuma from the northwest, blows it into the air, and imagines the hypostasized perspicacity (i.e., the Heavenly Eye) of the god Tai Yi suspended in the air before him. At this point the text provides a "Spell for Transforming the Body" (*bianshen zhou*). The Master then inhales the pneuma from the north and exhales it into the water basin. He orders the spirit-medium to swallow a mouthful of the mixture while the bystanders use some to rinse their eyes. Silently the Master intones a "Spell for Opening the Light" (*kaiguang zhou*). As a result, the spirit-medium becomes infused with a divine light that allows him either to see, or to illuminate so that others may see, the form of the deceased.

Although the spirit-medium is not actually possessed here by the soul of the deceased, this does not appear to have been ruled out by any means. The following commands close this chapter of Wang's work and appear in the text immediately after a demonic silhouette that depicts, I suspect, the Spirit-General Zhao Gongming, who is invoked in the passage and who is ubiquitous in exorcistic ritual (as we have seen in Chapter 6):

> The Emperor on High has ordered that the soul of the deceased quickly take possession! Child-Spirits of the Five Directions! Commanders Who Lead the *Hun*-Souls! By the Regulations of the Golden Porte, order so-and-so to come to the altar immediately, take possession of the body, and communicate its spirit! Quickly, quickly, respectfully receive the laws of the Most Venerable Tai Yi. Command the Spirit-General Zhao Gongming to quickly reveal its form. Spitting water, immediately take possession![60]

Which body—or, better, whose body—is the soul of the deceased being compelled to possess here? The term used for the possession of the body—"*futi*"—is exactly the one used in the exorcistic invocations for ordering the possession of a patient or spirit-medium. It is not, however, strictly necessary to dispel the ambiguity. Moreover, there is no compelling reason to privilege the canonical versions of the Yellow Register Retreat in our attempt to determine what actually and regularly transpired during these rituals as they were performed in the twelfth century. What I have been attempting to demonstrate is, first, that the possession of a child by the deceased, as described in the *Yijian zhi*, was not a serendipitous event; second, that it could only have occurred at one moment during the Retreat; and third, that this event was simply another version or interpretation of the specific ritual actions described in the canonical texts.

To re-characterize the second and central act of the Daoist "rites of deliverance," we might agree provisionally that it comprised two partially overlapping scenes: (1) the summoning of the soul into the ritual area, and (2) the appearance of and communication with the deceased. The soul might be summoned into a flag, into a puppet, or even into a human substitute; it might appear and talk directly to relatives, or its appearance and conversation might be mediated by another human being, whether a "divination youth" provided by the Master or a child of the deceased.

I would add, parenthetically, that the use of a puppet to represent the deceased, followed by the use of a spirit-medium to embody or communicate with him, is found in precisely the equivalent position within the modern liturgy. At the moment that corresponds to the "destruction of the earth-prisons" (*poyu*) in the Song-dynasty Retreat of the Yellow Register, the priest puts on the red turban of a *fashi* over his Daoist headdress and grasps a halberd with which he breaks open the gate of a "fortress" (*cheng*), a paper and wood-framed model of the earth-prison. At this point, according to the observations of Kristofer Schipper,

> The family members seize the fortress and shake it, wailing loudly and calling the name of the deceased, inviting him to return home to be washed, clothed and fed. When the officiant has opened the gate, the sedan chair bearers come into action. The deity is called by the officiant, the heavenly armies are marshalled again and again, until the chair charges the fortress, and beats it to shreds. The puppet representing the deceased is carefully taken out, tied on the back of the principal mourner and brought inside the Mourning Chapel. The doors are closed, and the family, after having presented bath water, clothes and his favorite dishes to the soul of the deceased, interrogates him through the intermediary of the medium. It is evident that this last part carries the greatest interest to the family and the neighbors.[61]

Indeed, we have shown that the interrogation of the deceased through an intermediary carried the greatest interest for Song-dynasty families as well. Schipper goes on to argue that this is also "the most original part of the entire ritual," by which he means that it is borrowed from vernacular rituals of exorcism, known as "*guoluguan*" or "*guan'ai*," in which the *fashi* undertakes a journey through the various earth-prisons in an attempt to retrieve the soul of the deceased that is blamed for the client's illness. At the conclusion of the journey, a fortress representing the earth-prison is destroyed and the deceased is interviewed through a spirit-medium.[62]

Rites for the Dead as Rites of Exorcism

The intersection of mortuary and therapeutic ritual was already a fact in the Song dynasty, and was so recognized by contemporaries. *The Record of the Numinous Efficacy of the Teachings of the Dao* (*Daojiao lingyan zhi*), preserved in the eleventh-century *Yunji qiqian*, includes seventeen anecdotes about the Yellow Register Retreat.[63] These anecdotes constitute an incomparable record of the diffusion and popularization of this ritual complex in the late Tang and Five Dynasties period (the ninth and tenth centuries). What is made eminently clear is that an enabling mechanism of this process of diffusion and popularization was the ability of a group of itinerant priests to use, and to defend their use of, the Yellow Register Retreat as a form of therapeutic ritual! All make the argument, in one way or another, that this mortuary rite is indispensable for treating illnesses caused by the souls of the dead. As one priest explains to a patient,

> Everything that has befallen the vengeful soul of the dead is reported to the Celestial Emperor. Receiving a "Celestial Talisman," the soul returns for retribution. The ritual techniques (*fangshu*) current among human beings are unable to offer any way out. Only the Yellow Register Retreat, by submitting a petition and memorializing Heaven (*baibiao zoutian*), can eliminate the crime.[64]

The claim here is that only the Yellow Register Retreat can provide the necessary access to the source legitimating the soul's retribution, although this argument seems to be a typical conceit of ritual experts whose analysis of a situation presupposes a solution that no one else can provide. The argument offered by another traveling priest seems more to the point:

> When the karma of crimes committed by the living weighs heavily upon them, nothing surpasses the Yellow Register Retreat (*Huanglu daochang*).

Supplicating, we proclaim it to Heaven and Earth. Then, for three days and nights, we burn incense and scatter flowers, hang pennants and suspend canopies, sing hymns and recite vows, confess sins and seek their pardon. By saving and delivering the soul of the dead, we eliminate the vengeful lawsuit (*miandui*). How great is the power and sublimity of this rite![65]

This explanation has the advantage of underscoring the perhaps obvious point that in saving the dead, the dead are necessarily transposed to an entirely separate plane of existence. Salvation entails the permanent removal of the dead from the living, which is a form of exorcism.

By the twelfth century, priests no longer needed to justify the use of the Yellow Register Retreat as therapeutic ritual; the souls of the dead return to remind the living that its performance would go a long way to assuaging their feelings of revenge. Moreover—and this is the point I have been working up to—mortuary ritual was not only used as therapeutic ritual but also began to reflect its content:

The Xu family of Yugan lived in Fujia village. Early in the Chunxi reign period [1174–1189], suddenly they were haunted by a demon. A band of spirit-mediums arrived together, but they weren't the slightest bit successful. They heard that in the neighboring county of Jinxian there was a certain Grand Chamberlain Chuan (Chuan Taichang) whose ritual power was so clever and lofty that he could subdue and control spirits and demons. They invited him to come to their home; he ordered them to set up a "Nine Obscurities Offering" (*Jiuyou jiao*) to exorcise (*xirang*) the demon.

During the night that Chuan brought down the spirits, he planted several dozen small yellow streamers in the middle of the courtyard. Amidst flashing lights, strange things moved up and down the flagpoles, striking each other. Chuan said, sighing, "These demons will not be easy to get rid of. Even in the presence of the Emperor on High and his retinue of Perfected [Ones], they still have the audacity to indulge themselves in such a manner; it is a sure indication that there is nothing that they fear. However, this gives me the opportunity to test the efficacy of my magical power."

Chuan had the master of the household put a small room .
in order, and in extreme secrecy they placed a vase in the
middle of it. He selected four sturdy retainers to each hold
an effigy, and from outside the home he worked his magical
rite. After a long time he heard agitated sounds coming
from inside the vase. He took it and looked inside, [where]
there were over one hundred varieties of insects, all tame
and immobilized. They threw them all away in the water,
and from that moment the spooky transformations (*guaib-*
ian) gradually subsided. Up to now there has been no
recurrence.[66]

Here we have a Daoist ritual for the dead being employed quite
specifically and self-consciously to exorcise a demon. It is paradoxical, therefore, that what deserves the exorcistic label is an entirely different ritual performed when the Daoist one has been concluded—a
ritual in which the demons are magically reduced to a material and
vermin-like form and then disposed of in water. Rituals such as this
were part of the basic repertory of Chinese exorcisms; they were the
stock-in-trade of spirit-mediums and sorcerers and were borrowed, as
we saw in Chapter 6, by Daoist and Buddhist Ritual Masters. The Nine
Obscurities Offering, in contrast, is not an exorcism at all. The demon
is neither removed nor driven away, but summoned so that it might be
examined, identified, and characterized. That the demon is not even
a soul of the dead is a mark of the extent to which this rite had been
separated from its mortuary context—and of the extent to which Daoist
rituals for the dead had come to look exactly like the therapeutic rituals of the twelfth century, which were not exorcisms either.

This anecdote is merely an instance of the convergence of Daoist
mortuary and therapeutic ritual in the twelfth century. At the most
general but also most basic level, the Daoist Yellow Register Retreat
was a "rite of summoning for investigation" (*kaozhao fa*), a rite in which
a demon or soul of the deceased was summoned and then investigated
(interrogated). More particularly, there was a convergence of constitutive elements of the rituals. If we treat the canonical and noncanonical descriptions of the Yellow Register Retreat as equally suggestive of the range of elements that any given ritual performance
might encompass, then we can find a sequence of elements not unlike the one that defined the Rite of Summoning for Investigation out-

lined in Chapter 5. Recall that the second act of the "rites of deliverance" opens with the "Metamorphosis of the Master" (A), usually into Tai Yi, and closes with the "Possession of a Surrogate" (D), whether a nonhuman substitute, a medium, or a child of the deceased. Between these two events, one may also find "Rites of Detection" (B) and/or "Rites of Seizure" (C). In the Yellow Register Retreat, however, the Rites of Seizure (in which the Divine Tiger and other divinities are commanded to bring the soul into the ritual area or into some object or person) are less prominent than in the Rites of Summoning for Investigation, while the Rites of Detection are much more so.

As we have seen, considerable space is awarded to instructions for making the dead appear to relatives or to a medium, while the processes by which the Master makes this happen—principally through the visualization and the exchange and projection of pneumas—are exactly those found in the Rites of Summoning for Investigation. The fact that the Rites of Summoning for Investigation and the Yellow Register Retreat were performed in sequence or as substitutes for each other, the fact that many priests who were expert in the therapeutic Rites of the Celestial Heart were also performing Yellow Register Retreats—all this might also account for the exchange and assimilation of the constitutive elements of therapeutic and mortuary ritual in the Song.

9

The Syncretic Field
of Chinese Religion

In my concluding remarks, I would like to talk explicitly about theory. Specifically, I want to discuss the current debate on civil society
among historians of modern China and its relevance to historians of
pre-twentieth-century China. This debate is relevant to us not because
it provides us with a model, but because the collective expertise of historians of religion can and should make an important contribution to
the debate. What I hope to show is that this debate is not only about
the presence or absence of civil society in the late Qing, and the implications of this for China's present and future, but also about the
nature of the pre-modern state, elites, and local society, the relations
among them, and the role that religion plays in those relations.

From "Civil Society" to "Cultural Nexus"

In 1987 and in 1989, the world was struck by two images from the com-
monwealth of communist nations: in Poland, we saw a church and a
trade union successfully negotiate freedom from an imperial state,
while in China we saw a single person valiantly but hopelessly block-
ing the path of a tank. To historians of modern China, these contrasting images could not have been starker, and they seemed to bring
to a head the question of whether China has, or has ever had, any institutions that could legitimately mediate society's demands on, or
from, the state. To some historians, the answer was yes; to others, a
clear no. As the debate matured, the yes people have continued to say

yes but have added that these institutions were lost or destroyed, whereas the no people have acknowledged the formal possibility of such institutions but have continued to say no by emphasizing their weakness and their permeability by the state or its representatives. I will concentrate on these more nuanced versions of the debate and take as its spokesmen Prasenjit Duara for the "yes, but no longer" school of thought and Frederic Wakeman for the "perhaps, but not really" contingent.

Duara locates a "potential" civil society in the Confucian tradition of literati dissent and autonomy that developed in the Ming-Qing transition and that was revived in the late nineteenth century under the rubric of "political feudalism" (*fengjian*). Its purpose, in the late Qing, was not to replace the imperial system (*junxian*) and return to the classical polity of the Zhou dynasty, but "to curb autocratic centralism and enhance the role of local elites and public opinion in national decision-making," carving out a "public realm" that would "preserve the autonomy of local society and simultaneously bring this society into the modernization project."[1]

The qualification of this public realm (*gong*) as "potential" is significant and is acceptable or not depending on whether one defines "potentiality" as something that might be actualized in the future or as something that must have been actualized, somewhere at some time, in the past. Duara implicitly argues for both these definitions at one and the same time. Yet what I find to be logically incoherent, Duara finds to be discursively paradoxical. He writes:

> The significance of civil society arose only with the European Enlightenment narrative of history. Because Chinese society until the late nineteenth century did not see itself within the European narrative of civil society versus the state, the elements of civil society existed only as potential history. . . . [These] very elements became retrievable as history only when two narratives— . . . that of the Enlightenment and . . . of Chinese feudalism—came together for a brief period in the late nineteenth century. In the unlikely space joining these two discourses, certain literati became positioned to actualize this potential history of societal autonomy—to mobilize a new history from the historical mosaic.[2]

In other words, the elements of feudal autonomy might be actualized as civil society because China was now seen as participating in a universal history in which civil society had been actualized at one point and in one place (i.e., in the eighteenth-century West). Yet all this takes place at the level of "discourse." Whether a discursive potential space positioned certain literati to actualize anything is as debatable as what they discursively meant to actualize—and whether what they meant to actualize would satisfy even our basic notions of civil society.

Wakeman is not so impressed by this discourse, and is prone to take what these literati did actualize as a better indication of what they discursively meant. In several rigorous critiques of the proponents of a late-Qing or Republican civil society (Rowe, Strand, Rankin), Wakeman uses their own empirical evidence to demonstrate that even they cannot mean what they say.[3] Wakeman is willing to acknowledge an expanding "public sphere" in the urban environment examined by these proponents, but he shows that those activities of the urban elite that can be classified as in the public realm (*gong*) collapse, more often than not, into official administration (*guan*) on the one hand and into private interest (*si*) on the other, and that they do not in any case carve out a civil society.

Wakeman's attribution of "cognitive dissonance" to these historians in the face of their own evidence produces a positive portrait as well as a harsh critique. Rather than exhibiting the municipal bourgeois autonomy of the public sphere, city life is riven by exclusions and conflicts drawn along ethnic, provincial, native-place, and sectarian lines. City life, in other words, is very close to rural life, and in particular to what Duara has called "the cultural nexus of power" in his book on North Chinese villages during the Republican period.[4] Thus we are back to Duara. The concept of "the cultural nexus" is a welcome addition to our analytic vocabulary, not least because it finally gives some legitimacy to something that historians and scholars of Chinese religion have long understood but that has been ignored or deemed irrelevant by those who focus on the gentry and on Confucianism.

"The cultural nexus" is defined as the set of segmentary hierarchies (lineages, markets), territorial hierarchies (temple cults), interpersonal networks (patron-client, master-disciple relationships), and voluntary associations (irrigation societies, guilds, spirit-writing cults). What is striking about the cultural nexus is that however secular all these hierarchies, networks, and associations may appear, they converge and diverge among themselves around temples, altars, and monasteries. The cultural nexus of power is more specifically a religious nexus, and might be so designated if the word "religious" were not thought to be somewhat old-fashioned.

Duara's conclusion—an important but not uncontroversial one— is that this cultural nexus was effectively destroyed first by Nationalist and then by Communist state-building during the second, third, and fourth decades of the twentieth century. This is another point on which Wakeman agrees with Duara: temples were replaced by police boxes.[5] Whether this initial destruction of the cultural nexus also destroyed a civil society is another matter (discussed below).

An emphasis on the cultural nexus, and on state-building, has many great advantages from our point of view. The greatest of these is that it gets us away from the gentry model of Chinese society that has guided research in pre-modern Chinese history for so long. (More accurately, it gets some of us historians away from this model, because others of us have never subscribed to it.) The gentry model insists that the gentry—consonant with their character as both a state-derived status group and a local land-holding economic class—were the mediators between state and society. And it insists that the gentry's ideology, Confucianism—consonant with its character as both *the* check on state autocracy and *the* source of a sense of responsibility for social welfare—was the hinge on which the stability and coherence of state-society relations depended.

The trouble with the gentry model (and not simply "the trouble with Confucianism") is not that it is wrong but that it is the view of the Chinese order most hospitable to the gentry themselves, and to their heirs—namely, the deracinated intellectuals of the Republic and their modern-day descendants. For those historians who have focused on the vagaries of gentry mediation *ad nauseam*, the trouble with this view is that it has taken the nature of Chinese society entirely for granted. Among these historians, Chinese society is of interest only to the extent that members of the gentry elite are seen as arresting or contributing to the private engrossment of land (and therefore to the enrichment or impoverishment of the state on the one hand and of the peasantry on the other). This is not an inconsequential matter, but in other respects the nature of society has remained largely unexamined. According to these historians, religion manifests itself only when debt-ridden tenants or hired laborers need a justification for rebellion. The advantage of the cultural nexus is that it throws the spotlight back on society and reveals that society to be what the

Chinese word for "society" once literally meant: an altar to the Earth God (*shehui*).

From our point of view, there are two weaknesses in Duara's account of the cultural nexus. The first is that Duara overstates the imperial metaphor and extends it throughout the nexus. He argues that the system of authority in the cultural nexus emanated not from one or the other of two parallel bureaucracies—a supernatural bureaucracy and a human one—but from "one cosmic universal bureaucracy," such that an official had power over the gods of a lower rank and performed rites only to gods of a higher rank. In this one cosmic bureaucracy, the supernatural and human bureaucracies interpenetrated each other to such an extent that a magistrate might be seen thrashing an uncooperative City God, just as villagers might neglect a Dragon God who failed to answer prayers for rain.[6]

The problem here is that although Duara asserts that this one cosmic bureaucracy extended through all levels of the nexus, his only two examples concern officials. It is not at all clear to me either that the power of village divinities derived from their rank within a bureaucratic hierarchy or that a magistrate's public thrashing of an uncooperative City God was the same thing as the neglect of a Dragon God who failed to answer prayers for rain. In the first case, the City God is thrashed because he failed to perform the role expected of its rank as an official. In the second case, however, the people withdraw their support because the god lacks *ling* (magical power).

Duara does admit that "this interpretation of a common underlying fount of authority in Chinese religion is not incompatible with significant differences in meanings and beliefs, and we will soon see how the various interpretations of a particular myth reflected as many different social interests."[7] In other words, there is one "fount of authority," the one cosmic bureaucracy, but many interpretations of it. Yet this manages to finesse the problem of difference because it presumes that a single cosmic bureaucracy is indeed a given, or a fact, when it may very well be one more meaning or belief or interpretation that differentiates one segment of society or one set of interests from another.

There is a second weakness in Duara's presentation of the cultural nexus of power. Although Duara is always careful to put "the nation" in quotation marks, to suggest, as he says, "that thinking of the nation as pre-existing in this mode—as a carrier of values of modernity—is problematic,"[8] he does not do the same for the "public sphere" or "civil society." Thus while he wants to "rescue history from the nation," he seems to want to restore civil society to history.

Duara strongly implies, if he does not state outright, that the cultural nexus of power was a potential civil society, in that it shared with an actual civil society the power to preserve the autonomy of society with respect to, and to curb the autocratic centralism of, the state. I agree that the cultural nexus shares this characteristic with civil society. He also argues, following an essay by Charles Taylor, that a strong but not autocratic state is necessary to guarantee the autonomy of civil society, and that what destroyed the civil society in China in the early decades of the twentieth century was not the state-building project per se but "the absence of a strong state capable of providing legal guarantees for civil society that ultimately had the effect of excluding societal initiative." Rather, a weak state that could not keep law and order was replaced by a strong statist ideology that "ended up de-forming and de-mobilizing civil society."[9] As a piece of historical analysis, I agree wholeheartedly. What is troubling is the rhetoric—and, ultimately, the logic.

Let us start from the last sentence. Duara has written an entire book encouraging us to deconstruct the Hegelian concept of the nation as the subject of History because the nation is a metaphysical entity that assumes its self-same identity even as it is transformed. But now, when he says that a strong statist ideology "ended up de-forming and de-mobilizing civil society," isn't he assuming the existence of a civil society that is to be de-formed and de-mobilized? And isn't "civil society" also one of Hegel's central metaphysical concepts?

Moving backward, Duara claims that China "lacked a strong state capable of providing legal guarantees for civil society," but a few sentences later he asks us to "qualify the determinist judgment that the absence of a Western-style legal and individualist tradition denied the possibility of an ideology of societal autonomy and initiative that checked the untrammeled expansion of state power."[10] Yet if a strong state that provides legal guarantees is necessary for a civil society, how can these legal guarantees be unnecessary when it is a civil society that one wants? Moreover, in the place of these legal guarantees, Duara offers the Chinese "tradition of literary autonomy," justified by "political feudalism," as precisely such an alternative "ideology of societal autonomy that checked the untrammeled expansion of state power." But

again, one could make a strong argument that it was precisely this tradition of literary autonomy and political feudalism that cannibalized
the state in the late nineteenth century through gentry-led militias and
tax-farming, thus ensuring only that the state would not be able to guarantee anything, much less a legal protection of civil society.

Finally—and here we come to the central issue—"the cultural
nexus of power" does share with civil society the characteristic of defending its autonomy against state power, but this similarity is entirely
formal. The fact that the two share this characteristic does not make
the cultural nexus a civil society or even potentially such a society. This
is why Duara makes no attempt to define civil society with any historical specificity or content, but merely considers it in its relation, both
dependent and oppositional, to the state, just as he guts modern nationalism by modeling it on a relation between self and others. Thus
we should adopt enthusiastically Duara's notion of the cultural nexus
but be very wary of its association with civil society, potential or actual.

Our notion of the cultural nexus can be refined by contrasting it
with civil society, but let me do this by first comparing it with what
Ernest Gellner has called "segmentary society," and what I would call
more broadly "agrarian bureaucratic empires." Segmentary societies
are characteristic of those agrarian empires that prevailed in river val-
leys where a sedentary, immobilized peasantry was easily vanquished,
disarmed, and subjected to a marked concentration of power and ex-
ploitation by a conquering ethnos or elite. But, as Gellner says, these
conditions do not prevail everywhere—nor, I might add, everywhere
equally or at the same time. Given the limitations of pre-modern tech-
nology and infrastructure, the imposition, and particularly the extension, of centralizing despotism is not a simple matter, and it is far
easier to allow local communities to administer themselves as long as
they supply produce and labor on pain of punishment. Therefore, in
these agrarian empires one finds "internally well-organized self-ad-
ministering and partly or wholly autonomous sub-communities" that
are also highly pluralistic and centralization-resistant.[11]

This high degree of pluralism and resistance to centralization is also
a characteristic of civil society, and it is this similarity, I believe, that
misleads those who argue for its potential or actual presence in China,
for here the similarities end. Although segmentary society can resist
centralization and the tyranny of kings, it does so (and can, perhaps,
only do so) at the cost of another tyranny: the subjugation of the in-

dividual to obligations of a familial, social, economic, and military nature in which all these spheres of obligation are superimposed on one another in a single idiom—an idiom that is held together and continually reinforced by ritual and the proliferation of rules. It subjugates the individual, in other words, to the cultural nexus of power.

For those who think that it is not a question of "subjugation," or even of "the individual," and for those who offer an alternative, nonindividualist conception of the Chinese self (legitimately, I might add), recall that such societies are equally characterized by a rampant clientism and by the opportunistic cultivation of personal connections. In such a society there are so many ways to go wrong, to fail to meet one's obligations of one kind or another, that it is essential to create a private fund of goodwill that one can draw on in the face of inevitable transgressions. Transgressions are inevitable not only because there are so many obligations but because the spheres of obligation overlap to such an extent that fulfilling one obligation brings one into conflict with another. In such a society, the individual person is under extreme pressure. This is why we also find a well-developed tradition of magic and the proliferation of magical therapies in such societies. These therapies are meant to defend the person against the sub-community and to cure him or her of illnesses that, it can be conclusively demonstrated, are a direct result either of the failure to meet one's group obligations or of harboring, even temporarily, a desire not to meet them. And just as particular conceptions of the self generate particular illnesses, so we might say that clientism, favoritism, and corruption are endemic to traditional and modern Chinese society because the ideologies of obligation refused, or were unable to find, a beneficial, legitimate role for private interest. Private interest (*si*) was always an illicit, partial, and selfish invasion of the public domain (*gong*). The result, in Wakeman's felicitous phrase, was a "sensible hypocrisy" that tolerated "moral speakeasies for officials on the take."[12]

From "Cultural Nexus" to "Syncretic Field"

Let me now proceed directly to a consideration of how we might refine the concept of "the cultural nexus of power." Duara calls this a "cultural" nexus because the nexus of hierarchies, networks, and associations converges and diverges around temples and is entirely underwritten by symbols (and, I would add, religious rituals). The problem is with what I have indicated to be the first weakness in Duara's account—his collapse of two parallel bureaucracies into one, and its extension throughout the nexus. These interpretive moves are made on far too little evidence, and the evidence he does offer is flimsy at best. If we were really dealing with one cosmic bureaucracy, we would expect to find some peasants paying their taxes with spirit-money and others burning copper coins for the gods. This is not trivial, but let me return to Duara's analogy between the magistrate publicly thrashing the City God and the withdrawal of popular support from the Dragon God. This, as I have said, is not really analogous: the City God is punished because he failed to perform what was expected of his role; the Dragon God is ignored because he lacks magical power. The difference is revealing and suggests the limits of the extension of the cosmic bureaucracy as well as the different principles by which segmentary sub-communities defend themselves against the state.

Indeed, there was a supernatural hierarchy that extended from one of various supreme divinities to the City Gods in the towns, and thence to the "Altars of the Land and Grain" (*sheji tan*) and "Altars to Those who Died [without Issue]" (*li tan*) in the countryside. This hierarchy roughly corresponded to the territorial divisions of imperial administration, and like its worldly counterpart, it was not really a bureaucracy but a status hierarchy of roles and obligations. The emphasis, as Stephan Feuchtwang has pointed out, was on conformity and harmony: conformity to the duties or obligations germane to a particular status, and harmony that is both a sign and result of such conformity.[13]

Now, I suggest, continuing to follow the work of Feuchtwang, that the cults that define each of the various hierarchies, networks, and associations of the cultural nexus are underwritten by a very different principle—a principle based not on the moral obligations relative to a position within a status hierarchy, but on the efficacy of the gods relative to boundaries that distinguish smaller from larger spatial units. These spatial units include the household, wards, and neighborhoods—areas defined by the division of domestic or temple incense, by festival processions, by regions of a town, and by region of origin. All these spatial units, which are also cult units, overlap to varying degrees, which is why they form a nexus, but there are several features that distinguish them from a status hierarchy, not to mention a bureaucracy:

*The boundaries that mark a cultic unit are not coterminous
with administrative or even marketing hierarchies.* The principle of a god's *ling* (magical power) is traced along pro-
cessional or pilgrimage routes that do not coincide with
administrative units and that are not extensions of the
lowest level of administration. In fact, the smallest units
of the cultural nexus are produced by the division of
household or temple incense, and more often than not
represent a new settlement beyond the administrative
or marketing area.

*The nexus of cults lacks both ultimate centralization and
a single unified cult or territorial entity.* Simply put, there
is no apex of the cultural nexus. The rituals and gods
of the nexus do not find their "fount of authority" in or
from a hierarchy, but appeal directly :o the highest god
of the unit, regardless of whether that is an Earth God,
an apical ancestor, a salvational god, or even Heaven.
Thus the highest god of the unit is a territorial patron.
The magical power that protects a territory marked by a
festival, procession, or pilgrimage defines itself directly
in relation to its neighbors, not as a unit in a nested
hierarchy; it is considered aberrant and potentially
subversive by all regimes because its organization may
be substituted for the central political channels.

*Finally, these gods define boundaries of inclusion and exclu-
sion that are produced by rituals of communion and exorcism
(rituals of alimentary sacrifice) and pervaded by a highly militaristic structure of command.* Territoriality in the nexus
is the marking of borders that distinguish inside from
outside and protection from invasion, whereas territoriality in the official system is a nested hierarchy of status
positions with boundaries (or responsibilities and jurisdictions) that are not clearly defined.[14]

· The militaristic, exorcistic nature of the gods, rituals, and festivals
of the cultural nexus has not been adequately recognized or explored.
History provides one reason for this. As Alexander Woodside remarks, the more richly developed and scholastic Confucianism be-

came, "the less capable it seemed to be of working out a legitimate permanent role for military men in the Chinese political system. . . . Emperors like Qianlong deliberately segregated soldiers from the world of literacy and learning, thus reinforcing their moral marginality."[15] This moral marginality, this preference for *wen* over *wu*, accounts for the marginality of military men and ideas as a subject of historical research, to the extent that historians have shared this literary bias. It also accounts for the overvaluation of the imperial or bureaucratic metaphor with respect to the cultural nexus, and for the misapprehension of the cultural nexus as a potential civil society.

One of the primary distinctions between civil and segmentary societies is the degree of military centralization. Coercive centralization is just as necessary as political centralization to the functioning of civil society, to guaranteeing its economic and ideological pluralism. The pluralism of segmentary societies, however, also extends to the sphere of coercion and order-maintenance.[16] This is evident in the long Chinese tradition of rural militias, gentry-led or not, in the peasant associations of the protective/predatory type, and in such groups as the Taipings and Boxers. The diffusion of coercion and order-maintenance throughout the system is the correlative of the exorcistic military nature of the gods, rituals, and processions of the nexus. In the nexus, the power of the emperor and his officials, in addition to that of the gods, may be viewed as more lethal than moral.

The status hierarchy, which seeks harmony through the interiorization of obligation, and the economy of magical power, which seeks protection or the integrity of boundaries through the exteriorization of exorcistic ritual, exist in a state of dynamic tension. Restricting ourselves for the moment to our small repertory of examples, this tension is easily perceptible in the cult of the City God, one of a limited number of points of convergence between the cosmic bureaucracy and the economy of magical power.

As a point within the cosmic bureaucracy, City Gods are recognized by their position or title, "God of Walls and Moats." Their cults are established automatically in every town, and their position within an imperial purgatorial judiciary reflects their function of controlling orphan-souls who are understood to be analogous to the subject masses. As a point within the economy of magical power, however, City Gods are identified with the name of a deified human being; their cults are established by the division of temple incense; and their participation

in a temple procession reflects their function as a territorial protector assisted by spirit-soldiers who are understood to be analogous to
local militiamen.

The tension between the cosmic bureaucracy and the economy of
magical power constitutes the context or framework of the cultural
nexus and should be carefully distinguished from the routine activities or repetitious practices of compromise and conflict that this context helps reproduce. The failure to distinguish formative contexts and
formed routines helps explain why many interpreters (particularly
those beholden to a discursive, hermeneutic, or deconstructionist approach) mistakenly overvalue the extent of the cosmic bureaucracy
or view the two principles of the nexus as different interpretations of
the same data. In times of routine compromise, such as the anniversary festival and temple procession of the City God, the principle of
magical power is rendered largely invisible because those local territorial deities participating in the procession appear to be subsumed
within a hierarchy. This routine compromise is then mistaken for the
entirety of the formative context. In times of routine conflict, however,
the two principles are rendered highly visible—and visibly antagonistic. For example, when a magistrate attempts to subsume a local tutelary divinity within the hierarchy—say by destroying the altar to an Earth
God or moving his effigy into the temple of the City God—these actions are successfully resisted by the irruption of spirit-possession,
which is a demonstration of the Earth God's magical power.

Even in cases of routine compromise, our interpretation can go seriously wrong if we fail to distinguish such cases from the formative
context. For example, at the end of Chapter 3, I translated and commented on a remarkable report of a village spirit-medium whose spirit-
soldier was called away by the City God to defend the region against
the invading Jurchens, resulting in the medium's inability to practice
his therapeutic art. The temptation is to interpret this as an example
of the extension of the cosmic bureaucracy, or of bureaucratic control, to the lower level of the cultural nexus. But if we better appreci-
ated the distinction between the formative context and formed routine, we would be able to see in this episode that the City God himself
is occupying a point within the economy of magical power, not a point
within the cosmic bureaucracy. The magical power of the City God is
defending a region with boundaries larger than those of the spirit-
medium's tutelary divinity. The magical power of the latter is mo-

mentarily trumped, but not permanently lost or sublimated or transformed. The tutelary deity's power is, in fact, conserved and returned
once the military crisis is over.

The formative context of the cultural nexus is therefore defined by
the tension between hierarchy and efficacy. In his recent exhaustive
monograph on the Three-in-One religion in Fujian, Kenneth Dean
presents the most sophisticated adumbration of this formative context
yet attempted by any student of Chinese society.[17] Dean calls the formative context the "syncretic field"—another happy addition to our
conceptual vocabulary. Like the earlier metaphor of a nexus, the
metaphor of a field has a number of advantages, not the least of which
is that it addresses the weaknesses in earlier formulations of the nexus
itself. As a description of the formative context, the syncretic field demands that we set our sights on "ritual events" rather than on institutions or texts. It argues that just as an inventory and typology of local
religious institutions, no matter how comprehensive, is inadequate as
a representation of the formative context, so an interpretation of religious discourse, however sophisticated, is neither transparently meaningful nor an adequate reflection of the institutional typology. Rather,
between institutions and text, just as between things and words, there
will always be a gap of desire that is only actualized in ritual events and
that can only be captured in the study of actual performances.

By shifting our attention to ritual events, Dean implicitly puts the
lie to C. K. Yang's still influential distinction between organized and
diffused religion, and to those who take this distinction as a model for
differentiating elite from popular culture.[18] Popular religion is diffused
only in a precise and positive sense: it is characterized by a "multiplicity
of spiritual manifestations" and seeks to maximize the forms that supernatural or magical power can take. As Dean remarks, in the syncretic field, the more manifestations of supernatural power, the better. But popular religion is not diffused in the sense of unorganized,
disorganized, or even less organized. Far from it: as a field of ritual
events, the syncretic field is both highly organized and, more importantly, self-organizing and autonomous.

Dean offers us a sketch of the parameters within which this self-
organization transpires. Briefly put, the parameters consist of spatial
planes and temporal flows that intersect at various points along a vertical axis defined by its two poles. The two poles are *sheng* (Confucian
sagehood) and *ling* (magical power/immediate efficacious spiritual

power), which correspond precisely to what we have defined as the two principles of the cultural nexus.

Sheng is "the embodiment of cosmic hierarchies" and "the exemplification of moral conduct." It seeks to channel all manifestations of material/spiritual power, including desire and sexuality, within the Confucian ideal of *ren*. I would like to translate *ren*, which is normally rendered as "humanity" or "benevolence," as "hierarchical solidarity," and offer it here for serious consideration as a supplement to the organic and mechanical forms of solidarity discovered by Durkheim.[19] *Ren* denotes that substance, or substantial connectedness, that subtends a vision of order and social regulation based on hierarchies achieved through ritualized relationships (*li*) and exemplified in filial piety (*xiao*) and loyal devotion (*zhong*).

Ling, in contrast, is "the imposition of supernatural power or efficacy into actualized resolutions." These actualized resolutions are ritual events, including dramatic acts of spirit-possession in which the priest or medium channels supernatural power and concentrates it in *any* spot in time or space. This "any spot" is not a position relative to other positions within a hierarchy but "a center appropriately oriented to a greater concentration of power on a transcendent plane."[20]

Where the polar attractor of Confucian sagehood is characterized by differentiation and exemplification, that of magical efficacy is characterized by nondifferentiation and identification. Where Confucian sagehood represents the forces of fusion whereby the various levels of the cultural nexus coalesce in a nested hierarchy of temples, magical power represents the forces of fission whereby this nested hierarchy is disrupted by everything from manifestations of supernatural power to the division of incense, thus pulling the various levels of the nexus toward the household or the *she* (altar of the Earth God), which are the smallest units in the syncretic field. Where Confucian sagehood is characterized by "hierarchical solidarity," the economy of magical power is characterized by an "organic hybridity" that we might describe as the continual production of new forms of collective religious experimentation defined by doctrinal syncretism and joint worship.

The "Syncretic Field" in the Song Dynasty

My own field of exploration—therapeutic ritual and its practitioners and clients in twelfth-century China—makes up a particular cross section of the syncretic field. This cross section includes a set of cultic units (spatial parameters) that can be situated along a vertical axis defined by the poles of efficacy and hierarchy, and that consists, from smaller to larger units, of (1) the *she* (but also rural monasteries), (2) village temple cults (but also ancestral shrines), and (3) temple networks (but also higher-order lineages).

The *she* has appeared in the present volume in the guise of "altars of trees and stones" (*congci*), the name given since the mid-Tang to the Earth God shrines of villages in South China. These shrines were served by spirit-mediums, and their tutelary divinities were called "Spirits of the Five Penetrations" (*wutong shen*). Hong Mai gives us a classic description:

> South of the Great River [the Yangzi], the land is mountainous and the popular custom is to worship demons—numinous prodigies that are extremely treacherous and eccentric. Many people construct natural altars (*congci*) using stones and trees and all the villages have one. In Zhejiang, the spirits are called *wutong*; in Jiangxi and Fujian, they are called *muxia sanlang* or *muke*.[21]

The rest of Hong Mai's long description lists the many forms of possession induced by contact with these spirits. He states that all who become possessed by these spirits initially become sad, emaciated, and dilatory, but that some "turn around" and become spirit-mediums; these are called "transcendents" (*xian*), and their initial symptoms are termed the "illness of transcendents." By the Southern Song, many of these cults became linked with rural monasteries, a fact reflected in the very name of these tutelary spirits, for the Spirits of the Five Penetrations are gods, or those who embody them, who possess the five supernatural powers of the Buddha.

Village temple cults have appeared here in the guise of territorial cults to Daoist and Buddhist divinities. Sometimes we have encountered these temple cults in their institutional form, as site of devotion or exorcism, but most often as they were inscribed in the scriptures or rituals of Daoist and Buddhist exorcists. The scriptures and rituals of all the Daoist and Buddhist Ritual Masters described in Chapters 2 through 7 were organized exclusively around the local temple cults to one or more martial divinities—Zhenwu, the Black Killer, Ucchuṣma, Nezha, and so on. The names and attributes of these martial deities, along with instructions about how to manipulate or identify with them, formed the exclusive content of the scriptures. These instructions, moreover, were passed down from a divine patriarch and a human transmitter, the latter most often identified with the late Tang or Five Dynasties period. The space occupied by village temple cults is also the space of ancestral graves and halls, and of the creation of descent groups through the production of genealogies and instructions. Although these descent groups have not been a concern here, we might usefully compare their genealogical focus on a distant mythical ancestor and a more recent pioneering ancestor (again, most often associated with the late Tang or Five Dynasties period) to the genealogies of the Daoist exorcistic lineages.

Temple networks have appeared in this book in the guise of Daoist and Buddhist rituals for the dead. My concern with these rituals has been restricted, on the one hand, to the experience of individuals and their families, and, on the other, to the broad structural features that these rituals shared with exorcism. But these delimited concerns should not blind us to the fact that these were ritual extravaganzas lasting several days, performed by dozens of priests and monks on the anniversary of the god, in settings that ranged from large-scale community temples in cities and market towns to suburban monasteries. The expenses incurred for such events were met by subscription and overseen by a manager, a reflection of the fact that the temple networks occupy a space whose identity is largely determined by the flow of capital.

These ritual events were also the occasion for processions in which the gods, priests, and residents of outlying neighborhoods or villages would make their way. These processions were in turn reflected in the divine pantheons of the rituals themselves, which were characterized by a vast hierarchy that extended from the high gods of Daoism and Buddhism through the god of the temple or monastery itself, his retinue of martial deities and spirit-generals, and thence to the Earth Gods, water deities, orphan-souls, and ancestral spirits of the outlying neighborhoods or villages. In such large-scale rituals we can see the outline of the temple networks that are described more concretely in the secular sources of the Yuan and Ming dynasties.

When we consider this cross section of cultic units within the temporal parameters defined by the Southern Song, two overwhelming facts deserve emphasis: the independence of local cultural forces, and the mediation of Buddhism. The Earth God shrines and village temple cults were proliferating everywhere at the same time that the latter were extending beyond the village and beginning the long process of individuation and alliance that produced overlapping temple networks. This proliferation and process was autonomous and self-organizing. The temple cults contested village cults to water deities and other officially recognized shrines on the one hand, and outgrew the village-based temples on the other.

These developments were, moreover, independent of the state. The intensifying conflict between officials and "illicit cults," described in Chapter 3, is *prima facie* evidence for this independence, as is the Southern Song canonization process, which must be seen as the fortuitous response of a regime (desirous of transforming religious control into legitimation) to the local initiative of one or two rich patrons (desirous of transforming their wealth into status). But the few cults that were lucky enough to get themselves "hierarchically inscribed" were just the tip of a cultural iceberg whose subsurface mass was burgeoning in response to the flow of capital rather than to desires of the state. Much later, the first Ming emperor would attempt to impose a hierarchy on the temple networks as part of his comprehensive administrative reorganization of local society. This effort collapsed within fifty years, however, and its cornerstone—the *sheji tan* that were to mediate between the village cults and the City God temples—mutated from official shrines into community temples (*shemiao*) that became the building blocks of the temple networks.[22]

The independence of local cultural forces is also apparent in the articulation of extended higher-order lineages that developed among those who were experimenting with new forms of ancestor worship. These higher-order lineages circulated around the worship of an apical Tang-dynasty ancestor of the Central Plains, a pioneering or immigrant ancestor of the ninth, tenth, or eleventh centuries, and his meritorious descendants. It was the literary distinction or examination success of these descendants in the eleventh, twelfth, or early thirteenth centuries that inspired such retrospective constructions. These constructions, in turn, sparked a Chinese version of the debate between Ancients and Moderns—between, as Dean has suggested, those who upheld the classical limitation of ancestor worship to five generations and those who defended their ritual experiments by appealing to the intentional, rather than normative, basis of ritual itself (*li yi yi qi*).[23]

The appeal to intention can already be found among the innovators of ancestor worship, whose merit-cloisters and tomb worship were mediated by Buddhist professionals. As we saw at the beginning of Chapter 8, when the lineage members of the minister Huang Lao of Jiangxi collectively rose up to oppose his son's attempt to exclude Buddhist and Daoist priests from his father's funeral, the mid-thirteenth-century Neo-Confucian Yu Wenbao remarked that, although the use of Buddhist and Daoist priests was both foreign and vulgar, it nevertheless expressed the sincerity and filiality of their intent. Yu Wenbao evidently hoped that this intent would be expressed in exclusively Confucian terms. For the most part, his hopes were realized.

In the Ming, the higher-order lineages not only became disarticulated from Buddhist or Daoist mediation (in contrast to the networks of temple cults that were moving in the opposite direction), but became the principal agents of land reclamation and irrigation maintenance, and slowly but methodically took over the landholdings of the Buddhist monasteries as well. By the end of the sixteenth century, monastic estates had declined in large parts of the Southeast from more than 30 percent of the total taxable property to less than 5 percent of it. Dean argues that the ritual reconstruction of lineages had achieved such a degree of consensus and confidence that these lineages no longer needed Buddhist mediation to justify the breaches in orthodoxy that such reconstruction had once entailed. If we appreciate that Buddhist mediation was not viewed as a cover for unorthodox practice at the time, this explanation seems perfectly sound. It does not explain, however, how these lineages were able to commandeer so much temple land. Certainly this did not happen overnight. The explanation, I believe, must be sought in the changing relationship between the *sangha* (monastic community) and local society after the Tang.

By the Southern Song, Buddhist institutions were themselves proliferating and becoming majority, if small-holding and tax-paying, landowners in large parts of the Southeast.[24] And each of the institutional and ritual foci of local society—the officially recognized cults of the irrigation systems, the temple festivals and sacrificial halls of single-lineage settlements, and the more isolated academies—reveals links with the monastery: Kanai Noriyuki has described the link between water deities and monasteries, while he and other scholars are now exposing those between Buddhist temples and the tutelary divinities of the Earth God shrines and village-based temples; Buddhist

"merit-cloisters" and "stewards" were defining features of the new experiments in ancestor worship, and extended from the eleventh century well into the fourteenth, as has now been demonstrated by
Miyamoto Noriyuki; and finally, as we learn from a recent series of ar-
ticles by Linda Walton, the academies, while exclusively Confucian in
curriculum and nativist in spirit, borrowed their institutional and cultic morphology directly from the monasteries and the Buddhist construction of the spiritual lineage.[25]

Although Buddhism has not been an exclusive or even organizing
focus of my investigations, it has loomed progressively larger as these
investigations concentrated more and more on rural and suburban
practitioners and their clients. The exorcistic and mortuary rituals of
the Daoist therapeutic lineages of the Southern Song have testified to
the pull of Buddhism. When the Daoist missionaries of the Celestial
Master lineage of Grand Protector Wen set out from Jiangxi to Fujian,
they confronted an entirely Buddhist landscape. Allowing for hyper-
bole, the organizations encountered by these Daoists are evidence of
the mediation of village festivals and ancestor worship by Buddhism.
Buddhism provided a point of orientation that Daoist practitioners recognized not only through differentiation and demonization, but
through assimilation and hybridization as well. This is not to say that
this point of orientation was itself an unmoving center of gravity. The
relation of the *sangha* to local society was also changing, but this is better addressed by taking a broader view of religious change.

The evidence is complex and would require a detailed exposition.
What seems clear to me at this point is that, in the Tang, the constitution of Chinese Buddhism around the institution of the lineage and
its focus on speculative, mystical, and/or soteriological issues had rein-
troduced a marked distinction between monks and laity. One manifestation of this distance was that in matters of patronage—which is
to say, in matters that concerned the organization and solicitation of
funds for the construction of temple buildings and for the performance of rituals—the abbots and monks took a decisive leadership
role with respect to their lay constituency. In the Song this lay deference to clerical direction begins to dissipate, if not reverse, and we find
over and over again not only that it is rural "landlords," "elders," or
"tax-paying households" who are taking the leadership role in monastic reconstruction or the solicitation of funds, but also that these village households refused to participate unless the monks themselves

showed a willingness to fill monastic vacancies with monks who had received their ordination locally.[26] The monks, in other words, were losing control over their own membership. The conclusion we must reach, therefore, is that even the mediation of local temple cults and lineage institutions by the monastery in the Song must be seen as part of the deference of the monastery to the surrounding villages, and that this shift laid the groundwork for regarding Buddhist mediation as ultimately dispensable—and Buddhist estates as ultimately exploitable.

The colonization of the *sangha* by the village underwrites the principal findings of my long chapter on Buddhist exorcists (see Chapter 6). In marked contrast to the exorcistic tradition of the Tang—the refined and courtly rites of *āveśa* that also confirmed the distance of monks from laymen—that tradition as practiced in the Song opened itself wide to the influences of village religion. The children recruited for Buddhist exorcism came from village households with which the monks were on intimate terms. Moreover, the characteristic practices of these village "divination youths" set the tone for the exorcisms. The monks, for their part, were becoming indistinguishable from Daoist Ritual Masters, either as foci of lay exorcistic associations of village adults or as officiants and initiators of village boys. And finally, the Buddhist involvement in village religion strongly influenced the village cults and ritual practices of both the Daoist Ritual Master and the traditional village spirit-medium (*wu*).

Thus we might conclude our discussion of the temporal aspect of the syncretic field by proposing that Song Buddhism was becoming more akin to Daoism, in the sense that both monks and priests were increasingly defined by their function as ritual experts responsive to the tastes, and dependent on the needs, of their lay constituencies. If there was a weakness to Buddhism in the Song, it was an institutional one, and this was less a consequence of the persecution of the ninth century than of an "institutional compromise" entailed in the construction during the Tang of the great lineages of Sinitic Mahāyāna (Tiantai, Huayan, Pure Land, and Chan)—a compromise that left the monastic community unable to respond to the great persecution in the same way that it had turned previous bans into opportunities.

The syncretic field is so named in part because it is subject to what Dean terms "collective experimentation." Dean has devised this category to describe forms of religious organization, such as the Three-

in-One religion of Lin Zhao'en or the sectarian religions of the sixteenth century, that transcended and traversed the temple networks.
But Dean also speaks of the plane of collective experimentation as a
plane of hybridization—of doctrinal syncretism and joint worship. Collective experimentation would therefore be, by definition, a characteristic of the syncretic field itself and, by logical inference, a characteristic of any particular plane within that field. In the context of my
investigations, collective experimentation or hybridization has appeared in several guises. The first and most obvious of these was the
creation of a milieu of lay exorcists, or Ritual Masters, in which elements of Daoism, Buddhism, and the village religion of spirit-mediums
all converged. From the perspective of ritual events, the Daoist Ritual
Master, the Buddhist monk, the village spirit-medium, and even the
Daoist priest all formed elliptical orbits around possessed children. The
trajectory of each individual orbit, moreover, was determined in large
part by the variety and frequency with which it intersected the other
orbits—points of cultural hybridization in which any given ritual element of one type of religious practitioner has been shown to be a characteristic of one or more of the others.

This form of cultural hybridization was reflected just as much in
the scriptures of these religious practitioners as in the local institutions
to which they were attached. The scriptures of the Daoist Ritual Masters or Tantric exorcists, for example, were saturated with the practical and discursive forms of the others (doctrinal syncretism), while the
pantheons of divinities and spiritual powers of any given lineage of
Daoist or Buddhist exorcists reflected the precise configuration of divinities of local temple cults (joint worship). We have encountered
numerous divinities, moreover, with three or even four forms, corresponding to the fact that the practitioner who called upon them
might be a priest, monk, ritual master, or spirit-medium. Moreover,
there is a direct link between these forms of cultural hybridization—
denigrated in the thirteenth century by Bo Yuchan as "mixed" or
"confused"—and the later appearance of such religious traditions as
the Sannai jiao, or of practitioners who will be called "neither Daoist
nor Buddhists."

This cultural hybridization has been accompanied in my work by a
kind of methodological hybridization. Instead of viewing any given cultural practice as exemplary of "Chinese culture," instead of taking the
part for the whole, I have chosen to place one cultural practice in re-

lation to another, to place a part in a certain relation to another part. Thus, in Chapter 5, Daoist therapeutic ritual was placed in relation to judicial trials and to theatrical performances, while in Chapter 8, Daoist mortuary ritual was placed in relation to classical ancestral ritual and to Tang- and Song-dynasty seances of spirit-mediums, and then in relation to the Daoist Rites of Summoning for Investigation of Chapter 5. In both these instances, chiasmus has replaced synecdoche as my primary trope, in an attempt to avoid the twin faults of essentialism and totalization. In both instances as well, the relation between the first cultural practice and the others—whether that relation is synchronic or diachronic—is one in which the first may be said to "reoccupy" the space of the others.

This reoccupation of space, a lesson learned from Hans Blumenberg, is meant to avoid the false choice between the continuity and discontinuity of cultural forms in history. Blumenberg's "reoccupation thesis" was devised to counter the "secularization thesis" according to which the modern Western idea of progress is simply a disguised version of medieval Christian eschatology. Rather, the Moderns reoccupied the position created by their inheritance of a set of medieval questions, although in answering these questions they attempted solutions that were legitimately new. History is indeed discontinuous—if there are re-occupations there are also vacancies—but these discontinuities are not absolute.[27] Blumenberg's "reoccupation thesis," by the way, should prove attractive to historians of Neo-Confucianism who have been locked in an unproductive debate between those who maintain Neo-Confucianism's radical discontinuity with China's medieval religious past and those who dismiss it as nothing more than a Confucianized Buddhism.

Before leaving the question of methodology, it should be admitted that, by itself, the replacement of synecdoche by chiasmus does not eliminate the threat of essentializing or totalizing views of culture. Letting the part speak for the whole can easily return by the back door if, along with Geertz, one goes on to read a given cultural practice as revelatory of the behavioral codes or logic of "society," or if, along with the poststructuralists, one collapses history into the text or into discourse.

For those who follow the radical Foucault, the dream of increasing emancipation in the "modern" narrative of progressive emergence is simply replaced with a nightmare of increasing control in a "modern" narrative of infinite containment. The costs of this kind of discourse itself are too high. One must dispense with the possibility of an effective opposition and accept that power is everywhere but nowhere *in particular.* Foucault has asked us to consider "power without a king," but even he has to acknowledge that the "humanity" that subjected man to new forms of inhuman practices once denoted a new space of power in opposition to the king. Must we always have to choose between the concentration of power and its dispersal? Must we always have to infer causes from effects? If we do, then one result will be to see the imperial metaphor everywhere in Chinese society, leaving the opposition to pick up the shards of what this metaphor represses or excludes. If we do, another result will be to construct a monological narrative of Western modernity in which a very limited number of texts, say of Hegel or Marx, are allowed to speak for the whole—a narrative that can only be achieved by repressing what the poststructuralists themselves owe to modernity.

What the poststructuralists, and indeed all of us, owe to modernity, and particularly to the great social theorists of modernity, beginning with Marx, is the idea that "society is made and imagined, that it is a human artifact rather than an expression of an underlying natural order."[28] This discovery, which inspired the great projects of social transformation of this century (liberalism, socialism, and communism), was accompanied by another discovery, one that speaks to us today with equal force in light of the widely shared perception that these projects have been a disappointment, to say the least. This is the discovery that although society is a human artifact, human activity is constrained by the very structures it individually and collectively conspires to erect. As Marx wrote so eloquently, "Human beings make their own history, but they do not make it just as they please; they do not make it under circumstances chosen by themselves, but under circumstances directly encountered, given and transmitted from the past" (*The 18th Brumaire of Louis Bonaparte*). The recognition that men and women make history but not on their own terms is a recognition that all human activity is conditioned and therefore contextual. It is also a recognition that all contexts are also conditional, and that contexts should be treated for what they are—a context and not a natural order.

To say that all practical or conceptual activity is contextual is to say, following Roberto Unger, that this activity depends on taking for granted, *at least provisionally*, many beliefs that define its nature and limits—beliefs about validity, explanation, how the world really is, even the structure of thought and language. To say, however, that a context is a context and not a natural order is to say that all contexts can be broken, that the incongruous insight or deviant experiment—which seems only to be a distraction from, or to register some uncertainty about, the fundamentals of the established context—may become contagious, and the fundamentals go under.

As Unger reminds us, however, such context-breaking remains both exceptional and transitory. Either it fails and leaves the context in place, or it generates another context that can sustain it. Hence we can never overcome context-dependence. *But we can loosen it.* The reason we can do so is that all contexts of representation and relationship differ in the severity of the limits they impose on human activity (as in Sahlins' cold and hot societies). The more severe the context, or the more it is immunized from activities that bring it into question, the greater the contrast between the context-preserving routines of conflict and compromise and the kind of extraordinary transformative act that seems necessary to sweep it away. The less severe the context, or the more the context is treated as the human artifact that it is, the less the contrast between context-preserving and context-breaking activities. "The more a structure of thought or society incorporates the occasion and instrument of its own revision, the less you must choose between maintaining it and abandoning it for the thing it excludes."[29]

To gain a higher freedom from a context is neither to be free of a context, which is impossible, nor to seek some meta-context, some context of contexts, some context of universal scope that will only make whatever it is you want to explain a prisoner of the social ideals and ideal texts of the particular society in which you happen to be thrown. In their attempt to see all contexts as broken, breaking, or breakable under the aegis of a limited set of textual authorities, the postmodernists manage to commit, at one and the same time, what Unger calls the opposite sins—and theoretical errors—of iconoclasm and idolatry. Rather, to gain a higher freedom from a context is to make the context more malleable, to be reminded of the conditionality of all contexts, and to incorporate into the context itself the principles and provisions for its own revision. Only then can the contrast between context-preserving and context-breaking activities be diminished, and only then can a routine conflict within a context become the occasion for the transformation of the context itself.

My discussion of the syncretic field has taken seriously the contrast between the formative context and formed routines. It has also attempted to enlarge what we understand to be the context of a particular historical society, and to do so by incorporating the principle of the plasticity of the context. This plasticity is captured in the tension between *sheng* and *ling*, Confucian sagehood and magical power, hierarchy and efficacy, between fusion and fission, solidarity and hybridity, *wen* and *wu*. This tension has manifested itself variously in the course of this book. In Chapter 1, it was foreshadowed in the debate between Strickmann and Schipper about the nature of Daoism, and more explicitly adumbrated in the announcement of the focus of my investigations—the relations between three groups of religious practitioners (Daoist priests, Daoist and Buddhist Ritual Masters, and spirit-mediums) arranged from top to bottom along a vertical axis. In Chapter 3, I showed this axis to be defined by the poles of *sheng* and *ling*. On the one hand, there is the sage—the Daoist priest, the Gentleman of the Dao (*daoshi*), the incarnation of the classical *ru*—who concentrates in his person, through a regimen of ritual meditation and ethical ascesis, the cosmic principle, the One. On the other hand, there is the spirit-medium, who embodies in himself, through a demanding regime of trance and martial prowess, the magical power of a god. In one, the quotidian is transformed into a space of the absolute that will identify the community with the values of centrality and harmony; in the other, the quotidian is transformed into a space of conditioned power that will identify the community with the limits of that power, with defensible boundaries. In one we have texts (*wen*), in the other we have weapons (*wu*).

From an abstract point of view, it was the creative tension between *sheng* and *ling* that produced the Ritual Master, whose ritual practices combined elements of Daoist meditation with the trances of spirit-mediums, whose deities were humanized forms of cosmic and ethical principles that subsumed the raw martial power of the gods of the spirit-mediums, and whose recruitment came from both priests and mediums. The tension between *sheng* and *ling* does not respect the commonplace distinction between geographical centers and peripheries. In Chapter 4, we saw how the magical efficacy of a god, the Black Killer, was harnessed at the Song court both to the Mandate of Heaven and to the defense of imperial borders. Nor does it respect the commonplace distinction among the Three Teachings or between elite and popular culture or organized and diffused religion. In Chapters 5 through 8, rituals of therapeutic and ancestral adjustment were shown to be rituals of possession or magical power, just as rituals of possession were brought under the hierarchical control of Ritual Masters, Tantric monks, and Daoist priests and made to serve the values of the Daoist or Confucian sage.

APPENDIX
HUANGLU JIAO
AND *SHUILU ZHAI*

The Daoist Retreat of the Yellow Register

The Daoist ritual for the dead, known everywhere else as the *Huanglu zhai,*
or "Retreat of the Yellow Register," is consistently referred to in Hong Mai's
Yijian zhi as an "offering" (*jiao*) rather than a "retreat" (*zhai*). Already, then,
we are confronted with an interpretive and historical problem that we cannot hope to untangle without some familiarity with the distinction between
these two basic forms of Daoist ritual, the *zhai* and the *jiao*. This distinction is not easy to make because the *zhai* and the *jiao* were often performed
sequentially and developed very much in tandem. Ultimately, both rituals came to include many of the same syntactical elements, so that by modern times the two can be fruitfully analyzed as a single all-encompassing
liturgy, distinguished primarily by the purpose for which it is performed:
when it is performed for the benefit of the dead, it is called a "*zhai,*"
whereas when it is performed for the benefit of the living, it is called a
"*jiao.*" Whether this was always the case, however, is not so clear, and there
are advantages to considering the two separately.

The *jiao* was a ritual of offering or libation in which the gods were summoned to an altar where wine, fruit, silk, and other items were displayed
and were asked either to mitigate a particular danger or to reaffirm their
alliance with an individual or community by granting protection or blessings. Several Tang and Song liturgists suggest that the *jiao* was just another
name for a sacrifice, though they also point out that what is sacrificed is
of a pure rather than bloody nature. Many scholars, however, question

the appropriateness of this comparison with a sacrifice, because techni-
cally the only objects that are transformed during a *jiao* are written requests, petitions, memorials, and talismans.[1]

The Daoist *zhai* was, above all, a ritual of purification and confession.
It has antecedents in pre-Daoist communal rites known as "kitchen
feasts"[2] and perhaps came to be influenced by the Buddhist *uposatha*, bi-
monthly assemblies of confession that date in China from the early fifth
century.[3] The early development of the Daoist *zhai* is inseparable from
the history of the Lingbao tradition of Ge Chaofu (fl. 397) and Lu Xiujing (406–477). It is a very complex subject that is still poorly understood.
The earliest enumeration of Daoist *zhai* is found in the single-chapter
Dongxuan lingbao wugan wen, composed by Lu Xiujing in 454 C.E. Here
we find the names and briefly stated functions of twelve different *zhai*, including the Retreat of the Yellow Register for the salvation of ancestors.[4]
For a description of this Retreat, however, we must turn to a chapter of
the Northern Zhou Daoist encyclopedia, the *Wushang biyao* (HY 1130).
John Lagerwey includes an abstract of this chapter in his historical study
of the encyclopedia,[5] while Henri Maspero has given us a stimulating, if
somewhat overdone, evocation of the ritual's performance based on an
interpretation of the same material.[6]

The ritual is preceded by the construction of an altar (*litan*) within a
sacred space defined by the gates of the ten directions (four gates at the
sides, four at the corners, and one each at the northeast and the southeast). At each gate are placed an incense burner and a lamp to attract the
spirits of the ten directions; nine lamps that illuminate, according to
Maspero's interpretation, the gates for the souls of the dead; and a golden
dragon and various pieces of embroidered silk to redeem the souls of the
dead. Finally, at the center of the ritual space, a large incense burner and
a nine-foot lamp are situated; it is here, after the installation of the priests
and a triple offering of incense at each of the ten gates, that the main ritual action occurs.

The ritual commences with the "Opening of the Incense Burner"
(*falu*), a rite of exteriorization (*chuguan*) in which the Master of Rites invokes Lord Lao the Most High (Taishang laojun) and calls upon the spirit-
officials or messengers of his own body to leave in order to inform (*guanqi*)
the local earth-spirit of the priest's desire to receive in his body the perfect and orthodox pneumas of the ten directions, enabling him to communicate his prayers to the Emperor on High.[7] The Master of Rites then
invites the transcendent officials (*qing xianguan*) "to assist in the ritual for

saving the souls of the dead (*sihun*) of nine generations of ancestors of the host" and makes another circuit of the gates of the ten directions, this time accompanied by the host and other mourners. At each gate, incense is offered three times (*san shangxiang*) while the Master of Rites recites a prayer directed to the Three Venerables (i.e., the Three Purities) asking that the merits of the ceremony redound to the benefit of the ancestors of the host. The climax of the retreat is the "Confession to the Ten Directions" (*xie shifang*). The Master describes the torments of the ancestors in purgatory and then expresses the host's wish to take refuge in the divinities of each direction. He presents gifts of silk and gold to release the souls of the ancestors and to have them ascend to the Celestial Hall. This confession is followed by others to the divinities of the sun, moon and stars, to the Five Sacred Peaks, to the Water-Official, and to the Three Treasures of Daoism—the Dao, the Scriptures, and the Master (*chaozhen*). The ritual concludes with the "Closing of the Incense Burner" (*fulu*), a rite of interiorization (*naguan*).

The sequence of rites from the opening to the closing of the incense burner became known as the "Audience with the Spontaneous" (*ziran chao*) and remained at the heart of the Retreat of the Yellow Register even as it expanded over subsequent centuries. The late Tang Daoist Du Guangting (850–933)[8] remarked over and over again that the *ziran chao* is the ancestor of the *zhai*, and indeed, we find that this sequence of rites forms the skeletal structure of the various retreats described in the *Wushang biyao*.[9] It is clear, moreover, that in the early Tang and before, this sequence was part of the daily routine of the Daoist priest, performed both morning and evening in his private oratory or in a Daoist abbey.[10] In Du Guangting's major and lengthy contribution to the Daoist liturgy for the dead, the *Taishang huanglu zhaiyi*,[11] the *ziran chao* is repeated three times a day—morning, noon, and evening—for three days. The daily cycle of morning, noon, and evening audiences (*zaochao*, *wuchao*, and *wanchao*) is called "Practicing the Way" (*xingdao yi*), while the three-day repetition of this cycle constituted the "Orthodox Retreat" (*zhengzhai*).[12]

Du Guangting also made some important additions to the *ziran chao* itself. The "Opening of the Incense Burner" (*falu*) is now introduced by a sequence of recitations and visualizations of divinities and internal meditations that populate the ritual area with pneumas generated out of the priest's own body;[13] the all-important Confession to the Ten Directions, meanwhile, is succeeded first by a recitation of cosmic purification called "Commanding the Demon[-King]" (*mingmo zhou*) and then by the famous celestial hymns and choreography known as "Pacing the Void" (*buxu*).[14] After each "evening audience," moreover, there is a "Ritual Homage to the Lamps" (*lideng yi*). Du Guangting's most important elaborations on the liturgy, however, concern the period both before and after the "Orthodox *zhai*."

The "Nocturnal Announcement" (*suqi*) is one of several rituals that, by the Song period, came to constitute the construction and consecration of the altar. The others include the "Sealing of the Altar" (*jintan*) and "Distribution of the Lamps" (*fendeng*). The central event of the *suqi* was, and still is, the installation of the "True Writs of the Numinous Treasure" (*Lingbao zhenwen*) in the Five Directions. These celestial talismans and their ritual re-creation go back to the very origin of the Lingbao tradition in the fourth century, though their historical relationship to the Nocturnal Announcement is problematic. Du Guangting suggests that the *suqi* was originally a sequence of four rites performed after a *ziran chao*: an announcement of the purpose of the retreat (*gaozhai*); an explanation of the various precepts to the priests and disciples (*shuojie*); the conferral of the documents of appointment on the six officials of the retreat (*bazhi*); and, finally, a thorough explanation of 36 prohibitions related to the performance of the retreat (*xuanjin*).[15] The history of the *suqi* is very complex and was perceived as such by Daoist liturgists.[16] Suffice it to say that, by the Song, the installation of the "true writs" and the rites related to the installation of the priest-officials had become fully integrated in descriptions of the Nocturnal Announcement.[17]

The "Announcement of Merit" (*yangong*) was performed on the morning after the last "evening audience." The central event of this rite was the submission of a memorial by the Daoist priest himself at the court of the Celestial Emperor. This event was embedded within rites for exteriorizing and interiorizing the spirits residing in the body of the priest (*chuguan* and *naguan*). The memorial was written in vermillion ink on yellow paper and was therefore referred to as the "*huangzeng zhubiao*." It announced the completion of the retreat and requested that the merit accumulated thereby be applied to the salvation of the dead.[18] The priest reads the memorial out loud and, parenthetically, expresses his hope that the Five Perfected Officials of his body correct any mistakes in the document before submitting it.[19] Then, in a dramatic meditation, the priest visualizes himself mounting a feathered chariot that is born aloft by a dragon in a purple pneumatic haze. The priest and his retinue pass through the gates of the Mysterious Capital (*xuandu*) and, finally, the Gate

of the Three Heavens (*santian men*), where the memorial and other petitions are submitted for a detailed examination.[20] At the conclusion of this
meditational journey, the various official messengers are returned to the
priest's body, and the written memorials are burned.[21] It appears, moreover, that the True Writs of the Numinous Treasure that had been installed
at the five cardinal points during the Nocturnal Announcement are dis-
mantled and burned along with other documents.

Following the Announcement of Merit, a *jiao*, or "offering," is performed in which the spirits are summoned to take part in a common banquet and to receive the gratitude of the priests and the host for the merit
created by the retreat. Offerings of wine, fruit, and vegetables are laid out,
and written requests are again read before the gods.[22] At the conclusion
of the *jiao*, the various Daoist priests return their documents of official
appointment to the Inspector of Merits (*nazhi*), and the ritual concludes.[23] An auspicious day might be selected, however, when special documents of penance and confession were tied together with a jade disc and
golden dragon and deposited in the mountains, in the earth, and in water.
This ritual is known as the "*toulongbi*" (or *toulongjian*).[24] It originated with
the Celestial Master sect, though it had long been absorbed and transformed by the Lingbao tradition.[25]

Du Guangting's Retreat of the Yellow Register can be considered the
culmination of the medieval Daoist ritual for the dead. With the Southern Song, we have a number of texts that are distinctly "modernist" in
their concern to address the ritual needs of a new and more complex
audience—and even "modern" in the sense that they form the basis of
the ritual as it is still performed today. The most important of these ritual compendia include Jiang Shuyu's (1162–1223) *Wushang huanglu
dazhai licheng yi* (HY 508); the *Lingbao wuliang duren shangjing dafa* (HY
219) and the *Lingbao yujian* (HY 547), both from the early thirteenth century; Jin Yuzhong's (fl. 1225) *Shangqing lingbao dafa* (HY 1212, early thirteenth century); Wang Qizhen's *Shangqing lingbao dafa* (HY 1213, late thirteenth century); and Lin Tianren's *Lingbao lingjiao zhidu jinshu* (HY 466,
dated to 1303).

These compendia are among the longest and most complex in the
Daoist canon. It is therefore impractical to analyze any one of these texts
in detail.[26] Taken as a group, however, we can say that these texts all preserve and even expand on Du Guangting's ritual sequence while introducing an entirely new series of rituals that significantly shift the emotional balance and change the character of the entire liturgy. These "new"

rituals all concern, in one way or another, various trips to the other world undertaken by the Daoist priest or his spiritual messengers in order to gain the release of the souls of the deceased from the earth-prisons, bring them into the ritual area, and then transform the deceased into a divinity and/or ancestor. These rituals are generally referred to as "rites of deliverance" (*kaidu*), to distinguish them from the "rites of merit" (*gongde*) that encompass the audiences, confessions, and recitations.

In the various summaries of the Yellow Register Retreat in the two texts entitled *Shangqing lingbao dafa*, we find references to petitions and rites for "Opening the Five Roads [of Taishan]" (*Kaitong wulu*).[27] Although in neither text is there a chapter devoted exclusively to the performance of this rite, Wang Qizhen's work includes a "Lamp-Chart for Opening the Five Roads" (*Kaitong wulu dengtu*), a chart that is preceded by the insistence that "when setting up a great retreat, one must first open the roads to liberate the *hun*[-souls] of the deceased (*shifang wanghun*)."[28] The ritual involved the installation of lamps and white flags in the five cardinal directions and the use of talismans and incantations that called upon the Great Gods of the Five Roads "to open up the dark roads of the five directions, lead the souls of the deceased unimpeded by heterodox and evil demons."[29]

The *Lingbao yujian* specifically compares these Great Gods of the Five Roads to the *fangxiang shi*,[30] the ancient Chinese exorcist and officiant at funerals who descended into the tomb on the day of burial and struck its four sides to drive away the *fangliang*-demons that sought to harm the corpse.[31] The apotropaic function of the *fangxiang shi* was played in Han tomb ordinances by the "Envoy of the Celestial Thearch" (*Tiandi shizhe*) and his guardian spirits of the four quarters, a function taken over more generally by Daoist grave-quelling writs in the Six Dynasties period. Among other things, these writs sought to compel the various spirits of the mound and tomb and other terrestrial demons not to harm the deceased.[32]

In addition to protecting the corpse from the wrath and depredations of the spirits of the tomb, the other function of the Han tomb ordinances and Daoist grave-quelling writs was to secure a pardon for the sins of the deceased—a pardon that would, at one and the same time, gain the release of the souls of the deceased from the earth-prisons and protect the living relatives from illness, which was thought to be caused by otherworldly lawsuits brought against the deceased. *The Almanac of Petitions of Master Red Pine*, for example, includes a petition addressed to the tomb-spirits requesting first that the deceased be pardoned and second that his souls be reunited with the corpse so that he might reside in the "heavenly bureaus."[33]

Similar documents reemerge in the Song liturgical compendia, where they constitute a discrete ritual within the Retreat of the Yellow Register. This ritual was loosely referred to as "Rite for Pardon and Release" (*Shiba zhi fa*). It involved the meticulous preparation of various orders and writs of pardon and a ritual in which various documents were issued and received from the celestial chancelleries (a rite known as "welcoming the pardon," or *yingshe*) and then dispatched by various agents and means to the earth-prisons.[34] In the modern period, the dispatch of the writ of pardon is undertaken by a mounted messenger—the officer of pardon—whose expedition to the other world is enacted in a piece of theater using a paper representation.[35]

In the Song period, "Opening the Five Roads" and "Sending the Writ of Pardon" were preliminary to, and minor compared with, the extravaganza that constitutes the "rites of deliverance" proper. The priest begins this ritual sequence with a dramatic segment known as "Lighting the Lamps and Destroying the Earth-Prisons" (*randeng poyu*). In Jin Yunzhong's version, the Daoist acolytes light the lamps at nine prison-altars (*yutan*) in order to illuminate the Nine Obscurities (*jiuyou*) of purgatory and reveal the souls within.[36] Then the Daoist Priest, the "One of High Merit" (*gaogong*), holding a "document-staff" (*cezhang*) in his hand and nine talismans for destroying the prisons in his sleeve, transforms himself, much like the Master of Rites of Summoning for Investigation, into the divine Heavenly Worthy "Savior from Distress" (*huashen wei Qiuku tianzun*) and walks the Dipper.[37] Then, at each of the nine directions, he burns the appropriate talisman while reciting a corresponding incantation; he also visualizes a light that floods the earth-prison, exposing thousands of prison guards and interrogators who face the prison gate and receive the talismans. These talismans break the locks and release the souls who will follow the light and come to the ritual area (*daochang*).[38] At this point, the priest burns a representation of Fengdu (*Fengdu shanxing*) and lights the prison lamps, this time with his staff, revealing that the prison itself is now empty. The rite concludes with the lighting of incense and an expression of gratitude for divine mercy.[39] A very similar ritual can be found in a chapter of Jiang Shuyu's liturgy in which the priest again transforms himself into the Heavenly Worthy "Savior from Distress" and destroys the earth-prisons with a slightly variant use of lamps, talismans, and visualizations.[40]

The second act in the deliverance of the deceased opens with a great "ritual for summoning the soul" (*zhaoling yi*) into the ritual area. In the various Song liturgical manuals, this rite comprises two episodes.[41] One focuses on the preparation and manipulation of a "soul banner" (*lingfan*), a Daoist interpretation, perhaps, of that moment in the ancient "summoning of the soul" (*zhaohun*) when the mourner mounted the housetop and waved a piece of white clothing belonging to the deceased. The second focuses on the priest's use of various talismans to compel the "divine tiger" (*shenhu*), the divinities in charge of the seven *po*-souls and the three *hun*-souls, and a host of soul-catchers to bring the souls of the deceased into the "ritual assembly" (*fahui*) so that they might benefit from the merit accumulated in the priest's performance of the "orthodox retreat" (*zhengzhai*). This ritual shares a deep structure with the exorcistic Rites of Summoning for Investigation and was the occasion for some rather dramatic encounters between the living and the dead. (We will return to all this below.) After the soul has been summoned, it is given a ritual bath (*muyu*) to remove the pollution and impurities associated with death and the corpse, and is then compelled to pay homage to the Three Treasures of Daoism and magically fed with celestial nourishment (*zhoushi*).[42]

All this is preparation for the soul's ultimate transformation. In a ritual of sublimation known as *liandu*, or "deliverance by refining," a new transcendent body is formed for the soul through a process of internal or physiological alchemy undertaken by the Daoist priest. The complex sequence of visualizations necessary to complete the transformation varies with the cosmic elements involved. In Jin Yunzhong's *Shangqing lingbao dafa*, the soul is purified and refined by passing through water and fire, "orthodox pneumas of *yin* and *yang*," that have been absorbed by the priest and assimilated with two organs in his own body.[43] In the fifty-seventh chapter of the early thirteenth-century *Lingbao wuliang duren shangqing dafa*, the dominant elements are the pneumas of the Nine Heavens.[44] This chapter is a variant of a twelfth-century text for refining souls produced by the Daoist lineage of Shenxiao.[45]

What is so interesting about both these versions is that they condense in one long meditative exercise the entire sequence of discrete rites for the soul's deliverance found in the late Song Retreat of the Yellow Register. The priest absorbs the nine celestial pneumas into his body and concentrates them to form an infant, a physical alter ego of the priest, who is transported from the Aquatic Court (in the bladder) to the Nirvana

Palace (of the brain). There the infant is transformed into the (Supreme Emperor of) Primordial Beginning. A ray of light is now emitted from between the eyebrows of the Supreme Emperor, confirming the identity between priest and divinity, since the cranial chamber sits behind the priest's eyebrows. The light illuminates the entire microcosm and smashes the Nine Obscurities of Fengdu (located below the navel), transforming them into pure lands. Meanwhile, various golden lads and jade lasses, among other divinities, descend with a talismanic decree from the Supreme Emperor to pardon and release the souls of the deceased. The souls then bathe in a great sea in the Aquatic Court, a boundless ocean located in the priest's bladder and fed by saliva from his mouth (i.e., the *huachi*, or Flower Pool). This purification also marks the beginning of the souls' conversion to the Dao. After the bath, the souls dress themselves in new white clothing, join the saints in singing a portion of *The Scripture of Salvation (Duren jing)*, and are fed with sweet dew. The same golden lads and jade lasses reappear to lead the souls across the "Great Bridge of the Law for Ascending to Heaven" (*Shengtian dafaqiao*), assimilated to the priest's spinal column. The souls now enter the Fire Pool (*huochi*) in the priest's heart, where they are melted down and refined, dressed in celestial vestments, and finally projected into the Heaven of Jade Purity, outside the priest's head, by way of his trachea and brain.

This twelfth-century ritual meditation anticipates, as we have noted, the sequence of distinct rituals that make up the Southern Song Daoist liturgy for the dead: namely, the illumination and destruction of the earth-prisons; the absolution and release of the souls of the deceased; the bath, clothing, and feeding; and the souls' purification by water and fusion by fire. Even the souls' conversion to the Dao, their "turning to the Correct Way," is given a more explicit and structured expression in the larger liturgy. In Jiang Shuyu's *Wushang huanglu dazhai licheng yi*, the rite of sublimation is followed by a rite of conversion and initiation.[46] The embodied soul is absolved from its sins by listening to sermons, by receiving instruction in the rules and prohibitions of the Daoist community, and by the transmission of documents of initiation along with talismans that function as a kind of celestial visa. The passage to Heaven is also represented in a final "Ritual for Crossing the Bridge" (*duqiao keyi*), a rite that has taken on a distinctly theatrical character in modern times.[47] The "rites of deliverance" are brought to a conclusion with the performance of a ritual for "the distribution of food and universal salvation" (*shishi pudu*), a ritual of salvation not only for the hungry ghosts (Skt. *preta*, Ch. *egui*) and orphan-souls (*guhun*) but also for all those who are, and have been, subject to rebirth.[48]

This Daoist *pudu* was obviously inspired by Buddhism. The question is to what extent the content of the Daoist "rites of deliverance," individual as well as universal, was actually influenced by this assimilation of Buddhist liturgy, to which we now turn.

The Buddhist Retreat of Water and Land

The *Shuiluzhai*, or "Purificatory Fast [for the Spirits] of Water and Land," was only one, if the most extravagant one, of the many Buddhist rites of "universal salvation" (*pudu*) practiced in Song China. The *Shuilu zhai* was a distinctively Song phenomenon. A full analysis, however, would have to explore its continuities with the medieval ghost festival and with rituals for "distributing food to the hungry ghosts" (*shi egui*).[49] In a pioneering investigation more than twenty years ago, Makita Tairyō assembled most of the relevant historical references to the *Shuilu zhai*.[50] Since that time, at least one set of *shuilu* paintings used during monastic performances in the fifteenth century has been reproduced and/or studied.[51] More recently, Michel Strickmann and now Daniel Stevenson have examined all this textual and graphic material in greater detail and organized it in a more chronological and coherent fashion. Strickmann has also provided an interpretation of the rite that attempts to locate it within the context of East Asian Tantric Buddhism.[52]

Buddhist tradition attributes the creation of the *Shuilu zhai* to the sixth-century monk Baozhi, who was encouraged to do so by Emperor Wudi of the Liang. The emperor personally attended the first performance at Gold Mountain Monastery (Jinshan si), just as he went, in 538, to the Tongtai Monastery to take part in the first celebration of an Avalambana festival.[53] The monk Daoying supposedly revived the ritual a century and a half later in Chang'an.[54] It is not, however, until the tenth century that we find independent confirmation of the performance of the retreat from non-Buddhist sources,[55] and it is only in the eleventh century that its popularity becomes manifest. The monk Zunshi (964–1032) observed that throughout the ancient kingdoms of Wu and Yue (i.e., throughout the Southeast), monasteries maintained separate cloisters devoted entirely to the performance of the *shuilu* and other rituals for feeding *pretas*, or hungry ghosts.[56] He suggests, parenthetically, that the name of the rite derived from the fact that the food offerings for the gods were placed in running water and those for the ghosts were placed on land. This gloss is repeated in a thirteenth-century Buddhist encyclopedia, although I have yet to find any internal evidence in the extant ritual texts that would support it.[57]

The other center of *shuilu* practice was Szechwan. About 1071, a layman named Yang E (*jinshi* degree 1034) from Dongchuan composed a manual for performing the *shuilu*, extracts of which are preserved in another thirteenth-century Buddhist encyclopedia.[58] The extracts reveal that Yang E's rite focused on invocations and offerings to sixteen categories of beings, divided into two groups of eight. The first group, worshipped at an upper altar, includes the buddhas, the Dharma, the Sangha, the bodhisattvas, pratyekabuddhas, arhats, and, interestingly, the Saints of the Five Supernatural Powers (*wutong shen*) and the Dragons Who Protect the Law (*hufa longshen*); the second group, worshipped at a lower altar, includes, among others, those who are subject to the six modes of rebirth—officials, gods, demigods (or *asuras*), people, hell-beings, and hungry ghosts. Another extract involves a very brief inventory of the ritual's highlights, including the interesting suggestion that the food offerings be sprinkled with water that has been transformed by the priest into the "sweet dew" of immortality. (We will return to this below.) Twenty-two years after Yang E composed his manual, Su Shi, the most famous literatus of Sichuan, had a *shuilu* ritual performed for his deceased wife. He personally composed a poem for each of the sixteen classes of beings invoked during the rite—the same sixteen classes as in Yang E's manual—and even created some of the paintings used to represent them.

The involvement of officials and wealthy laymen was crucial to the popularity and institutionalization of the *shuilu* ritual, even in the Southeast. In the twelfth century, after witnessing a performance of the *shuilu* at Gold Mountain Monastery, the official Shi Hao (1106–1194) returned home to Zhejiang and donated 100 *mu* of land to a monastery on Yueboshan so that it could perform the rite all year round. The ritual was called a "Four Seasons *Shuilu*" (*sishi shuilu*) and was dedicated specifically "to Heaven and Earth and to the lords and their kin" (*tiandi zhunqin*).[59] Shi Hao edited and published the ritual texts and recorded the fact that that part of the monastery set aside for *shuilu* rituals had been graced with a plaque from the Xiaozong Emperor (in the manner, we might add, of the "merit-cloisters" commandeered by high Song officials). Meanwhile, in response to the aristocratic and exclusive pretensions of Shi Hao's dedication, upward of three thousand supporters of the nearby monastery of

Zunjiao si collected contributions and donated land for the performance of their own "Four Seasons *Shuilu*" and convinced the editor of our source, Zhi Pan (ca. 1220–1275), to compose a new ritual for a more universal, egalitarian audience. The text of Zhi Pan's new ritual was revised and edited by the sixteenth-century monk Zhu Hong (1535–1615) and has come down to us in this form.[60] The many continuities between Zhu Hong's text and both earlier descriptions and later versions of the *Shuilu zhai* suggests an overwhelming conservatism; thus I am confident that we can use this sixteenth-century manual as an accurate reflection of Song practice.[61]

Zhu Hong's revision (*chongding*) of Zhi Pan's instructions is entitled *Liturgy for the Cultivation of the Purificatory Fast of the Victorious Assembly of Water and Land for the Saints and Commoners of the Dharma-World* (*Fajie shengfan shuilu shenghui xiuzhai yigui*). It is divided into six chapters that correspond, more or less, to significant shifts in the ritual action. I summarize the ritual as three movements. The entire liturgy occupied a couple of days, and later versions, which lasted much longer, are quite specific about the hour at which each ritual segment was to begin:

(A) Zhu Hong's Retreat of Water and Land begins at dawn with the construction and purification of the ritual area (*kaiqi fa*) [1.1a]. Guardian deities are invited to occupy positions at the five cardinal points: the Vajra[-Being] of Impure Traces (Huiji jin'gang) in the center; the Ten Great Kings of Light (*shi da mingwang*) to the left and the Celestial Dragons (*tianlong*) to the right; to the sides of one of the doors sit the monastic tutelary divinities (*qielan shen*), while to the sides of the other sit the City God and the Dukes and Kings of the Various [Local] Temples (*chenghuang zhumiao houwang*) [1.4a].

After the purification of the ritual area with water and incense [1.6b], the priest undertakes a rite of announcement known as "Sending the Talismans" (*fafu fa*) [1.13b]. On one table is placed the seat (or effigies?) of the Emissaries of the Four Talismans (*sifu shiwei*), along with various offerings and paper money (*caima*); on another table are placed the written invitations, memorials, talismans, decrees, and other documents [1.13b]. The Four Messengers are then invited to descend into the ritual area [1.15a–b]. The various documents are read and the messengers dispatched, bearing the talismans that announce the Retreat to the saints and spirits throughout the universe [1.18a–b]. Finally, all the documents and paper money are burned [1.18b].

(B) The second chapter of Zhu Hong's manual is devoted to the summoning of the saints to the upper hall, or inner altar (*shangtang zhaoqing fa*) [2.1a]. There are ten classes of saints: (1) the buddhas; (2) the Dharma; (3) the bodhisattvas; (4) the patyekabuddhas; (5) the śrāvakas; (6) the patriarchs of the Tantric, Chan, and Vinaya lineages; (7) the Saints of the Five Supernatural Powers; (8) various Protectors of the Dharma, including the ten Vidyārājas and Ucchuṣma; (9) various tutelary divinities, including guardians of reliquaries, pagodas, monasteries, feasts, the nation, and domiciles; and, finally, (10) the "ten great gentlemen" identified with the creation, performance, and propagation of the *Shuilu zhai*. The last of these gentlemen are none other than Su Shi and Yang E. Each of these classes and constituents is called upon individually, and each invitation is accompanied by mantras and visualizations [2.3a–10b]. After the saints have assembled at the inner altar, they all undergo a communal bath and receive a meal [2.11a–12a]. Food and drink, sacralized by the sweet dew of Heaven, are offered to each of the ten classes of saints, along with a new set of clothing and other offerings [2.13a–29b]. The Ritual Master then presents a sermon on the history and efficacy of the Retreat of Water and Land [2.29b–34b], while an Announcer expounds on the purpose and significance of rites of universal salvation and goes on to enumerate the merit that will accrue— to the living as well as to the dead—from the performance of the Retreat [2.35a–37a].

(C) The invitation to "the commoners" occupies the third, fourth, and fifth volumes of Zhu Hong's manual. Ten classes of commoners are summoned to the lower hall of the inner altar (*xiatang zhaoqing fa*): various celestial and terrestrial deities (classes 1 and 2); various well-known figures from China's ancient past, including dynastic founders, classical philosophers, and Daoist ascetics (class 3); ordinary human beings, differentiated by occupational and moral criteria, including diviners, sorcerers, actors, and the ancestors of the ritual's patron (class 4); *asuras* (class 5); orphan-souls (class 6); gods of the underworld (class 7); hellbeings (class 8); birds and beasts (class 9); and those in the forty-nine-day limbo after death, waiting to be reborn (class 10). Each of these ten classes of commoners encompasses ten subclasses, all of which are invoked [3.3a–10b]. The priest then summons two additional sets of commoners. The first comprises five classes: (1) the City Gods and gods of the local temples of Hangzhou, site of Zhu Hong's monastery; (2) the tutelary divinities of the monastery and its buildings; (3) all the ancestors of the patron and his relatives; (4) the spiritual ancestors of the monks; and (5) various and sundry souls of the dead. The second set comprises twelve classes of orphan-souls of those who have suffered violent deaths (*hengsi guhun*), from emperors and their consorts to those who died in prison to those who were murdered by pirates or eaten by tigers. Page after page is devoted to these unfortunates and their gruesome deaths [3.10b–25a].

When the last of the hungry ghosts have been summoned (those that died at the hands of hunters and fishermen), the Ritual Master begins a series of recitations for releasing the hell-beings who have been incarcerated in the earth-prisons. The Ritual Master first recites a mantra for the "Destruction of the Earth-Prisons" (*po diyu*), after which he visualizes that the doors of each of the ten subterranean prisons rattle and open, and that the prisoners, overcome by the sound of the mantra and the desire to be saved, rush out to join the assembly [3.25a–b]. There follows a "Mantra for the Opening of the Roads" (*kaidaolu zhenyan*) and a visualization in which the confused and disoriented prisoners find their way along the roads that lead from purgatory [3.26a–b]. Having been released from prison, the hell-beings are now divested of their emotional shackles and physical handicaps. The Ritual Master recites three mantras: one that "separates them from fear" (*libuwei zhenyan*), one that "opens their throats" (*kaiyanhou zhenyan*), and one that "liberates them from the bonds of resentment" (*jieshi yuanjie zhenyan*) [3.26b–28b]. The middle mantra refers to the needle-thin throats of the hungry ghosts, which prevented them from eating. All these mantras were anticipated in the scriptures for feeding the hungry ghosts translated by Śikṣānanda and Amoghavajra in the seventh and eighth centuries. Then, in a final stage of purification, the hungry ghosts are joined by those subject to rebirth in a great communal bath and change of clothing [3.28b ff.].

The spirits now sit around the periphery of the ritual area and listen attentively to the recitations and lectures performed by the priests on their behalf. These include the singing of hymns, a lecture on the Dharma, a recitation of the litanies of confession, an enumeration and explanation of the ten grave precepts of Buddhism, and so forth [4.1a–14b]. Throughout all this, the Ritual Master imagines the souls' spiritual transformation and conversion. The souls join the priests in the invocation and contemplation of the Buddha (*nianfo*) [4.15a–b], a ritual that realizes the essential identity between the subjects and object of contemplation. The souls have now become the "Buddhas of the Six Roads of Rebirth." They are led by the Ritual Master before each of the saints in a ritual of homage and communion. They enter and take their seats within the ritual area, where the retreat will conclude in a great feeding of the hungry ghosts [4.16a–17b]. Further purifications, lectures, and a collective recitation of *The Scripture of the Flaming Mouth* (*Yankou jing*) [5.1a–4b] preface the consecration of the food and drink offerings and their transformation into *amṛta*, the sweet dew that is "the divine tonic of deathlessness" [5.4b–5a]. One by one, the commoners are invoked and invited to take part in the feast [5.5b–23a]. As a result of this and their dedication to the Dharma, the *pretas*, ancestors, and all the commoners will gain liberation, though the text is somewhat ambiguous as to whether this means immediate rebirth in the Western Paradise or progressive and improved rebirths that will ultimately lead to such a blessed condition [5.23a].

The Retreat for the Souls of Water and Land was truly ecumenical, egalitarian, and universal in its promise of redemption. This promise was extended not merely to the nine generations of ancestors of the Avalambana feast or to the hosts of hungry ghosts of the many "feeding rituals" (*shishiyi*), but to notorious figures from China's past and to representatives of all the social classes of her present as well. The Retreat of Water and Land was, in this respect, not unlike the Feast of All Souls established by Odilo, Abbot of Cluny, in 998.[62] The feast, inspired by the torments of the dead in the other world,[63] was dedicated literally to all souls who lived "from the beginning of time to the end" (*ab initio mundi fuerunt usque in finem*).[64] It envisioned a totality in time that rivaled the totality of space claimed by the Roman emperor. The feast, moreover, followed immediately upon All Saints Day and presaged the unity at the end of time, when all the saints and all the souls would be joined *in saecula saeculorum*. The unity of saints and souls in the Buddhist festival, in contrast, was less eschatological than ontological, based on the universal buddhahood of all beings.

NOTES

Chapter 1: Introduction

1. *Pingfu* literally means "to lean on and adhere to" (compare with L. *incubus*).
2. Gibert Rouget, *Music and Trance: A Theory of the Relations between Music and Possession* (Chicago: The University of Chicago Press, 1985), 25–28 and 325.
3. Gananath Obeyesekere, "The Idiom of Demonic Possession: A Case Study," *Social Science and Medicine* 4 (1970), 97–111 (esp. 105–106), and idem, *Medusa's Hair: An Essay on Personal Symbols and Religious Experience* (Chicago: The University of Chicago Press, 1981).
4. Piet van der Loon, "Les origines rituelles du théâtre chinois," *Journal Asiatique* 265 (1977), 168.
5. Stephen J. Teiser, *The Ghost Festival in Medieval China* (Princeton: Princeton University Press, 1988), 145, note.
6. See Mircea Eliade, *Shamanism: Archaic Techniques of Ecstacy* (Princeton: Princeton University Press/Bollingen Series, 1974), 210–212.
7. Rouget, *Music and Possession*, 23.
8. In the debate on the evidence for and importance of shamanism in Shang and Zhou religion, I find the arguments of David Keightley, "Royal Shamanism in the Shang: Archaic Vestige or Central Reality?" a paper prepared for the Workshop on Chinese Divination and Portent Interpretation (Berkeley, June 20–July 1, 1983), much more compelling than those of K. C. Chang, *Art, Myth and Ritual: The Path to Political Authority in Ancient China* (Cambridge: Harvard University Press, 1983), 44–55. For a judicious analysis of the functions and attributes of the Chinese spirit-medium in the Zhou-dynasty state,

see now Lothar von Falkenhausen, "Reflections on the Political Role of Spirit-Mediums in Early China: The *Wu* Officials in the *Zhou Li*," *Early China* 20 (1995), 279–300. For shamanism and/or spirit-possession in the state of Chu, see John S. Major, "The Characteristics of Late Chu Religion," in Constance A. Cook and John S. Major, eds., *Defining Chu: Image and Reality in Ancient China* (Honolulu: University of Hawai'i Press, 1999), esp. 135–139.

9. Microhistory has been primarily associated with the Italian historians Carlo Ginzburg and Giovanni Levi. For an English introduction to the theoretical aspect of their approach, one might begin with Ginzburg's article, "The Name and the Game," in Edward Muir and Guido Ruggiero, eds., *Microhistory and the Lost Peoples of Europe* (Baltimore: The Johns Hopkins University Press, 1991), 1–10, and Levi's article, "On Microhistory," in Peter Burke, ed., *New Perspectives on Historical Writing* (University Park: The Pennsylvania State University Press, 1991), 93–113.

10. Kristofer Schipper, *Le corps taoïste* (Paris: Fayard, 1982), 21. Also, John Lagerwey, *Le continent des esprits: La chine dans le miroir du taoïsme* (Bruxelles: La Renaissance des Livres, 1991), 15.

11. Schipper, *Le corps taoïste*, 30.

12. Ibid., 31.

13. Ibid., 32.

14. Ibid., 21.

15. Schipper, *Le corps taoïste*, 29; John Lagerwey, *Taoist Ritual in Chinese Society and History* (New York: Macmillan, 1987), 276. I should mention parenthetically that even those sinologists who see the historical relationship of the state to Chinese religion in a more neutral light insist on the distinction between Buddhism and Daoism, which are religions, and Confucianism, which is not: "The oft-mentioned 'Confucianism' is . . . best seen as something else, not strictly comparable—more a Paideia, a system of culture and its gradual inculcation, rather than a faith professed by a guild of ritual technicians claiming otherworldly authority. The paradigm later styled 'Confucian' was simply a broad base of Sinic letters, a fundamental view of the cosmos and society which we might better term 'common Chinese,' for it was also shared by Daoist priests and Chinese Buddhist monks" (Michel Strickmann, "India in the Chinese Looking Glass," in D. Klimburg-Salter, ed., *The Silk Route and the Diamond Path* [Los Angeles: UCLA Art Council, 1982], 55). I, too, would insist—along with Strickmann and many before him, including C. K. Yang—that Confucianism is not a religion. Strickmann's identification of Confucianism with "the broad base of Sinic letters" seems particularly germane to the Six Dynasties period, although it would, I believe, leave us hard pressed to account for de-

velopments after the Tang and would certainly be rejected by *daoxue* scholars. Strickmann's use of the word "paideia" in the context of Confucianism is fine as long as we do not press the comparison between Greek and Chinese cultures too far. For some wise words on the difference, see Chris Connelly, *The Empire of the Text: Writing and Authority in Early Imperial China* (Lanham: Rowman & Littlefield, 1998), 44.

16. I therefore disagree strongly with attempts to define the *shi* class in exclusively Confucian terms. See, especially now, Peter Bol, *'This Culture of Ours': Intellectual Transitions in T'ang and Sung China* (Stanford: Stanford University Press, 1992), 18–19.

17. Michel Strickmann, "Magical Medicine: Therapeutic Rituals in Medieval China," unpublished ms. (Berkeley, 1987), chapter 1, "Disease and Daoist Law," 3. Strickmann's manuscript has been edited by Bernard Faure and will be published posthumously as *Chinese Magical Medicine* (Stanford: Stanford University Press, 2001).

18. Ibid., 5. In keeping with his portrayal of Daoism as a religious revolution and of the chasm that separated it from popular religion, Strickmann insists, "This systematic bureaucratisation of the unseen world was not an adventitious evolution of so-called 'popular religion,' but rather the conscious, studied creation of Daoism from its very beginnings" (ibid.). Yet this would seem hard to maintain in light of an article by Anna Seidel which demonstrates that the Daoist bureaucratization of the other world and of the means of dealing with it were already a part of Han, pre-Daoist village religion: "It is clear that Daoism, rather than opposing or reforming this religion, adopted all its features without essential changes" (see her "Traces of Han Religion in Funeral Texts Found in Tombs," in Akizuki Kan'ei, ed., *Dōkyō to shūkyō bunka* [Tokyo: Hirakawa shuppan, 1987], 47). Seidel is thereby forced to ask, "What was new in Daoism?" though her answer—a "new soteriological paradigm" (the "saving grace of the Dao," exclusively mediated by a divinized Laozi and an apostolic priesthood, combined with a beatific vision of immortality)—is frustratingly brief and noticeably Catholic.

Other scholars—notably Peter Nickerson, Angelika Cedzich, Stephen Bokenkamp, Terry Kleeman, and Christine Mollier—are exploiting the creative tension between the work of their teachers to produce an increasingly sophisticated dialectic between the old and the new in the formative period of the Daoist religion. It should be mentioned, however, that the developmental model worked out by Strickmann, Seidel, Robinet, and others, and assumed or elaborated on by their students—a model that identifies the formation of Daoism with three distinct movements, traditions, or lineages

(Celestial Master, Highest Purity, and Numinous Treasure)—is being seriously and forcefully contested in the work of Kobayashi Masayoshi. See, most recently, his *Chūgoku no Dōkyō* (Tokyo: Sōbunsha, 1998). For a brilliant study of the relationship between the Celestial Master organization and Highest Purity texts in light of Kobayashi's argument, see Shawn Eichman, "Converging Paths: Highest Purity and Celestial Master Traditions of Taoism during the Six Dynasties" (Ph.D. diss., University of Hawai'i, 1999).

19. Kristofer Schipper, "Exposé de titres et travaux," unpublished ms. (Paris, 1983), 31–32.

20. Kristofer Schipper, "Vernacular and Classical Ritual in Daoism," *Journal of Asian Studies* 45.1 (Nov. 1985), 21–51. Even the distinction between black-head and red-head priests (between *daoshi* and *fashi*, between those who perform the large-scale rites of "offering" and "merit" and those who only perform the small-scale rites of exorcism) based on Schipper's fieldwork in southern Taiwan loses some of its paradigmatic value when we look to other regions. In the Taibei basin of northern Taiwan, John Lagerwey found that the *daoshi* perform "offering rituals" but not "merit rituals," which were in fact being performed by those claiming to be Buddhists, while the small-scale exocistic rites were considered superior to the "offering rituals." And in several counties in Fujian, Guangdong, and Zhejiang, Lagerwey found so-called Buddhists performing "offering rituals," so-called Daoists who only perform "merit rituals," and individuals who do both but who change their religion in order to do so. Lagerwey concludes that in these areas, the distinction between "red" (auspicious) and "white" (inauspicious) rituals trumps the distinction between black-head and red-head priests, and even that between Daoism and Buddhism. For all of this, see John Lagerwey, "Questions of Vocabulary, or How Shall We Talk about Chinese Religion?" in Lai Chi Tim, ed., *Daojiao yu minjian zongjiao yanjiu lunji* (Hong Kong: Xuefeng wenhua shiye gongsi, 1999), 165–191, especially 173–179 and his publications based on recent fieldwork listed in the bibliography.

21. Kristofer Schipper, "An Outline of Taoist Ritual," paper prepared for the International Conference on Asian Rituals and the Theory of Ritual, Berlin (Wissenschaftkolleg), June 1984, 1.

22. Schipper, "Vernacular and Classical Ritual in Daoism," 45.

23. Schipper, *Le corps taoïste*, 29.

24. *Mister Lu's Abridged Codes for Followers of the Way* (*Luxiansheng daomen kelüe*, HY 1119) is attributed to Lu Xiujing (406–477) but was most likely redacted by his disciples. A partial translation and commentary by Peter Nickerson can be found in Donald Lopez, ed., *Religions of China in Practice* (Princeton: Prince-

ton University Press, 1996), 347–359. The text tells us more about the construction of the Celestial Master organization in the Liu Song dynasty (420–479) than about Daoism's historical relation to popular religion since the end of the Han. As such, this text should be paired with *The Great Highest Scripture on the Inner Explanations of the Three Heavens* (*Taishang santian neijiejing*, HY 1196), which refers specifically to the legitimization of the Liu Song dynasty and to its descent from the ruling family of the Han (see HY 1196, 1.8–9). The *Inner Explanations* takes Buddhism as its primary (but not exclusive) rival, and at the very least complicates Strickmann and Schipper's programmatic definition of Daoism exclusively with respect to "popular religion." For a partial translation and commentary of this text, see Stephen Bokenkamp, *Early Daoist Scriptures* (Berkeley: University of California Press, 1997), 186–229. For Lu Xiujing, see Giovanni Vitiello, "Studio sul taoista Lu Xiujing (406–477)," *Annali dell'Instituto Universitario Orientale di Napoli* 47.3 (1987), 293–332.

25. Schipper, "Vernacular and Classical Ritual in Daoism," 47.

26. See Tanaka Issei, *Chūgoku saishi engeki kenkyū* (Tokyo: Tōkyō daigaku shūppansha, 1981), 18–31 and 269–277.

27. Subsequent references to the texts of the Daoist canon are by title number in the *Combined Indices to the Authors and Titles of Books in Two Collections of Taoist Literature: Harvard-Yenching Institute Sinological Index Series* No. 25 (abbr., HY); references to the scriptures of Buddhist canon are by title number in the *Taishō shinshū daizōkyō* (abbr., T.) and the *Dai-Nihon Zokuzōkyō* (abbr., Z.); and references to Dunhuang manuscripts are by Stein number in the Stein Collection of Tun-huang Manuscripts (abbr., Stein). (See the List of Abbreviations in the front matter of this volume.) References to the anecdotes of the *Yijian zhi* are by page number in Hong Mai, *Yijian zhi* (Beijing: Zhonghua shuju, 1981).

28. These scholars include John Lagerwey, Judith Boltz, Franciscus Verellen, and Poul Andersen.

29. John Lagerwey, "Taoist Ritual: An Integral Part of Elite Culture," paper presented at the Conference on the Rituals and Scriptures of Chinese Popular Culture, Bodega Bay, California, Jan. 2–8, 1990.

30. Ibid., 2 and 6–7.

31. Ibid., 13–15.

32. Valerie Hansen, *Changing Gods in Medieval China, 1127–1276* (Princeton: Princeton University Press, 1990), 21.

33. Ibid., 21, note 25.

34. Ibid., 22. Despite my disagreements here, there is much to admire in Hansen's discussion of the *Yijian zhi*, esp. 18–21.

35. G. Genette, *Narrative Discourse: An Essay in Method*, trans. J. E. Lewin (Ithaca: Cornell University Press, 1980), 244–245.

36. John J. Winkler, *Auctor and Actor: A Narratological Reading of Apulius's The Golden Ass* (Berkeley: University of California Press, 1985), 73–76.

37. Joel Fineman, "The History of the Anecdote: Fiction and Friction," in H. Aram Veeser, ed., *The New Historicism* (New York: Routledge, 1989), 64.

Chapter 2: Therapeutic Movements in the Song: Texts

1. Poul Andersen, "Taoist Ritual Texts and Traditions" (Ph.D. diss., University of Copenhagen, 1991), 81–131. For earlier but much more impressionistic treatments of the Rites of Tianxin, see Michel Strickmann, "The Taoist Renaissance of the Twelfth Century," paper presented at the Third International Conference on Daoist Studies, Unterägeri (Switzerland), Sept. 3–9, 1979, and Judith Boltz, *A Survey of Taoist Literature, Tenth through Seventeenth Centuries* (Berkeley: Institute of East Asian Studies, 1987), 33–38.

2. For the relation of Chen Shouyuan and various mediums to the Min emperors, see Edward Shafer, *The Empire of Min* (Rutland and Tokyo: Charles Tuttle, 1954), 96–109. For Tan Zixiao, see now John Didier, "Messrs. T'an, Chancellor Sung, and the *Book of Tranformation* (*Hua Shu*): Texts and Transformations of Traditions," *Asia Major* 3rd ser., 11.1 (1998), 99–151 (esp. 117–124).

3. *Nan-Tang shu*, Lu You, 14. 3a–b (also in Lu You, *Lu Fangwen quanji*, vol. 1, p. 72).

4. *Nan-Tang shu*, Ma Ling, 24. 2b–3a. The text says that Tan "performed 'offerings' (*jiao*) to the stars, served the Spirit-Lord Black Killer, walked the dipper, and exorcised demons."

5. See Chapter 4, "The Four Saints."

6. See *Huagaishan Fouqiu-Wang-Guo san zhenjun shishi* (HY 777) 5.4b–5b.

7. *Shangqing tianxin zhengfa* (HY 566) preface, 1a–b.

8. Poul Andersen, "Taoist Ritual Texts and Traditions," 82–83.

9. *Shangqing tianxin zhengfa* 3.1a–9a. For additional references to the *heisha fu*, see *Fahai yizhu* (HY 1158), 6.10b, and *Wushang xuanyuan santianwang yudang dafa* (HY 220), 25.3a–4a.

10. *Shangqing tianxin zhengfa* , 3.9b–21a.

11. Ibid., 3 passim.

12. For an analysis of all the Tianxian talismans from a literary as well as religious point of view, see Monika Drexler, *Daoistische Schriftmagie: Interpretatione zu den*

Schriftamulleten Fu im Daozang (Stuttgart: Franz Steiner, 1994), 24–85, and the criticisms of Poul Andersen, "Taoist Talismans and the History of the Tianxin tradition," *Acta Orientalia* 57 (1996), 141–152.

13. *Shangqing gusui lingwan guilü* preface, 3a.

14. Ibid., preface, 2b.

15. Ibid., preface, 1b.

16. Poul Andersen has identified an impressive array of texts related to the Rectifying Rites of the Celestial Heart. I see these texts as divisible into three general groups, which I enumerate for future reference: (1) those texts that derive directly or in part from the Tianxin tradition, such as the *Wushang xuanyuan santianwang yudang dafa* (HY 220, composed in the second half of the twelfth century by Lu Shizhong), the late Song *Shangqing tianshu yuan huiche bidao zhengfa* (HY 549), the late fourteenth-century *Guandou zhongxiao wulei wuhou bifa* (HY 585), and the *Tianxin xiuzhen daochang shejiao* (HY 806); (2) those texts that influenced the Tianxin tradition, such as the ninth- or tenth-century *Jinsuo liuzhu yin* (HY 1009), the tenth- or eleventh-century *Tai-shang yuanshi tianzun shuo beidi fumo shenzhou miao jing* (HY 1401), and the eleventh-century *Yisheng baode zhuan* (HY 1275), discussed in Chapter 3; and, finally, (3) those texts that intersect with the Tianxin tradition by virtue of the divinities invoked or the kinds of therapeutic methods employed. These include the *Taishang chiwen tongshen sanlu* (HY 589), the *Sanhuang nei biwen* (HY 854), the *Guiguzi tiansui lingwen* (HY 866), the *Beidou zhifa wuwei jing* (HY 869), among others.

17. See Michael Saso, *The Teachings of Daoist Master Chuang* (New Haven: Yale University Press, 1978), 234–266. While enlightening on contemporary practice, Saso's historical sketch of Thunder Magic revolves around rather impenetrable notions of orthodoxy. See also Liu Zhiwan, "Raishin shinkōto raihō no tenkai," *Tōhō Shūkyō* (1990), 121. Liu has amassed an impressive array of references to practitioners of Thunder Magic in the Song, Yuan, and Ming periods, but he makes little attempt to analyze these either in their own right or with reference to any texts in the Daoist canon. Michel Strickmann, "Sō-dai no raigi: Shinshōundō to dōka nanshū ni tsuite no ryaku setsu" (Thunder Rites of the Song: Concerning the Divine Empyrean Movement and the Southern School of Daoism), *Tōhō Shūkyō* 46 (1975), 15–28, is not so much about Thunder Rites as about the Divine Empyrean Movement. Matsumoto Kōichi, "Sōdai no raihō," *Shakai bunka shigaku* 17 (1979), 45–65, is still unsurpassed as a judicious introduction but will soon be superceded by the work of Lowell Skar, for which see "Administering Thunder: A Thirteenth-Century

Memorial Deliberating the Thunder Rites," *Cahiers d'Extrême-Asie* 9 (1996–1997), 159–202.

18. From the third century B.C.E., we find references to a deity variously known as "Leizi," "Leishi," or "Leigong," and to a triad of other divinities—Tianmu, Fengbo, and Yushi—with whom he is linked. All four retain their importance in the Thunder Magic texts of the Song.

19. See Liu Zhiwan, "Raishin shinkō," 2 and 18, note 7.

20. A *fangshi* in Jiangsu, for example, summoned thunder and lightning to eliminate the plaintiffs in a land dispute with his disciples (*Shenxian zhuan* 5, "Liu Ping," as quoted in Liu, "Raishin shinkō," 4–5).

21. *Shenxian ganyu zhuan* 1.3a–4a.

22. See *Yijian zhi* 487–488.

23. Here I follow Matsumoto Kōichi, whose early article on Thunder Magic is still the best introduction to the subject.

24. For confirmation of this point in the Song, see *Yijian zhi* 71, 504, 633, 638, 732–733, 1447–1448, 1449.

25. See Miyakawa Hisayuki, "Rin Reiso to Sō no Kisō," *Tōkai daigaku kiyō: Bungaku-bu* 24 (1975), 18; Michel Strickmann, "The Longest Taoist Scripture," *History of Religions* 17 (1978), 331–354.

26. *Shenxiao jinhuo tianding dafa* is found in chapters 198–205 of the *Daofa huiyuan* (HY 1210). For the identity of Liu Yu, see Judith Boltz, *A Survey of Taoist Literature*, 206, note 59. Lu Ye, otherwise known as Lu Boshan, may have played the most important role as a textual transmitter. He is mentioned in connection with the transmission of other exorcistic traditions, including the *Taiyi huo leifu Zhu jiangjun kaofu dafa* (*Daofa huiyuan* 227), the *Diqi fa* (*Daofa huiyuan* 253), and the *Beiyin fengdu taixuan zhimo heilu lingshu* (*Daofa huiyuan* 265).

27. *Wushang jiuxiao yuqing dafan zuwei xiandu leiting yujing* (HY 15). Undated, but attested in the early thirteenth century, this is one of the central texts of Shenxiao. Here the "Master of the Thunderclap" is identified with none other than the Most High Monarch of Everlasting Life, Perfect King of Jade Purity of the Divine Empyrean. The text seems intent on distinguishing this deity from the one of the same name of which Huizong claimed to be an incarnation, intent on integrating the overblown claims for Shenxiao within traditional Daoist cosmology. In the Lin/Huizong scheme, the Monarch of Everlasting Life was the *eldest son* of the Jade Emperor, the Divine Empyrean over which he ruled was the highest Daoist heaven, and the teaching of Shenxiao was the highest Dao, above even that associated with the Celestial Venerable of Primordial Commencement (Yuanshi tianzun). In the present text, the Monarch of Everlasting Life is the *ninth son* of Fuli yuanshi tianzun and Yuch-

ing shenmu yuanjun and the *younger brother* of Yuqing yuanshi tianzun (i.e., the Celestial Venerable of Primordial Commencement).

28. *Gaoshang shenxiao yuching zhenwang zishu da fa* (HY 1209).

29. *Lishi zhenxian tidao tongjian xubian* (HY 296) 53.1b–2a.

30. Ibid., 53.4b–5a.

31. Included in *Daofa huiyuan* 198.

32. I therefore find it difficult to accept the preference of Paul Katz "to treat the Divine Empyrean movement as a *local* ritual tradition." See his discussion in Katz, *Demon Hordes and Burning Boats: The Cult of Marshal Wen in Late Imperial Chekiang* (Albany: State University of New York Press, 1995), 32–38 and 146–147.

33. *Yijian zhi* 487.

34. Ibid., 1049.

35. Ibid., 832.

36. See Yu Ji, *Daoyuan xue gu lu* 25.15a–18b, "Linghui zhongxu tongmiao zhenjun Wang Shizhen ji" (reprint ed., Shanghai: Shangwu yinshu guan, 1937, 423–426.)

37. For the rather laconic biography of this legendary(?) figure, see *Lishi zhenxian tidao tongjian xubian* 5.10a–b.

38. *Daofa huiyuan* (HY 1210) 56, "Shangqing yufu wulei dafa yushu lingwen," 1a–3b; 61, "Gaoshang Shenxiao yushu zhankan wulei dafa," 1a–2a; 67, "Leiting xuanlun," 21a–25a; 69, "Wang Shichen [= Wang Wenqing] qidao baduan jin"; 70, "Xuanzhu ge," 1a.

39. *Daomen shigui* (HY 1222) 11a.

40. Miyakawa Hisayuki, "Nansō no dōshi Haku Gyokusen no jiseki," in *Uchida Gimpu Hakushi shōju kinen tōyōshi ronshū* (Kyoto, Dōhōsha, 1978), 499–517; Judith Berling, "Channels of Connection in Sung Religion: The Case of Pai Yü-ch'an," in Patricia Ebrey and Peter Gregory, eds., *Religion and Society in T'ang and Sung China* (Honolulu: University of Hawai'i Press, 1993), 307–333; and especially Lowell Skar, "Administering Thunder."

41. See *Xiuzhen shishu* (HY 263) 47.10b.

42. *Song Bai zhenren Yuchan quanji* 5.13.

43. See, for example, Bo's commentary to *The Precious Scripture of the Jade Pivot* in *Song Bai zhenren Yuchan quanji* 7.1–22.

44. See *Qingwei xianpu* (HY 171) preface; *Lishi zhenxian tidao tongjian xubian* 5.9a–10a; and especially *Daomen shigui* (HY 1222) 11a.

45. *Lishi zhenxian tidao tongjian xubian* 5.11a–b.

46. *Daofa huiyuan* 111, 146, 188, 246.

47. For brief introductions to this compendium, see Piet van der Loon, "A Taoist

Collection of the Fourteenth Century," in Wolfgang Bauer, ed., *Studia Sino-Mongolica, Festschrift für Herbert Franke* (Wiesbaden: Franz Steiner, 1979), 401–405, and Judith Boltz, *A Survey of Taoist Literature*, 47–49. Several scholars have suggested that the Qingwei lineage, and particularly Zhao Yizhen and/or several of his students, were primarily responsible for this collection. For the arguments, see Piet van der Loon, *Taoist Books in the Libraries of the Sung Period: A Critical Study and Index* (London: Ithaca Press, 1984), 63, note 50; Judith Boltz, *A Survey of Taoist Literature*, 47; and especially Kristofer Schipper, "Master Chao I-chen (?–1382) and the Ch'ing-wei School of Taoism," in Akizuki Kan'ei, ed., *Dōkyō to shūkkyō bunka* (Tokyo: Hirakawa shūppan, 1987), 720–719 (from the back).

48. For analysis of the cult to one such deity, see Barend J. ter Haar, "The Rise of the Guan Yu Cult: The Taoist Connection," in Jan A. M. De Meyer and Peter M. Engelfriet, eds., *Linked Faiths: Essays on Chinese Religions and Traditional Culture in Honour of Kristofer Schipper* (Leiden: E. J. Brill, 2000), 184–204 (esp. 199–202). For others, see Edward L. Davis, "Arms and the Tao, 1: Hero Cult and Empire in Traditional China," *Sōdai no shakai to shūkyō: Sōdai-shi kenkyūkai kenyū hōkoku*, 2 (Tokyo: Kyūko sho'in,1985), 1–56, and idem, "Arms and the Dao, 2: The Xu Brothers in Tea Country," forthcoming in Livia Kohn and Harold Roth, eds., *Daoist Identity in Practice* (Honolulu: University of Hawai'i Press, 2001); and the essays by Kleeman and Hansen in Ebrey and Gregory, eds., *Religion and Society in T'ang and Sung China* (Honolulu: University of Hawai'i Press, 1993), 45–113. More generally, see now Lowell Skar, "Ritual Movement, Deity Cults and the Transformation of Daoism in Song and Yuan Times," in Livia Kohn, ed., *Handbook of Daoism* (Leiden: E. J. Brill, 2000).

49. Strickmann, "The Taoist Renaissance of the Twelfth Century," 7.

50. A more fundamental criticism of Strickmann's "shift" awaits elaboration. It is by no means certain that those who specialized in Highest Purity (Shangqing) scriptures and practices, exclusive of Tao Hongjing (456–536), ever formed a discrete entity that was separate from and/or dominant over the Celestial Master organization. Many, if not most, of the prominent transmitters of Shangqing scriptures in the Tang were Celestial Master Daoists (see Kobayashi, *Chūgoku no Dōkyō*, 284–295). T. H. Barrett, *Taoism Under the T'ang: Religion and Empire During the Golden Age of Chinese History* (London: Wellsweep, 1996), sheds little light on this issue.

51. See, for example, *Sandong xiudao yi* (HY 1227), passim.

52. Valerie Hansen argues that the rise of these lay exorcists, or "uneducated pratitioners" as she calls them, in the twelfth century was prompted by "doctrinal changes and the suspension of government-administered examinations for

Buddhists and Daoists" (see her *Changing Gods in Medieval China, 1127–1276*, 43). Her argument seems to be that with the eventual abolition in the Southern Song of examinations as the means for receiving official certification as a Buddhist monk or Daoist priest, and with the sale of ordination certificates, those who could not obtain these certificates—either because their number was limited or because they couldn't afford one—were forced to become lay practitioners. I find this argument difficult to accept. The rise of "lay exorcists" or "uneducated practitioners" had nothing to do with what the government did or did not do with respect to certifying examinations, though the growing and successful practice of an uneducated or lay exorcist might lead him to buy a certficate (see *Yijian zhi* 989).

53. Christine Mollier, *Une apocalypse taoïste du Ve siècle: Le livre des incantations divines des grottes abyssales* (Paris: Mémoires de L'Institut des Hautes Études Chinoises 31, 1990).

54. See ibid., 44–46, for Mollier's arguments against the view that the use here of the term "Three Caverns" refers to the divisions of the Daoist canon.

55. Christine Mollier, "La Méthode de l'empereur du Nord du Mont Fengdu: Une tradition exorciste du taoïsme médiévale," *T'oung Pao* 83, 4–5 (1997), 329–385.

56. Mollier, *Une apocalypse taoïste*, 86.

57. See, for example, Shizutani Masao, "Hōshi (dharma–bhānaka) ni tsuite," *Indogaku bukkyōgaku kenkyū* 3.1 (1954), 131–132, and idem, "Daijōkyōdan no seiritsu, 1," *Bukkyō shigaku* 13.3 (1967), 17–44; and Hirakawa Akira, *Shoki daijō bukkyō no kenkyū* (Kyōto: Shunjusha, 1968).

58. Kristofer Schipper, "Taoist Ordination Ranks in the Dunhuang Manuscripts," in Gert Naundorf et al., eds., *Religion und Philosophie in Ostasien: Festschrift für Hans Steininger zum 65: Geburtstag* (Würzburg: Königshausen & Neumann, 1985), 127–148 (esp. 140).

59. We may trace this influence already on Ye Jingneng, a prototype of the Song Daoist Ritual Master, who lived during the first half of the eighth century. His biography, preserved in a Dunhuang manuscript (Stein 6836, translated by Arthur Waley, *Ballads and Stories from Tun-Huang* [London: George Allen & Unwin, 1960], 124–144, and more recently by Alfredo Cadonna, *Il Taoista di sua Maesta* [Venezia: Cafoscarina, 1984]), is, however, a product of the ninth or tenth century. Ye was an acolyte of the Huiji Abbey in Zhejiang. At age twenty he became a Daoist monk, but it was not as a monk that he built his career. Through the intermediary of an unnamed spirit, the god Indra, Monarch of the Daluo Heaven, conferred upon Ye a book of talismans (*fuben*) that allowed him to control all the demons, spirits, and sprites listed therein.

Ye set out for Chang'an to make his name as an exorcist and thaumaturge. After his arrival in the capital, Ye Jingneng was invited by a commoner named Kang Taiqing to cure his adolescent daughter, who had been possessed by a fox-spirit. (Cadonna points out, following Pulleyblank, that the name "Kang" suggests a person of Sogdian origin. It was derived from the Sogdian "Rwxšn," the name also of An Lushan [Middle Chinese: Lukshan]. "Rwxšn," by the way, meaning "light," is the origin of the English name Roxanne.) Ye grasped a sword, cut the girl into three sections, and placed her remains under a piece of matting that was then nailed to the floor. After considerable hysteria on the part of her family and the arrival of the chief of police, the matting was finally removed to reveal the girl unharmed and a fox-spirit lying next to her, cut into three pieces.

This rather dramatic piece of exorcistic theater represents a fictional literalization of the kind of exorcistic practices being performed at precisely the same time not by Daoist priests but by Tantric monks. In the case of a particularly persistent case of demonic illness, an eighth-century Tantric text composed in China advises the practicant, the "Master of the Spell" (*chizhou ren*), to have the patient sit down in the middle of a ritual space that has been constructed out of mud. Next, the practicant makes an effigy or representation of the patient out of rice flour and recites the Noose Dhāraṇī while calling out the patient's name. Finally, he grasps a sword and cuts the effigy of the patient into several pieces. Hearing and witnessing all this, the patient will become terrified, and the demon departs, never to return. (See *Bukong juansuo tuoluoni Zizai wang zhou jing* [T. 1097], 426c, translated by Bao Siwei [Skt. Ratnacinta], a Kashmiri monk who arrived in Luoyang in 693. This comparison was first made by Ogawa Yōichi, "Dōkyō setsuwa," in *Tonkōto chūgoko dōkyō* [Tokyo: Tokyo Shuppansha, 1983], 301–302.) Ye Jingneng's book of talismans and spells, we recall, was conferred on him by a Vedic god, and Ye himself was venerated after his death by the popular devotees of a therapeutic cult who invoked and summoned him along with various Tantric and Buddhist divinities (see Stein 2615 and Ogawa Yīchi, "Dōkyō setsuwa," 300–301).

60. See Miyakawa Hisayuki, "Sō no kisō to dōkyō," in *Tōkai daigaku kiyō: Bungakubu* 23 (1975), 34.

61. *Zizhi tongjian changbian jishi benmo* (Taibei: Wenhai chubanshe, 1967), 127, "Daoxue," 6a.

62. For Wang Laozhi, Wang Zixi, and still others, see Jin Zhongshu, "Lun Bei Song monian zhi chongshang daojiao," in *Songshi yanjiu ji* 7 (Taibei: Taiwan shuju, 1974), 297–302; and Miyakawa Hisayuki, "Sō no kisō to dōkyō," 45.

63. See Strickmann, "The Longest Taoist Scripture," 331–354 (esp. 342–344).

64. Piet van der Loon, *Taoist Books in the Libraries of the Sung Period,* 44.

65. Ibid., 58–59.

66. Ibid., 42, note 49.

67. See note 27.

68. These massive compilations of classical liturgy produced by the Ritual Service include a *Daguan lishu* in 231 *juan;* a continuation (*xubian*) of the previous in 497 *juan,* renamed the *Wuli xini;* a *Jifu zhidu* in 16 *juan;* a *Jifu tu;* and a *Zhenghe wuli xini* in 226 *juan* with prefaces.

69. Piet van der Loon, *Taoist Books in the Libraries of the Sung Period,* 39.

70. Strickmann, "The Longest Daoist Scripture," 349. (See 346–350 for more on Huizong's anti-Buddhist policies.)

71. *Zizhi tongjian changbian jishi benmo* 127, "Daoxue," 5a. The restoration of this "ancient and happy unity" also undergirds Huizong's reform of the examination system. Huizong established Daoist schools in 1116, and two years later these became part of the public school system envisioned by Wang Anshi as a substitute for the civil service examinations and partially implemented by Shenzong. The curriculum of these Daoist schools was divided between Daoism (which initially included the *Huangdi neipian, Laozi, Zhuangzi, Liezi, Kang Sangzi,* and *Wenzi,* but later dropped the first, leaving the five Daoist classics established by Tang Xuanzong) and Confucianism (which included the *Yijing* and *Mencius.*) In 1118, the *Shenji jing*—a work of medical prescriptions and Daoist talismans—as well as the *Laozi* became required reading in all public schools. For this and much more, see Chao Shih-yi, "Daoist Examinations and Daoist Schools during the Northern Song Dynasty" (unpublished paper, UCLA, 1995).

72. *Taishang zhuguo jiumin zongzhen biyao* (HY 1217) 4.1a, for example, states that the nine Tianxin talismans that were collected under the rubric of the "Spinal Numinous Writ" also derived from Zhang Daoling, while Zhang himself was divinized in the Tianxin pantheon as the Commissioner of the Department of Exorcism (1.2b; 2.6a); by the Southern Song, the *Shangqing beiji Tianxin zhengfa* (HY 567), 1a quotes the thirtieth Celestial Master to the effect that the Rites of Tianxin had descended from Heaven and were transmitted to Zhang Daoling on Mount Guming in Sichuan.

73. See *Wushang jiuxiao yuqing dafan zuwei xiandu leiting yujing* (HY 15), 15a; *Jiutian yingyuan leisheng puhua tianzun yushu baojing* (HY 16), 4b.

74. See *Daofa huiyuan* 227, "Taiyi xilei Zhu jiangzhun kaofu dafa," 2b; *Daofa huiyuan* 253, "Diqi fa," 3a.

75. *Lishi zhenxian tidao tongjian xubian* 19.16b.

76. *Yuanshi* 202.8a.
77. For an analysis of one such exorcistic text in this way, see Chapter 6, note 14.
78. *Shangqing lingbao dafa* (HY 1213), 10.9a–b.
79. Ibid., 10.11a.
80. For an analysis of these anecdotes, see Chapter 3, note 55.
81. See *Lishi zhenxian tidao tongjian xubian* 18.8b–9a and *Han Tianshi shijia* (HY 1451), 2.3b–4a.
82. Michel Strickmann, "Magical Medicine: Therapeutic Rituals in Medieval China" (unpublished ms., 1987; to be published as *Chinese Magical Medicine*, Stanford University Press, 2001), 1. See also his "Therapeutische Rituale und das Problem des Bösen im frühen Daoismus," in G. Naundorf, ed., *Religion und Philosophie in Ostasien* (1985), 185–200, which presents some of the ideas explored more fully in "Magical Medicine."
83. *Santian neijie jing* (HY 1169), 1.6b, quoted in Kobayashi Masayoshi, "The Celestial Masters under the Eastern Jin and Liu-Song Dynasties," *Taoist Resources* 3.2 (May 1992), 24.
84. For the details of all this, see Strickmann, "Magical Medicine," 8–13.
85. *Nüqing guilü* (HY 789).
86. I realize that there is a tension in *The Demon Statutes of Nüqing* between what Peter Nickerson has called the moral and magical traditions of therapy, but with the exception of a single, highly circumstantial reference to exorcism (2.5b–6a: *zhigui fa*), the text gives no account of the actual therapeutic process. This must be inferred from the text as a whole.
87. See Chapter 2, "The Rites of the Celestial Heart."
88. *Daofa huiyuan* 151–152, "Taishang hundong chiwen nüqing zhaoshu tianlu," and 167, "Taixuan fengdu heilü yige."
89. See Chapter 5, "The Daoist Rite of Summoning for Investigation."
90. See Edward L. Davis, "Women and Psychosomatic Illness in the Song," paper presented at the Triangle East Asia Colloquium, Durham, North Carolina, Feb. 27, 1999.
91. Strickmann, "Magical Medicine," 19–24.

Chapter 3: Therapeutic Movements in the Song: Practitioners

1. *Yijian zhi* 1458.
2. Ibid., 804–805.
3. Ibid., 1457–1458.
4. Ibid., 1751–1752.
5. Ibid., 54–55.

6. Ibid., 1180–1181. Kristofer Schipper has rendered this sentence differently, and I suspect that he has brought his understanding of contemporary nomenclature to bear too heavily upon the Song material: "But he was not a daoshi; hence this appellation (of fashi)." See his "Vernacular and Classical Ritual in Taoism," *Journal of Asian Studies* 45.1 (Nov. 1985), 37.

7. *Yijian zhi* 603: "Mei xiangshe zhu xi zuo yagu shi, ze wei daoshi; gu mu wei Hu daoshi."

8. The identification of exorcistic practices of certain Ritual Masters with Maoshan is also found in present-day Guangdong, Jiangxi, and Taiwan. For a discussion of this phenomenon, see John Lagerwey, "Introduction," in Fang Xuejia, ed., *Meizhou Heyuan diqi di cunluo wenhua*, vol. 5, *Traditional Hakka Society Series*, ed. John Lagerwey (Hong Kong: EFEO, Overseas Chinese Archives of the Chinese University of Hong Kong, 1977), 1–48, especially "Concluding Remarks."

9. *Yijian zhi* 1429–1430.

10. For a discussion of these eighth- or ninth-century texts, see Chapter 6.

11. See Chapter 6, note 50.

12. *Yijian zhi* 1101.

13. One may choose to dismiss this ending as generic moralizing, but one should remember that the form of the ending itself derives its power from the very real way in which biological death might follow upon the literal or internalized social isolation that results from the breaking of communal or religious norms.

14. I must respectfully disagree with Professor Schipper's interpretation of Wang's punishment, which he describes as a result of his "wearing the stellar crown and ritual vestments without being a daoshi" (Schipper, "Vernacular and Classical Ritual," 37). Clearly, such was not Wang's transgression, nor is there any indication that Wang's clerical attire was anything more than a social presumption. This is not to say that a Daoist priest might not have seen things differently, even if the gods didn't. Valerie Hansen believes that because Wang relied on another to prepare the written documents, Wang was himself illiterate (see Hansen, *Changing Gods in Medieval China*, 46). This seems probable, though the possibility that there was simply a division of labor here must be kept in mind.

15. Hansen, *Changing Gods in Medieval China*, 41.

16. See the Appendix to the present volume.

17. See above and Kristofer Schipper, "Taoist Ordination Ranks," 139–141.

18. See *Yijian zhi* 1456 for a Tianxin *fashi*; 797, for a Hunyuan *fashi*; 1356–1357, for a Tianxin zhengfa Wu *daoshi*; 1717, for "a *fashi* of the Tianqing Abbey"

(*Tianqing guan yi fashi*), who must have been a Daoist priest; 1755–1756, for "Liu Shouzhen, the *fashi* of the Zhengyi Palace" (*Zhengyi gong fashi Liu Shouzhen*), who practices the "Rectifying Rites of the Five Thunder [Gods] of the Celestial Heart of the Most High" (*Taishang Tianxin wulei zhengfa*), and who must also have been a Daoist priest; 1198–1199, for "the Daoist priest of Maoshan, Liu *fashi*" (*Maoshan daoshi Liu fashi*); 1342, for a notary (*qianpan*) who invites a "Daoist priest who practices rites" (*xingfa daoshi*), which I take to indicate a *daoshi* acting as a *fashi*.

19. *Yijian zhi*, 311–312.
20. Ibid., 1461; 1140.
21. Ibid., 1096.
22. Ibid., 1252–1253. For Ucchuṣma and his relation to lay exorcists, Buddhist and Daoist, see Chapter 6, "The Rites of Ucchuṣma" and subsequent sections.
23. Ibid., 364–367. For more on Xue Jixuan, see Winston Lo, *The Life and Thought of Yeh Shih* (Shatin N. T. : The Press of the Chinese University of Hong Kong, 1974), 43–44.
24. Lo, *The Life and Thought of Yeh Shih*, 308. See also *Yijian zhi* 695 for *Muxia sanlang*.
25. If the *fashi* emerged in a mediating position between the Daoist priest and the spirit-medium, then he also shared this plane with a series of lay religious practitioners variously identified as *fangshi, shushi, buzhe, xiangshi*, and *daoren*. Where the *fashi* has been seen primarily as an expert in exorcism, the others were experts in various arts of ancient derivation. The source material is too extensive and complex to adequately treat these practitioners here. The *shushi*, or "occultist," appears to have been primarily a geomancer whose services were sought most often with respect to burial. Geomancy, however, by no means exhausted the techniques (*shu*) in which someone designated by this term might specialize. The *buzhe* and *xiangshi* were diviners and physiognomists, respectively. The term "*daoren*" is less amenable to such limiting definitions. It denotes a class of individuals who, to a greater or lesser degree, had retreated from social life to pursue various arts of longevity, enlightenment, or self-improvement. The term might be applied to some Daoist priests and even immortals, but also to those who chose a Buddhist path. "Holy man" might be an adequate translation. Yet, as if to confirm the plane they shared with the *fashi*, or at least an elasticity of nomenclature, we find a *daoren* who called himself "He *fashi*" (*Yijian zhi* 1697–1698), another who specialized in the Rites of the Five Thunders (ibid., 1315–1316), and still another whose speciality was the Rites of the Celestial Heart (ibid., 1422–1424). The Rites

of Tianxin, moreover, found devotees among "occultists" (ibid., 1327), and there were *fangshi* who were also called *fashi*.

26. See *Yijian zhi* 582.
27. Ibid., 1049.
28. Ibid., 65–66.
29. Ibid., 487–488.
30. Ibid., 832–833.
31. Ibid., 582–583.
32. Ibid., 232.
33. For Hong Mai's assessment of conflicting accounts of Shizhong's relation to Lu Quan, see ibid., 479 and 684–685.
34. Ibid., 479.
35. *Wushang xuanyuan santianwang yudang dafa.*
36. Poul Andersen, "Taoist Ritual Texts and Traditions," 97–101.
37. Ibid., 100.
38. *Yijian zhi* 237.
39. Ibid., 1594.
40. Ibid., 1362–1363.
41. Ibid., 237–239.
42. Ibid., 684–685.
43. Ibid., 1362.
44. Ibid., 866–867.
45. Ibid., 1089–1091. For the translation and analysis of this anecdote, see Chapter 7, "Confucian Literati and Child-Mediums."
46. *Yijian zhi*, 244.
47. Ibid., 837–838.
48. Ibid., 347.
49. Ibid., 1191.
50. Ibid., 235–236. See also 504, where Zhao performs a Yellow Register Retreat; 111–112, where a Daoist priest employs the "Talismanic Register of the Six Ding Spirits of the Celestial Heart" (*Tianxin liuding fulu*) in an exorcism; and 313, where a commoner serves the Six Jia and Six Ding spirits and is petitioned by someone to exorcize a dragon-spirit that is capsizing boats on the Wusong River.
51. Ibid., 653–654.
52. Ibid., 846. For a summary and analysis of this anecdote, see Chapter 7, "Daoist Priests and Child-Mediums" (under the subsection "In an Official Compound in Jiangsu").
53. *Yijian zhi*, 419–420.

54. Ibid., 949–950.

55. Liu Zhugan from Hengzhou acquired the "Sublime Arts of Bajing" (*Bajing miaoshu*) and the "Rectifying Rites of the Celestial Heart" while a student in the capital, and went on to cure a man possessed by a *wutong* spirit after numerous mediums had failed (*Yijian zhi* 1484–1486); also in Hengzhou, a literatus (*junshi*) named Xu Zhuzhan practiced the "Rites of the Great Cavern" (*dadong fa*) and exorcized a woman possessed on the eve of her marriage by placing a talisman in the stove and another in her mouth (ibid., 1191–1192); in Yugan, a literatus (*xiangshi*) practiced Thunder Magic (*leibu fa*) and thereby disposed of a demon first identified by a Daoist priest (ibid., 1435–1436); and in Chuzhou, another literatus (*shiren*), Ye Sheng, who had traveled to Hangzhou to study at the Imperial University, received the "Ritual Registers of the Divine Empyrean" (*shenxiao falu*) and performed exorcisms for commoners, among others (ibid., 1489–1490 and 1493–1494).

I should mention parenthetically, however, that the older lineages of Daoism at Maoshan and Longhushan also still found a following among the elite. Hong Xingzu, the uncle of Hong Mai and author of an influential commentary on the *Songs of Chu*, became an initiate on Maoshan while acting as a provincial judge (ibid., 91–92). The son of an official whose brothers had all passed the *jinshi* examination personally received the "Register of Highest Purity" on Maoshan from its twenty-fifth patriarch, Liu Hunkang (ibid., 565), and officials both civil and military were also promoting and attending Daoist "offerings" on Maoshan (ibid., 330; 1197).

The Celestial Master sect seems to have attracted a much wider social audience. While those who received the exorcistic services of the Celestial Master himself or his priests on Longhushan were primarily courtiers and ministers (ibid., 1438–1439; 1102–1103), laymen or commoners were often favored with registers and spells (ibid., 406–407; 596–597; 674). In the process of appropriating the new therapeutic rites of the Song, the Celestial Master became the premier exorcist of all, and some twelfth-century demons declared that they were not afraid of anyone but him (ibid., 328–330). Entire communities might turn to him in particularly desperate situations. During the Zhenghe reign period (1111–1118), in the administrative city of Tongzhou, a demon had so devastated its residents, both official and commoner, that no bureaucrat would knowingly take up his post. It required an edict from the emperor Huizong himself to bring the Celestial Master Zhang Xuqing to this town, and in a dramatic and truly frightening piece of exorcistic theater, the Celestial Master constructed a five-tiered altar and placed the clerks of the yamen on top of it to act as bait (ibid., 1098–1100).

56. Ibid., 568. See also 320–321, where Song Ankuo was invited to exorcize the daughter of another official and employed a bamboo pole held by a small boy as a demonic conduit.

57. Ibid., 1070–1071. Cheng passed his technique on to Liu Dayong, a famous doctor about whom we have several anecdotes (1072–1073, 1116–1117, 1117–1118). See also 1245, for another magistrate who sets up a Daoist "offering" to rid his community of snakes.

58. Ibid., 745.

59. Ibid., 830.

60. Ibid., 853.

61. See below. For other examples of local functionaries, spirit-mediums, or landlords who advise officials to respect customary sacrifices at local temples, see *Yijian zhi* 217–218, 945–946, and so forth.

62. Ibid., 995.

63. Based on a close reading of several stories in the *Taiping guangji,* Jean Levi has shown how, in the Six Dynasties and Tang periods, the magistrate's mission to civilize or reform local customs and to transform the physical landscape for productive use often took the form of a personal confrontation with local gods and their servants—spirit-mediums, or sorcerers, as he calls them (Jean Levi, "Les fonctionnaires et le divin: Luttes de pouvoirs entre divinités et administrateurs dans les contes des Six Dynasties et des Tang," *Cahiers d'Extrême-Asie* 2 [1986], 81–106; see also his "Les Fonctions religieuses de la bureaucratie céleste," *L'Homme* 101 [1987], 27 [1]: 35–37). In this confrontation, the magistrate adopted the profile of an exorcist: in some cases he would function as a kind of double of the local god; in others he would be put in the position of the sacrificial substitute, an archaic role once assumed by the spirit-medium himself; in still other cases, the magistrate himself might be honored with a cult that would replace the one he had successfully eradicated. (For some of these themes, see also David Johnson, "The City-God Cults of T'ang and Sung China," *Harvard Journal of Asiatic Studies* 45:2 [Dec. 1985]: 363–457.)

For the historian, the endless play of thematic substitutions here manages to finesse the complex reality of the spirit-medium's position and functions in Tang society, and gives a false impression of the infrequency with which the magistrate's civilizing mission might be seriously contested in that society. In the subprefecture of Shanshi, for example, a spirit-medium, a monk, and even the local earth-spirit all found common cause in the successful defense of a rural cult against the depredations of an outgoing magistrate. The magistrate was lectured on the necessity of upholding local customs and criticized in precisely the same language with which officials criticized local cults for being licentious and perverse. This lesson was not lost on the magistrate's successor, who personally honored the altar and thereby quickly won over even the urban population (*Taiping guangji*, 2433.) Still, Levi's subtle analysis is important for drawing attention here and there to the parallel function of the Confucian magistrate and Daoist priest in controlling forces of anarchy, both natural and supernatural (which often amount to the same thing). And in particular, he demonstrates how the official proclamations (*jiao*, *zhao*, and *xi*) of the magistrate work on the gods in precisely the same manner as the talismans (*fu*) and invocations (*zhou*) of the Daoist.

64. See *Daofa huiyuan* 56, preface; 158, second preface; *Qingwei shenlie bifa* (HY 222), shang; *Song Bai zhenren Yuchan quanji*, 2; and so forth.

65. See, now, Judith Boltz, "Not by the Seal of Office Alone: New Weapons in Battles with the Supernatural," in Ebrey and Gregory, eds., *Religion and Society in T'ang and Sung China* (1993), esp. 269–283.

66. Nakamura Jihei, "Tōdai no fu," *Shien* 105–106 (August 1971), 61–92.

67. Nakamura Jihei, "Godai ni okeru fu," *Tōyō Bunka* 55 (March 1975), 1–14.

68. Ibid., 10–11. This account, written on a stone tablet, is preserved in the Qing gazetteer, *Zhangqiu xian zhi* 14, "Jinshi lu."

69. Nakamura Jihei, "Godai ni okeru fu," 4–6; Makita Tairyō, *Godai shūkkyōshi kenkyū* (Kyoto: Heirakuji Shoten, 1971), passim.

70. Nakamura Jihei, "Hokusōchō to fu" *Chūō daigaku kiyō; Bungakubu shigakka* 88 (1978), 63–78, and "Sōdai no fu no tokuchō" *Chūō daigaku kiyō ; Bungakubu shigakka* 104 (1982), 51–75.

71. Nakamura, "Hokusōchō to fu," 69.

72. Ibid., 74.

73. Kanai Noriyuki, "Sōdai no sonsha to bukkyō," *Bukkyō shigaku kenkyū* 18.2 (1976), 38.

74. See Sawada Mizuho, *Chūgoku no juhō* (Tokyo: Hirakawa, 1984), 290–304 and 305–310.

75. See Sawada Mizuho, *Chūgoku no minkan shinkō* (Tokyo: Kosakusha, 1982), 332–373.

76. See Chikusa Masa'aki, *Chūgoku bukkyō shakai shi kenkyū* (Tokyo: Dōhōsha, 1982), 199–227.

77. *Song huiyao jigao* 20.14.

78. See Ursula Angelika Cedzich, "Wu-Tong: Zur bewegten Geschichte eines Kultes," in Gert Naundorf, ed., *Religion und Philosophie in Ostasien* (Würzburg: Königshausen & Neumann, 1985), esp. 44–46.

79. *Chunxi Sanshan zhi* 8.21a–22a (esp. 21b, lines 8–9) and 8.22b–23a (esp. 22b, lines 2–6); *Zhi-zheng Jinling xinzhi* 11.16b–17a; *Xiandun Lin'an zhi* 71.13a–14a.
80. *Yijian zhi* 1074–1075.
81. Ibid., 1235–1236. See also 1437 for another anecdote about this temple.
82. Ibid., 1084–1085.
83. Ibid., 1034.
84. *Liangxi manzhi*, Fei Gun, 10.9b–10a.
85. *Yijian zhi* 780.
86. Ibid., 782.
87. Ibid., 585.

Chapter 4: The Cult of the Black Killer

1. This and the following three paragraphs are based on the texts collected by Sun Kekuan, *Song Yuan daojiao zhi fazhan* (Taizhong: Donghai University, 1965), 71–93; Michel Soymié, *Annuaire de l'École Pratique des Hautes Études, IVe Section* (1975–1976), 997–1002, and (1976–1977), 1027–1034; and Suzanne Cahill, "Taoism at the Sung Court: The Heavenly Text Affair of 1008," *Bulletin of Sung-Yuan Studies* 16 (1980), 23–44.
2. See *Songchao shishi* 7, "Wang Jie."
3. Soymié, *Annuaire de l'École Pratique des Hautes Études* (1976–1977), 10–33. At the end of the Northern Song, the emperor Huizong , as we have seen, would exploit the religious culture of another southerner to make claims for himself and his dynasty that exceeded even those of his predecessors.
4. *Yunji qiqian* 103.10b.
5. Ibid., 103.10b.
6. *Yisheng baode zhuan* (HY 1275). Zhenzong's preface to this work is wrongly attributed to his successor, Emperor Renzong. An earlier version, however, is preserved in chapter 103 of the Daoist encyclopedia *Yunji qiqian* (HY 1026), compiled by Zhang Junfang around 1028. It is this version to which I refer.
7. *Yunji qiqian* 103.2b–3a.
8. Ibid., 103.3b. The Tower Abbey in the Zhongnan mountains marked the holy site where Laozi had revealed *The Scripture of the Way and Its Power* (*Daodejing*) to the Guardian of the Pass Yin Xi. This tradition has been traced to a fifth-century priest of the Tower Abbey, Yin Tong (398–499), who also claimed descent from Yin Xi. The putative ancestry of the priests of the Tower Abbey was strengthened in the Tang when its abbot, Yin Wencao (622–688), further identified Laozi's mother as the daughter of the Yin family of Tianshui, Gansu—the family residence of Yin Wencao himself. Moreover, because of

the Tang dynasty's own claim of descent from Laozi, the emperor Gaozu rebuilt the Tower Abbey and renamed it the "Abbey of the Holy Ancestor." In
679, in fact, Yin Wencao performed an "offering" (*jiao*) in which Laozi himself descended before the imperial court, resulting in a commission to write
a new hagiography of Laozi (i.e., *The Holy Record of the Emperor of the Mysterious Prime*). The Daoist lineage of Tower Abbey took Laozi as its high god, with
Yin Xi as its "Ancestral Patriarch" and Yin Gui as its "High Transcendent."
While religious practice focused on the soteriological value of the *Daodejing*,
the Tower Abbey Daoists also situated themselves within the reformed practices of Kou Qianzhi's northern Celestial Masters and absorbed alchemical
and other practices associated with the southern traditions of Shangqing and
Lingbao. All this had already occurred by the fifth and sixth centuries.

In the Tang, the emphasis on genealogy so characteristic of the elite and
the ruling house seems just as crucial to the priests of Tower Abbey as to the
successful effort of the Zhang family in Jiangxi to reconstitute the Celestial
Master lineage on Longhushan. A comparison of these genealogies is in-
structive. The latter's seems distinctly patriarchal and characteristic of a lineage of *married priests* who claim direct descent from the Han founder of Celestial Master Daoism, Zhang Daoling. The lineage of the Tower Abbey priests,
in contrast, was based on an entirely different principle. These priests are related to Laozi through his mother, who is believed to have conceived Laozi
without the benefit of a male phallus. And even the abbot Yin Wencao's own
birth was said to be the result of an exchange between Laozi's mother and
his own, again excluding the phallus. This way of figuring descent seems characteristic of a lineage of *unmarried priests* who seek to exclude male desire in
pursuit of a feminine (mystical) enjoyment. For the history of the Tower
Abbey before the Song, see now Otagi Hajime, "Tōdai rokan kō," in Yoshikawa Tadao, *Chūgoku kodōkyō shi kenkyū* (Kyoto: Dōhōsha, 1992), 275–322;
and Livia Kohn, "Yin Xi: The Master at the Beginning of the Scripture," *Journal of Chinese Religions* 25 (1997), 83–139, and idem, "The Northern Celestial Masters," in Kohn, ed., *Handbook of Daoism* (Leiden: E. J. Brill, 2000).
For a biography of Liang Quan, who died in 978, see *Zhongnan shan Shuojingtai lidai zhenxian beiji* (HY 955), 17a–b.

9. *Yunji qiqian* 103.3b–5a.

10. Ibid., 103.5b: "Wu jianglai yunzhi Taiping jun Songchao di'er zhu."

11. Ibid., 103.5b–6a.

12. Ibid., 103.6b.

13. For these rumors and the problem of imperial succession, see Chikusa
Masa'aki, *Sō-no Taiso to Taisō* (Tokyo: Shimizu sho'in, 1975), 134–147.

14. *Yunji qiqian* 103.6b. For the Qionglin yuan, see Zhou Cheng, ed., *Song Dongjing kao* (Beijing: Zhonghua shuju, 1988), 193.

15. *Yunji qiqian* 103.6b–7b.

16. *Jinshi cuibian* 125.19a–25b, "Shangqing taiping gong zhong ji."

17. See note 8 above. For this suggestion, see Otagi Hajime, "Sō Taiso satsugai-setsu to jōshintaiheikan," *Shirin* (1984), 70–73.

18. See Yamauchi Kōichi, "Hokusō no kokka to gyokkō," *Tōhōgaku* 62 (1981), 83–97.

19. *Yunji qiqian* 103.9a.

20. *Xu Zizhi tongjian changbian*, entry dated tenth month, ninth year of Kaibao (976).

21. *Huangchao shishi leiyuan* 44. 9a.

22. Ibid., 44.9b.

23. Su Shi, *Sushi shizhi* (Beijing: Zhunghua shuju, 1982), 3.

24. *Daofa huiyuan* 156, "Shangqing fumo tianpeng dafa," 3b.

25. Marc Kalinowski, *Cosmologie et divination dans la Chine ancienne: Le compendium des cinq agents (Wuxing dayi, VIe Siècle)*, (Paris: École Française d'Extrême Orient, 1991), 384–387.

26. Ibid., 386: "Tianfeng favorise la sécurité des frontières et la protection des points stratégiques."

27. *Zhen Gao* 10.10b–11a (See also *Dengzhen yinque* [HY 421] 2.11a.) For a translation of this spell, see Michel Strickmann, "The Taoist Renaissance of the Twelfth Century," 18–19. The spell, with certain variations, remains central in the Song exorcistic "rites of Tianpeng," for which see *Daofa huiyuan* 156.5; 157.18; 159.2, and the analysis in Liu Zhiwan, "Tenhōshin to tenhōju ni tsuite," in Akizuki Kanei, ed., *Dōkyō to shūkyō bunka* (Tokyo: Hirakawa shūppan, 1987), 403–424.

28. See *Daojiao lingyan ji* (HY 590) 13.11a–12a, and *Yunji qiqian* 120.14b–15b.

29. See *Zhiqing zashuo*, compiled by Wang Mingqing, as quoted in Liu Zhiwan, "Tenhōshin to tenhōju ni tsuite," 407–408. For the cult to Tianpeng in the Song and its ubiquitous presence in the *Yijian zhi*, see Sawada Mizuho, *Chūgoku no juhō* (Tokyo: Hirahawa, 1984), 478–480.

30. Nakano Miyako, *Chūgoku no yōkai* (Tokyo: Iwanami shoten, 1983), 115–116 and illustration #35, a rubbing from Shanxi.

31. For Mount Wudang, see now John Lagerwey, "The Pilgrimage to Wudang Shan," in Susan Naquin and Chunfang Yu, eds., *Pilgrims and Sacred Sites in China* (Berkeley: University of California Press, 1992), 293–332. There is disagreement about the dating and interpretation of the *Xuanting shangdi qisheng lu*. Chuang Huang-i has demonstrated the inaccuracy of many of the

historical references in the hagiography, for which see Chuang, "Les croyances concernant la divinité taoïste Xuanwu, Xème-XIIIème siècles" (Ph.D. diss., EHESS, Paris, 1994). This has inspired Pierre-Henri de Bruyn to interpret the entire work as the invention of a Ming imperial propagandist (see his "Wudang Shan: The Origins of a Major Center of Modern Taoism," paper prepared for the International Conference on Religion and Chinese Society, Chinese University of Hong Kong, Shatin, N.T., May 29–June 2, 2000). John Lagerwey, Judith Boltz, and others, myself included, believe that despite the "historical mistakes," many of the passages in *juan* 2–8 reflect the political as well as the religious importance of the cult to Zhenwu in the Song dynasty, as suggested in this chapter. (See also John Lagerwey, *Taoist Ritual in Chinese Society and History*, 257–258.) Still, de Bruyn's work on Wudangshan is authoritative, and we look forward to the publication of his thesis.

32. *Xuanting shangdi qisheng lu* 1.19b–24a.

33. Ibid., 3.5b–6b. For over thirty years, Zhuan Hong had placed his personal devotion to the Perfected Warrior at the disposal of others. Literati, in particular, made their way to Hong's door in Yangzhou in the hope of exchanging their poetry and prose for some auspicious words from the god. Ultimately, Zhuan Hong grew tired of the market atmosphere created by the horses and carriages always parked at his gate. He decided to enter the religious life (*chu-jia*) and spend his last years "wandering like the clouds." Actually, he was on a pilgrimage, for he made his way to the Palace of Great Peace on Zhong-nanshan, where he lived in a tiny hut, no doubt to be in close proximity to the Palace's western pavilions, which were dedicated to the Perfected Warrior. There he attracted the attention of Zhang Shouzhen, who took him into the Palace as a disciple and priest.

One evening three year later, Zhang Shouzhen heard Zhuan Hong talking in his sleep and then noticed a bright light emanating from Hong's hut, about which he inquired the next morning. Hong told Zhang that his life was about to come to an end. He proceeded to bathe, change clothing, and mount the main altar to the Perfected Warrior. There, in a trance from which he never emerged, Hong became possessed by the Perfected Warrior, who claimed that "the Mandate would be renewed and the Barefoot Transcendent would be welcomed at the spring sacrifices." Although these lines were written down, no one knew what they meant.

With hindsight, we may perhaps understand the reference better than the original witnesses. As late as the twelfth century, a rumor still persisted that the emperor Zhenzong's son and successor was the issue of a palace maid and not of his officially designated mother, the empress Liu. The union, more-over, was the result of conversations between the emperor and the maid in which the latter confided that she had had a dream in which a Barefoot Transcendent told her that he was destined to be her son. When the future emperor Renzong was born the following year, he liked to walk around the palace grounds without shoes or socks and was nicknamed the Barefoot Transcendent. For this rumor, see Wang Mingqing (1127–1214), *Huizhu yuhua* 2, summarized in Ting Ch'uan-ching, *A Compilation of Anecdotes of Sung Personalities* (Taipei: St. John's University Press, 1989), 31.

34. Ibid., 2.12a–b.
35. *Daofa huiyuan* 171–178. See also 169–170.
36. See *Xuanting shangdi qisheng lu* 2.17b–18b.
37. See, for example, *Xuanting shangdi qisheng lu* 2.18b; 4.1a–2a, and many other passages in *juan* 4; see also, *Yijian zhi* 250–251, 551, 905, 989, 1100, 1231–1232, 1397, 1538–1539, 1690–1692, 1769–1770.
38. *Yijian zhi* 1100.
39. Ibid., 777 and 996; *Xuanting shangdi qisheng lu* 4.21b–23b.
40. *Xuanting shangdi qisheng lu* 1a–15b. In view of the ancient iconographical representation of Xuanwu as a turtle/snake (see above, note 30), the mythological representation of these animals as his defeated assistants suggests that Xuanwu has overcome his own demonic nature.
41. *Yijian zhi*, 1425: "with loosened hair and bare feet, [the medium] defiantly came forward, beating drums and blowing horns"; 364–369 (365, line 7); 705–706. For earlier examples, see, for instance, *Song Shu* 79.39 (p. 2040), where several people who "diligently served spirit-mediums, often loosened their hair and bared their feet and bowed their heads before the divinity of the Northern Pole."
42. For references, see Chapter 2, "The Rites of the Celestial Heart," and notes 2–7 of that chapter.
43. The three fundamental talismans are the Talisman of the Three Luminosities (*Sanguang fu*), the Talisman of the Black Killer (*Heisha fu*), and the Talisman of the Celestial Outline (*Tiangang fu*). See *Shangqing tianxin zhengfa* (HY 566) 3.1a–9a.
44. Ibid., 3.5a–7a.
45. Ibid., 2.3a–b; 3.1a; 3.8b.
46. Ibid., 3.17a and 19a.
47. *Yunji qiqian* 103.14a–21b.
48. *Jinshi cuibian* 134.7b–13a, "Shengsong zhuanying da fashi xingzhuang" (see 9a.5 for the reference to Zhang Heisha).

49. See, for example, *Yijian zhi* 97.

50. The link between Zhang Shouzhen and the Celestial Master tradition is drawn more tenuously in *The Transmissions* (see 28a, where the Perfected Lord indicates to Zhang Shouzhen's son that he should carry on the priesthood in the same way that the office of the Celestial Master was passed on from father to son.)

51. See Chapter 2. The relocation or, better, the assumption of the Celestial Master lineage by a certain Zhang family of Jiangxi occurred sometime between the end of the eighth and beginning of the tenth century. See Kristofer Schipper, *Annuaire de l'École Pratique des Hautes Études* (1985–1986), 133–135, and T. H. Barrett, "The Emergence of the Taoist Papacy in the T'ang Dynasty," *Asia Major* 3rd ser., 7.1 (1994), 89–106.

52. *Wushang xuanyuan santianwang yudang dafa* (HY 220), 28.7b.10–28.8a.1. See Poul Andersen, "Taoist Ritual Texts and Traditions," 98. For Lu Shizhong and the *Yudang dafa*, see ibid., 72–73. For spirit-writing as a point of convergence between early Daoism and mediums, see R. A. Stein, "Un exemple de relations entre Taoïsme et religion populaire," in *Fukui Hakase shōju kinen Tōyō bunka ronshū* (Tokyo, 1969), 79–90.

53. For this process, see Sudō Yoshiyuki and Nakajima Tōshi, *Chūgoku no rekishi 5: Godai-Sō* (Tokyo: Kodansha, 1974), 29–44 and 55–64; Peter Bol, "This Culture of Ours," 49–50.

54. Zhao is referring here to his spirit-general who has bribed "a spirit-general in the law courts" and who is identified below. The spirit who has made the bribe known to Zhao, the one who has possessed someone in order to be questioned, is another spirit entirely.

55. Ibid., 831–832.

56. The ambivalence with which the Ritual Master approached these local spirits is mirrored here by the ambivalence of responsibility for their excesses. Theoretically, the Ritual Master had not "presumed upon his authority"; the responsibility for the bribe fell upon the spirits who offered and accepted it. In fact, however, the Ritual Master's identity was so bound up with that of his spirit-general, his efficacy so tied to local worship, that he was forced to reform himself and give up his own commission rather than try to defend himself. What I am trying to argue here is that it was not simply a matter of the priest being implicated in the transgression of a subordinate, nor was it simply a matter of his thinking that it was his fault for not having adequately paved the way procedurally for the use of his spirit-general as a bureaucratic emissary. All of this is probably true. The Ritual Master's complex response must be explained by the realization that his own integrity as a local exorcist de-

pended very much on the integrity of the local cult, which was now compromised.

57. See *Taishang zhuguo jiumin zongzhen biyao* (HY 1217) 3.7b–8a, where the Ritual Master transforms himself into Tianpeng (*hua shen wei Tianpeng dajiang*) before writing the talismans; 5.6a, where the Ritual Master visualizes his body to be that of Zhenwu (*xiang shen wei Zhenwu*), with disheveled hair, weapons in hand, and the demonic snake and tortoise at his feet; and so forth.

58. Gilbert Rouget, *Music and Trance*, 312.

59. *Yijian zhi* 617–618.

Chapter 5: The Daoist Ritual Master and Child-Mediums

1. Kristofer Schipper, "Vernacular and Classical Ritual in Daoism," 27.

2. Ibid., 29. Schipper's descriptions, here and in other places, of *fashi* rituals are based on his personal observation and/or on manuscripts acquired during fieldwork. For otherworldly journeys employing a spirit-medium, the reader might begin with Kokubu Naoichi, "Taiwan ni okeru shamanizumu no sekai—toku ni tanki no rakugoku tankyu o megutte," *Minzokugaku hyoron* 6 (1971), 1–22. In the therapeutic rite known as "*Luoyu tangong ke*," the Daoist first dons a red turban and transforms himself (*bianshen*) into a divine personality; then, blowing on a water-buffalo horn, he commands one of his divinities to descend and possess a "divination youth" (*tongji*). The entranced medium spends the rest of the time immobile and covered under a table, suggesting his absence. The medium is said to be traveling through the courts of the twelve earth-prisons in order to retrieve the *hun*-soul of the sick client, a journey and mission described in literary Hokkien by the *fashi*. For the divine transformation of the Master, and its significance, see Poul Andersen, "The Transformation of the Body in Taoist Ritual," paper presented for the conference "Religious Reflections on the Human Body," Cornell University, Ithaca, N.Y., April 19–21, 1991. For other descriptions of rituals of contemporary *fashi* and/or of their relation to spirit-mediums, see Brigitte Baptandier-Berthier, "Enfant de divination, voyageur du destin," *L'Homme* 101 (Jan.-Mar. 1987), XXVII (1): 86–100; John Lagerwey, "'Les têtes des démons tombent par milliers': Le *fachang*, rituel exorciste du nord de Taiwan," *L'Homme* 101 (Jan.-Mar. 1987), XXVII (1): 101–116; Ōfuchi Ninji, *Chūgokujin no shūkyū girei* (Tokyo: Fukutake shoten, 1983), 1008–1083; James R. Wilkerson, "The 'Ritual Master' and His 'Temple Corporation' Rituals," in Lin Ru, ed., *Minjian xinyang yu Zhongguo wenhua: Guoji yantao huilun wenji 2* (Taibei: Hanxue yanjiu zhongxin, 1994), 471–522.

3. See discussion in Chapter 1, in the section "Historians, Sinologists, and the Song Period."

4. *Yijian zhi*, 1002.

5. N. H. Van Straten, *Concepts of Health, Disease and Vitality in Traditional Chinese Society* (Wiesbaden: Franz Steiner, 1983), 61.

6. Ibid., 62 and 145–164.

7. Ibid., 59.

8. *Yijian zhi*, 913.

9. *Taiping guangji* 325: "Meng Xiang" (2577–2578), an anecdote from the *Fayuan zhulin*.

10. See the anecdotes collected and paraphrased in Sawada Mizuho, "Kenkikō," reprinted in his *Chūgoku no juhō* (Tokyo: Hirakawa, 1984), 3–39 (esp. 13–22). The Master Demon Seers flourished in market towns and villages.

11. *Baopuzi neipian*, Ge Hong, "Dengshe bian."

12. For the magical as well as metaphorical use of mirrors in Daoism, one might begin with Fukunaga Mitsuji, "Dōkyō ni okeru kagami to tsurugi," *Tōhō Gakuhō* 45 (1973), 59–120.

13. See *Yunji qiqian* 19.

14. See Sawada Mizuho, "Kokuki kō," reprinted in his *Chūgoku no juhō* (Tokyo: Hirakawa, 1984), 40–55.

15. Toward the end of the Tianbao reign period (742–756), the Prefect of Yanzhou (Shandong), Su Shen, was hoping to marry his only son into a particular family named Lu. This family, however, had three nubile daughters, and the prefect did not know which one was the most beautiful. He therefore asked a friend—a woman from Chang'an named Ma Erniang—to intervene and bring the three girls for the perusal of the boy's mother. Ma Erniang then proceeded to make the most extraordinary introduction. She marked off a ritual space within a Buddhist hall and performed a rite of "summoning for investigation." After a while the *hun*-souls of the three girls arrived, and the mother examined them up close. Lady Ma herself then made an assessment of the relative merits of each girl, and Su Shen selected the second eldest. See *Taiping guangji* 358, under the title "Su Shen" (vol. 8, p. 2833), an anecdote from the *Guangyi ji*. Here *kaozhao* appears close to *shehun* ("controlling the *hun*-soul").

16. See the section later in this chapter on "The Daoist Rite of Summoning for Investigation."

17. See *Taishang zhuguo jiumin zongzhen biyao* (HY 1217), 7.1a.

18. *Jinsuo liuzhu yin*, preface, 2a–b.

19. See biographies in *Jiu Tangshu* 79.5b–7a, and *Xin Tangshu* 204.1a–b.

20. For the early date, see Michel Strickmann, *Mantras et mandarins: Le bouddhisme tantrique en Chine* (Paris: Gallimard, 1996), and David Johnson, "The City-God Cults of Tang and Song China," 436; for the later date, Judith Boltz, *A Survey of Taoist Literature* (1987), 262.

21. For the arguments, subtle but persuasive, see Poul Andersen, "Taoist Ritual Texts and Traditions," 73–77, and T. H. Barrett, "Towards a Date for the Chin-So Liu-Chu Yin," *Bulletin of the School of Oriental and African Studies*, 53.2 (1990), 292–294.

22. *Jinsuo liuzhu yin* 23.8a–9a and 11.2a–b.

23. Ibid., 4.5b.

24. Ibid., 4.5b–6a.

25. Ibid., 4.6a–7b.

26. Ibid., 4.7b–8b.

27. Ibid., 28:2a–b.

28. Ibid., 29:3b–4a.

29. What I would call proto-*kaozhao* rites can also be found in the *Protocols for the Precious Memorials from the Jade Records and Golden Book of the Most High* (*Taishang jinshu yudie baozhang yi*, HY 805, 1b, 7a–b, 9b–10a, 12b–13a). John Lagerwey, who dates this Zhengyi text to the Tang, has succinctly described the content relevant to the issue of *kaozhao fa*: "the master, after he has exteriorized the relevant officers on his registers, tells them 'to report' (*guanqi*) the problem which made the ritual necessary to the local 'prefect officer' of the soil, as well as to the officers and clerks on his staff who are in charge of 'investigating on the four sides' and 'of searching out and summoning' (*kaozhao*) those guilty of causing the problem" ("Introduction to Taoist Ritual through the Tang," unpublished ms., 1985, 16). On the one hand, the term "*kaozhao*" appears in this text exclusively in apposition to various officers (HY 805, 1b, "*sanyuan kaozhaojun*," and 4a, line 10 through 4b, line 1, "*zhuqi jiancha kaozhao jiazi zhuguan*"). On the other hand, the work clearly anticipates the *kaozhao* rites of the Song in the critical role it gives to the god of the soil and his minions, who are to "search out and summon" the guilty spirits—a role that is demonstrated in many of the anecdotes that I translate in Chapters 6 and 7 (though, as is more charactertistic of the Song, the god of the soil is often abused).

30. In another Daoist text attributed to the seventh-century official Li Chunfeng, the *Taishang chiwen dongshen sanlu* (HY 589), Michel Strickmann has discovered, summarized, and analyzed a set of ritual procedures in which a child-medium is employed in a form of "dream therapy" (see Strickmann, "Dreamwork of Psycho-Sinologists: Doctors, Daoists, Monks," in Carolyn Brown, ed.,

Psycho-Sinology: The Universe of Dreams in Chinese Culture [Lanham: University Press of America, 1988], 36). The use of a child-medium in a seventh-century Daoist exorcism would appear to present a serious qualification to my argument that the use of such mediums was a characteristic of Song-dynasty Daoism. There are grounds, however, for questioning the assignment of this text to the seventh century. Because I also have a rather different interpretation of this passage, I offer first a translation (which nonetheless benefits from Strickmann's "tentative reading," as he calls his summary):

> *Method of the Patriarch [for Treating] Hun-Souls Which, Having Roamed to Various Regions during a Night Dream, Have Been Beguiled by Jade Maidens:* In the first stage, the priest has a small child go to sleep. First, he twice intones the spell, "The Immovable, Venerable Saint [i.e., Acala vidyārāja], take control!" and takes a piece of paper, folds it in half, and has the child hold it between his teeth. After he wraps the head of the child with two pieces of silk cloth, he first takes two mouthfuls of pneumas from the sleeping one [i.e., the patient] and intones the spell, "I send the Four Great Spirit-Generals to capture the Jade Maiden who has beguiled the *hun*-soul!" After the spell is finished, he exhales into the mouth of the sleeping small child. Then, using the thumbs of his two hands, the priest presses them above the temples of the sleeping person [i.e., the patient]. While this person remains asleep, the priest takes the pneumas of the five directions and blows them onto his body. After the time it takes to drink two cups of tea, the priest sits still in a formal manner and intones, "The Immovable, Venerable Saint, take control!" and he goes off searching for the *hun*-soul. After he has seen it, he intones again, "I send the Four Great Spirit-Generals to capture the *hun*-soul which has been beguiled by a Jade Maiden! I call upon the soul to quickly return!" Then he calls out the patient's personal name and causes him to awaken. (HY 589, 6a–b)

Strickmann accurately and insightfully calls this a treatment for "pathological dreaming," and more specifically either for "debilitating erotic dreams" or for "a more serious instance of soul-loss and consequent disorientation, even delirium." However, Strickmann also characterizes the treatment per se as "a case of 'setting a dream to catch a dream,'" which seems to me inaccurate. On my reading, the action involves two steps. In the first, the priest inhales the patient's pneumas that embody the Jade Maiden (i.e., his erotic thoughts and delirium), mixes them with his own pneumas that embody the command to capture the Jade Maiden, and finally exhales them into the mouth of the medium. The paper is meant to absorb the erotic delirium/Jade Maiden embodied in the pneumas, while the silk cloth wrapped around the child's head was probably intended to prevent anything (another Jade Maiden?) from getting in. With the transfer of the Jade Maiden to the child-medium, the patient is now an empty vessel. In the second step, the *hun*-soul is located, captured, and restored to the patient.

Strickmann concludes, "This particular seventh century text reveals Buddhist influence. I know of no other cases from so early a period in which Daoists use a child-medium. But such practices are found at the time in Tantric Buddhism." While it is true, as Strickmann has shown elsewhere, that Tantric Buddhists were performing such practices in the Tang (for which see Chapter 6), Poul Andersen has argued, based on various internal references in the text, that the date of this scripture cannot be earlier than the middle of the tenth century and is probably later (see Andersen, "Taoist Ritual and Traditions," 61–62). The attribution to Li Chunfeng, as in the case of the *Jinsuo liuzhu yin*, is pseudo-epigraphical. I would argue, moreover, that the use of a medium in this text is evidence of its Song provenance. And, as we shall see, the transfer of breaths from the patient to a medium is precisely the method employed in Song Daoist exorcisms.

31. This symptomatic behavior is described in the Daoist ritual texts as *diankuang* ("deranged and mad") or *dianxie* ("deranged and deviant"). See, among other texts, *Shangqing tianxin zhengfa* (HY 566), 4.1a.

32. See Michel de Certeau, *La Possession de Loudun* (Paris: Julliard, 1970), 61 and 207.

33. For the Tianxin tradition, see *Taishang zhuguo jiumin zongzhen biyao* 2.2a–b (the earliest occurrence of the *bianshen* spell used by the Daoist priest in the modern *jiao* liturgy), and especially, 7.9a: "At the time when you perform the rite above, first visualize a fire within your heart enveloping your entire body. The fire cleanses and refines your form and spirit. Then envision your body becoming the Envoy of Summoning for Investigation (*kaozhao shi*), an awful spirit, fiery with rage and booming like thunder." The Ritual Master's transformation here occurs almost incidentally within the context of "Rites of Entrapment," for which see the end of this section of Chapter 5. For a more explicit reference to *bianshen* within the same text, see 7.34b, where "the Ritual Master lights incense and transforms himself into the Envoy of the Department of Exorcism," who is none other than Zhang Daoling, the founder of

the Celestial Master tradition. (For Zhang's connection to the Tianxin tradition, see toward the end of Chapter 2.) See also *Shangqing tianxin zhengfa* (HY 566), 3.1a, where the Master again transforms himself into Zhang Daoling before he copies the three talismans of the Tianxin tradition; and 4.1b, 4.2b, 4.9a, and especially 5.1a, where he transforms himself into the god Zhenwu, for which see also Chapter 6, under "Tantric Cults and Village Spirit-Mediums." In addition, see *Daofa huiyuan* (HY 1210), 227, "Taiyi huoxi leifu Zhujiangjun kaofu," 6b; 228, "Leifu Zhushuai kaoxie dafa," 1b; and many other texts in this collection. See also *Fahai yizhu* 1.12b: "My spirit enters the Master's spirit; the Master's spirit enters my spirit / My body is Lord Xin, Lord Xin is my body." An interesting and perhaps very early reference to *bianshen* is found in a text identified with the Celestial Master tradition, *The Scripture for Spell-Binding Demons, of Orthodox Unity of Taishang* (*Taishang zhengyi zhougui ching*, HY 1184). See especially 2a–b: "The Celestial Master says, 'On behalf of Heaven and Earth, I drive away myriad disasters; transforming my body as a human being, I become the Demon King (*bianshen renjian zuo guiwang*); my body is six *zhang* in length, and my head faces all directions.'" Kobayashi Masayoshi has dated this text to the Eastern Jin (*Rokuchō dōkyō shi kenkyū* [Tokyo: Sobunsha, 1990], 378–379), although I suspect a later date. The substance of the text is purported to have been transmitted to the Celestial Master by Lord Huang-Lao, not in Sichuan, but on Taishan (2b.4).

34. See *Taishang zhuguo jiumin zongzhen biyao* 7.9a–10b, "Zhaogui xianxing fa"; 7.11a, "Shuizhao fa"; 7.12a, "Anchu zhaogui xianxing fa."

35. Obeyesekere, *Medusa's Hair*, and Chapter 1, passim.

36. See Michel de Certeau, "Discourse Disturbed: The Sorcerer's Speech," in idem, *The Writing of History* (New York: Columbia University Press, 1988), 244–268.

37. *Taishang zhuguo jiumin zongzhen biyao* 7.12b–13b, "Shi'er shenjiang zhuogui jiafu kaoze"; 7.13b–14b, "Dali tianding zhuizhuo xiemo egui fa."

38. Ibid., 7.24a–b, "Siling zhuogui fa"; 24b–25a, "You zhuofa," where the inhaled pneumas are exhaled into a basin of water from which the patient is then compelled to drink, the reverse of the "rites of reflection"; 25a–b, "Fugui fa."

39. Ibid., 7.24b.45 (commentary): "Shen zhan shi yen ye."

40. Ibid., 7.31b, "Yijiang fa," or "Rites of Descent and Transference." For "Rites of Transfer" and the possession of a medium in the Shenxiao tradition, see *Gaoshang shenxiao yuqing zhenwang zishu dafa* (HY 1209), 3.20b–25a.

41. Ibid., 7.32a, "Youfa," or "Additional Rites [of Descent and Transference]."

42. *Daofa huiyuan* 138, "Taiyi tianzhang yanglei bili dafa," 12b; 196, "Hunyuan

yiqi bagua dongshen tianyi wulei dafa," 13b ; 222, "Zhengyi hum shen ling-guan huoxi daxian kaozhao bifa," 25b–30a; 224, "Jinbi yuanguang huoxi da-xian zhengyi lingguan Mayuanshuai bifa," 19a–24b; 227, "Taiyi huoxi leifu Zhujiang jun kaofu fa," 22b–23b; 229, "Lingguan Chen-Ma-Zhu sanshuai kaozhao dafa," 23b–24a, esp. "Bamowang menghun zhou" and "You meng-zhou." This list is not exhaustive. For mediums in the Thunder Magic tradi-tion, see *Daofa huiyuan* 101, "Wulei qidao xingchi bifa," 10a–b. See also *Fa-hai yizhu* 33, 7b–10b; 34, 3b–4a; 36, 12–13; and 37, 22b–end.

43. Ibid., 243, "Nanji huolei lingguan Wang yuanshuai bifa," 3b–4a: "Pu daomeng fa."

44. Ibid., 196, "Hunyuan yiqu bagua dongshen tianyi wulei dafa," 13b–14b; 229, "Lingguan Chen-Ma-Zhu sanshuai kaozhao dafa," 22b–26a; and so forth. Poul Andersen reports that during certain exorcisms on Taiwan, the *hun*-souls of the actor who will transform himself into the exorcistic Zhongkui must first be removed through the ears (= *jiao'er*) and deposited either in the incense burner or into the character for "well" (*jing*), which has been written on the ground (= *zanghun*).

45. *Taishang zhuguo jiumin zongzhen biyao* 7.12a, "Rites for Illuminating Demons and Manifesting their Forms in a Dark Place" (*Anchu zhaogui xianxing fa*).

46. Ibid., 7.12b–13b, "Rites of the Twelve Spirit-Generals for Seizing, Yoking, Binding, Investigating, and Accusing the Demon" (*Shi'er shenjiang zhuogui jiafu kaoze fa*).

47. *Shangqing tianxin zhengfa* 4.3a, "Zhuofujiakao sizhou jue." See also *Daofa huiyuan* 59, "Shangqing yuchu wulei zhenwen," 5a–10b, for a complete rit-ual sequence in the Thunder Magic tradition.

48. *Daofa huiyuan* 157–168, "Shangqing tianpeng fumo dafa." For the ashes and boiling sesame oil, see esp. 157.21a–b, 166.2b, and passim.

49. Ibid., 166,1b–2a and 16a.

50. Ibid., 166, 15a–b.

51. Ibid., 167, esp. 16a on.

52. For Song prisons see Brian McKnight, *Law and Order in Sung China* (Cam-bridge: Cambridge University Press, 1992), 353–384; Michael Dutton, *Polic-ing and Punishment in China* (Cambridge: Cambridge University Press, 1992), 131–134.

53. Miyazaki Ichisada, "The Administration of Justice during the Sung Dynasty," in Cohen, Edwards, and Chen, eds., *Essays in China's Legal Tradition* (Prince-ton: Princeton University Press, 1980), 61.

54. Xu Daoling, "Songlu zhongde shenpan zhidu," *Dingfang zazhi fukan* 4.4.

55. Li Yuanbi, *Zuoyi zizhen* (preface dated 1117). Reprinted in *Sibu congkan xubian*, vol. 48 (Shanghai: Shanghai shudian, 1984). For the treatment of trials and criminals, see esp. *juan* 2 and 3.

56. See John A. Evans, "Chinese Criminal Law in *All Men Are Brothers*," paper presented at the conference on "The History of Chinese Law," Bellagio, 1969.

57. *Taiping guangji* 470, "Xue Erniang" (vol. 10, p. 3872), an anecdote from the *Tongxuan ji*.

58. See note 57 above.

59. This is particularly true among the Muslim brotherhoods of medieval Morocco and Iraq. For the link between fakirism and possession, see Rouget, *Music and Trance*, 273–279.

60. For the role of anger and violence here, compare with an exorcism described in the sixth-century Tantric text, *Scripture of Dhāraṇīs Presented to the Buddha by Aṭavaka, the General of Demons and Spirits* (*Azhapoju guishen dajiang shangfo tuoluoni jing*, T. 1238), 183c–184d: "Rites of Dispersal and Exorcism." The master sits before an effigy of Aṭavaka and forms the mudrā of Great Anger with his hand. Then the person afflicted with a demonic illness is brought in, and the master tells him to sit down. "Beside himself with anger, the master reviles the patient, hoping to strike fear into him. Then he yells, 'How much longer must the gods wait?! Quickly, tie him up!' His assistants respond immediately and bind the afflicted, and the master intends to beat the demon out of him. All the while he uses few words. This is the method of dispersing demons of the Great General. There is no need to recite spells." In view of this, one wonders what is meant by the reference to the "barbarian fashion" in which Xue Erniang "cried out . . . commanding the patient to bind herself."

61. See the end of Chapter 2.

62. *Taishang zhuguo jiumin zongzhen biyao* 7.28a.7–8.

63. Ibid., 7.26a–b, "Additional Rite [for Yoking Demons]."

64. Ibid., 7.26b–27a, "Additional Rite [of the Five Dippers for Flogging Demons]."

65. *Yijian zhi* 814.

66. Ibid., 908.

67. See Wilt Idema and Stephen H. West, *Chinese Theater 1100–1450: A Sourcebook* (Wiesbaden: Franz Steiner, 1982), 188 ff.

68. A translation of this anecdote, told to Hong Mai by a military inspector and native of Kaifeng, can be found in Idema and West, *Chinese Theater*, 124.

69. Stephen Greenblatt, "Shakespeare and the Exorcists," in idem, *Shakespearean Negotiations* (Berkeley: University of California Press, 1988), 94–129 (esp. 111–114).

70. See *Zhouli* 31; *Liji* 15; *Houhan shu* 15.5.
71. See Meng Yuanlao, *Dongjing menghua lu* 10, and Wu Zimu, *Mengliang lu* 6.
72. See Tanaka Issei, *Chūgoku saishi engeki kenkyū*, 186–254.
73. See Tanaka Issei, *Chūgoku fukei engeki kenkyū* (Tokyo: Tōkyō daigaku shuppansha, 1993), 139–141.
74. See *Jiangxi shiwei* 24, "Observing a Nuo" (*Guannuo*) by Liu Tang, as reproduced in Tanaka Issei, *Chūgoku fukei engeki kenkū*, 43–46.
75. One may also demonstrate this shift at the level of the Daoist "offering" (*jiao*). By the Song, the cause of pestilence and drought has been attributed to "orphan-souls," an attribution revealed in, and effected by, the Daoist Retreat of the Yellow Register. On this point, see Tanaka Issei, *Chūgoku fukei engeki kenkyū*, 359–367. The character, function, and history of Daoist and Buddhist rites for the dead are explored in Chapter 8 and in the Appendix. The anonymous Song manual, *Huanglu jiuyou jiao wu'ai yezhai cidi yi* (HY 514), lists ten categories of orphan-souls, the first of which are the souls of heroes who have died in battle. On this score, see the commemorative poem by Zhang Jinyan (*Yijian zhi* 394–396), in which the illness and deprivation of the population of Liyang (Huainan West Circuit) are attributed to the powerful souls of the magistrates and members of the local elite, who were cut down defending the region against the invading Jurchens. The author recommends that their spirits become the focus of a *shehui* and Daoist "offering" (*jiao*) as a means of reconstituting a regional community: "the rule of the city (*zhunzhi*) will become peaceful"; "the sovereignty of the region (*bangjun*) resides in the people's altars (*minshe*)"—a form of nonethnic *Landespatriotismus*, which seems a better description than incipient nationalism of the Chinese response to the Jurchen invasions.
76. See the four volumes by Tanaka Issei: *Chūgoku saishi engeki kenkyū* (Tokyo: Tōkyō daigaku shuppansha, 1981), *Chūgoku zonso to engeki* (Tokyo: Tōkyō daigaku shuppansha, 1985), *Chūgoku goson saishi kenkyū* (Tokyo: Tōkyō daigaku shuppansha, 1989), *and Chūgoku fukei engeki kenkyū* (Tokyo: Tōkyō daigaku shuppansha, 1993); Wang Qiugui, *Minsu quyi congshu*, vols. 1–80 (Taibei: Minsu quyi, 1993–).

Chapter 6: Tantric Exorcists and Child-Mediums

1. *Yijian zhi*, 1396–1397.
2. In fact, Xu Jia, a disciple of Laozi and putative originator of red-head rituals, is described in a legend as the "Ritual Master of the Three Altars." Kristofer Schipper, to whom this legend was orally transmitted by a *fashi* in southern

Taiwan, remarks that the "Three Altars (*Santan*) is yet another common name
for the traditions of the *fashi* in Taiwan and among the *daoshi* from Quanzhou
in Singapore. Nothing is known about the origin or significance of this name"
(Schipper, "Vernacular and Classicial Ritual in Daoism," 41, note 73.)

3. Among the many accounts, see Liu Zhiwan (Riu Shiman), "Taiwan no shyamanisumu," in Sakurai Tokutarō, ed., *Shyamanisumu no sekai* (Tokyo: Shunjūsha, 1979), 91–94.

4. Ibid., 94–99.

5. Ibid., 99.

6. The use of three boys (or rather two sets of three boys) seems unusual. Can
we conclude from this anything about the nature of the Rite of the Three Altars? For instance, did the rite involve a cult to three different divinities or
fierce bodhisattvas, each represented by a different altar, each possessing a
different boy? And if the first set of boys was to be possessed by divinities, was
the second set to be possessed by demons? (One of the boys in this second
group claims that the demon had descended into his hand, an eventuality
that is anticipated in certain Tantric texts mentioned below.)

7. Kenneth Dean (Ding Hesheng) and Zheng Zhenman, "Group Initiation and
Exorcistic Dance in the Xinghua Region," in Wang Qiugui, ed., *Zhongguo
Nuoxi: Nuo wenhua gouji yantaihui lu wenli* (*Minsu quyi* 85.2, 1993), 105–214.
See also Brigitte Baptandier-Berthier, "The Kaiguan Ritual and the Construction of the Child's Identity," in Lin Ru, ed., *Minjian xinyang yu Zhongguo
wenhua: Guoji yantao huilun wenji 2* (Taibei: Hanxue yanjiu zhongxin, 1994),
523–596; Ye Mingsheng, "Fujiansheng Longyanshi Dongxiaozhen Lushan-
jiao Guangjitan keyiben huibian," in Wang Qiugui, ed., *Zhongguo chuantong
keyiben huibian* (Taibei: Xinwenfeng, 1998); Wu Yongmeng, "Penghu gongmiao xiaofa de Pu An Zushi zhi shenyuan," in *Donfang zongjiao yanjiu 4*,
165–181; and Kenneth Dean (Ding Hesheng) and Zheng Zhenman, "Min-
Tai daojiao yu minjian zhushen chongbai chukao," *Bulletin of the Institute of
Ethnology, Academia Sinica* 73 (1993), 33–52.

8. Dean and Zheng, "Group Initiation and Exorcistic Dance in the Xinghua Region," 116–117.

9. *Daofa huiyuan* (HY 1210), 253, "Diqi fa."

10. Ibid., 254, "Dongyue Wen taibao kaozhao bifa."

11. Ibid., 255–256, "Diqi Wen yuanshuai dafa."

12. Ibid., 254.7b–8a.

13. Ibid., 253.10a–12a.

14. *Diqi shangjiang Wen taibao zhuan* (HY 779. For a more comprehensive treatment of this text from a very different point of view, see John Lagerwey, *Taoist*

Ritual in Chinese Society and History, 241–252, and Paul R. Katz, *Demon Hordes and Burning Boats: The Cult of Marshal Wen in Late Imperial Chekiang*, 80–88. Grand Protector Wen was born Wen Qiong in the subprefecture of Pingyang, Wenzhou, during the Tang dynasty. Wen was a soldier and suppressor of bandits, until, that is, he quarreled with his commander, the general Guo Ziyi, and fled to Taishan. There he became a butcher and wine merchant (*Diqi shangjiang Wen taibao zhuan*, 1a). The story of how Wen Qiong abandoned these unsavory and paradigmatically impure professions and became, first, a "master of transformations" in the Temple of the Eastern Peak and, then, after his own transformation (i.e., death), a subordinate divinity in the service of the Dao is an absolute masterpiece of Daoist revisionism. Everywhere, Wen Qiong is seen refusing the fruits of cultic worship that he clearly enjoyed; everywhere, the text attempts to efface the traces of a local spirit-medium cult supported by the citizens of a city whose identity and rising fortunes found expression in a hero and protector, one who perhaps even gave that city Wenzhou its name. In 961, according to the *Biography*, during a drought, Wen Qiong graced these citizens with rain. Wen Qiong then possessed a commoner named Wang Jiu'er, only to say that he had little interest in temple sacrifices or imperial enfeoffments because he hoped for nothing but to enter the Dao and become a minor clerk in "the assemblies of rites" (*fahui*, ibid., 3a). That a self-respecting local hero would want to become a minor clerk seems the height of Daoist presumption.

And one presumption is then followed by another. In the twelfth century, Wen Qiong's cultic indifference attracts the attention of the thirtieth Celestial Master, Zhang Xujing, who makes Wen an earth deity in charge of the talismans, spells, and hand-seals of the rectifying rites (*zhengfa*, ibid., 4a). The presumption lies in the portrayal of Zhang Xujing as the crucial figure in the dissemination of "Grand Protector Wen's Secret Rites of the Earth-Spirits." The Celestial Master transmits these rites to a Daoist, Wang Zongjing, who passes them on to his disciple, Wu Daoxian, who in turn passes them on to 532 disciples, whereupon "Wen's Secret Rites" come to be considered "an inferior degree of the Orthodox Rites" and lose their efficacy (ibid., 10a–b). This tale of popularization and degeneration, I believe, masked a self-serving bid on the part of the Celestial Master lineage for control over a local ritual tradition that originated among precisely those practitioners (lay exorcists?) who had supposedly contributed to its demise.

15. Ibid., 8a.
16. Ibid., 8b–9a.
17. Ibid., 11a–12b, though these two individuals are first mentioned at 3b, where

they are said to have struck terror into the hearts of officially recognized earth deities, and where their religion is called the "Teaching of the Three Altars."

18. *Weinan wenji* 5.7b–8b, quoted in Éd. Chavannes and P. Pelliot, *Un Traité manichéen retrouvé en Chine* (Paris: Imprimerie Nationale, 1913), 305–310.

19. *Xueshan ji* 3.26, quoted in Samuel Lieu, *Manichaeism in the Later Roman Empire and Medieval China* (Manchester: Manchester University Press, 1985), 240.

20. See Chavannes and Pelliot, *Traité*, 315–324.

21. Chikusa Masa'aki, *Chūgoku bukkyō shakai shi kenkyū* , 203–204.

22. The various dictionaries and encyclopedias of Esoteric Buddhism do, in fact, include entries for "Rites of the Three Altars" (*Santan fa*), as well as for "Rites of the Five Altars" (*Wutan fa*), which are in some accounts an elaboration and expansion of the former. We must be extremely cautious in exploiting these entries, however. First, there is no reason to suppose that the types of altars, divinities, and rituals described therein correspond at all to those employed by our Buddhist Ritual Masters. Second, these dictionaries and encyclopedias are Japanese and are heavily weighted toward ritual practices specific to the Japanese Shingon and Tendai traditions. In fact, the Rites of the Three or Five Altars (*sandanhō*, *godanhō*) as described appear to have formed part of the repertoire of "imperial rites" (*mishuhō*—large-scale, occasional, and solemn rituals performed by dozens of monks for the benefit of the imperial family). See, especially, *Mochizuki Bukkyō daijiten*, p. 1613a–b, "Sandan mishuhō," and p. 1246, "Godanhō"; *Koji ruien*, pp. 329–335, quoting at length historical references to the "Rites of the Three Altars" and "Rites of the Five Altars." See also *Mikkyō jiten*, p. 816b, "Sandan gamae," and p. 620b–c, "Godanhō," which includes discussion of "Sandanhō"; *Mikkyō daijiten*, p. 619b–c, "Godan gamae," and p. 620b–c, "Godanhō."

23. *Yijian zhi*, 1437–1438.

24. Sun Wei, *Huanyi zhi*, paraphrased in Sawada Mizuho, *Chūgoku no juhō*, 148.

25. T. 2057. *Gaoseng zhuan*, 712a, quoted in Zhou Yiliang, "Tantrism in China," *Harvard Journal of Asiatic Studies* 8 (1945), 284.

26. See T.2057, 711c, and Zhou, "Tantrism in China," 278–279.

27. The following account of the *āveśa* ritual is based on:

> T. 1277 (vol. 21) *Su ji li Yanmoxishouluotian shuo aweishe fa*, 329b–331a
>
> T. 895 (vol. 18) *Supodi tongzi qingwen jing*, zhong, 725a–c; xia, 741c–742c
>
> T. 867 (vol. 18) *Jingangeng louge yiqie yujia yuqi jing*, xia, 268c–269c
>
> T. 896 (vol. 18) *Miaobi pusa suo wen jing*, 3.754b–755b.
>
> T. 1202 (vol. 21) *Budong shi zhe tuoluoni bimi fa*, 24b ff.
>
> T. 1217 (vol. 21) *Miaojixiang zuisheng gen ben da jiao jing*, xia, 92a.

For an introduction to the subject, see *Hōbōgirin* (*Dictionnaire encyclopédique du bouddhisme*), vol. 1, p. 452, "*āvesá*," and now Michel Strickmann, *Mantras et mandarins: Le bouddhisme tantrique en Chine*, "Exorcisme et spectacle," where long passages from several of the above-mentioned Chinese texts are translated. Strickmann also comments on two historical references to the practice of *āveśa*-like rituals at the Tang court: the first was performed by the Indian Tantric master Vajrabodhi for the benefit of emperor Xuanzong's daughter (T. 2061, 711c, referred to above), and the second was performed by the Chinese Tantric master Huiguo for emperor Taizong (T. 2057, 295a). Although neither performance is explicitly referred to as an *āveśa* ritual, Strickmann makes an argument for why the first should be so considered (and the first was apparently so considered by Japanese Buddhist exegetes, who included this anecdote in discussions of *āveśa* [see *Nihon Daizōkyō*, vol. 38, 531a–b]). The second performance is called an "enchantment of summoning for investigation," though its content better conforms to what we will come to expect from *āveśa* rituals as they are described in the canonical texts.

For *āveśa* (J. *abisha*) in Japan and other rituals employing child-mediums (*yorimashi*), consult *Minakata Kumagusu zenshū* (Tokyo: Heibonsha, 1973), vol. 9, 186–187, and *Teihon Yanagida Kunio shū* (Tokyo: Chikuma shobō, 1962), vol. 9, 238–248. Yanagida also discusses *yorimashi* in the contexts of Shintō and Shugendō (see vol. 5, 133; vol. 7, 280; vol. 9, 54–55, 76–77, 313; vol. 10, 258–260, 264, 404–406). Among Japanese Buddhist canonical sources, *āveśa* is formally treated in *Nihon Daizōkyō* vol. 38, 531–533; vol. 36, 84–85; vol. 17, 322; *Taishō Daizōkyō Zuzōhen* vol. 7, 355b–356a; vol. 8, 677a–678a; *Shingonshū zenshū* vol. 3, 107b–108a. Performances of Buddhist exorcisms employing child-mediums are described in *The Tale of Genji* and *The Pillow Book of Sei Shōnagon*. See also William H. McCullough, "Spirit Possession in the Heian Period," in *Studies on Japanese Culture*, vol. 1 (Tokyo: The Japan P.E.N. Club, 1973), 91–98, and Doris Bargen, *A Woman's Weapon: Spirit Possession in the Tale of Genji* (Honolulu: University of Hawai'i Press, 1997).

28. T. 895, 728a, lines 19–21 and 728c, lines 11–12; T. 867, 268c, line 24, and 269b, line 28; T. 1202; 24b, line 18.

29. T. 895, 728a, 297–298b, line 13; 742a, lines 19–22; T. 1202, 24b. For catoptromancy and the ritual or divinatory use of child-mediums in the Greek, Late Antique, and Byzantine worlds, see A. Delatte, *La catoptromancie grecque et ses dérivés* (Liège-Paris: Bibliothèque de la Faculté de Philosophie et Lettres de l'Université de Liège, Fasc. XLVIII, 1932); E. R. Dodds, *The Ancient Concept of Progress and Other Essays on Greek Literature and Belief* (Oxford: Oxford University Press, 1988), 185–210; idem, *The Greeks and the Irrational* (Berkeley:

University of California Press, 1951), 295–299; Richard Greenfield, *Traditions of Belief in Late Byzantine Demonology* (Amsterdam: Adolf Hakkert, 1988), 262–268; and now, especially, Hans Dieter Betz, *The Greek Magical Papyri in Translation*, vol. 1 (Chicago: University of Chicago Press, 1986), p. 5, line 86; p. 14, lines 55–56; p. 108, line 376; p. 133, line 544, and so forth.

30. T. 895, 728c, lines 20–21, and 742c, line 15.

31. See, especially, *Taiping guangji* 346; "Li Xiang" (2739–2740), an anecdote taken from the *Xu yuguai lu*. Daoism, too, had similar divinatory seances in the late Tang. See the eighth- or ninth-century text of the Sanhuang tradition, *Dongshen badi yuanbian jing* (HY 1202), 25b–27b, where one or more of the Eight Archivists (*bashi*) are summoned, seen, and interrogated by the practitioner (*shushi*). Here, however, there is no possession of a medium, and the elaborate rules and instructions that surround the seance were clearly intended to maintain a strict boundary between gods and men. For more on this text, see Poul Andersen, "Taoist Ritual Texts and Traditions," 58–60, and idem, "Talking to the Gods: Visionary Divination in Early Taoism (Sanhuang Tradition)," paper prepared for the Western Conference of the Association of Asian Studies, University of Arizona, Oct. 23–24, 1992.

32. T. 1277. 330a, line 4.

33. Ibid., 330a, lines 15 ff.

34. Ibid., 330a, lines 24–25.

35. *Yijian zhi* 171.

36. Ibid., 525. I am tempted here to compare these young boys to the temple mediums (*to dōji*) of late Heian Japan who became possessed by several tutelary divinities collectively known as "Youths Who Protect the Dharma" (*gohōdōji*), so called, it has been surmised, because they were conceived of in terms of the young mediums who embodied them. See *Teihon Yanagida Kunio shū* vol. 9, 407–416 and Wada Akio, "Gohō dōji," *Mikkyō Bunka* 104 (1973), 19–41.

37. For this description of the *āveśa* mediums both before and during trance, see T. 895, 728b–c and 742b–c.

38. Marie-Thérèse de Mallman, *Introduction à l'iconographie du tântrisme bouddhique* (Paris: Maisonneuve, 1986), 297.

39. Iyanaga Nobumi, "Récits de la soumission de Mahésvara par Trailokyavijaya—d'après les sources chinoises et japonaises," in Michel Strickmann, ed., *Tantric and Taoist Studies*, vol. 3 (Bruxelles: Mélanges Chinois et Bouddhiques, 1985), 693–694.

40. T. 1225, 1226, 1227, 1228, and 1229.

41. *Song Bai zhenren Yuchan quanji*, Bo Yuchan (Taiwan: Committee to Publish Bo Yuchan's Works, 1976), 424 (*Yulu* 6a–b).

42. T. 1228, *Huiji jin'gang shuo shentong daman tuoluoni fashu ling yaomen.*
43. Iyanaga, "La soumission de Mahésvara," 697.
44. *Song Bai zhenren Yuchan quanji* 424 (*Yulu* 6b).
45. M. Walleser, *The Life of Nāgārjuna from Tibetan and Chinese Sources* (Dehli: Nag, 1979), 25–30.
46. *Song Bai zhenren Yuchan quanji* 424 (*Yulu* 6b).
47. Snowy Mountain has been identified with Mount Sumeru in the Himalayas, and Incense Mountain with a peak or range in the Transhimalayas. The two are associated in Buddhist scripture (see the passage from the *Guan fo san wei jing* cited in Morohashi, *Dai kanwa jiten*, 44518.134). The important point is that Incense Mountain is identified as being to the north of Snowy Mountain.
48. The Two Great Lords Swine Head and Elephant Trunk are to be understood not simply as a pair, but as the bifurcation of a single deity known as the "Heaven of Felicity and Joy" or the "Deva of Bliss" (Huanxi tian), which was represented iconographically by male and female elephants or by elephant- and swine-headed divinities (male and female, respectively) in sexual embrace. The single elephant-headed figure is none other than Gaṇeśa, from whom the ecstatic, bifurcated divinity derived. Gaṇeśa is the child of Pārvatī and Śiva. He is also known as "Gaṇapati" (Jia'nabodi), the "Lord of the Gaṇas" (a group of demigods and attendants of Śiva) and as "Vināyaka" (Binayejia), the "Lord [or Remover] of Obstacles." In the Chinese canonical scriptures from the fifth century on, Gaṇeśa reveals himself most often as Vināyaka, the Lord of Obstacles, a quasi-demonic figure who prevents the practitioner from attaining his vows and who must be propitiated and controlled. See Lewis Lancaster, "Gaṇeśa in China," in Robert L. Brown, ed., *Ganesh: Studies of an Asian God* (Albany: State University of New York Press. 1991), 277–288. The dual Gaṇeśa (Huanxi tian), however, is predominant in a strand of the Chinese Esoteric Buddhist tradition and Japanese Shingon. The important scriptures of this strand are T. 1266, 1267, 1268, 1270, 1271, and 1275.

The female half of the dual Gaṇeśa—here appearing in the form of a swine-headed divinity—has been identified with, among others, Avalokiteśvara (Guanyin). See, for example, the opening of T. 1270, *Da Sheng Huanxi shuangshen Dazihai tian Pinayejia wang guiyi niansong gongyang fa.* Some passages on the dual Gaṇeśa in the Japanese *Besson* manuals of the Heian period have been clearly inspired by this text. Here Avalokiteśvara takes the form of a female *vināyaka* in order to seduce and thereby convert the demonic Gaṇeśa (Vināyaka); see James Stanford, "Literary Aspects of Japan's Dual-Gaṇeśa Cult," in Brown, *Ganesh*, 297–298. It is uncertain, however, whether we can identify the swine-headed figure of our dual Gaṇeśa with Avaloki-teśvara. The swine-headed divinity certainly brings to mind the "Diamond Sow" of the *Hevajra Tantra*; in the Tibetan *Tantra of the Great Gānapati*, more-over, Gaṇeśa's consort is Arcikāri, the adamantine pig-faced woman. (See Christopher Wilkinson, "The Tantric Gaṇeśa: Texts Preserved in the Tibetan Canon," in Brown, *Ganesh*, 247.) Yet James Stanford doubts this association, and suspects that "the female of the dual [Deva of Bliss] represents, not a borrowing of a Buddhist form of Gaṇeśa, but a fairly direct amplification of or adoption of the attendant devi of the boon-giving Ucchiṣṭa Gaṇapati form of Hinduism" (see Stanford, "Literary Aspects" in Brown, *Ganesh*, 313). For more on these Hindu devotees of an "Impure" (Ucchiṣṭa) Gaṇeśa, see Paul Courtright, *Gaṇeśa* (New York: Oxford University Press, 1985), 218–220. The association with the *ucchiṣṭa*-form of Gaṇeśa is suggestive, given our dual Gaṇeśa's association with Ucchuṣma.

We may learn more about the Song conception of the Two Lords, Swine Head and Elephant Trunk, from the fact that, in the thirteenth and four-teenth centuries, this bifurcated divinity had found its way into the texts of certain Daoist exorcistic lineages. *The Secret Rites of Prime Marshal Zhao of the Dark Altar* (*Xuantan Zhao yuanshuai bifa*) offers a list of divinities subordi-nate to the eponymous Zhao Gongming, an early medieval grave demon (see *Zhen Gao* 10.17a.9 and 17b.5) who has now become a powerful Daoist spirit-general. These secondary divinities include the Swine Head and Elephant Trunk gods, here identified as the Two Spirit Lords, Yang and Zhu (Zhutou xiangbi Yang-Zhu shenjun), as well as another who, it turns out, is a permuta-tion of, or substitute for the first: "the Saintly Monk Wan Hui, the Old Man, Detached from Affairs, of Harmony and Unity (Wanhui shengseng hehe san-shi laoren)" (*Daofa huiyuan* 231.7a). As Rolf Stein has pointed out, the hyper-active monk Wan Hui ("He who comes and goes a thousand times in an in-stant") was worshipped in China as a single person, "Harmony-Unity (*hehe*)"—usually a comic and obese monk like Budai—or as two persons, "Har-mony" (*he*) and "Unity" (*he*)"—usually two young monks called "Felicitous Heaven and Joyous Earth" (*Hantian xidi*); see R. Stein, *Annuaire du Collège de France* (1972–1973) 62. Other texts related to the cult of Zhao Gongming and this Daoist exorcistic lineage reinterpret the concept of "Harmony-Unity" in terms of Daoist cosmological notions and meditational operations, identifying "harmony" and "unity" with two discrete divinities corresponding to different directional pneumas united by the Master (*Daofa huiyuan* 232, "The Secret Rites of Prime Marshal Zhao of the Dark Altar of Orthodox-Unity," 14b–15b).

49. The Bodhisattva Flower Radiance (Huaguang pusa) is the protagonist of the

Ming novel *Journey to the South* (*Nanyou ji*), where he is described as an embodiment of fire. (The first incarnation of Huaguang, in fact, was nothing but an incarnation of the Buddha who had transformed the radiance of a lamp that had intensified, while he preached, into the deity Miao Jixiang.) In the twelfth century, Flower Radiance was the object of popular cult, though our main source for this is Daoist. In the addenda to *The Biography of Grand Protector Wen, Commander of the Earth-Spirits*, Flower Radiance is identified as the fourth of the five divinities worshipped in the Temple of the Five Manifestations (Wuxian miao) in Jizhou (Anhui). This identification was made in the course of a "Rite of Summoning for Investigation" performed in the marketplace by a Daoist *fashi* named Cao Kefu for the benefit of a concubine of the local Prefect. The woman had become utterly transfixed by the beauty of the god's temple effigy and had wasted away. Cao raised the corpse of the concubine and then caused her to become possessed by the god of the effigy, who identified himself as Flower Radiance (*Diqi shangjiang Wen taibao zhuan, buyi* [addenda] 1b–2a).

The identification of Huaguang as one of the Five Manifestations (*Wuxian*) is revealing. The Five Manifestations—whose main temples were built in the subprefectures of Wuyuan and Dexing in Jiangxi during the latter half of the twelfth century—were none other than semiofficial and urban transformations of the "Spirits of the Five Supernatural Powers" (*Wutong shen*)—the gods par excellence of the spirit-medium cults in southern villages in the Song. For the history of the cult to these divinities in the Song, Yuan, and Ming, see Cedzich, "Wu-T'ung: Zur bewegten Geschichte eines Kultus," and idem, "The Cult of the Wu-t'ung/Wu-hsien in History and Fiction: The Religious Roots of the *Journey to the South*," in David Johnson, ed., *Ritual and Scriptures in Chinese Popular Religion: Five Studies* (Berkeley: Chinese Popular Culture Project, 1995), 137–218; and Richard Von Glahn, "The Enchantment of Wealth: The God Wutong in the Social History of Jiangnan," *Harvard Journal of Asiatic Studies* 51.2 (1991), 651–714. These Spirits of the Five Supernatural Powers were most often conceived as latter-day versions of the ancient mountain sprites (*shanxiao*), who were now thought to reside primarily among rocks and trees. Their gradual association with the five supernatural powers (Skt. *abhijñā*) of the Buddha and Buddhist monks is evidence of the abiding links being formed in the Song between rural monasteries and village religion. I suspect that, on the one hand, gods of the villages and of village spirit-mediums were becoming guardian deities of Buddhist monasteries and temples; on the other hand, there appears to have been an assimilation of the Buddhist magical powers to the transformational powers of the *Wutong shen* and their spirit-mediums.

Specific evidence for the identification of Flower Radiance with a Spirit of the Five Supernatural Powers appears in a discussion of the latter found in a Daoist legislative text of a lineage of Ritual Masters specializing in the "Secret Rites of Fengdu":

> All Wutong are evil demons (*mogui*) who have attained spiritual efficacy (*ling*). The upper class of Wutong are formed from the pneumas (*qi*) of [the five elements]: metal, wood, water, fire, and earth. Among the middle class of Wutong is none other than Flower Radiance (Huaguang). He is formed from the pneuma of mountains, streams, and the Five Peaks. He usurps the halo of the Buddha and takes the title "Head of the Gods" (*shenshou*). The "Numinous Officers" (*lingguan*) of the middle class are gods who have attained spiritual efficacy and take the title "Transcendent Saints" (*xiansheng*). The lower class of Wutong are formed from the pneuma of grass and trees. Some take the appellation "Muxia," and they reside in grasses and trees, out of which their altars are made. These gods let fly misfortune upon human beings and crave blood sacrifices. (*Daofa huiyuan* 267, "The Ritual Models and Black Codes of Taixuan Fengdu," 14b.)

This passage recapitulates synchronically the history of the cult to these remarkable gods. The lower class of Wutong corresponds to the village gods of the spirit-mediums (indeed, as we learn from the *Yijian zhi*, they lived in trees and many were known as "*muxia*"). The upper class of Wutong corresponds to the rarefied saints (*wuxian* or *wusheng*) of the urban temples. Finally, the middle class of Wutong corresponds to the gods of Tantric and Daoist Ritual Masters, who mediated between these other worlds. This middle class is said to include "Numinous Officers" (*lingguan*), the appellation by which the Daoist Ritual Master or Ritual Officer referred to his spirit-generals and cultic divinities. One of these Numinous Officers, Ma Sheng (the "Horse Vanquisher"), was the focus of his own cult and Daoist lineage. He was a god of the south and of fire, and none other than the Daoist version of the Bodhissatva Flower Radiance (for exorcistic texts belonging to the Daoist cult of Ma Sheng, see *Daofa huiyuan* 222–226).

The "Ritual Models and Black Codes of Taixuan Fengdu" has one more thing to say about this middle class of divinities:

> Among the worldly [i.e., the vernacular, nonclerical world], there are the "Three Martial Spirits of the Penetrations" (*Sanxiong tong-*

shen), who are those in whom the hexagrams *qian* and *kun* have attained spiritual efficacy. *They are called Xiongwei, Huaguang, and Nezha* [my italics]. Although these spirits have received the mandate from the Jade Emperor of the Divine Empyrean (*Shenxiao yudi*) and are unable to harm human beings, their natures are difficult to control. (*Daofa huiyuan* 267.15a)

There can be no better statement of the mediating nature and function of the gods of Buddhist and Daoist Ritual Masters than the description of these gods, whose volatile nature betrays their popular origin but who have been tamed and enfeoffed by the high god of Song Daoism as his fierce lieutenants and protectors of the faith. Moreover, there can be no better statement of the interpenetration of the cults of Daoist and Tantric Ritual Masters. This triad of worldly Daoist divinities—Xiongwei, Huaguang, and Nezha—has been taken over unchanged from Ucchuṣma's pantheon, though the latter represents the triad in the expanded form of two pairs: the Two Great Lords Xiongwei and Huaguang, and Prince Nezha and the Saintly King Dinglun. I have been unable to identify Xiongwei.

50. Nezha (abbreviated transliteration of Nalakūbara, son of Kubera, from the *Mahābhārata*) is the third and youngest son of Vaiśravaṇa (Pishamen), guardian of the north and one of the Four Mahārāja Devas (Si da tianwang). The cult to Nezha, like that to his father, originated in Khotan in the eighth century; see *Da Tang Xihuo ji* (T. 2087), Xuanzang, 12.943ab; *Da Song seng shi lüe* (T. 2126), Zanning, 254b. As mentioned in Chapter 3, their cult inspired a number of scriptures attributed to but originating several generations after the death of Amoghavajra; for the dating of these scriptures, probably to the mid-ninth century, see Yoritomi Motohiro, *Chūgoku mikkyō no kenkyū* (Tokyo: Daitō shuppansha, 1979), 152. The central text, the *Pishamen yigui* (T. 1249), describes Amoghavajra's successful effort to enlist the aid of Vaiśravaṇa in defending the Western Protectorate (Anxi cheng), which had been surrounded by various Central Asian kingdoms in 742. In the presence of Emperor Xuanzong himself, Amoghavajra's continuous mantra recitations produced the epiphany of over two hundred soldiers led by the second son of Vaiśravaṇa, Du Jian. Two months later, a report arrived from the Western Protectorate that, shortly after this ritual had been performed, the enemy had been forced into retreat by the thunderous sound of drums and horns, and that their weapons had been cut in half by, of all things, a band of golden-haired desert rats; for the link between these desert rats and Khotan, see *Da Tang Xihuo ji* (T. 2087),

12.944a–b. Vaiśravaṇa, moreover, finally appeared atop the city's northern tower in a flash of light.

Almost as an afterthought, the scripture interjects, somewhat later, that Vaiśravaṇa's third son, Nezha, had accompanied his father during the city's defense, carrying the pagoda that was Vaiśravaṇa's signature. Nezha, however, is the central focus of another scripture in this series, the *Beifang Pishamen tianwang suijun hufa yigui* (T. 1248). Here, Nezha appears to replace his elder brother as Vaiśravaṇa's principal lieutenant. This short and fragmentary text includes a list of various rites and *homa* offerings whose purpose is overwhelmingly aggressive, resulting in the defeat of one's enemies, both human and demonic. Nezha assumes the function of Vaiśravaṇa as protector of the emperor, his ministers, and the bureaucracy, and the rites decribed therein are said to have been instrumental in the defense of the empire during the reign of Xuanzong. Among the iconographical instructions, moreover, we find Nezha depicted with a *yakṣa* at his feet.

In the late Tang and Five Dynasties period, the cult to Vaiśravaṇa spread beyond the Tantric milieu of the Tang court, particularly among military men (see *Jiu Wudai shi* 25 and 47). In 947, for instance, artisans of the Later Jin dynasty were instructed by a member of the staff of the Military Commissioner Who Returns to Righteousness, Yuan Zhong, to construct a Buddhist mural in which Vaiśravaṇa was featured along with his army of prairie rats; see Yoritomi, *Chūgoku mikkyō no kenkyū*, 153.

By the twelfth and thirteenth centuries, Nezha had been fully absorbed into the pantheons of a number of therapeutic lineages of Daoist Ritual Masters. Among some, he was invoked as a kind of multivalent figure with three forms, identified with the Daoist Prime Marshals (*yuanshuai*), Chen Danian, Ma Sheng, and Zhu Luqi (see *Daofa huiyuan* 229, esp. 27b–28a; 224; 4b; 230, 1a). Among others, he had become an assistant commander of the demon devotee Zhao Gongming (see *Daofa huiyuan* 231, 8a–9b; 232, 3a; 233, 5b; 234, 14a–b; 235, 1a and 1b; 236, 6b). As we have seen in Chapter 3, Hong Mai offers a brief sketch of a lay Daoist Master of the "Rites of Maoshan" who employed a "Spell of Nezha's Fireball." In the Yuan and Ming, Nezha became a demon-quelling protagonist in several plays; see W. L. Idema, *The Dramatic Oeuvre of Chu Yu-tun (1379–1439)*, (Leiden: E. J. Brill, 1985), 33; Sawada Mizuho, "Shakkyōgeki joroku," *Tenri daigaku gakuhō* 44 (1964), 39–43. In the play *Erlang shen zui she suo mo jing*, Nezha even claims to have been invested by the Jade Emperor as commander of an army that included Tianpeng and Heisha; see Liu Zhiwan, "Tenhōshin to tenhōju ni tsuite," 410. In the Ming, Nezha became the subject of a full-blown myth as well as the object of ritual. His story occupies several chapters of the *Romance of Divine Investiture (Fengshen yanyi)*; see Liu Tsun-yan, *Buddhist and Taoist Influences on Chinese Novels*, 1 (Wiesbaden: Harrassowitz, 1962), 217–242; and Ho Kinchung, "Nezha: Figure de l'enfant rebelle," in *Études Chinoises* 7.2 (1988), 726. In the *Journey to the West* and *Journey to the South*, he plays confrontational roles with respect to the main protagonists, Sun Wukong and Huaguang, respectively. In modern times, Nezha's cult (both myth and ritual) has become central to the practices of spirit-mediums and Daoist Ritual Masters; see Schipper, "Classical and Vernacular Ritual," 28; Cheu Hock Tong, *The Nine Emperor Gods: A Study of Chinese Spirit-Medium Cults* (Singapore: Times Books International, 1988), 28–51; and David K. Jordan, *Gods, Ghosts and Ancestors: The Folk Religion of a Taiwanese Village* (Berkeley, University of California Press, 1972), 71–72. The association, in Ucchuṣma's pantheon, of Nezha with Dinglun shengwang escapes me. The Sagely King Dinglun is an hyposticization of the Buddha's cognitive powers. He appears to have been at the center of his own mandala and sequence of Tantric rituals in the Tang (see, for example, T. 959).

51. The God of Deep Sands was represented iconographically as a serpentine monster who presided over the semi-mythical River of Flowing Sands (Liusha he). His very name recalls the desert terrain west of Gansu. By the ninth century, at the very latest, this fierce demon became the object of Tantric cult and was identified as an incarnation of none other than Vaiśravaṇa, father of Nezha. All this we learn from a bibliography brought from China in the ninth century by the Japanese Shingon monk Jyōgyō (see T. 2163, 1070c–1071d). The God of Deep Sands was perhaps the model for one of Xuanzang's three companions, Sha Wujing, in *The Journey to the West*. He is best remembered, however, as an opponent, and then protector, of the monk.

The God of Deep Sands is paired here with a divinity I have yet to identify to my satisfaction: Jiedi shen (lit., "God who Manifests the Truths [*satya*]"?). In *The Journey to the West*, we find mention of the "Wufang jiedi," or "Fierce Protectors of the Five Quarters" in Anthony Yu's translation. Yu, most likely, is following Morohashi, who identifies Jiedi as the name of a "fierce divinity who protects the Dharma" (*Dai kanwa jiten*, 12389.35, also citing *Shuihu zhuan* 4). Nakano Miyako, in contrast, asks us to compare these five divinities with a rather enigmatic spell found toward the end of the scripture *Boruo xinjing*: "Jiedi; jiedi; boluo jiedi; boluoseng jiedi; pudiseng jiedi"; see Nakano Miyako, *Seiyuki no himitsu* (Tokyo: Fukutake shooten, 1984), 207. In the Ming play *Menglie Nezha sanbian hua*, we find four Jiedi gods who aid Nezha in a battle with female demons. They are called Jintou jiedi, Yintou jiedi,

Boluo jiedi, and *Boluoseng jiedi.* (See Sawada Mizuho, "Shakkyōgeki joroku," 40.) Similarly, in Zhu Yudun's *Xiang shizi,* Mañjuśrī leads four Jiedi generals in capturing a green lion after Nezha has failed. See Idema, *The Dramatic Oeuvre of Chu Yu-tun,* 33.

52. For the meaning and significance of these names and epithets, see T. 310, *Da baoji jing* 10.52c.

53. Rolf Stein, *Annuaire du Collège de France* (1973–1974), 513. Elsewhere, Stein refers to two paintings from Dunhuang, dated by inscription to the tenth century, which depict a doubled form of Ucchuṣma on the right and a doubled form of Vajrapāṇi on the left. At their feet, moreover, lie an elephant-headed demon and a pig-headed demon, respectively—Vināyaka/Vinākaya, the dual form of the demonic Gaṇeśa; see Stein's "The Guardian of the Gate: An Example of Buddhist Mythology, from India to Japan," in Yves Bonnefoy and Wendy Doniger, eds., *Asian Mythologies* (Chicago: University of Chicago Press, 1993), 129. See also the early fourteenth-century T. 1688, *Miji lishi daquan shenwang jing jiesong,* 778a–779c, where the story of Ucchuṣma's suppression of Brahma Śikhin is repeated and Ucchuṣma is designated by the appellation of Vajrapāṇi—the "Stalwart of Mysterious Traces" (Miqi lishi).

54. Rolf Stein, *Annuaire du Collège de France* (1972–1973), 61.

55. Ibid., 63. For an expanded version of these ideas, see Stein's essay, "The Guardian of the Gate," referred to in note 53 above.

56. The Great Lord of Incense Mountain, Nezha, and the God of Deep Sands can all be safely identified with the north, suggesting that all first terms of the pairs may be so identified as well; the Great Lord of Snowy Mountain and Flower Radiance, gods in the second position, have so far been identified with the south.

57. See notes 48, 49, and 50 above.

58. *Song Bai zhenren Yuchan quanji* 424 (*Yulu* 6b).

59. T. 1229, *Huiji jingang jin baibian fa jing.*

60. For the illustrations of the talismans, as well as instructions for their application and function, see T. 1229, 160a–c. See also Strickmann, "Magical Medicine."

61. T. 1420, *Longshu wuming lun.* For a preliminary study of this text, see Osabe Kazuo, *Tō-Sō mikkyōshi ronkō* (Kyoto: Nagada bunshōdō, 1982), 234–247. Other texts worthy of comparison include T. 1238, *Azhapoju guishen dajiang shangfo tuoluoni jing* (esp.184a–185b); T. 1265, *Changqulidu nü tuoluoni jing;* T.1275, *Sheng Huanxitian shi fa* (esp. 324 for Daoist talismans); and so forth.

62. *Longshu wuming lun,* 956, note 1.

63. Ōmura Seigai, *Mikkyō hattatsushi* (Tokyo: Bussho kankokai zuzobu, 1918), vol. 5, Furoku (appendix), "Kyōkishōsho ichiran," p. 17.

64. T. 1420, 957a, lines 710.

65. Ibid., 961–962.

66. Ibid., 957b–958b.

67. Ibid., 958b–961a.

68. Ibid., 963a–967a.

69. Ibid., 964b, lines 19–20; 964c, lines 17–18; and passim.

70. Ibid., 966a, lines 78, lines 19–20, and so forth. See also Strickmann, "Magical Medicine."

71. Ibid., 963c, lines 12–23.

72. Aśvaghoṣa was traditionally taken to have been the teacher of Nāgārjuna.

73. Two incense burners for the bodhisattvas, two for the vajra-beings (i.e., Vajrapāṇi in bipartite form), two for the eight spirit-kings, and one for the practitioner.

74. T. 1420, 967b–c.

75. Osabe Kazuo, *Tō-Sō mikkyōshi ronkō*, 150–181.

76. T. 1420, 963b, lines 1416.

77. Ibid., 956b.

78. *Yijian zhi*, 304–305.

79. See *Song Bai zhenren Yuchan quanji* 436 (*Yulu* 18b), where Bo Yuchan is describing "ritual-studying literati of his day" (*jin zhi xue fa zhi shi*), who take neither the Dao nor self-cultivation seriously; who are autodidacts and self-proclaimed Masters (*shi*); who take "the opening of light and bodily possession" to be the most sublime of arts; who pollute orthodox rituals with the instructions of spirit-mediums; and who receive secret transmissions through the automatic writing of spirits. Bo is describing here that group of lay Daoist Ritual Masters who had close connections with spirit-mediums, and whom we described in Chapters 3 and 4.

80. *Yijian zhi*, 195.

81. Ibid., 1713.

82. Ibid., 1252–1253. (For Liang Hun's relation to Ren Daoyuan, see ibid., 1089).

83. HY 575, buyi (addenda), 4a–b.

84. *Daofa huiyuan* 253, 10b–11a.

85. *Yijian zhi*, 814–815.

86. *Daofa huiyuan* 243, "Nanji huolei lingguan Wang yuanshuai bifa," 3b.

87. Ibid., 243, 1a–b and 4a.

88. Ibid., 417. With this anecdote, we may surmise that the cult to Ucchuṣma had spread from southern Fujian (from Zhang and Quan prefectures) in two

directions—overland, in a northwesterly direction into Jiangxi, and along the coast, in a northeasterly direction to Fuzhou. Below we will consider other anecdotes that show the cult had extended to Poyang in Jiangxi and as far north as Yangzhou in Jiangsu.

89. Ibid., 919.

90. Ibid., 1172.

91. See the tenth-century account of a medium discussed in Chapter 3, note 68.

92. See Wang Yucheng (954–1001), *Xiaochu ji* (Taipei: Sibu congkan ji, 1936), 3.7a–b, "He yayi jiao"; the discussion of the medium's "child underlings" (*tongli*) in the 1023 memorial of Xia Song, requesting permission to eliminate sorcery in Hongchou (*Xu Zizhi tongjian changbian* 101, "Hongzhou qing duan yaowu zou"); and *Yijian zhi* 986, where a medium in Fuzhou arrives at an exorcism with a "boy-retinue" (*putong*) numbering several dozen.

93. See *Jiannan shikao*: 37, "Qiu Han," Lu You (1125–1210), reprinted in *Lu Fangweng quanji* (Beijing: Zhonghua shuju, 1986), vol. 2, 571; the poem by Liu Yun (971–1031), quoted in Nakamura Jihei, "Sōchō no kiu ni tsuite," *Ajia no kyōiku to shakai* (Tokyo: Fumaitō shuppan, 1980), 111, which distinguishes between ten-odd "elderly mediums" (*laoxi*), and a group of "child-mediums" (*tongwu*) and "actors and actresses" (*lingchang*); and, from the Tang, *Quan Tang Shi* 396, "Han Shen" by Yuan Zhen.

94. *Yijian zhi* 996.

95. Consider, in the context of Tantric Buddhism, T. 1246, *Mo he fei shi luo mo na ye ti po he luo she tuoluoni yigui*, 221a–b, "Dao Tang jinhuo fa" ("Rites for Walking Through Boiling Water and Exorcising Fire"). At *Yijian zhi* 1299, a Daoist priest of the Tianqing Abbey in Leizhou "walks through boiling water without being aware," evidently in trance, but he is suffering from a demonic illness.

96. See Ōfuchi Ninji, *Chūgokujin no shūkyō girei*, 1008–1044, passim.

97. John Lagerwey, most recently, has found in the counties of Ninghua, Taining, and Jiangle (West Central Fujian) the same divinities to be central to offering rituals of the Buddho-Daoist ritual masters of the Pu'an jiao: Ucchuṣma (Miji jingang), Nāgārjuna and Zhenwu, and Nezha, but also the Four Saints (Tianpeng, Tianyou, Yisheng, and Yousheng), Huaguang, various *luo*-spirits, etc. In Taining county, these ritual masters are called "Molangxian" (Demon-Son Transcendents). Lagerwey writes: "According to [the priest] Chen [Shengzhong], Molangxian . . . do both 'light' and 'dark' rituals, but primarily the latter. They cannot be called 'monks' because they marry and know magic (*fashu*), but they are at once Buddhist

and Taoist. [The priest] Xiao [Fujian] added: 'We are Taoists. Taishang lao-jun taught the ancestral master Pu'an, so it can be called the Pu'an school.' There is another type of priest in the area who belong to the Three-Altar school (Santan jiao). Their specialty is crossing barefoot on beds of hot coals (*guohuolian*)—'if this needs to be done, we must invite them'—and 'call-ing down the Wulang' (*jiang wulang*) (both of these are normally Lüshan rituals): 'The Wulang can catch demons. In addition they blow buffalo horns (*niujiao*), but otherwise their rituals are the same as ours, and we can work together. We are both called Molangxian. They are Taoists with an admixture of Pu'an teachings; we are Taoist with Buddhist scriptures.'" For this and much more, see John Lagerwey, "Popular Ritual Specialists in West Central Fujian (Taibei: Proceedings of the International Colloquium on Chinese Society, Ethnicity, and Cultural Performance, 2000), 1–33. The commitment to Tantric Buddhism of Linshui furen—the putative founder of the Lüshan sect who lived in the eighth century in Putian, Fujian—is emphasized in Ōfuchi Ninji, *Chūgokujin no shūkyō girei*, 1013, line 22 through 1014, line 1. See also Brigitte Baptandier-Berthier, *La Dame au bord de l'eau* (Nanterre: Societé d'ethnologie, 1988), and idem, "The Lady Lin-shui: How a Woman Became a Goddess," in Meir Shahar and Robert P. Weller, eds., *Unruly Gods: Divinity and Society in China* (Honolulu: Univer-sity of Hawai'i Press, 1996), 105–149.

Chapter 7: Daoist Priests, Confucian Literati, and Child-Mediums

1. *Yijian zhi*, 1198–1199.
2. Ibid., 846.
3. For these Daoist rites for the dead, see Chapter 8.
4. This, by the way, is further proof that, despite later criticism, twelfth-century priests who practiced the funeral liturgy of the *Lingbao dafa* also practiced exorcisms.
5. *Yijian zhi*, 1759–1761.
6. Ibid., 1382–1383.
7. Denis Twitchett, "The Fan Clan's Charitable Estate, 1950–1760," in David Nivison and Arthur Wright, eds., *Confucianism in Action* (Stanford: Stanford University Press, 1959), 97–133, and idem, "Documents on Clan Adminis-tration 1: The Rules of Administration of the Charitable Estate of the Fan Clan," *Asia Major* 3rd ser., 8 (1960), 1–35.
8. Patricia Ebrey, "Early Stages of Descent Group Organization" in Ebrey and

Watson, eds., *Kinship Organization in Late Imperial China, 1000–1940* (Berkeley: University of California Press, 1986), 42–43.

9. See, for example, the Dunhuang document (Stein 6537v) translated and analyzed by Chikusa Masa'aki, *Chūgoku bukkyōshakai shi kenkyū*, 497–500 (document #7).

10. Twitchett, "The Fan Clan's Charitable Estate," 116. The list of familial encroachments continues at some length.

11. Compare with the temple-medium of Ucchuṣma (Chapter 6), who also stands on a table.

12. In 720, statues and offerings to the "ten wise" disciples of Confucius were dedicated by imperial decree in the Confucian Temple at Yanzhou. See David McMullen, *State and Scholars in T'ang China* (Cambridge: Cambridge University Press, 1988), 45.

13. *Yijian zhi*, 1089–1091.

14. For *liandu* and the Yellow Register Retreat, see Chapter 8 and Appendix.

15. See Chapter 4, under the section "Spirit-Mediums and Daoist Revelation."

16. See Chapter 6, under "Tantric Cults and Daoist Ritual Masters," and this chapter, under "Confucian Literati and Child-Mediums."

17. *Yijian zhi*, 1260.

Chapter 8: Spirit-Possession and the Grateful Dead

1. Yu Wenbao, *Chuijian silu*, as reproduced in Matsumoto Kōichi, "Sōrei-sairei ni miru Sōdai shūkyōshi no ichi keikō," in *Sōdai no shakai to bunka* (Tokyo: Kyūko shoin, 1983), 172.

2. The tendency of many historians to examine mortuary ritual from the perspective of Song Neo-Confucianism at best grossly simplifies a very complex religious situation, and at worst seriously distorts the actual state of religious practice in the twelfth and thirteenth centuries. Typical of this perspective is Evelyn Rawski's introduction to the recent conference volume, James Watson and Evelyn Rawski, eds., *Death Ritual in Late Imperial and Modern China* (Berkeley: University of California Press, 1988), 20–40. Her article is entitled "A Historian's Approach to Chinese Death Ritual," though Rawski has a very narrow view of what counts as ritual and what constitutes a historian's approach to it. In contrast to the anthropologist, she writes, "The historian's understanding of death ritual . . . is dominated by the texts that are constantly cited in writings on ritual, beginning with the *Li ji* (Treatise on ceremonial usages), a work from the fourth century B.C., which was one of the 'Five Canons' (*Wujing*), and the *Yili* (Rites and ceremonial usages), dating

from the same period. These texts were the reference points for subsequent compilations of ritual into the late Qing period, and for historians one major question is To what extent were these texts the guide to actual ritual practice?"

The historian's understanding of and approach to mortuary ritual are limited here to classical Confucian texts and their historical permutations. The relation of these texts to actual ritual practice is indeed an important question, but Rawski makes no attempt to answer it. Rather than posing the question of their relation to different historical periods, the development of Chinese mortuary ritual is read entirely in terms of the supposed convergence of classical text and ritual practice in the Ming and especially Qing dynasties. Rawski appears to divide pre-Qing China into two periods. Before the Song, death ritual and the ancestor cult were denied to commoners, and "the effect of limiting the audience for classical ritual prescriptions to the ruling elite was to permit other belief systems, notably Buddhism and Daoism, to dominate popular practice" (ibid., 20). Buddhism and Daoism, therefore, managed to dominate popular practice by default.

In addition to being a completely inadequate explanation for the prevalence of non-Confucian mortuary ritual, the implication of this view is that, as historians, we might have been spared the necessity of even mentioning Buddhism and Daoism had the audience for classical ritual not been so circumscribed. That this is indeed an implication of Rawski's view is borne out by the fact that she goes on to attribute the same mechanism to the decline of Buddhist and Daoist influence as she does to its rise: "In the eleventh and twelfth centuries, a newly vigorous Confucian officialdom began to look closely at and to correct popular mores through reform of marriage and mourning customs" (ibid., 30–31). In particular, "the Neo-Confucian philosophical attack on Buddhism and Daoism . . . sought to replace errant practices among commoners with approved classical rites and signaled an important reorientation toward the propagation of standards that would cover commoners as well as gentleman-officials" (ibid., 30). Rawski believes that "the impact of the Neo-Confucian concern with the social transformation of commoners" was facilitated by two long-term secular trends: first, the development of printing, which was both cause and effect of the dissemination of Confucian norms, and, second, the central government's reliance on indirect means of social control through the educational efforts of "a group of degree-holders educated in the Confucian curriculum, committed to the dynasty, and strategically placed throughout China." Once, in other words, the Neo-Confucian elite decided in the Song to expand the audience for classical ritual, Buddhist and Daoist ritual progressively collapsed under the weight of compelling philosophical argument and a rising tide of books and lectures that left no social shore of the empire uncovered. The history of Chinese religious practice since the Song is a linear narrative of standardization and normalization driven exclusively by the paternalistic instincts of a uniform and monovocal elite such that, "by the Qing, one could truly say that the mourning observances for an emperor were in their essentials the same as the mourning observances for commoners" (ibid., 32).

A number of unfortunate consequences follow from this approach. By limiting the historian to classical ritual, we not only deny the historian a significant body of textual evidence but we will never see that, long before the Qing, the death rituals of emperors were often the same as those of commoners, only these rituals were not Confucian. By linking the fortunes and fate of Buddhist and Daoist death ritual with the ritual prescriptions of the state or the elite, we miss what was compelling about these rituals in themselves: how they came to satisfy individual needs or familial aspirations that the very nature of classical ritual precluded it from addressing; how they emerged and flourished within a particular society and gave shape to a particular configuration and historical vision of social and economic relations; and how they functioned as *the* vehicle for the transmission and perpetuation of archaic Chinese ritual practices and for the dissemination of distinctly Chinese, even Confucian, values.

Most importantly, by maintaining a hard distinction between elite and commoners, and by further identifying the elite with the practice of classical ritual and the espousal of Neo-Confucianism, we blind ourselves to the fact that through the Song, Yuan, and Ming dynasties, and to a more differentiated extent in the Qing, the most ardent practitioners of Buddhist and Daoist death ritual were members of the bureaucratic class and local gentry. A "common Confucian curriculum" did not guarantee that the elite spoke with a single voice on this issue, nor did the label "popular" (*su*), applied by Neo-Confucians to nonclassical rituals, guarantee that those who practiced them were primarily commoners.

It has been argued, furthermore, that Zhu Xi's *Family Rituals* did not become historically significant or influential until the sixteenth and, especially, the seventeenth century, when the gentry began to ensure their dominance of local society—and to undermine the horizontal, economic ties of class—by organizing their less fortunate kin along the vertical lines of lineage. See Timothy Brook, "Gentry Dominance in Chinese Society: Monasteries and Lineages in the Structuring of Local Society, 1500–1700" (Ph.D. diss., Harvard

University, 1984), esp. ch. 8, 262–295, and idem, "Funerary Ritual and the Building of Lineages in Late Imperial China," *Harvard Journal of Asiatic Studies* 49 (1989), 465–499, esp. 483–489; for Zhu Xi's *Family Rituals*, see also Patricia Ebrey, trans., *Chu Hsi's Family Rituals: A Twelfth-Century Manual for the Performance of Cappings, Weddings, Funerals and Rites* (Princeton: Princeton University Press, 1991), and Ebrey, *Confucianism and Family Rituals in Imperial China: A Social History of Writing About Rites* (Princeton: Princeton University Press, 1991), esp. ch. 6 and 7. Ebrey wants to indicate the success of Zhu Xi's book as a guide to actual practice by enumerating the many editions, abridgments, and commentaries it spawned from the Song through Ming dynasties, a success that seems to be contradicted by the evidence analyzed by Brook.

In the Song and Yuan dynasties, we do find what Robert Hymes has called a "lineage orientation" among elite families—what from a slightly different point of view Patricia Ebrey has called "group consciousness." See Hymes, "Marriage, Descent Groups, and the Localist Strategy in Song and Yuan Fuzhou," in Ebrey and Watson, eds., *Kinship Organization in Late Imperial China, 1000–1940* (Berkeley: University of California Press, 1986), 133; and Ebrey, "The Early Stages of Descent Group Organization," also in Ebrey and Watson, eds., *Kinship Organization*, 23. More often than not, however, the desire of individuals to express their descent from a common apical ancestor was made within the context of Buddhist institutions and observances.

At a more abstract level, the problem with examining death and other ritual practices from the perspective of Neo-Confucianism is that it necessarily tends to marginalize Buddhism and Daoism and to distract us from the extent to which the Neo-Confucians represented an extremely radical, minority position within the Song-dynasty elite. In a recent conference paper on the "State Response to Popular Funeral Practices in Song China" (presented at the Symposium on Religion and Society in China, Urbana-Champaign, Nov. 1988), Ebrey defines these popular practices as those that were "perceived as objectionable by the educated elite or state officials." Her evidence for the position of the educated elite, however, is drawn entirely from the writings of a small group of (Neo-)Confucian writers, most notably Sima Guang, Cheng Yi, and Yu Wenbao. In her final paragraph, at the end of a long analysis of their objections to Buddhist death ritual, geomancy, and the exorcism of the *sha* spirits, Ebrey does admit that "the educated elite" were not uniform in their attitudes to these popular funerary customs and that some actually left poems commemorating their participation in Buddhist rituals, yet she draws no conclusions from this.

When Ebrey turns to the state, she finds that, for the most part, it not only took a very tolerant attitude toward the popular practices criticized by the Neo-Confucians but actually engaged in these practices itself. Yet again, Ebrey draws nothing positive from this. Instead of offering a historical and cultural analysis of what the state actually did, she feels compelled to explain how the Song state could possibly tolerate or adhere to such a contradictory and fragmented set of practices (Confucian, Buddhist, geomantic, and folk) at one and the same time. Ebrey offers a series of "sociological explanations" for how each and every one of these practices served state interests in a different and special way. In the end she writes, "As a historian I would prefer to look at the issue historically, analyzing why particular practices spread when they did. Unfortunately it is difficult to date with any confidence the penetration of grave geomancy and Buddhist services throughout the population. Certainly geomantic theories were known and discussed by the elite in the early Tang; whether typical peasants in that period consulted geomancers is not so clear. Buddhist services and the related idea of Buddhist purgatories and transferring merit seem to have spread during the Tang, but there is not enough evidence to estimate the proportion of the population performing Buddhist services in mid-Tang and mid-Song" (ibid.)

While it is certainly true that we cannot attach a numerical figure to the proportion of the Tang and Song population that performed Buddhist services for the dead, we can chart with a fair degree of confidence and specificity, I believe, the historical development and social diffusion not only of Buddhist but also of Daoist, and other, death rituals. We cannot do this, however, by relying on the writings of Song Neo-Confucians or state edicts.

3. Examples of what would appear to be indisputable Buddhist influence on the Daoist ritual are the "bathhouse" (*wenshi* or *mushi*), where the souls are washed, and the "sweet dew" on which they feed. Compare, for example, *Fajie shengfan shiulu shenghui xuizhai yigui*, Zhu Hong, 2.12a and 3.28a with *Wushang huanglu dazhai licheng yi* 26.8a and 29.6a, and with *Shangqing lingbao dafa*, Jin Yunzhong, 37.3b and 38.23a. In the Daoist *pudu*, moreover, the souls of the dead line up and are bathed by gender, a detail borrowed directly from the *shuilu*. Michel Strickmann, by the way, in his attempt to place the *shuilu* within the Tantric tradition, found parallels to the bathing of the saints in the devotional bathing of icons, and parallels to the bathing of the commoners in the purificatory use of water to exorcise demons (*Mantras et mandarins*, 308). I find these parallels unconvincing, as I do the entire project of identifying the *shuilu* as a Tantric ritual. A more significant comparison would be with the bathhouses (*mushi*) maintained and sponsored by

Song-dynasty monasteries in which over a thousand monks and laymen (= the saints and commoners of the *shuilu*) might be washed at the same time. These bathhouses had their origin in the Tang, when they were restricted to monks. (See Huang Minzhi, *Songdao fojiao shehui jingji shi lunji*, 432–434.)

Be that as it may, it is difficult to know how to assess these examples of Buddhist influence on Daoist rites for the dead. At a deep level, the bathing and feeding and even clothing of the soul resonates with the ancient Chinese funerary practice of bathing, clothing, and feeding the corpse. See the passages from the *Liji* and *Yili* translated and analyzed in J. J. M. de Groot, *The Religious System of China* (Taipei reprint, 1976), vol. 1, ch. 2–3. Moreover, in a Daoist context, the bathing, clothing, and feeding of the soul can already be seen in a text that belongs to the original corpus of Lingbao scriptures revealed at the end of the fourth century, *The Marvelous Scripture of Salvation through Extinction by Revivification of Corpses through Fivefold Refinement* (*Taishang dongxuan lingbao miedu wulian shengshi miaojing*, HY 369). This scripture contains "talisman-orders" (*fuming*) addressed to the Spirits of the Five Directions. They were to be painted on stone and buried in the tomb. One of these has been translated by Stephen Bokenkamp ("Death and Ascent in *Lingbao* Daoism," *Taoist Resources* 1.2 [1989], 8–9) and, more recently, by Peter Nickerson: "Let Taishan, the Eastern Marchmount, open to the light the Offices of the Long Night of the Nine Stygia, and let out the *hun*-spirit of (so-and-so). Shampoo, bathe, cap and gird him, and send him to the southern mansion. Supply him with clothing and food, and let him be eternally in the light" (Nickerson, "Taoism, Death, and Bureaucracy in Early Medieval China," [Ph.D. diss., Berkeley, 1996], 224). Similar instructions are made to the spirits of the tomb in the fifth-century Daoist tomb ordinances translated and analyzed by Nickerson, (ibid., 17): "All the divinities of the mound and tomb should . . . open and show the deceased the passage, putting to rest his cadaverous form, shampooing and bathing, capping and girding him."

4. See *Yijian zhi* 416, for a *shuilu* performed in a village near Wenzhou, ostensibly for those who died at sea. Examples of urban *shuilu* will be encountered below.

5. *Yijian zhi* 1149 and 1209.

6. Ibid., 326, for a *Huanglu jiuyou jiao* performed at the Yusi Abbey on Gezaoshan.

7. For the *shuilu*, see ibid., 465; for the *huanglu*, see ibid., 1422.

8. Ibid., 443.

9. Ibid., 1237. This monk, befitting his elite clientele, was also expert in Sanskrit.

10. Ibid., 1259.

11. Ibid., 589.

12. Ibid., 988.

13. Ibid., 456–457.

14. Ibid., 443.

15. Ibid., 761, 983, and so on.

16. Ibid., 461.

17. Ibid., 750.

18. Ibid., 162.

19. Ibid., 560.

20. Ibid., 746.

21. Ibid., 1398.

22. Ibid., 471.

23. Ibid., 774.

24. Ibid., 1528–1529.

25. Ibid., 545.

26. Ibid., 1405–1406.

27. Ibid., 588–589.

28. Ibid., 1100.

29. *Song Bai zhenren Yuchan quanji* 428–429 (*Yulu* 6.10b–11a.)

30. For the appearance of the individual or collective dead at Buddhist funerary ritual, see *Yijian zhi* 360, where the dead return during a *Yulanpen zhai* following a funeral; 385–386, where a vision of the dead following Buddhist rites leads a community to replace a Daoist *Huanglu luohan zhaihui*; 457, where Buddhist nuns appear in a dream during a *shuilu* performed by neighbor; 497, where a dead wife appears to her husband following a *shuilu,* and his appearance is identified by monks as a "Living Heavenly Image" (*sheng-tianxiang*); 742, where a monk summons the orphan-soul during a *shuilu* and causes it to appear; 916, where a dead uncle appears during a Buddhist *Sanqi zhaihui* sponsored by his niece and her husband, and converses with relatives; 1142, where dozens of roaming dead appear during a *shuilu*; 1209, where a *shuilu* performed at Gold Mountain Monastery has the power not only to cause the dead to appear but actually to restore the dead to life(!); and 1415, where a dead husband appears at a *Jiqi daochang* performed by monks forty-nine days after his death.

31. *Yijian zhi* 1319.

32. Ibid., 767.

33. Ibid., 1704–1705.

34. The *Rites of Zhou* specifies that in funerals one should have performed "the

ritual of the spirit-medium (*wu*) bringing down [or being possessed by] the ancestral spirit" (*Zhouli zhengyi* 26.9a–b).

35. *Taiping guangji* 388 "Seng Daojie" (p. 3096).

36. See, for example, *Yijian zhi* 739: "Xiang Ming, a commoner from Mount Kang-liang in the canton of Hongyayi, Yugan subprefecture, took a singing girl, née Hu, as a wife. Over ten years later, she died giving birth to a daughter. In 1164, a spirit-medium arrived from another canton, claiming that (s)he could cause the *hun-* and *po-*souls of the dead to return. Xiang had the medium summon his wife. As soon as the medium commanded it, she came, but Xiang couldn't see anything; only the daughter, who was then already twelve years old, saw that she was truly her mother. . . . All her demands she would announce through the girl."

37. For other examples of sons or grandsons who play the role of spirit-medium during a Yellow Register Retreat, see *Yijian zhi*, 188–189 and 448–449.

38. See, for example, *Shi jing* 248: "The wild ducks are on the King river; the representative of the (dead) princes comes and feasts and is at peace and (approves =) finds it good; your wine is clear, your viands are fragrant; the representative feasts and drinks; felicity and blessings come and (achieve, complete you =) make you perfect," translated by Bernhard Karlgren, *The Book of Odes* (Stockholm: Museum of Far Eastern Antiquities, 1974), 204.

39. See C. H. Wang, *From Ritual to Allegory: Seven Essays in Early Chinese Poetry* (Hong Kong: The Chinese University Press, 1988), 47.

40. See, for example, *Li ji* 2, "Ki Thung," 9: "of the pantomimic evolutions there was none more important than representing (King) Wu's (army) on the night (before his battle)." James Legge, trans., *Li Chi: Book of Rites* (New Hyde Park: University Books, 1967).

41. Arthur Waley, trans., *The Book of Songs: The Ancient Chinese Classic of Poetry* (New York: Grove Weidenfeld, 1988), 211.

42. This interpretation would seem to be supported by *Li ji* 2, "Kiao Theh Sang" 26: "The *shi* personated the spirit; the officer of prayer was the medium of communication between him and the sacrificer" (Legge, *Li Chi*, 446).

43. As translated by Henry Dore, *Researches into Chinese Superstitions*, vol. 1 (Taipei: Chengwen, 1966), 100.

44. Ibid., 99.

45. Legge, *Li Chi*, 337–338.

46. Dore, *Researches into Chinese Superstitions*, 101–102.

47. Ibid., 102. The words that are translated here by "reposes therein" were often used in the Song to designate bodily possession. The passage, not specified by Dore, can be found in *Zhuzi yulei* 90.18a–b. I am pleased to see

that this passage has been discussed recently by Julia Ching under the fine heading "Spirit-Possession Reinterpreted by Philosophy." See her *Mysticism and Kingship in China: The Heart of Chinese Wisdom* (Cambridge: Cambridge University Press, 1997), 117–118.

48. *Daoshu yuanshen qi* (HY 1221), 5a.

49. Ibid., 1a–b.

50. Ibid., 2a–7a.

51. Possession within the Yellow Register Retreat, I would argue, should be contrasted with nonstructural/spontaneous possession following death. See *Yijian zhi* 561–562, concerning the Record-Keeper of Haimen subprefecture in Tongzhou who died while assisting in police matters: "The coffin was lodged in a nunnery. The wife had not overcome her fear and hired two nuns to keep her company during the night. Just as they passed by the spirit-curtain, one of the nuns agitatedly got up and then calmly sat down. She assumed the voice of the deceased, ordering them to summon the magistrate of the subprefectural office, Sun Su. Sun arrived and engaged in very detailed questions and answers with the deceased. The deceased begged Sun to have several clerks named so-and-so flogged for their transgressions. Sun followed his advice. Thereupon he proclaimed on matters of ethics, 'Your sincerity has not attained favor, and your death has been fated. If it is the same for those whom you hold dear [i.e., your relatives], how will you attain transcendence?' And he had the monk Hui Yu invited to explain the Dharma. A day passed, and the nun regained consciousness. But with the funeral, the deceased returned, and the nun again assumed his voice, commanding his wife, 'If you want to marry, then go ahead; not at all will you bring shame and pollution upon the affairs of our household, nor will I be angry with you!'" See also *Yijian zhi* 1693–1694, where a concubine becomes possessed by her dead master during ancestral sacrifices and addresses his son.

52. See *Wushang huanglu dazhai licheng yi* (HY 508), 25 and 26.

53. Ibid., 26.1a and 26.3a.

54. Ibid., 26.3b. For more detailed instructions see the early fourteenth-century *Lingbao lingjiao jidu jinshu* (HY 466), 283.6b–16b.

55. *Shangqing lingbao dafa* (Jin Yunzhong), 36.14b–15a.

56. Ibid., 36.12a.

57. Ibid., 36.16a; also, *Shangqing lingbao dafa* (Wang Qizhen), 38.9b–10a.

58. *Shangqing lingbao dafa* (Wang Qizhen), 35.9b–10a. The rituals that bring the soul to the altar and cause it to reveal its form and/or to speak are collectively referred to as "Rites of Attracting and Summoning" (*shezhao fa.*) See *Lingbao lingjiao jidu jinshu* 260 for the instructions for "The Rites of Attract-

ing and Summoning [as explained in the] Numinous Book of the Purple
Flower of the Great Rites of Lingbao," prefaced by a fascinating account of
their historical transmission and alteration.

59. *Shangqing lingbao dafa* (Wang Qizhen), 38.18b–19b.

60. Ibid., 38.25a.

61. Kristofer Schipper, "Mulien Plays in Daoist Liturgical Context," in David Johnson, ed., *Ritual Opera, Operatic Ritual* (Berkeley: Chinese Popular Culture Project, 1989), 139–140. Much more detailed accounts of the destruction of the
fortress can be found in Ōfuchi Ninji, *Chūgokujin no shūkyō girei*, 502–510,
and Lagerwey, *Taoist Ritual in Chinese Society and History*, 221–228.

62. Schipper, "Mulien Plays," 140. Tanaka Issei has found references to the inclusion of *nuo*-type rituals already in the Song-dynasty *jiao*. These rituals,
found in the *Lingbao lingjiao jidu jinshu* 256–258, were performed by *falei
deng* (the Ritual Masters and their entourage). See Tanaka Issei, *Chūgoku fukei
engeki kenkyū*, 40–44.

63. *Lingbao lingjiao jidu jinshu* 120 and 121.

64. Ibid., 120.25a.

65. Ibid., 120.24a.

66. *Yijian zhi* 1536.

Chapter 9: The Syncretic Field of Chinese Religion

1. Prasenjit Duara, "State and Civil Society in the History of Chinese Modernity," in Frederic Wakeman, Jr., and Wang Xi, eds., *China's Quest for Modernization* (Berkeley: Institute of East Asian Studies, University of California at
Berkeley, Research Papers and Policy Studies 41, 1997), 300–324.

2. Ibid., 304–305.

3. Frederic Wakeman, Jr., "Civil Society in Late Imperial China," in Wakeman
and Wang, eds., *China's Quest*, 325–351.

4. Prasenjit Duara, *Culture, Power, and the State: Rural North China, 1900–1942*
(Stanford: Stanford University Press, 1988), 5.

5. Frederic Wakeman, Jr., "Models of Historical Change: The Chinese State and
Society, 1839–1989," in Lieberthal et al., eds., *Perspectives on Modern China:
Four Anniversaries* (Armonk: Sharpe, 1991), 68–102, esp. 81–87.

6. Duara, *Culture, Power, and the State*, 134–135.

7. Ibid., 135.

8. Prasenjit Duara, *Rescuing History from the Nation: Questioning Narratives of Modern China* (Chicago: University of Chicago Press, 1995), 7.

9. Duara, "State and Civil Society in the History of Chinese Modernity," 316.

10. Ibid.

11. Ernest Gellner, *Conditions of Liberty: Civil Society and Its Rivals* (London: Penguin reprint, 1996), 6–9.

12. Frederic Wakeman, Jr., "Boundaries of the Public Sphere in Ming and Qing China," *Daedalus* 127.3 (Summer 1998), 182; Ray Huang, *1587: A Year of No Significance* (New Haven: Yale University Press, 1981) is still the best study of this "sensible hypocrisy."

13. Stephan Feuchtwang, *The Imperial Metaphor: Popular Religion in China* (London: Routledge, 1992), 56–57.

14. Ibid., 56, 81–85, 91–125.

15. Alexander Woodside, "Emperors and the Chinese Political System," in Lieberthal et al., eds., *Perspectives on Modern China*, 10–11. In the Song, especially, the *shi* came to define themselves more specifically in contrast to the military. See Peter Bol, *"This Culture of Ours,"* 55.

16. I would argue that pluralism in China, in contrast to historical examples of civil society, must be characterized as exclusive rather than inclusive. Religious syncretism notwithstanding, membership in one cultic unit was exclusive of membership with respect to a neighboring cultic unit. Such units were invariably defined by rituals of alimentary sacrifice—performative rituals of communion (feasts) and exclusion (exorcisms).

17. Kenneth Dean, *Lord of the Three in One: The Spread of a Cult in Southeast China* (Princeton: Princeton University Press, 1998), 30–63 and 273–295.

18. Recently, for example, Patricia Ebrey and Peter Gregory have tried to produce a "metaphor for Chinese religion" derived from the picture of three mountains, each representing one of the "Three Religions," all sitting on a base of "popular religion" (*Religion and Society in T'ang and Sung China*, Introduction). What is defended as "only a metaphor" is nonetheless presented as a model. It is the Buddhist mountain, and not reality, that in fact provides the model for the other two mountains. The Buddhist mountain includes a celibate clergy at the summit, lay believers in the middle, and a broad base of laymen who do not identify themselves as Buddhist yet who on occasion worship a Buddhist deity. (This broad base appears to merge with the base of popular religion.) Corresponding to the celibate clergy of Buddhism are Daoist priests and Confucian officials, scholars, and teachers, despite the facts that Daoist priests were neither celibate nor monastic and that Confucian officials were neither clerics, celibates, nor monks. Corresponding to the Buddhist lay believer are the lower ranks of the Daoist priesthood and those who merely read a Confucian book, despite the fact that the lower ranks of the Daoist priesthood were priests and not laymen,

while those who read Confucian books included many priests and priests-to-be.

At this point Ebrey and Gregory even question whether there was such a thing as a Confucian lay believer. Corresponding to the Buddhist worshipper-but-nonbeliever are those who do not identify themselves as Daoists yet supplicate a Daoist divinity in a Daoist temple, as well as those who do not identify themselves as Confucian but who either accept certain Confucian values (e.g., filiality), practice Confucian rituals such as ancestor worship, or simply refuse to practice non-Confucian rituals. Yet there were no Daoists in Chinese society except for Daoist priests and Ritual Masters, so the contrast between believing Daoist laymen and nonbelieving supplicants of Daoist divinities is meaningless. Furthermore, those who accepted Confucian virtues included Buddhist monks and Daoist priests; those who practiced ancestor worship included Buddhist monks, Daoist priests, and Buddhist laymen; and those who refused to practice non-Confucian rituals were, sad to say, only a small group of Confucian officials, at least in the Song.

This house of cards is all built on the firm base of popular religion—the repository for everything that does not quite fit into the "Three Religions," including divination, ancestor worship, and spirit-mediumship, despite the fact that these three (and almost everything else that is mentioned) have ancient and very learned pedigrees. For a very fine historical introduction to Chinese religions—one that is still organized along the lines of the traditional categories but that manages to avoid such incoherence, see Stephen Teiser's introduction to Donald Lopez, Jr., ed., *Religions of China in Practice* (Princeton: Princeton University Press, 1996), 3–37.

19. Here I am combing different suggestions of François Jullien and Marshall Sahlins.

20. Dean, *Lord of the Three in One* 26, note 29, quoting Stephan Feuchtwang.

21. *Yijian zhi* 690.

22. Kenneth Dean, *Lord of the Three in One*, 50; idem, "Transformations of the *She* (Altars of the Soil) in Fujian," *Cahiers d'Extrême-Asia* 10 (1998); esp. 33–41; and Romeyn Taylor, "Official and Popular Religion and the Political Organization of Chinese Society in the Ming," in Liu Kwang-ching, ed., *Orthodoxy in Late Imperial China* (Berkeley: University of California Press, 1991), esp. 143–148.

23. Dean, *Lord of the Three in One*, 49.

24. See Chikusa Masa'aki, *Chūgoku bukkyō shakai shi kenkyū*, 145–198 and 261–319; Huang Minzhi, *Songdai fojiao shehui jingji shi lunji* , 119–200.

25. See Kanai Noriyuki, "Sōdai-no gōsha-to dojishin," *Nakajima Satoshi-sensei*

koki kinen ronshū (Tokyo: Kyūko shoin, 1980–81), esp. 401–403, and idem, "Nansō saishi shakai-no tenkai" *Shūkyō shakaishi kenkyū* (Tokyo: Yūzankaku, 1977), esp. 594–597, on monasteries and the "altars to the spirits of the land and grain"; Miyamoto Noriyuki, "Sō-Gen jidai ni okeru fun'an-to sosen saishi," *Bukkyō shigaku kenkyū* 35.2 (1992), 112–135; Linda Walton, "Southern Sung Academies as Sacred Places," in Ebrey and Gregory, eds., *Religion and Society in T'ang and Sung China*, 335–363. In the recent and most sophisticated study of Buddhism and literati in the Tang and Song, Mark Halperin explores the partnership between the Song state and Buddhist church whereby selected Buddhist monasteries served as memorials for the war dead, as religious spaces to mark imperial birthdays and death-days, as repositories of imperial calligraphy, and as galleries of imperial portraits. See his "Pieties and Responsibilities: Buddhism and Chinese Literati, 780–1280" (Ph.D. diss., University of California at Berkeley, 1997), 186–259.

26. Kanai Noriyuki, "Sōdai-no sonsha-to bukkyō," esp. 50–53. Mark Halperin makes a similar point from a different perspective: "Literati, not the sangha, came to determine how Buddhist institutions should be presented. The distance separating sangha and lay people had diminished markedly after the T'ang. First many of the eminent monks of the time such as Tsan-ning (919–1001), Tsun-shih (964–1032), Ch'i-sung (1007–1072), Te-hung (1071–1128) and Ta-hui (1089–1163) cultivated close ties with the state and scholar-officials. Although they largely continued old patterns of clerical-lay ties, the search for patrons amid partisan debates within the Buddhist church might have intensified the level of this association. To a much greater degree than in the T'ang, elite clergy composed work with lay audiences in mind. Moreover, Sung administrative changes granted prefects the power to appoint the abbots of large, public monasteries. *Shi* thus were obliged in their government duties to know something about monks. Given the sangha's great diversity, this new familiarity might at times have bred contempt, but it often led to considerable admiration. In many cases, lay and religious elites treated each other as peers" ("Pieties and Responsibilities: Buddhism and Chinese Literati, 780–1280," 37–38).

27. Hans Blumenberg, *The Legitimacy of the Modern Age*, trans. Robert Wallace (Cambridge: MIT Press, 1983), 37–51 (esp. 48–50).

28. Roberto Mangabeira Unger, *Politics: The Central Texts: Theory Against Fate* (London: Verso, 1997), 3.

29. Ibid., 22.

Appendix

1. Schipper, *Le corps taoïste*, 122–125; Cedzich, "Das Ritual der Himmelmeister," 137–141.

2. Rolf Stein, "Les fêtes de cuisines du taoïsme religieux," *Annuaire du Collège de France* 69 (1968–1969): 431–440; and idem, "Spéculations mystiques et thèmes relatifs aux 'cuisines' du taoïsme," *Annuaire du Collège de France* 72 (1971–72): 489–499.

3. Michel Soymié, "Les dix jours de jeûne du taoïsme," in *Dōkyō kenkyū ronshū, Dōkyō no shisō to bunka* (Tokyo: Kokushōkankōkai, 1977), 1–21.

4. *Dongxuan lingbao wuganwen* (HY 1268), 5b–7a. The twelve *zhai* include two associated with the Shangqing tradition, nine with the Lingbao tradition, and one with the Celestial Master tradition (the *zhai* of the Three Primordials of Mud and Soot). The nine *Lingbao zhai* are distinguished by function. Some, like the Retreat of the Golden Register, are dedicated to the salvation of the state; others, like the Yellow Register Retreat, are dedicated to "banishing the sins of nine generations of ancestors"; and still others appear to be particularly concerned with the salvation and immortalization of the Taoist master or practicant. All nine of these *Lingbao zhai*, however, may be specific adaptations of the *zhai* described in the earlier *Taiji zhenren fu lingbao zhaijie weiyi zhujing yaojie* (HY 532), as suggested by Catherine Bell. This *zhai* includes (a) an opening sequence in which the priest enters the oratory and makes an announcement before the incense burner, (b) a rite for exteriorizing the spirits who will announce the *zhai* to all corners of the universe, (c) a rite of petition, three of which are read and burned in the incense burner, and, finally, (d) a rite of supplication performed in each of the ten directions. See Catherine Bell, "Medieval Taoist Ritual Mastery: A Study in Practice, Text and Rite" (Ph.D. diss., University of Chicago, 1983), 111–114. The three petitions include one for the deliverance of ancestors, another for the salvation of the state (the emperor, dynasty, and ministers), and a third for the salvation of the master. These three petitions, therefore, anticipate the tripartite functions of the nine *Lingbao zhai*.

5. John Lagerwey, *Wu-shang pi-yao, Somme taoïste du VIe siecle* (Paris: EFEO, 1981), 163–165.

6. Henri Maspero, *Taoism and Chinese Religion* (Amherst: The University of Massachusetts Press, 1981), 293–298.

7. For the differentiation between and elaboration of the *falu* and *chuguan* rites in the Tang and Song, see *Jiao santong zhenwen wufa zhengyi mengwei lu licheng*

yi (HY 1202), 6b–8b, and the *Wushang huanglu dazhai licheng yi* (HY 508), 16.3a–5a and 32.11a–13a, respectively.

8. See Franciscus Verellen, *Du Guangting (850–933): Taoïste de cour à la fin de la chine médiévale* (Paris: Mémoires de l'Institut des Hautes Études Chinoises 30, 1989).

9. *Wushang biyao* (HY 1130), 49–57.

10. See the *Dongxuan lingbao sandong fengdao kejie yingshi* (HY 1117), 6: "Chang-chao yi." For different and earlier procedures, see *Dengzhen yinjue* (HY 421), 3, and Strickmann, "Magical Medicine," 8–11.

11. HY 507, in 58 *juan*.

12. *Taishang huanglu zhaiyi* 1–9. For different *zhai* of varying length, see *juan* 10 through 40.

13. These meditations, and those of the *falu* that immediately follow, are based partly on Tao Hong jing's (456–536) *Dengzhen yinjue* (HY 421). See especially 3.5b–10a, "Rujing." For the importance of this Shangqing text as a reposi-tory of ritual practices of early Daoism and the Celestial Master sect, see Cedzich, "Das Ritual der Himmelmeister im Spiegel früher Quellen Über-setzung und Untersuchung des liturgischen Materials im dritten *chuan* des *Tengchen yinchueh*."

14. See, for example, *Taishang huanglu zhaiyi*, 1.10a–11a, "Buxu shiyuan"; 2.4a–b; 3.3a–b; and so forth.

15. See *Taishang huanglu zhaiyi* 53, "Zanzun," 3a–4a.

16. See the comments at *Wushang huanglu dazhai licheng yi* (HY 508), 16.12a–13a, and *Shangqing lingbao dafa* (HY 1213), 56.1a–3a, both Song compilations. The *suqi* deserves its own historical monograph, including an analysis of these very passages. One might begin with *Wushang biyao* 35 and 48, and the comments found in Lagerwey, *Wu-shang pi-yao*, 31.

17. See *Wushang huanglu dazhai licheng yi* 16, "Gufa suqi jianzhai yi," passim. This text purports to go back to Lu Xiujing (406–477) and then to have been re-worked by Tang and Song exegetes.

18. The "Announcement of Merit" (*yangong*) may have originally applied to the merit acheived by otherworldy officials in carrying out their duties, and was subsequently extended, under Buddhist influence, to the living and dead. See the "announcements of merit" that conclude many of the petitions in the *Chisongzi zhangli* (HY 615).

19. See *Taishang huanglu zhaiyi* 49, "Yangong baibiao," 6a–b.

20. Ibid., 49.7b–8a. For a dramatic account of the meditational journey under-taken during the submission of the petition, see the account of a *jiao* per-formed in 1174 in Huzhou at *Yijian zhi* 1765–1766. In the Song dynasty, what

transpired during this ritual moment might have momentous consequences for cultural politics. See *Yijian zhi* 1765, where Hong Mai gives the real reason for the lifting of the ban, instituted by the minister Cai Jing, on the works of Su Shi. According to Hong Mai, everyone believed that the relaxation occurred at the insistence of Su Shi's son Liang Shicheng, but this in fact was not true: "At that time the Abbey of the Precious Registers of Shangqing (Shangqing baolu gong) had been built and 'Offerings' (*jiao*) and 'Retreats' (*zhai*) were being performed there with great sincerity and reverence. Very often the emperor Huizong personally attended these ceremonies. One evening, the emperor ordered the priest to send up a memorial to Heaven. After many hours, the priest got up, and the emperor asked why he had taken so long. The priest answered, 'At the moment when I arrived at the palace of the Celestial Emperor, the *gui* constellation was memorializing. After a long time he finally finished, and I was just now able to submit my own petition.' Huizong was amazed and asked who was this *gui* constellation and what did he memorialize about. The priest answered, 'I heard nothing of his memorial; however, this constellation is none other than the former scholar of the Duanming Palace, Su Shi!' The facial expression of the emperor changed noticeably. Subsequently he relaxed the former restrictions." For yet another example, see the anecdote about the *fashi* Li Mingwei translated in Chapter 3, in the section "The Ritual Master as Exorcist."

21. *Taishang huanglu zhaiyi* 49.8a.

22. Ibid., 50, "Santan shejiao."

23. For the *nashi*, see *Taishang huanglu zhaiyi* 50.7b.

24. See *Taishang huanglu zhaiyi* 55.

25. In the Celestial Master tradition, writs of penance were sent to the Three Officials (*sanguan shoushu*) in the event of illness. For the early Lingbao tradition, see the "burial of the documents" (*maijian*) in the *Taishang dongxuan lingbao chisu yujue miaojing* (HY 352), 3. The *toulongbi* has been studied by Edouard Chavannes, "Le Jet des Dragons," *Mémoires concernant l'Asie orientale*, vol. 3 (Paris, 1919).

26. For such a detailed analysis, see the entries by John Lagerwey in Kristofer Schipper and Fransciscus Verellen, eds., *Catalogue raisonné du canon taoïste* (Chicago: University of Chicago Press, forthcoming).

27. See Wang Qizhen's *Shangching lingbao dafa* 54, "Zhaifa zongji men," and Jin Yunzhong's *Shangching lingbao dafa* 16, "Huanglu zixu," 4b. See also *Taishang jidu zhangshe* 2.6b–7b, for a representative petition.

28. *Shangching lingbao dafa* (Wang Qizhen), 34.14a.

29. *Lingbao yujian* 29.11b.

30. Ibid., 29.8a, "Wushen bing ru Fangxiangshi."

31. *Zhouli* 31.12b.

32. See Anna Seidel, "Traces of Han Religion in Funeral Texts Found in Tombs," esp. 34–39; for a translation and analysis of five Taoist tomb documents dating from the fifth and sixth centuries, see Peter Nickerson, "Taoism, Death, and Bureaucracy in Early Medieval China," chapters 2 and 3; see also *Chisongzi zhangli* (HY 615), 4.7a–9b. For a Southern Song example from Jiangxi, see Zhang Xunliao, "Jiangxi Gao'an chutu Nan-Song Chunxi liunian Xu Yong mu 'Fengdu luoshan baku chaosheng zhengui shenxing' tu shike," *Daojiao wenhua yanjiu* 6 (Shanghai: Guji chubanshe, 1995), 300–311.

33. *Chisongzi zhangli* 6.1b–2a.

34. *Shangching lingbao dafa* (Wang Qizhen), 44 (entire) and 54.14b–15a; *Wushang huanglu dazhai licheng yi* 44.6a–b; *Lingbao lingjiao jidu jinshu* 6a; and esp. *Taishang jidu zhangshe* 2.14a–15b.

35. See Ōfuchi Ninji, *Chūgokujin no shūkyō girei*, 496–502 (esp. 500), and John Lagerwey, *Taoist Ritual in Chinese Society and History*, 202–215 (esp. 206–207).

36. See *Shangqing lingbao dafa* (Jin Yunzhong), 34.3a–6b. This lamp ritual was already the centerpiece of the earliest Taoist text for the salvation of souls, the *Dongxuan lingbao changyezhifu jiuyu yukui mingzhen ke* (HY 1400, fifth to sixth century), for which see John Lagerwey, *Wu-shang pi-yao*, 158–159. At 34.1a and 34.9b, Jin Yunzhong compares the Lighting of the Lamps to the *Lideng zhi fa* of Du Guangting, mentioned above.

37. *Shangqing lingbao dafa* (Jin Yunzhong), 34.7a.1–6. The staff embodies the Divine Soldiers of the Five Peaks and is prepared in a rite that precedes the destruction of the earth-prisons (see *juan* 33).

38. *Shangqing lingbao dafa* (Jin Yunzhong), 34.7a.–67b.1.

39. Ibid., 34.7b.1–4.

40. *Wushang huanglu dazhai licheng yi* 24, "Rites of the Divine Lamps for Destroying the Earth-Prisons."

41. See *Wushang huanglu dazhai licheng yi* 25 and 26; *Shangqing lingbao dafa* (Jin Yunzhong), 36; and *Shangqing lingbao dafa* (Wang Qizhen), 35, 36, 37, and 38.

42. *Wushang huanglu dazhai licheng yi* 26.8a–11b, "Muyu wangling yi"; 26.11–b12a, "Fen chaozhen yi deng"; 26.12a–17b, "Zhushi yi"; *Shangqing lingbao tafa* (Jin Yuzhong), 37.3b–7b, "Zheng jian muyu yi"; 37.7b–9a, "Yinhun chaoye"; 37.9a–14a, "Zhushi."

43. *Shangqing lingbao dafa* (Jin Yuzhong), 37, "Shuihuo liandu," 14b–34a.

44. This chapter, entitled "Yuanshi lingbao ziran jiutian shenghua chaodu yinlian bijue," has been translated and copiously annotated by Judith Boltz, "Opening the Gates of Purgatory. A Twelfth-Century Taoist Meditation Tech-

nique for the Salvation of Lost Souls," in Michel Strickmann, ed., *Tantric and Taoist Studies*, vol. 2 (Bruxelles: Mélanges Chinois et Bouddhiques 21, 1983), 487–511.

45. *Lingbao dalian neizhi xingchi jiyao* (HY 407). This version has been translated by John Lagerwey, *Taoist Ritual in Chinese Society and History*, 233–235.

46. *Wushang huanglu dazhai licheng yi* 28, "Lingbao tazhai zhuanshou jiefu shengdu wang lingyi"; *Shangqing lingbao dafa* (Jin Yunzhong), 37.34a–39a.

47. See the historical discussion at *Shangqing lingbao dafa* (Jin Yunzhong), 37.39a–b; also *Wushang huanglu dazhai licheng yi* 28.12a–b.

48. See *Wushang huanglu dazhai licheng yi* 30 and 31; *Shangqing lingbao dafa* (Jin Yunzhong), 38.

49. For the ghost festival, or *Yulanpen zhai* (Skt. *Avalambana*), see Stephen F. Teiser, *The Ghost Festival in Medieval China*, and idem, "The Ritual Behind the Opera: A Fragmentary Ethnography of the Ghost Festival, A.D. 400–1900," in David Johnson, ed., *Ritual Opera, Operatic Ritual* (Berkeley: Chinese Popular Culture Project, 1990), 191–223. With respect to the feeding rituals, see the nine scriptures translated in the Tang by Amoghavajra and/or his school and others, T. 1313–1321; Marinus de Visser, *Ancient Buddhism in Japan: Sūtras and Ceremonies* (Leiden: E. J. Brill, 1935) for the Sino-Japanese and tantric traditions; and Hirai Yukei, "Tonkō no shigakihō," *Buzan kyogaku taikai kiyō* 8 (1980): 135–151, for Dunhuang. On Chinese tantrism and rites for the distribution of food, see now Charles Orzech, "Esoteric Buddhism and the Shishi in China," in Henrik H. Sorensen, *The Esoteric Buddhist Tradition*, SBS Monograph Series 2 (Copenhagen Seminar for Buddhist Studies, 1994), 51–72. For a more exacting comparison of the pre-*shuilu* Buddhist esoteric rituals for the dead and the Daoist rites of universal salvation (*pudu*), see Orzech, "*Fang yen-k'ou* and *P'u-tu*: Metaphor and Translation," to appear in Livia Kohn and Harold Roth, eds., *Daoist Identity in Practice* (Honolulu: University of Hawai'i Press, 2001).

50. Makita Tairyō, "Zuiriku-e kokō," in *Chūgoku kinsei bukkyōshi kenkyū* (Kyoto: Heiryakuji shoten, 1957), 169–193.

51. See Wu Liansheng, *Baoning si Mingdai shuilu hua* (Peking: Wenwu chubanshe, 1985); Wang Hailang and Chen Yaolin, *Pilu si he Pilu si bihua* (Shijiazhuang: 1984); Caroline Gyss-Vermande, "Démons et merveilles: Vision de la nature dans une peinture liturgique de XVe siècle," *Arts Asiatiques* 43 (1988): 106–122; and idem, "The All Chinese Pantheon of the Shuilu chai," paper presented at JCCS conference on "The Rituals and Scriptures of Chinese Popular Culture," Bodega Bay, California, 1990.

52. Michel Strickmann, *Mantras et mandarins*, 369–411; Daniel B. Stevenson, "The

Buddhist Rite for the Creatures of Water and Land: Text and Image in the History of the *Shuilu fahui*" (unpublished ms., 1997).

53. *Fozu tongji*, edited by Zhi Pan, 33. Makita Tairyō, "Hōshi oshō denkō," in *Chūgoku kinsei bukkyōshi kenkyū* (Kyoto: Heirakuji shoten, 1957), 31–63.

54. Strickmann, *Mantras et mandarins*, 292; Makita, "Zuiriku-e kokō," 177–178.

55. Makita Tairyō, *Godai shūkyōshi kenkyū*, 89, 97, and 147.

56. Zun Shi, "Shishi zhengming," quoted in Makita, "Zuiriku-e kokō," 177.

57. *Shimen zhengtong* (1237 C.E.), quoted in Strickmann, *Mantras et mandarins*, 297.

58. *Shishi tonglan*, "Shuilu da zhai lingqiji." See Makita, "Zuiriku-e kokō," 178; Strickmann, *Mantras et mandarins*, 293.

59. *Fozu tongji* 33.

60. *Fajie shengfan shuilu shenghui yigui*, Zhu Hong, *Yunxi fahui*, vols. 18 and 19. For intellectual background, consult Zhunfang Yu, *The Renewal of Buddhism in China: Chuhung and the Late Ming Synthesis* (New York: Columbia University Press, 1981).

61. For late nineteenth-century versions based on Zhu Hong's work, Makita Tairyō mentions Zhi Guan's (fl. 1864), *Jiyuan shuilu tonglun*, and his *Falun baochan*; for another version, also based on Zhu Hong and compiled by the early nineteenth-century abbot Yi Run, see Yi Run, *Shuili yigui* (Yangzhou: Yangzhou zangjing yuan, 1917) and idem, *Shuilu yigui huiben* (Yangchou: Yangzhou zangjing yuan, 1924). For the contemporary ritual, see now *Shuilu yizhe huiben* (Shanghai: Shanghao foxue shuju, n.d.).

62. See Robert G. Heath, *Crux Imperatorum Philosophia: Imperial Horizons of the Cluniac Confraternitas, 964–1109* (Pittsburgh: University of Pittsburgh Press, 1976), 87–108.

63. Compare the authorizing legend of the Cluniac All Souls in Jotsald's *Life of Saint Odilo* (*Vita S. Odilonis, Patrologia Latina* 142, 926–927) with the legend justifying Buddhist offerings to hungry ghosts in Śikṣānanda (652–710), *Jiu mianran egui tuoluoni shengzhou jing* (T. 1314) and referred to repeatedly during the *Shuilu zhai*.

64. Jotsald, *Vita S. Odilonis, Patrologia Latina* 142, 1037–1038.

GLOSSARY

An Lushan　安禄山
Anxi cheng　安西城
aweishe　阿尾奢
baban　八班
baibiao zoutian　拜表奏天
Baishi　白石
Baitian　白田
baizhang fuci　拜章伏詞
Bali shenwang　八力神王
bangjun　邦君
baoan jiao　保安醮
Baofu ge　寶符閣
Baojian　寶劍
Baozhi　寶誌
bazhi　罷職
bei　碑
Beidi　北帝
Beidi gong　北帝宮
Beidi sanmei fashi　北帝三昧法師
Beidi shagui zhi fa　北帝煞鬼之法
Beifang Rengui jinhuo dafa　北方
　壬癸禁火大法

Beiji sisheng guan　北極四聖觀
ben miao　本廟
benxin　本心
bi　辟
bi qiu qi lei er yi　必求其類而依
bianshen　變身（神）
bianshen renjian zuo guiwang　變身
　人間作鬼王
bianshen zhou　變身咒
bishu　秘書
Bo Yuchan　白玉蟾
Budai heshang　布袋和尚
bugang　步罡
bugang nianjue　步罡捻訣
buxu　步虛
buzhe　卜者
Cai Jing　蔡京
caima　財馬
Caizhou　蔡州
canyi　參議
Cao Kefu　曹可復
chan　禪

313

Changbaishan 長白山

Changsheng dadi 長生大帝

Changshu 常熟

Changtian 昌田

changxiao 長嘯

Changzhou 常州

chaozhen 朝真

Chen Danian 陳大年

Chen Daoyi 陳道一

Chen Guoqian 陳國潛

Chen Mao 陳茂

Chen Shouyuan 陳守元

Chen Tiebian 陳鐵鞭

Chen Wei 陳威

Chen Yuancheng 陳元承

Cheng 程

Cheng *fashi* 程法師

cheng 城

Cheng Yi 程伊

Chenghuang 城隍

chenghuang miao 城隍廟

chenghuang shemiao 城隍社廟

chenghuang zhumiao houwang
    城隍諸廟侯王

Chenzhou 陳州

chizhang 赤章

chimei 魑魅

Chizhou 池州

chizhou ren 持咒人

Chong'an 崇安

chongding 重訂

Chongxian guan 崇仙觀

Chuan Taichang 傳太常

chuguan 出官

chujia 出家

Chuzhou 處州

Chuzhou 楚州

ci 詞

cizhang 刺杖

congci 叢祠

cun 存

cunmin 村民

cuntong 村童

cunwei 存為

Da zhen zhi lu 達真之路

dabei 大悲

Dafan yinyu 大梵隱語

daizhi 待制

dairen 代人

Dayizhen xunjian 大儀真巡檢

dangki 童乩

danuo 大儺

dao tang jinhuo fa 蹈湯禁火法

dao tanghuo 蹈湯火

dao zhi yong 道之用

daochang 道場

Daojie 道傑

daoliu 道流

daoren 道人

daoshi 道士

daosu 道俗

daozhe 道者

Daozhen tang 道真堂

Daozhou 道州

dawu 大巫

Daxi si 大喜寺

dazhai 大齋

Dean fu 德安府

deng 登

Deng Yougong 鄧有功

Deqing 德清

Dexing 德興

Dezhou 德州

diankuang 癲狂

Dinglun 頂輪

Dizang yuan 地藏院

Dizhou 棣州

Dong Shen 董佚

Dong Song 董松

Dongjia zidi 董家子弟

Dongyue 東岳

Dongyue xingmiao 東嶽行廟

Dongyue jun 東嶽君

douzhang 斗章

Du Guangting 杜光庭

du jian 都監

Du You 杜佑

duanqi daochang 斷七道場

dunjia jiushen 遁甲九神

duqiao keyi 度橋科儀

egui 餓鬼

ernü 兒女

Ezhou 鄂州

fa 法

fafu fa 發符法

faguan 法官

Faguan si 法觀寺

Faguang 法廣

fahui 法會

falei deng 法類等

falu 發爐

Fan An 范安

Fan Songnian 藩松年

Fan Zhongyan 范仲淹

fangshi 方士

fangshu 方術

fangxiang shi 方相師

Fanyang 番陽

fashi 法師

fatang 法堂

fawen 法文

fayin 法印

fayuan 法院

fayuan shenjiang 法院神將

fei daoshi 非道士

fendeng 分燈

feng 封

Fengdu 酆都

Fengdu shanxing 酆都山形

Fenghua 奉化

Fengxiang 鳳翔

Fenglin si 鳳林寺

Fengwang ci 蜂王祠

Feng Xingji 馮行基

Fouliang 浮梁

Fu San 傅三

Fu Xuan 傅選

fuben 符本

fufan xianxing 附旛現形

fugu 復古

Fujia li 富甲里

Fujian 福建

fujiang 副將

fulu 復爐

furen 附人

futi 附體

Fuyang 滏陽

Fuzhou 福州

gaogong 高功

Gaoshang Shenxiao lu 高上神霄籙

gaoshi 高士

gaozhai 告齋

Gezaoshan 閣皂山

genchen 庚辰

godanhō 五壇法

gohōdōji 護法童子

gong 公

gongde 功德

gongde si 功德寺

gongzhu 工祝

guaibian 怪變

guan 關

guan tongji 關童乩

guan'ai 關隘

guanci 觀伺

guanfu 官府

Guang Fu Yuan 廣福院

guanjie 關戒

guanqi 關啓

guanren 官人

guantong 關童

gudu 蠱毒

guhun 孤魂

Guiji (Kuaiji) guan 會稽觀

guimen 鬼門

guilü 鬼律

Guo 郭

Guo Ziyi 郭子儀

guoluguan 過路關

Gusui lingwen 骨髓靈文

Haikou xian 海口縣

Haimen 海門

Haiqiong 海瓊

Hao Bian 郝邊

He Niang 和孃

hechang 鶴氅

Hehe 和合

Heisha 黑殺

Heisha fu 黑殺符

Heisha jiangjun 黑殺將軍

Helin Peng 鶴林彭

Hong Gua 洪适

Hong Jinggao 洪景高

Hong Mai 洪邁

Hong Xingzu 洪興祖

Hong Xun 洪迅

Hongzhou 洪州

Houguan 侯官

Housheng 後聖

Hu jialuo 虎伽羅

Hu Wu 胡五

huachi 華池

Huagaishan 華蓋山

Huaguang pusa 華光菩薩

Huaidong zongling 淮東總領

Huang E 黃塄

Huang Gongjin 黃公瑾

Huang Shunshen 黃瞬申

Huangcheng si 黃城司

huangguan 黃冠

Huanglu dajiao 黃籙大醮

Huanglu daochang 黃籙道場

Huanglu jiao 黃籙醮

Huanglu zhai 黃籙齋

huangzeng zhubiao 黃繒朱表

Huantian xidi 歡天喜地

Huanxitian 歡喜天

huashen wei Tianpeng dajiang
　　化身為天蓬大將

huashen wei Qiuku tianzun 化身
　　為求苦天尊

Huating 華亭

hufa longshen 護法龍神

Huiji fa 穢跡法

Huiji jin'gang 穢跡金剛

Huiji jin'gang fa 穢跡金剛法

Huiji shengbing 穢跡神兵

Huiji zhou 穢跡咒

Huilan Daoren 慧蘭道人

Huili si 慧力寺

Huizong 徽宗

Hukou 湖口

hun 魂

huochi 火池

huoshi 火師

hutiao hanwu 胡跳漢舞

Huzhou 湖州

Jialu wang 伽嘍王

Jialuo wang 伽羅王

jiamiao 家廟

jianfa 劍法

jiang 降

Jiang Yanyan 姜延言

jiangbi 降筆

Jiangdong 江東

jiangui shi 見鬼師

jiangjun 將軍

jiangli 將吏

Jiangnan 江南

jiangui 見鬼

jiangling 降靈

Jiangxi 江西

jiangyan 降言

Jianyang 建陽

Jiangzhe 江浙

Jiankang 建康

Jianning 建寧

Jianzhou 建州

jiao 醮

jiao'er 攪耳

jiaoxi 醮席

Jiedi shen 揭諦神

jieshi yuanjie zhenyan 解釋怨結
真言

jietan fa 結壇法

jietian 界田

jieti tongzhuan 借體通傳

jiewen 誥問

jieyin 結印

jijiu 祭酒

Jin 金

jitian 祭田

Jin Yunzhong 金允中

jin zhi xue fa zhi shi 今之學法
之士

Jin Zhongshu 金中樞

jing 井

Jin'gang chan 金剛禪

Jin'gang lishi 金剛力士

Jin'gang shou 金剛手

Jinlun huiji zhou 金輪穢蹟咒

Jinshan si 金山寺

jinshe 禁蛇

Jinsuo liuzhu 金鎖流珠

jintan 禁壇

Jintou luo 金頭羅

Jinwang 晉王

Jinxian 進賢

Jiuhuashan 九華山

jiuxiao 九霄

Jiuyi guan 九疑觀

jiuyou 九幽

Jiuyou jiao 九幽醮

Jixian guan 集仙觀

Jizhou 吉州

Jōgyō 常曉

jue 訣

jue 覺

juedixi　角觝戲

Jue Fei　覺非

junxian　郡縣

kaidaolu zhenyan　開道路真言

kaidu　開度

Kaifeng　開封

kaiguang　開光

kaiguang zhou　開光咒

kaiqi fa　開啓法

Kaitong wulu　開通五路

Kaitong wulu dengtu　開通五路
　燈圖

kaiyanhou zhenyan　開咽喉真言

Kang Taiqing　康太清

kaofu　考附

kaogui zhaoshen　考鬼召神

kaowen zuosui zhi zhe mingzi　考照
　作祟之者名字

kaozhao　考召

kaozhao　考照

kaozhao fa　考召法

kaozhao shi　考召使

kaozhao suihuo　考照祟惑

kaozhi　考治

ke　科

Kong Guipin　孔貴嬪

Kou Zhun　寇準

koujue　口訣

laoxi　老覡

leibu fa　雷部法

leifa　雷法

Leigong　雷公

Leizhou　雷州

Leping　樂平

li　里

li　禮

Li Chunfeng　李淳風

Li Henglao　李衡老

Li Mingwei　李明微

Li Renshi　李仁師

Li Sheng　李生

Li Shimei　李十美

li yi yi qi　禮以義起

Li Yuanbi　李元弼

Li Zhongyong　李仲永

liandu　練度

Liangcuo　梁厝

Liang Hun　梁緄

Liang Quan　梁荃

Liang Shicheng　梁師成

Liang Wudi　梁武帝

libuwei zhenyan　離怖畏真言

lideng yi　禮燈儀

limin　里民

Lin Lingsu　林靈素

Lin'an　臨安

Linchuan　臨川

ling　令

ling　靈

Lingbao　靈寶

Lingbao dafa　靈寶大法

Lingbao zhenwen　靈寶真文

lingfan　靈旛

lingguan　靈官

Lingbi　靈壁

Linjiang　臨江

Linshui furen　臨水夫人

lisu　里俗

litan　厲壇

Liu Cunli　劉存禮

Liu Dayong　劉大用

Liu *fashi*　劉法師

Liu Hunkang 劉混康

Liu Yanshi 劉彥適

Liu Yu 劉玉

Liu Zhuhui 劉居晦

liujia liuding 六甲六丁

Liusha he 流沙河

liwu 里巫

Liyang 歷陽

lizhe ren 立者人

Long *fashi* 龍法師

Longche fengnian 龍車鳳輦

Longhushan 龍虎山

Longshu yiwang 龍樹醫王

Longshu wang 龍樹王

Longshu zhou 龍樹咒

Louguan 樓觀

lu 籙

lü 律

Lu 盧

Lu Boshan 盧伯善

Lü Chunnian 呂椿年

Lü Deqing 呂德卿

Lü Dongbin 呂洞賓

Lu Guan 路瓘

Lu Shizhong 路時中

Lu Xiujing 陸修靜

Lu Yanghao 盧養浩

Lu Ye 盧埜

Lu You 陸游

Lu Zhenguan 路真官

lüe shengtong 掠生童

luji 路歧

Luoyu tangong ke 落嶽探官科

Lüshan jiao 閭山教

Lushi canjun 錄事參軍

Ma Erniang 馬二娘

Ma Huaguang 馬華光

Ma jialuo 馬伽羅

Ma Sheng 馬勝

maijian 埋簡

Maming 馬鳴

Maoshan 茅山

Maoshan fa 茅山法

Maoshan zhengfa 茅山正法

mei 魅

miandui 免對

Miji lishi 密跡力士

Miji jin'gang 密跡金剛

Mile 彌勒

ming tongzi futi 命童子附體

ming tongzi guan yan 命童子觀焉

ming zhuling Jiangnan daojiao
命主領江南道教

Mingge 明哥

mingmo zhou 命魔咒

Mingshan miao 鳴山廟

Mingxi 明溪

Mingzhou 明州

Minqing 閩清

minshe 民社

minsu 民俗

mishuhō 御修法

Mizhu jin'gang 密主金剛

mo 魔

Mo Yueding 莫月鼎

mogui 魔鬼

Mowang 魔王

muke 木客

Muping sanlang 木平三郎

mushi 沐室

muxia 木下

muxia sanlang 木下三郎

muyu　沐浴

naguan　納官

Nanchang　南昌

nanfa　南法

Nanjing　南京

Nankang　南康

Nanyang　南陽

Nanyuan　南原

nazhi　納職

Nezha　那吒

Nezha huoqiu zhou　那吒火毬咒

Nezha taizi Dinglun shengwang
　　那吒太子頂輪聖王

nianfo　念佛

Ningming dian　凝命殿

Ningming lou　凝命樓

ningmo zhou　寧魔咒

Ningyuan　寧遠

Niutou luo　牛頭羅

nuo　儺

Ouyang Wenbin　歐陽文彬

Ouyang Xuan　歐陽暄

Pan Jiangui　潘見鬼

Peng *fashi*　彭法師

pifa xianzu　披髮跣足

Piling　毗陵

pingfu　憑附

Ping jiang　平江

Pingyang　平陽

Pishamen　毗沙門

Poyang　鄱陽

poyu　破獄

Puan jiao　普庵教

pudu　普度

Puzhao si　普照寺

qi　氣

Qiandao zhai　千道齋

qianhe　譴劾

Qianlong Erlang　錢用二郎

qielan shen　枷藍神

qing xianguan　請仙官

qingci　青詞

Qinghua dijun　青華帝君

Qingwei　清微

Qingxi maobao　慶喜貓報

qingxin dizi　清信弟子

Qionglin yuan　瓊林苑

Qiongzhou　瓊州

Qiu Xian　丘先

Qiyuan　七元

Qizhou　齊州

Quan Qing　全清

Quan Shi　全師

Quanzhou　泉州

Quxie yuan　驅邪院

randeng poyu　燃燈破獄

Rao Dongtian　饒洞天

Raozhou　饒州

ren　仁

Ren Boxian　仁伯賢

Ren Daoyuan　任道元

Ren Wenjian　任文薦

renwu　壬午

Renzong　仁宗

ru wu pingfu　如物憑附

Ruochong　若沖

Sa Shoujian　薩守堅

san shangxiang　三上香

sandanhō　三壇法

Sandong fashi　三洞法師

sanguan shoushu　三官手書

Sanguang fu　三光符

Sannai jiao　三奶教

sanqi zhaihui　三七齋會

Sanshan fulu　三山符籙

Santan fa　三壇法

Santan sengjia zhi dao　三壇僧伽
　之道

Santan wubu fa　三壇五部法

Santan zhengfa　三壇正法

santian men　三天門

Sanwu dougong lu　三五都功籙

Sanxiong tongshen　三雄通神

sanyue　散樂

Sengjia　僧伽

sengshe　僧舍

Sha Wujing　沙悟靜

Shang Rixuan　商日宣

Shangdi　上帝

Shangqing　上清

Shangqing baolu gong　上清寶
　籙宮

Shangqing lu　上清籙

Shangqing taiping gong　上清太
　平宮

shangshu　尚書

shangshu sheng　尚書省

Shangshui　商水

shangtang zhaoqing fa　上堂召
　請法

shangtian　上天

shanxiao　山魈

sharen jigui　殺人祭鬼

she　社

sheba zhi fa　赦拔之法

shehui　社會

shehun　攝魂

sheji tan　社稷壇

Shen Anzhi　沈安之

shen zhan shi yen ye　身戰是驗也

shenbao　神保

shenci　神祠

sheng　聖

Sheng Qiniang　聖七娘

shengmu　生母

Shengtian dafaqiao　升天大法橋

Shengtian dazhuan　升天大篆

shengtianxiang　生天象

shengtong　聖童

shengzhe　聖者

shenhu　神虎

shenjiang　神將

shenmiao　神廟

Shensha shen Jiedi shen　深沙神
　揭諦神

shenshou　神首

shentang　神堂

shenxian jiayu　神仙家語

Shenxiao　神霄

shenxiao falu　神霄法籙

Shenxiao leishu　神霄雷書

Shenxiao yudi　神霄玉帝

shezhao fa　攝召法

shenzhi　神祇

shi　尸

shi egui　施餓鬼

Shi Hao　史浩

Shi Jiangjun　石將軍

shi shen xiang ye　尸神象也

shi tongzi zhaoshi　使童子照視

Shixiao ruoshen zhi zui　尸酵若神
　之醉

shi zhe　十哲

shi da mingwang　十大明王

shidaifu 士大夫

shifang wanghun 釋放亡魂

shigui 視鬼

Shili cun 石里村

shiren 士人

shishiyi 施食儀

shiwu 師巫

shiyi 使役

shiyushi 侍御史

shouban 手板

shu 術

Shu Xindao 舒信道

shuaishou 帥守

shuiguan 稅官

Shuilu zhai 水陸齋

shuojie 說戒

shushi 術士

Si da tianwang 四大天王

Sichuan 四川

sifu shiwei 四符使位

sihun 死魂

Siming zhenjun 司命真君

Siniang miao 四娘廟

sishi shuilu 四時水陸

Sizhou yuan 泗州院

Song Anguo 宋安國

songshi 送尸

su 俗

Su Shi 蘇軾

suqi 宿啓

Sui fei daoshi, er de ci cheng 雖非
    道士而得此稱

Sun Gu 孫古

Sun Wukong 孫悟空

suren 俗人

sushi 俗師

Tai Yi 太乙

Taichang si 太常寺

Taichang xiaoqing 太常小卿

Taibu shu 太卜署

Taishan 泰山

Taishang daode fashi 太上道得
    法師

Taishang laojun 太上老君

Taishi ling 太史令

taishou 太守

Taixiao dijun 太霄帝君

Taiyi tianzun 太一天尊

Taizong 太宗

Taizu 太祖

tamiao 塔廟

Tan *fashi* 譚法師

Tan Shiyi 譚師一

Tan Zhenren 譚真人

Tan Zixiao 譚紫霄

Tang Xianzu 湯顯祖

Tang Xuanzong 唐玄宗

tangki 童乩

tangnuo 堂儺

Tao Hongjing 陶弘景

ti 題

Tianchang 天長

Tiandi shizhe 天帝使者

tiandi junqin 天地君親

Tiangang fu 天罡符

tianguan 天官

tianlong 天龍

Tianpeng 天蓬

Tianpeng da yuanshuai 天蓬大
    元帥

Tianqing guan 天慶觀

tianshu 天書

Tianxin　天心

Tianxin fa　天心法

Tianxin zhengfa　天心正法

tianyin　天印

Tianyou　天猷

Tianyuan kaozhao Deng jiangjun　天元考召登
將軍

tishen　替身

to dōji　堂童子

tong tianmu fu　通天目符

Tongchu dafa　童初大法

tongji　童乩

Tongling xiansheng Zhang Heisha　通靈先生張黑殺

tongpan　通判

tongwu　童巫

tong xingming　通姓名

Tongzhou　通州

tongzhuan　通傳

tongzi　童子

tongzi shen　童子身

toulongbi　投龍壁

toulongjian　投龍簡

tudi shen　土地神

waidao　外道

wanchao　晚朝

Wang Chang　王昶

Wang Fu　王富

Wang Jiu'er　王九二

Wang Laozhi　王老志

Wang Qinruo　王欽若

Wang Shan　王善

Wang Shi　王師

Wang Shichen　王侍晨

Wang Wenqing　王文卿

Wang Zhi　王質

Wang Zihua　汪子華

Wang Zixi　王仔昔

Wang Zongjing　王宗敬

Wanhui　萬回

Wei Sheng　魏生

Weituo　韋陀

wen　文

Wen *fashi*　文法師

Wen Huigong　文惠公

Wen Qiong　溫瓊

Weng Jishi　翁吉師

wenshi　溫室

Wenxuan wang　文宣王

Wenzhou　溫州

wu　巫

Wu Daoxian　吳道顯

Wu jianglai yunzhi Taiping jun Songchao di'er zhu　吾將來運值太
平君宋朝第二主

wubu　五部

wubu fa　五部法

wuchao　午朝

Wuchusema　烏雛澀麼／烏樞
瑟麼

Wudangshan　武當山

Wufang jiedi　五方揭諦

wugong daifu　武功大夫

Wujiang　吳江

wulei fa　五雷法

wulei shu　五雷術

Wulei yuanshuai　五雷元帥

Wu shen bingru Fangxiang shi　吾神並如方相氏

Wushang dongxuan fashi　無上洞
玄法師

Wushang sandong fashi 無上三洞法師

wusheng 五聖

wushi 巫師

wutan fa 五壇法

wutong 五通

wutong shen 五通神

wuxian 五顯

Wuxian miao 五顯廟

Wuyishan 武夷山

Wuyuan 婺源

wuzhe 巫者

wuzhu 巫祝

xi 覡

xian 仙

xiang 想

xiang shen wei Zhenwu 想身為真武

Xiangshan yunshan er dasheng 香山雲山二大聖

Xiangdun 香屯

xianghuo tian 香火田

xiangnuo 鄉儺

xiangren 鄉人

xiangshe 鄉社

xiangshi 相士

Xiang Tong 項通

Xiangzhou 相州

xianshe 縣舍

xiansheng 先生

xianwei ling 顯威靈

Xiao Chunli 蕭淳禮

xiao'er 小兒

xiaofa 小法

xiaosun 孝孫

xiaotong 小童

xiaowu 小巫

xiatang zhaoqing fa 下堂召請法

xie shifang 謝十方

Xie Shiting 謝時享

xie'en 謝恩

xieshi 邪師

Xijiang 西江

ximin 細民

Xin 辛

Xinchang 新昌

Xinding 新定

Xindu Yuanfang 信都元方

xing Huiji fa tongling 行穢跡法通靈

xingdao 行道

xingdao yi 行道儀

xingfa daoshi 行法道師

xingfa guan 行法官

Xingfu si 興福寺

xinghua daitian famiao quxie 行化代天伐廟除邪

xingsu 星宿

xingzhe 行者

xinsi 幸巳

Xinzhou 信州

Xiong 熊

Xiongwei 雄威

Xiongwei Huaguang er dasheng 雄威華光二大聖

Xishan 西山

Xu Baowen 許寶文

Xu Chaofeng 徐朝奉

Xu Dake 徐達可

Xu Shisan 徐十三

Xu Wen 許溫

Xu Yuquan 許與權

Xu Jixian 許吉先
Xu Zhongshi 徐仲時
xuandu 玄都
xuanjin 宣禁
Xuanwu 玄武
Xuanwu fashi 玄武法師
Xuanwu fushi 玄武符使
Xuanyuan huangdi 軒轅黃帝
Xuanzhou 宣州
Xue Erniang 薛二娘
Xue Jixuan 薛季宣
Xun 迅
xuyi 虛夷
yamen 衙門
Yan Fu 閻歡
Yang Jingchang 楊耕常
Yang E 楊鍔
Yang Zhonggong 楊中弓
yangong 言功
Yangzhou 揚州
Yanzhou 袞州
Yao Jiangshi 姚將仕
yaoshu 妖術
Ye Dao 葉道
Ye Daoshi 葉道士
Ye Jingneng 葉淨能
Ye Qianshao 葉遷韶
Yi 益
Yihuang 宜黃
Yili ju 儀禮局
Yin Gui 尹軌
Yin Tong 尹通
Yin Wencao 尹文操
Yin Xi 尹喜
yinbing 陰兵
yinci 淫祠

Yingcheng 應城
yingshe 迎赦
yinshi 陰士（隱士）
yiren 邑人
Yisheng baode 翊聖保德
Yisheng jiangjun 翊聖將君
Yisheng zhenjun 翊聖真君
yishi 義式
yitian 義田
yiwu 醫巫
yizhai 義宅
yizhuang 義莊
Yongjin Gate 湧金門
Yongning si 永寧寺
yorimashi 尸童／寄坐
youcong zhenglang 右從正郎
You Da 郁大
Yu Kui 玉匱
Yu miao 禹廟
Yu Ronggu 余榮古
Yuan Fuyi 袁復一
Yuan Miaozong 元妙宗
Yuan Zhong 元仲
yuanben 院本
Yuanshi tianzun 元始天尊
yuanshuai 元帥
Yubu 禹步
Yugan 餘干
yuge 玉格
Yuhuang 玉皇
Yuhuang shangdi 玉皇上帝
Yulanpen zhai 孟蘭盆齋
Yuqing zhaoying gong 玉清照
應宮
Yusi guan 玉筍觀
yutan 獄壇

Yuzhang 豫章

zaijia 在家

zaju 雜劇

zanghun 藏魂

Zanning 贊寧

zaochao 早朝

zhai 齋

Zhan 詹

Zhan Cong 詹聰

Zhang 張

Zhang Daoling 張道靈

Zhang Dexiang 張德隆

Zhang Jinyan 張晉彥

Zhang Junfang 張君房

Zhang Keda 張可大

Zhang Lihua 張麗華

Zhang Ruhui 張如晦

Zhang Shouqing 張守清

Zhang Shouzhen 張守真貞

Zhang Xujing 張虛靖

Zhang Xun 張勛

Zhang Xuqing 張虛清

Zhang Yuanduan 張元瑞

zhang jiao 章醮

Zhang Jixian 張繼先

Zhang jun an 張君庵

Zhangqiu 章邱

Zhangzhou 漳州

Zhang Zifang 張子房

Zhao Boxu 趙伯虛

Zhao Gongming 趙公明

Zhao Ruhui 趙汝澮

Zhao Rui 趙芮

Zhao Shandao 趙善蹈

Zhao Sheng 趙昇

Zhao Yuanlang 趙元郎

Zhao Ziju 趙子舉

Zhao Zujian 趙祖堅

zhaofa 罩法

zhaohe 召劾

zhaohun 招魂

zhaoling yi 召靈儀

zhaotiao chuzhan 照條處斬

Zhe 浙

Zhedong Anwusi canyi guan 浙東
　安撫司參議官

Zhejiang 浙江

Zheng Daoshi 鄭道士

zhengfa 正法

Zhengyi 正一

Zhengyi daoshi 正一道士

Zhengyi mengwei lu 正一盟威錄

zhengzhai 正齋

zhenren 真人

Zhenwu 真武

Zhenwu yin 真武印

Zhexi 浙西

zhi 制

Zhi Pan 志盤

zhiguan 知觀

Zhiquan 知權

Zhong Kui 鍾馗

zhongsong 冢訟

Zhongnanshan 終南山

zhongcheng 中丞

Zhou 周

zhou 咒

Zhou Si 周四

Zhoujin boshi 咒禁博士

Zhoujin gong 咒禁工

Zhoujin shi 咒禁師

zhoushi 咒食

Zhoutian dajiao 周天大醮

Zhouzhi 盩厔

Zhu Bajie 豬八戒

Zhu Hong 袾宏

Zhu Sengqi 朱僧奇

Zhu Xi 朱熹

Zhu Yan 朱彥

Zhu Yancheng 朱彥誠

zhuhun tan 居魂壇

Zhutou xiangbi er dasheng 豬頭象鼻二大聖

Zhutou xiangbi Yang-Zhu shenjun 豬頭象鼻楊朱神君

ziran chao 自然朝

Zishan 芝山

Ziwei 紫微

Ziyi 妲己

Zizhou 淄州

Zongjian 宗鑑

Zou 鄒

Zu Shu 祖舒

Zunjiao si 尊教寺

Zunshi 尊式

zuodao 左道

zuoshi 佐使

zushi 祖師

BIBLIOGRAPHY

Andersen, Poul. "Taoist Ritual Texts and Traditions." Ph.D. diss., University of Copenhagen, 1991.

———. "The Transformation of the Body in Taoist Ritual." Paper prepared for the conference "Religious Reflection on the Human Body," Cornell University, Ithaca, N.Y., April 19–21, 1991.

———. "Talking to the Gods: Visionary Divination in Early Taoism (Sanhuang Tradition)." Paper prepared for the Western Conference of the Association of Asian Studies, University of Arizona, Oct. 23–24, 1992.

———. "Taoist Talismans and the History of the Tianxin Tradition," *Acta Orientalia* 57 (1996): 141–152.

Azhapoju guishen dajiang shangfo tuoluoni jing 阿吒婆拘鬼神大將上佛陀羅尼經 Anonymous (early sixth century). T. 1238.

Baopuzi neipian 枹朴子內篇. Ge Hong 葛洪 (283–343). HY 1177.

Baptandier-Berthier, Brigitte. "Enfant de divination, voyageur du destin." *L'Homme* 101 (Jan.-Mar. 1987) XXVII (1): 86–100.

———. *La Dame au bord de l'eau.* Nanterre: Societé d'ethnologie, 1988.

———. "The Kaiguan Ritual and the Construction of the Child's Identity." In Lin Ru 林如, ed., *Minjian xinyang yu Zhongguo wenhua: Guoji yantao huilun wenji* 2 民間信仰與中國文化國際研討會論文集 2. Taibei: Hanxue yanjiu zhongxin, 1994: 523–596.

———. "The Lady Linshui: How a Woman Became a Goddess." In Meir Shahar and Robert P. Weller, eds., *Unruly Gods: Divinity and Society in China.* Honolulu: University of Hawai'i Press, 1996: 105–149.

Bargen, Doris. *A Woman's Weapon: Spirit Possession in the Tale of Genji.* Honolulu: University of Hawai'i Press, 1997.

Barrett, T. H. "Towards a Date for the Chin-So Liu-Chu Yin." *Bulletin of the School of Oriental and African Studies* 53:2 (1990): 292–294.

———. "The Emergence of the Taoist Papacy in the T'ang dynasty." *Asia Major* 3rd ser., 7.1 (1994): 89–106.

———. *Taoism Under the T'ang: Religion and Empire During the Golden Age of Chinese History.* London: Wellsweep, 1996.

Bell, Catherine. "Medieval Taoist Ritual Mastery: A Study in Practice,Text and Rite." Ph.D. diss., University of Chicago, 1983.

Berling, Judith. "Channels of Connection in Sung Religion: The Case of Pai Yü-ch'an." In Patricia Ebrey and Peter Gregory, eds., *Religion and Society in T'ang and Sung China.* Honolulu: University of Hawai'i Press, 1993: 307–333.

Beifang Pishamen tianwang suijun hufa yigui 北方毘沙門天王隨軍護法儀軌. Attributed to Amoghavajra (705–744). T. 1247.

Betz, Hans Dieter. *The Greek Magical Papyri in Translation.* Chicago: University of Chicago Press, 1986.

Blumenberg, Hans. *The Legitimacy of the Modern Age.* Robert Wallace, trans. Cambridge: MIT Press, 1983.

Bokenkamp, Stephen. "Death and Ascent in *Lingpao* Taoism." *Taoist Resources* 1:2 (1989): 1–20.

———. *Early Daoist Scriptures.* Berkeley: University of California Press, 1997.

Bol, Peter. *"This Culture of Ours": Intellectual Transitions in T'ang and Sung China.* Stanford: Stanford University Press, 1992.

Boltz, Judith. "Opening the Gates of Purgatory. A Twelfth-Century Taoist Meditation Technique for the Salvation of Lost Souls." In Michel Strickmann, ed., *Tantric and Taoist Studies,* vol. 2. Bruxelles: Mélanges Chinois et Bouddhiques XXI, 1983: 487–511.

———. *A Survey of Taoist Literature, Tenth through Seventeenth Centuries.* Berkeley: Institute of East Asian Studies, China Research Monograph 32, 1987.

———. "Not by the Seal of Office Alone: New Weapons in Battles with the Supernatural." In Patricia Ebrey and Peter Gregory, eds., *Religion and Society in T'ang and Sung China.* Honolulu: University of Hawai'i Press, 1993: 241–305.

Brook, Timothy. "Gentry Dominance in Chinese Society: Monasteries and Lineages in the Structuring of Local Society, 1500–1700." Ph.D. diss., Harvard University, 1984.

———. "Funerary Ritual and the Building of Lineages in Late Imperial China." *Harvard Journal of Asiatic Studies* 49 (1989): 465–499.

Budong shi zhe tuoluoni bimi fa 不動使者陀羅尼祕密法. Attributed to Vajrabodhi (?–751). T. 1202.

Bukong juansuo tuoluoni Zizai wang zhou jing 不空羅索陀羅尼自在王咒經. Attributed to Ratnacinta (?–721). T. 1097.

Cadonna, Alfredo. *Il Taoista di sua Maesta.* Venezia: Cafoscarina, 1984.

Cahill, Suzanne. "Taoism at the Sung Court: The Heavenly Text Affair of 1008." *Bulletin of Sung-Yuan Studies* 16 (1980): 23–44.

Cedzich, Ursula-Angelika. "Wu-T'ung: Zur bewegten Geschichte eines Kultes." In G. Naundorf, ed., *Religion und Philosophie in Ostasien. Festschrift für Hans Steininger zum 65. Geburstag.* Würzburg: Königshausen & Neumann, 1985: 33–55.

———. "Das Ritual der Himmelmeister im Spiegel früher Quellen Übersetzung und Untersuchung des liturgischen Materials im dritten *chuan* des *Tengchen yinchüeh.*" Ph.D. diss., Würzburg, 1987.

———. "The Cult of the Wu-t'ung/Wu-hsien in History and Fiction: The Religious Roots of the *Journey to the South.*" In David Johnson, ed., *Ritual and Scriptures in Chinese Popular Religion: Five Studies.* Berkeley: Chinese Popular Culture Project, 1995: 137–218.

Certeau, Michel de. *La Possession de Loudun.* Paris: Julliard, 1970.

———. "Discourse Disturbed: The Sorcerer's Speech." In idem, *The Writing of History.* New York: Columbia University Press, 1988: 244–268.

Chang, K. C. *Art, Myth and Ritual: The Path to Political Authority in Ancient China.* Cambridge: Harvard University Press, 1983.

Changqulidu nü tuoluoni zhou jing 常瞿利毒女陀羅尼咒經. Attributed to Qu Duo 瞿多 (Skt. Gupta?). (Tang, before 865). T. 1265.

Chao Shih-yi. "Daoist Examinations and Daoist Schools during the Northern Song Dynasty" (unpub. paper; UCLA, 1995).

Chavannes, Édouard. "Le jet des dragons." *Mémoires concernant l'Asie orientale* 3. Paris: Éditions Ernest Leroux, 1919.

Chavannes, Éd., and P. Pelliot. *Un Traité manichéen retrouvé en Chine.* Paris: Imprimerie Nationale, 1913.

Cheu Hock Tong. *The Nine Emperor Gods: A Sudy of Chinese Spirit-Medium Cults.* Singapore: Times Books International, 1988.

Chikusa Masa'aki. *Sō no Taiso to Taisō* 宋の太祖太宗. Tokyo: Shimizu sho'in, 1975.

———. 竺沙雅章 *Chūgoku bukkyō shakai shi kenkyū* 中國佛教社會史研究. Tokyo: Dōhōsha, 1982.

Ching, Julia. *Mysticism and Kingship in China: The Heart of Chinese Wisdom.* Cambridge: Cambridge University Press, 1997.

Chingwei xianpu 清微仙譜. Compiled by Chen Cai 陳采 (1293). HY 171.

Chisongzi zhangli 赤松子章歷. (Six Dynasties to Tang). HY 615.

Chunxi Sanshan zhi 淳熙三山志. Song-Yuan difang zhi congshu, vol. 12. Taibei: Dahua shuju, 1980.

Combined Indices to the Authors and Titles of Books in Two Collections of Taoist

Literature: Harvard-Yenching Institute Sinological Index Series No. 25. Weng Tu-chieh, ed. (Peking, 1925). Taipei: Ch'eng-wen reprint, 1966.

Connelly, Chris. *The Empire of the Text: Writing and Authority in Early Imperial China.* Lanham: Rowman & Littlefield, 1998.

Courtright, Paul. *Ganesa.* New York: Oxford University Press, 1985.

Da baoji jing 大寶積經. Bodhiruci (572–726). T. 310.

Da Sheng Huanxi shuangshen Dazizhai tian Pinayejia wang guiyi niansong gongyang fa 大聖歡喜雙身大自在天毘那夜迦王歸依念誦供養法. T. 1270.

Da Song seng shi lue 大宋僧史略. Zanning 贊寧 (919–1001). T. 2126.

Da Tang Xihuo zhi 大唐西域記. Xuanzang 玄奘 (602–664). T. 2087.

Dainihon kōtei zōkyō 大日本校訂藏經. Kyoto: Zōkyō shoin, 1902–1905.

Dai-Nihon Zokuzōkyō 大日本續藏經. Kyoto: Zōkyō shoin, 1905–1912. Abbreviated herein as Z.

Daofa huiyuan 道法會元. Compiled by Zhao Yizhen 趙宜真 (?–1382). HY 1210.

Daojiao lingyan ji 道教靈驗記. Du Guangting 杜光庭 (850–933). HY 590.

Daomen shigui 道門十規. Compiled by Zhang Yuchu 張宇初 (1361–1410). HY 1222.

Daoshu yuanshen qi. HY 1221.

Davis, Edward L. "Arms and the Tao, 1: Hero Cult and Empire in Traditional China." In *Sōdai kenkyū no shakai to shūkyō. Sōdai-shi kenkyūkai kenkyū hōkoku,* 2. Tokyo: Kyūko sho'in, 1985: 1–56.

———. "Arms and the Dao, 2: The Xu Brothers in Tea Country." In Livia Kohn and Harold Roth, eds., *Daoist Identity in Practice.* Honolulu: Univeristy of Hawai'i Press, 2001.

———. "Women and Psychosomatic Illness in the Song." Paper presented at the Triangle East Asia Colloquium, Durham, North Carolina, Feb. 27, 1999.

Dean, Kenneth. *Lord of the Three in One: The Spread of a Cult in Southeast China.* Princeton: Princeton University Press, 1998.

———. "Transformations of the *She* (Altars of the Soil) in Fujian." *Cahiers d'Extrême-Asia* 10 (1998): 19–75.

Dean, Kenneth (Ding Hesheng), and Zheng Zhenman. "Group Initiation and Exorcistic Dance in the Xinghua Region." In Wang Qiugui, ed., *Zhongguo Nuoxi: Nuo wenhua gouji yantaihui lu wenli.* In *Minsu quyi* 85.2 (1993): 105–214.

———. "Min-Tai daojiao yu minjian zhushen chongbai chukao 閩台道教與民間諸神崇拜初稿." *Bulletin of the Institute of Ethnology, Academia Sinica* 73 (1993): 33–52.

Delatte, A. *La catoptromancie grecque et ses dérivés.* Liège-Paris: Bibliothèque de la Faculté de Philosophie et Lettres de l'Université de Liège 48, 1932.

Dengzhen yinjue 登真隱訣. Tao Hongjing 陶弘景 (456–536). HY 421.

Didier, John. "Messrs. T'an, Chancellor Sung, and the *Book of Tranformation (Hua Shu)*: Texts and Transformations of Traditions." *Asia Major* 3rd ser., 11.1 (1998): 99–151.

Diqi shangjiang Wen taibao zhuan 地祇上將溫太保傳. Huang Gongjin 黄公瑾 (fl. 1274). HY 779.

Dodds, E. R. *The Greeks and the Irrational.* Berkeley: University of California Press, 1951.

————. *The Ancient Concept of Progress and Other Essays on Greek Literature and Belief.* Oxford: Oxford University Press, 1988.

Dongshen badi yuanbian jing 洞神八帝元變經. HY 1202.

Dongxuan lingbao changyezhifu jiuyou yukui mingzhen ke 洞玄靈寶長夜之府九幽玉匱明真科 (fifth–sixth century). HY 1400.

Dongxuan lingbao sandong fengdao kejie yingshi 洞玄靈寶三洞奉道科戒營始. HY 1117.

Dongxuan lingbao wuganwen 洞玄靈寶五感文. Lu Xiujing 陸修靜 (dated 454). HY 1268.

Dore, Henry. *Researches into Chinese Superstition,* vol. 1, Taipei: Ch'eng-wen reprint, 1966.

Drexler, Monika. *Daoistische Schriftmagie: Interpretatione zu den Schriftamulleten Fu im Daozang.* Stuttgart: Franz Steiner, 1994.

Duara, Prasenjit. *Culture, Power, and the State: Rural North China, 1900–1942.* Stanford: Stanford University Press, 1988.

————. *Rescuing History from the Nation: Questioning Narratives of Modern China.* Chicago: University of Chicago Press, 1995.

————. "State and Civil Society in the History of Chinese Modernity," In Frederic Wakeman, Jr., and Wang Xi, eds., *China's Quest For Modernization.* Berkeley: Institute of East Asian Studies, University of California at Berkeley, Research Papers and Policy Studies 41, 1997: 300–324.

Dutton, Michael. *Policing and Punishment in China.* Cambridge: Cambridge University Press, 1992.

Ebrey, Patricia. "Early Stages of Descent Group Organization." In Patricia Ebrey and James Watson, eds., *Kinship Organization in Late Imperial China, 1000–1940.* Berkeley: University of California Press, 1986: 16–61.

————. "State Response to Popular Funeral Practices in Sung China." Paper presented at "The Symposium on Religion and Society in China, 750–1300," Urbana-Champaign, Nov. 1988.

————. *Confucianism and Family Rituals in Imperial China: A Social History of Writing About Rites.* Princeton: Princeton University Press, 1991.

————, trans. *Chu Hsi's Family Rituals: A Twelfth-Century Chinese Manual for the Performance of Cappings, Weddings, Funerals and Rites.* Princeton: Princeton University Press, 1991.

Ebrey, Patricia, and Peter Gregory, eds., *Religion and Society in T'ang and Sung China.* Honolulu: University of Hawai'i Press, 1993.

Eichman, Shawn. "Converging Paths: Highest Purity and Celestial Master Traditions of Taoism during the Six Dynasties." Ph.D. diss., University of Hawai'i, 1999.

Evans, John A. "Chinese Criminal Law in *All Men Are Brothers.*" Paper presented at the conference on "The History of Chinese Law," Bellagio, 1969.

Fahai yizhu 法海遺珠. HY 1158.

Fajie shengfan shuilu shenghui xiuzhai yigui 法界聖凡水陸勝會修齋儀軌. Zhu Hong 袾宏 (1535–1615). *Yunxi fahui* 雲棲法彙, vols. 18–19. Nanjing: Jingling kejing chu, 1897.

Fengshen yanyi 封神演義. Hong Kong: Zhonghua shuju, 1985.

Feuchtwang, Stephan. *The Imperial Metaphor: Popular Religion in China.* London: Routledge, 1992.

Fineman, Joel. "The History of the Anecdote." In H. Aram Veeser, ed., *The New Historicism.* London: Routledge, 1989.

Fozu tongji 佛祖統記. Edited by Zhi Pan 志盤 (thirteenth century). T. 2035.

Fukunaga Mitsuji 福永光司. "*Dōkyō ni okeru kagami to tsuguri* 道教における鏡と劍." *Tōhō Gakuhō* 45 (1973): 59–120.

Gaoshang shenxiao yuqing zhenwang zishu da fa 高上神霄玉清真王紫書大法 (fourteenth century). HY 1209.

Gellner, Ernest. *Conditions of Liberty: Civil Society and Its Rivals.* London: Penguin reprint, 1996.

Genette, G. *Narrative Discourse: An Essay in Method.* Translated by J. E. Lewin. Ithaca: Cornell University Press, 1980.

Ginzburg, Carlo. "The Name and the Game." In Edward Muir and Guido Ruggiero, eds., *Microhistory and the Lost Peoples of Europe.* Baltimore: The Johns Hopkins University Press, 1991: 1–10.

Greenblatt, Stephen. "Shakespeare and the Exorcists." In idem, *Shakespearean Negotiations.* Berkeley: University of California Press, 1988: 94–129.

Greenfield, Richard. *Traditions of Belief in Late Byzantine Demonology.* Amsterdam: Adolf Hakkert, 1988.

Groot, J. J. M. de. *The Religious System of China.* Taipei: Ch'eng Wen Publishing Co. (reprint ed.), 1976.

Gyss-Vemande, Caroline. "Démons et merveilles: Vision de la nature dans une peinture liturgique du XVe siècle." *Arts Asiatiques* 43 (1988): 106–122.

———. "The All Chinese Pantheon of the Shuilu chai." Paper presented at the JCCS conference on "The Rituals and Scriptures of Chinese Popular Culture," Bodega Bay, 1990.

Haiqiong Bai Zhenren yulu 海瓊白真人語錄. Bo Yuchan 白玉蟾 (fl. 1209–1224). HY 1296.

Halperin, Mark. "Pieties and Responsibilities: Buddhism and Chinese Literati, 780–1280." Ph.D. diss., University of California at Berkeley, 1997.

Han Tianshi shijia 漢天師世家 (fourteenth–sixteenth centuries). HY 1451.

Hansen, Valerie. *Changing Gods in Medieval China, 1127–1276.* Princeton: Princeton University Press, 1990.

Heath, Robert G. *Crux Imperatorum Philosophia: Imperial Horizons of the Cluniac Confraternitas, 964–1109.* Pittsburgh: University of Pittsburgh Press, 1976.

Hirai Yukei 平井宥慶 "Tonkō no shigakihō 敦煌の施餓鬼法." *Buzan kyogaku taikai kiyō* 8 (1980): 135–151.

Hirakawa Akira 平川彰. *Shoki daijō bukkyō no kenkyū* 初期大乗佛教の研究. Kyoto: Shunjūsha, 1968.

Ho Kinchung. "Nezha: Figure de l'enfant rebelle." *Études Chinoises* 7.2 (1988): 726.

Hōbōgirin: Dictionnaire encyclopédique du bouddhisme d'après les sources chinoises et japonaises. Fascicule annexe. Tokyo: Maison Franco-Japonaise, 1931.

Hong Mai. *Yijian zhi.* See under *Yijian zhi.*

Huagai shan Fouqiu-Wang-Guo san zhenjun shishi 華蓋山浮丘王郭三真君事實 (fourteenth century). HY 777.

Huang Minzhi 黄敏枝. *Songdai fojiao shehui jingji shi lunji* 宋代佛教社會經濟史論集. Taibei: Xuesheng shuju, 1989.

Huang, Ray. *1587: A Year of No Significance.* New Haven: Yale University Press, 1981.

Huangchao shishi leiyuan 皇朝事實類苑. Jiang Shaoyu 江少虞 (?–after 1145). Kyoto: Chūbun shuppansha, 1981.

Huanglu jiuyou jiao wu'ai yezhai cidi yi 黄籙九幽醮無碍夜齋次第儀. HY 514.

Huiji jingang jin baibian fa jing 穢跡金剛禁百變法經. T. 1229.

Huiji jin'gang shuo shentong daman tuoluoni fashu ling yaomen 穢跡金剛説神通大滿陀羅尼法術靈要門. T. 1228.

Hymes, Robert. "Marriage, Descent Groups, and the Localist Strategy in Sung and Yuan Fuchou." In Patricia Ebrey and James Watson, eds., *Kinship Organization in Late Imperial China, 1000–1040.* Berkeley: University of California Press, 1986: 95–169.

Idema, W. L. *The Dramatic Oeuvre of Chu Yu-tun (1379–1439)*. Leiden: E. J. Brill, 1985.

Idema, Wilt, and Stephen H. West. *Chinese Theater 1100–1450: A Sourcebook*. Wiesbaden: Franz Steiner, 1982.

Iyanaga Nobumi. "Récits de la soumission de Mahésvara par Trailokyavijaya—d'après les sources chinoises et japonaises." In Michel Strickmann, ed., *Tantric and Taoist Studies*, vol. 3. Bruxelles: Mélanges Chinois et Bouddhiques, 1985: 633–745.

Jiannan shigao 劍南詩稿. Lu You 陸游 (1125–1210). *Lu Fangweng quanji* 陸放翁全集 vol. 2. Beijing: Zhongguo shuju, 1986.

Jiao sandong zhenwen wufa zhengyi mengwei lu licheng yi 醮三洞真文五法正一盟威籙立成儀. Zhang Wanfu. HY 1202.

Jin Zhongshu 金中樞. "Lun Bei Song monian zhi chongshang daojiao 論北宋末年之崇尚道教." *Songshi yanjiu ji* 宋史研究集 7–8. Taibei: Taiwan shuju, 1974: 291–392 and 207–278.

Jingangfeng louge yiqie yujia yuqi jing 金剛峰樓閣一切瑜伽瑜祇經. Attributed to Vajrabodhi (?–741). T. 867.

Jinshi cuibian 金石萃編. Compiled by Wang Chang 王昶. (1725–1806). Jingxun tang, 1872.

Jinsuo liuzhu yin 金鎖流珠引 (ninth or tenth century). HY 1009.

Jiu mianran egui tuoluoni shenzhou jing 救面然餓鬼陀羅尼神咒經. Attributed to Śikṣānanda (652–710). T. 1314.

Jiu Tangshu 舊唐書. Liu Xu 劉昫 (887–946). Beijing: Zhonghua shuju, 1975.

Jiu Wudai shi 舊五代史. Xue Juzheng 薛居正 (912–981). Beijing: Zhonghua shuju, 1976.

Jiutian yingyuan leisheng puhua tianzun yushu baojing 九天應元雷聲普化天尊玉樞寶經 (early thirteenth century?). HY 16.

Johnson, David. "The City-God Cults of T'ang and Sung China." *Harvard Journal of Asiatic Studies* 45:2 (Dec. 1985): 363–457.

Jordan, David K. *Gods, Ghosts and Ancestors: The Folk Religion of a Taiwanese Village*. Berkeley: University of California Press, 1972.

Jotsald. *Vita S. Odilonis, Patrologia Latina* 142. Paris: J. P. Migne, 1884–1864. Reprint edition. Turnhout: Brepols, 1977.

Journey to the West. Translated and edited by Anthony C. Yu. 4 vols. Chicago: The University of Chicago Press, 1977.

Kalinowski, Marc. *Cosmologie et divination dans la Chine ancienne: Le compendium des cinq agents (Wuxing dayi, VIe Siècle)*. Paris: Ecole Française d'Extrême-Orient, 1991.

Kanai Noriyuki 金井德幸 "Sōdai no sonsha to bukkyō 宋代の村社佛教." *Bukkyō shigaku kenkyū* 18:2 (1976): 31–57.

————. "Nansō saishi shakai-no tenkai南宋祭祀社會の展開." In *Shūkyō shakaishi kenkyū*. Tokyo: Yūzankaku, 1977: 591–610.

————. "Sōdai-no gōsha-to dojishin 宋代の郷社土地神." In *Nakajima Satoshi-sensei koki kinen ronshū*. Tokyo: Kyūko shoin, 1980–1981: 385–407.

Karlgren, Bernhard. *The Book of Odes.* Stockholm: Museum of Far Eastern Antiquities, 1974.

Katz, Paul R. *Demon Hordes and Burning Boats: The Cult of Marshal Wen in Late Imperial Chekiang.* Albany: State University of New York Press, 1995.

Keightley, David. "Royal Shamanism in the Shang: Archaic Vestige or Central Reality?" Paper prepared for "The Workshop on Chinese Divination and Portent Interpretation," Berkeley, June 20–July 1, 1983.

Kobayashi Masayoshi 小林正美. *Rokuchō dōkyō shi kenkyū* 六朝道教史研究. Tokyo: Sōbunsha, 1990.

————. "The Celestial Masters under the Eastern Jin and Liu-Sung Dynasties." *Taoist Resources* 3:2 (May 1992): 17–44.

————. *Chūgoku no Dōkyō* 中国の道教. Tokyo: Sōbunsha, 1998.

Kohn, Livia. "Yin Xi: The Master at the Beginning of the Scripture." *Journal of Chinese Religions* 25 (1997): 83–139.

————. "The Northern Celestial Masters." In Livia Kohn, ed., *Handbook of Daoism.* Leiden: E. J. Brill, 2000.

Koji ruien 古事類苑. Tokyo: Yoshikawa kōbunkan, 1967.

Kokubu Naoichi. 国分直一. "Taiwan ni okeru shamanizumu no sekai—toku ni tanki no rakugoku tankyu o megutte 台灣におけるシャーマニズムの世界—乩の落獄探宮をめぐって." *Minzokugaku hyoron* 6 (1971): 1–22.

Lagerwey, John. *Wu-shang pi-yao: Somme taoïste du VIe siècle.* Paris: Ecole Française d'Extrême-Orient, 1981.

————. "Introduction to Taoist Ritual through the Tang" (unpub. ms., 1985).

————. "'Les têtes des démons tombent par milliers': Le *fachang*, rituel exorcists du nord de Taiwan." *L'Homme* 101 (Jan.–March 1987) XXVII (1): 101–116.

————. *Taoist Ritual in Chinese Society and History.* New York: Macmillan, 1987.

————. "Taoist Ritual: An Integral Part of Elite Culture." Paper prepared for the Conference on the Rituals and Scriptures of Chinese Popular Culture, Bodega Bay, Jan. 2–8, 1990.

————. *Le continent des esprits: La chine dans le miroir du taoïsme.* Bruxelles: La Renaissance des Livres, 1991.

————. "The Pilgrimage to Wutang Shan." In Susan Naquin and Chunfang Yu, eds., *Pilgrims and Sacred Sites in China*. Berkeley: University of California Press, 1992: 293–332.

———. "Introduction." In Fang Xuejia, ed., *Meizhou Heyuan diqi di cunluo wenhua* (vol. 5, *Traditional Hakka Society Series*, ed. John Lagerwey). Hong Kong: EFEO, Overseas Chinese Archives of the Chinese University of Hong Kong, 1997: 1–48.

———. "Questions of Vocabulary, or How Shall We Talk about Chinese Religion?" In Lai Chi Tim, ed., *Daijiao yu minjian zongjiao yanjiu lunji*. Hong Kong: Xuefeng wenhua shiye gongsi, 1999: 165–181.

———. "Popular Ritual Specialists in West Central Fujian." Taibei: Proceedings of the International Colloquium on Chinese Society, Ethnicity, and Cultural Performance, 2000: 1–33.

Lancaster, Lewis. "Ganesa in China." In Robert L. Brown, ed., *Ganesh: Studies of an Asian God*. Albany: State University of New York Press, 1991): 277–286.

Legge, James, trans. *Li Chi: Book of Rites*. New Hyde Park: University Books, 1967.

Levi, Giovanni. "On Microhistory." In Peter Burke, ed., *New Perspectives on Historical Writing*. University Park: The Pennsylvania State University Press, 1991: 93–113.

Levi, Jean. "Les fonctionnaires et le divin: Luttes de pouvoirs entre divinités et administrateurs dans les contes des Six Dynasties et des Tang." *Cahiers d'Extrême-Asie* 2 (1986): 81–106.

———. "Les Fonctions religieuses de la bureaucratie céleste." *L'Homme* 101 (1987), XXVII (1): 35–57.

Li Yuanbi 李元弼. *Zuoyi zizhen* 作邑自箴. *Sibu congkan xubian*, vol. 48. Shanghai: Shanghai shudian, 1984.

Liangxi manzhi 梁谿漫志. Fei Gun 費袞 (*jinshi* in 1205). Xuehai leibian 學海類編, vol. 6. Zhexi: Wenyuan shuju, 1920: 3604–3669.

Lieu, Samuel. *Manichaeism in the Later Roman Empire and Medieval China*. Manchester: Manchester University Press, 1985.

Liji jijie 禮記集解. Edited by Sun Xidan 孫希旦. Shanghai: Shangwu yinshu guan, 1930.

Lingbao dalian neizhi xingchi jiyao 靈寶大煉內旨行持機要. HY 407.

Lingbao lingjiao jidu jinshu 靈寶領教濟度金書. Edited by Lin Tianren 林天任 (1303). HY 466.

Lingbao yujian 靈寶玉鑑 (early thirteenth century). HY 547.

Lishi zhenxian tidao tongjian 歷世真仙體道通鑑. Zhao Daoyi 趙道一 (fl. 1294–1307). HY 296.

Liu Tsun-yan. *Buddhist and Taoist Influences on Chinese Novels, 1*. Wiesbaden: Harrassowitz, 1962.

Liu Zhiwan 劉枝萬. "Taiwan no shyamanisumu 台灣のシャーマニズム." In

Sakurai Tokutarō, ed., *Shyamanisumu no sekai* シャーマニズムの世界. Tokyo: Shunjūsha, 1979.

———. "Tenhōshin to tenhōju ni tsuite 天蓬神と天蓬咒について." In A-kizuki Kanei 秋月觀暎, ed., *Dōkyo to shūkyō bunka* 道教宗教文化. Tokyo: Hirakawa shuppan, 1987: 403-424.

———. "Raishin shinkō to raihō no tenkai 雷神信仰と雷法の展開. *Tōhō Shūkyō* (1990): 121.

Lo, Winston. *The Life and Thought of Yeh Shih.* Shatin, N.T.: The Press of the Chinese University of Hong Kong, 1974.

Longshu wuming lun 龍樹五明論. T. 1420.

Loon, Piet van der. "Les origines rituelles du théâtre chinois." *Journal Asiatique* 265 (1977): 141–168.

———. "A Taoist Collection of the Fourteenth Century." In Wolfgang Bauer, ed., *Studia Sino-Mongolica, Festschrift für Herbert Franke.* Wiesbaden: Franz Steiner, 1979: 401–405.

———. *Taoist Books in the Libraries of the Sung Period: A Critical Study and Index.* London: Ithaca Press, 1984.

Lopez, Donald, ed. *Religions of China in Practice.* Princeton: Princeton University Press, 1996.

Lu xiansheng daomen kelüe 陸先生道門科略. Lu Xiujing 劉修靜 (406–470). HY 1119.

Major, John S. "The Characteristics of Late Chu Religion." In Constance A. Cook and John S. Major, eds., *Defining Chu: Image and Reality in Ancient China.* Honolulu: University of Hawai'i Press, 1999.

Makita Tairyō 枚田諦亮. "Hōshi oshō denkō 寶志和尚傳考." *Chūgoku kinsei bukkyō shi kenkyū* 中国今世佛教史研究. Kyoto: Heirakuji shoten, 1957: 31–63.

———. "Zuirikue kokō 水陸會一考." *Chūgoku kinsei bukkyō shi kenkyū* 中国今世界佛教史研究. Kyoto: Heirakuji shoten, 1957: 169–193.

———. *Godai shūkkyō shi kenkyū* 五代宗教史研究 Kyoto: Heirakuji shoten, 1971.

Mallmann, Marie-Thérèse de. *Introduction à l'iconographie du tāntrisme bouddhique.* Paris: Maisonneuve, 1986.

Maspero, Henri. *Taoism and Chinese Religion.* Translated by Frank A. Kierman, Jr. Amherst: The University of Massachusetts Press, 1981.

Matsumoto Kōichi 松本浩一. "Sōdai no raihō 宋代の雷法 *Shakai bunka shigaku* 17 (1979): 45–65.

———. "Sōrei-sairei ni miru Sōdai shūkyōshi no ichi keikō 葬礼祭礼にみる宋代宗教史の一傾向." In *Sōdai no shakai to bunka* 宋代の社會と文化. Sōdai-shi kenkyūkai kenkyū hōkoku. Tokyo: Kyūko shoin, 1983: 169–194.

McCullough, William H. "Spirit-Possession in the Heian Period." In *Studies on Japanese Culture,* vol. 1. Tokyo: The Japan P.E.N. Club, 1973: 91–98.

McKnight, Brian. *Law and Order in Sung China.* Cambridge: Cambridge University Press, 1992.

McMullen, David. *State and Scholars in T'ang China.* Cambridge: Cambridge University Press, 1988.

Meng Yuanlao 孟元老. *Dongjing menghua lu* 東京夢華錄 (1147).

Miaobi pusa suo wen jing 妙臂菩薩所問經. Faxian 法賢 (?–1001). T. 896.

Miaojixiang zuisheng genben da jiao jing 妙吉祥最勝根本大教經. Faxian 法賢 (?–1001). T. 1217.

Mikkyō daijiten 密教大辞典. 6 vols. Mikkyō Jiten Hensenkai, 1966.

Mikkyō jiten 密教辞典. Kyoto: Hōzōkan, 1975.

Miji lishi daquan shenwang jing jiesong 密跡力士大權神王經偈頌. Edited by Guangfu dashi 廣福大師 (early fourteenth century). T. 1688.

Minakata Kumagusu zenshū 南方熊楠全集. Tokyo: Heibonsha, 1973.

Miyakawa Hisayuki 宮川尚志. "Rin Reiso to Sō no Kisō 林靈素と宋の徽宗. *Tōkai daigaku kiyō: Bungakubu* 24 (1975): 1–8.

———. "Sō no kisō to dōkyō 宋の徽宗と道教. *Tōkai daigaku kiyō: Bungakubu* 23 (1975): 1–10.

———. "Nansō no dōshi Haku Gyokusen no jiseki 南宋の道士白玉蟾の事蹟." *Uchida Gimpu Hakushi shōju kinen tōyōshi ronshū* 内田吟風博士頌壽記念東洋史論集. Kyoto: Dōhōsha, 1978: 499–517.

Miyamoto Noriyuki 宮本則之. "Sō-Gen jidai ni okeru fun'an-to sosen saishi 宋元時代における墳庵と祖先祭祀." *Bukkyō shigaku kenkyū* 35.2 (1992): 112–135.

Miyazaki Ichisada. "The Administration of Justice during the Sung Dynasty." In Cohen, Edwards, and Chen, eds., *Essays in China's Legal Tradition.* Princeton: Princeton University Press, 1980.

Mo he fei shi luo mo na ye ti po he luo she tuoluoni yigui 摩訶吠室囉末那野提婆喝囉闍陀羅尼儀軌 (ninth century). T. 1246.

Mochizuki Bukkyō daijiten 望月佛教大辞典. 10 vols. Tokyo: Sekai seitan kankō kyōkai, 1960–1966.

Mollier, Christine. *Une apocalypse taoïste du Ve siècle: Le livre des incantations divines des grottes abyssales.* Paris: Mémoires de l'Institut des Hautes Études Chinoises 31, 1990.

———. La méthode de l'empereur du Nord du Mont Fengdu: Une tradition exorciste du taoïsme médiévale." *T'oung-Pao* 83, 4–5 (1997): 329–385.

Morohashi Tetsuji 諸橋轍次. *Dai kanwa jiten* 大漢和辞典. Tokyo: Taishūkan shoten, 1955–1960.

Nakamura Jihei 中村治兵衛. "Tōdai no fu 唐代の巫." *Shien* 105–106 (August 1971): 61–92.

———. "Godai ni okeru fu 五代における巫." *Tōyō Bunka* 55 (March 1975): 1–14.

————. "Hokusōchō to fu 北宋朝と巫." *Chūō daigaku kiyō; Bungakubu shigakka* 88 (1978): 63–78.

————. "Sōchō no kiu ni tsuite 宋朝の祈雨について." *Ajia no kyōiku to shakai*. Tokyo: Fumaitō shuppan, 1980: 102–113.

————. "Sōdai no fu no tokuchō 宋代の巫の特徴." *Chūō daigaku kiyō: Bungakubu shigakka* 104 (1982): 51–75.

Nakano Miyako 中野美代子. *Chūgoku no yōkai*中国の妖怪. Tokyo: Iwanomi shoten, 1983.

————. *Seiyuki no himitsu* 西遊記の秘密. Tokyo: Fukutake shoten, 1984.

Nan-Tang shu 南唐書. Lu You 陸游 (1125–1210). *Sibu congkan xubian*, vol. 15. Shanghai: Shanghai shudian, 1984.

Nan-Tang shu 南唐書. Ma Ling 馬令 (early twelfth century). *Sibu congkan xubian*, vol. 15. Shanghai: Shanghai shudian, 1984.

Nanyou ji 南遊記. In *Zhongguo gudian wenxu: Si you ji* 中國古典文學：四遊記. Taibei: Wenhua tushu gongsi, 1984.

Nickerson, Peter. "Taoism, Death, and Bureaucracy in Early Medieval China." Ph.D. diss., University of California at Berkeley, 1996.

Nüqing guilü 女青鬼律 (third century). HY 789.

Obeyesekere, Gananath. "The Idiom of Demonic Possession: A Case Study." *Social Science and Medicine* 4 (1970): 97–111.

————. *Medusa's Hair: An Essay on Personal Symbols and Religious Experience*. Chicago: The University of Chicago Press, 1981.

Ōfuchi Ninji 大淵忍爾. *Chūgokujin no shūkyō girei*中国人の宗教儀礼. Tokyo: Fukutake shoten, 1983.

Ogawa Yōichi 小川陽一. "Dōkyō setsuwa 道教説話." *Tonkō to chūgoku dōkyō* 敦煌と中国道教. Tokyo: Tōkyō shuppansha, 1983: 291–304.

Ōmura Seigai 大村西崖. *Mikkyō hattatsushi* 密教發達史. Tokyo: Bussho kankokai zuzobu, 1918.

Orzech, Charles. "Esoteric Buddhism and the Shishi in China." In Henrik H. Sorensen, *The Esoteric Buddhist Tradition*. SBS Monograph Series 2. Copenhagen Seminar for Buddhist Studies, 1994: 51–72.

————. "*Fang yen-k'ou* and *P'u-tu*: Metaphor and Translation." In Livia Kohn and Harold Roth, eds., *Daoist Identity in Practice*. Honolulu: University of Hawai'i Press, 2001.

Osabe Kazuo 長部和雄. *Tō-Sō mikkyōshi ronkō* 唐宋密教史論考. Kyoto: Nagada bunshōdō, 1982.

Otagi Hajime 愛宕元. "Sō Taiso satsugai-setsu to jōshintaiheikan 宋太祖殺害説と上清太平宮." *Shirin* (1984): 51–79.

————. "Tōdai rokan kō 唐代樓觀考." In Yoshikawa Tadao 吉川忠夫, ed., *Chūgoku kodōkyōshi kenkyū* 中國古道教史研究. Kyoto: Dōhōsha, 1992: 275–322.

Pishamen yigui 毘沙門儀軌. Attributed to Amoghavajra (705–744). T. 1249.

Quan Tang Shi 全唐詩. Compiled by Tsao Yin 曹寅. Shanghai: T'ungwen, 1898.

Rawski, Evelyn. "A Historian's Approach to Chinese Death Ritual." In James Watson and Evelyn Rawski, eds., *Death Ritual in Late Imperial and Modern China*. Berkeley: University of California Press, 1988: 20–40.

Rouget, Gilbert. *Music and Trance: A Theory of the Relations Between Music and Possession*. Chicago: The University of Chicago Press, 1985.

Sandong xiudao yi 三洞修道儀 (Song). HY 1227.

Saso, Michael. *The Teachings of Taoist Master Chuang*. New Haven: Yale University Press, 1978.

Sawada Mizuho 澤田瑞穗. "Shakkyōgeki joroku 釋教劇敘録." *Tenri daigaku gakuhō* 44 (1964): 39–43.

———. *Chūgoku no minkan shūkyō* 中国の民間宗教. Tokyo: Kosakusha, 1982.

———. *Chūgoku no juhō* 中国の咒法. Tokyo: Hirakawa, 1984.

———. "Kenkikō 見鬼考." In Sawada, *Chūgoku no juhō*. Tokyo: Hirakawa, 1984: 3–39.

———. "Kokukikō 劾鬼法." In Sawada, *Chūgoku no juhō*. Tokyo: Hirakawa, 1984: 40–55.

Schipper, Kristofer. *Le corps taoïste*. Paris: Fayard, 1982.

———. "Exposé de titres et travaux," (unpub. ms., Paris, 1983).

———. "An Outline of Taoist Ritual." Paper prepared for the "International Conference on Asian Rituals and the Theory of Ritual," Berlin, June 1984.

———. "Taoist Ordination Ranks in the Tunhuang Manuscripts." In G. Naundorf, ed., *Religion und Philosophie in Ostasien: Festschrift für Hans Steininger zum 65. Geburstag*. Würzburg: Königshausen & Neumann, 1985: 127–148.

———. "Vernacular and Classical Ritual in Taoism." *Journal of Asian Studies* 45:1 (Nov. 1985): 21–51.

———. *Annuaire de l'École Pratique des Hautes Études* (1985–1986): 133–135.

———. "Master Chao I-chen (?–1382) and the Ch'ing-wei School of Taoism." In Akizuki Kan'ei 秋月觀暎, ed., *Dōkyō to shūkyō bunka* 道教と宗教文化. Tokyo: Hirakawa shuppan, 1987: 1–21 (from the back).

———. "Mulien Plays in Taoist Liturgical Context." In David Johnson, ed., *Ritual Opera, Operatic Ritual*. Berkeley: Chinese Popular Culture Project, 1989:126–154.

Seidel, Anna. "Traces of Han Religion in Funeral Texts Found in Tombs." In Akizuki Kan'ei 秋月觀暎, ed., *Dōkyō to shūkyō bunka* 道教と宗教文化. Tokyo: Hirakawa shuppan, 1987: 21–57 (from the back).

Shafer, Edward. *The Empire of Min*. Rutland: Charles Tuttle, 1954.

Shangqing beiji Tianxin zhengfa. HY 567.

Shangqing gusui lingwen guilü 上清骨髓靈文鬼律. HY 461.

Shangqing lingbao dafa 上清靈寶大法. Jin Yunzhong 金允中 (early thirteenth century). HY 1213.

Shangqing lingbao dafa 上清靈寶大法. Wang Qizhen 王契真 (late thirteenth century). HY 1211.

Shangqing tianxin zhengfa 上清天心正法. Deng Yougong 鄧有功 (early twelfth century). HY 566.

Sheng Huanxitian shi fa 聖歡喜天式法. T. 1275.

Shenxian ganyu zhuan 神仙感遇傳. Du Guangting 杜光庭 (850–933). HY 592.

Shimen zhengtong 釋門正統. Zong jian 宗鑑 (Song). Z. 2B, 3:5.

Shishi tonglan 施食通覽. Zongxiao 宗曉 (thirteenth century). Z. 2A, 6:3.

Shizutani Masao 靜谷正雄. "Hōshi (dharma-bhānaka) ni tsuite 法師 (dharma-bhānaka)について." *Indogaku bukkyōgaku kenkyū* 3.1 (1954): 131–132.

———. "Daijō kyōdan no seiritsu ni tsuite, 1 大乘教團の成立について." *Bukkyō shigaku* 13.3 (1967): 17–44.

Shuilu yigui huiben 水陸儀軌會本. Shanghai: Shanghao foxue shuju, n.d.

Skar, Lowell. "Administering Thunder: A Thirteenth-Century Memorial Deliberating the Thunder Rites." *Cahiers d'Extrême-Asie* 9 (1996–1997): 159–202.

———. "Ritual Movement, Deity Cults and the Transformation of Daoism in Song and Yuan Times." In Livia Kohn, ed., *Handbook of Daoism*. Leiden: E. J. Brill, 2000.

Snellgrove, D. L. *The Hevajra Tantra*. London Oriental Series, vol. 6. London: Oxford University Press, 1959.

Song Bai zhenren Yuchan quanji 宋白真人玉蟾全集. Bo Yuchan. Taiwan: Committee to Publish Bo Yuchan's Works, 1976.

Song Gaoseng zhuan 宋高僧傳. Zanning 贊寧 (919–1001). T. 2061.

Song huiyao jigao 宋會要輯稿. Compiled by Xu Song 徐松. Reprint edition. Taibei: Shijie shuju, 1964.

Songchao shishi. Li You (early twelfth century). *Siku quanshu*. 1698–1699. Reprint edition. Taipei: Commercial Press, 1971.

Soymié, Michel. *Annuaire de l'École Pratique des Hautes Études, IVe Section* (1975–1976): 997–1002.

———. *Annuaire de l'École Pratique des Hautes Études, IVe Section* (1976–1977): 1027–1034.

———. "Les dix jours de jeûne du taoïsme." *Dōkyō kenkyū ronshū, Dōkyō no shisō to bunka*. Tokyo: Kōkushō kankōkai, 1977: 1–21.

Stanford, James. "Literary Aspects of Japan's Dual-Ganesa Cult." In Robert L. Brown, ed., *Ganesh: Studies of an Asian God*. Albany: State University of New York Press, 1991: 287–335.

Stein, R. A. "Les fêtes de cuisines du taoïsme religieux." *Annuaire du Collège de France* (1968–1969): 431–440.

———. "Un exemple de relations entre Taoïsme et religion populaire." *Fukui Hakase shōju kinen Tōyō bunka ronshū*. Tokyo, 1969: 79–90.

———. "Spéculations mystiques et thèmes relatifs aux 'cuisines' du taoïsme." *Annuaire du Collège de France* (1971–1972): 489–499.

———. *Annuaire du Collège de France* (1972–1973): 60–65.

———. *Annuaire du Collège de France* (1973–1974): 512–515.

———. "The Guardian of the Gate: An Example of Buddhist Mythology, from India to Japan." In Yves Bonnefoy and Wendy Doniger, eds., *Asian Mythologies*. Chicago: The University of Chicago Press, 1993: 122–136.

Stevenson, Daniel B. "The Buddhist Rite for the Creatures of Water and Land: Text and Image in the History of the *Shuilu fahui*" (unpub. ms., 1997).

Strickmann, Michel. "Sōdao no raigi: Shinshō undō to dōka nanshū ni tsuite no ryaku setsu 宋代の雷儀：神霄運動と道家南宗についての略説." *Tōhō Shūkyō* 46 (1975): 15–28.

———. "The Longest Taoist Scripture." *History of Religions* 17 (1978): 331–354.

———. "The Taoist Renaissance of the Twelfth Century." Paper prepared for the Third International Conference of Taoist Studies, Unterägeri, September 39, 1979.

———. "India in the Chinese Looking Glass." In D. Klimburg-Salter, ed., *The Silk Route and the Diamond Path*. Los Angeles: UCLA Art Council, 1982: 53–63.

———. "Therapeutische Rituale und das Problem des Bösen im frühen Taoismus." In G. Naundorf, ed., *Religion und Philosophie Ostasien: Festschrift für Hans Steininger zum 65. Geburstag*. Würzburg: Königshausen & Neumann, 1985: 185–200.

———. "Magical Medicine: Therapeutic Rituals in Medieval China" (unpub. ms., Berkeley, 1987, forthcoming in 2001 as *Chinese Magical Medicine* from Stanford University Press, ed. Bernard Faure).

———. "Dreamwork of Psycho-Sinologists: Doctors, Taoists, Monks." In Carolyn Brown, ed., *Psycho-Sinology: The Universe of Dreams in Chinese Culture*. Lanham: University Press of America, 1988.

———. *Mantras et mandarins: Le bouddhisme tantrique en Chine*. Paris: Gallimard, 1996.

Su ji li Yanmoxishouluotian shuo aweishe fa 速疾立驗魔醯首羅天説阿尾奢法. Amoghavajra (705–774). T. 1277.

Su Shi 蘇軾. *Sushi shiji* 蘇軾詩集. Annotated by Wang Wengao 王文誥. Beijing: Zhonghua shuju, 1982.

Sudō Yoshiyuki 周藤吉之 and Nakajima Toshi. *Chūgoku no rekishi 5: Godai-Sō* 中国の歴史 vol. 5: 五代－宋. Tokyo: Kodansha, 1974.

Sun Kekuan 孫克寬. *Song Yuan daojiao zhi fazhan* 宋元道教之發展. Taizhong: Donghai University, 1965.

Supodi tongzi qingwen jing 蘇婆呼童子請問經. T. 895.

Taiji zhenren fu lingbao zhaijie weiyi zhujing yaojue 太極真人敷靈寶齋戒威儀諸經要訣 (Six Dynasties). HY 532.

Taiping guangji 太平廣記. Compiled by Li Fang 李昉 (978). Beijing: Zhonghua shuju, 1961.

Taishang chiwen dongshen sanlu 太上赤文洞神三籙. Attributed to Li Chunfeng (seventh century). HY 589.

Taishang dongxuan lingbao miedu wulian shengshi miaojing 太上洞玄靈寶滅度五鍊生尸妙經 (Six Dynasties). HY 369.

Taishang huanglu zhaiyi 太上黃籙齋義. Du Guangting 杜光庭 (850–933). HY 507.

Taishang jidu zhangshe 太上濟度章赦 (early fourteenth century). HY 316.

Taishang santian neijiejing 太上三天内解經 (early fifth century). HY 1196.

Taishang zhengyi zhougui jing 太上正一咒鬼經 (Six Dynasties?). HY 1184.

Taishang zhuguo jiumin zongzhen biyao 太上助國救民總真祕要. Yuan Miaozong 元妙宗 (1116). HY 1217.

Taishō shinsū daizōkyō 大正新修大藏經. Takakusu Jinjirō and Watanabe Kaikyoku, eds. (Kyoto, 1905–1912). Tokyo: Daizōkyō, 1924–1935. Abbreviated herein as T.

Tanaka Issei 田仲一成. *Chūgoku saishi engeki kenkyū* 中国祭祀演劇研究. Tokyo: Tōkyō daigaku shuppansha, 1981.

———. *Chūgoku no zonso to engeki* 中国の宗教と演劇. Tokyo: Tōkyō daigaku shuppansha, 1985.

———. *Chūgoku gōson saishi kenkyū* 中国郷村祭祀研究. Tokyo: Tōkyō daigaku shuppansha, 1989.

———. *Chūgoku fukei engeki kenkyū* 中国巫系演劇研究. Tokyo: Tōkyō daigaku shuppansha, 1993.

Taylor, Romeyn. "Official and Popular Religion and the Political Organization of Chinese Society in the Ming." In Liu Kwang-ching, ed., *Orthodoxy in Late Imperial China.* Berkeley: University of California Press, 1991: 126–157.

Teihon Yanagida Kunio shū 訂本柳田國男集. Tokyo: Chikuma shobō, 1962.

Teiser, Stephen F. *The Ghost Festival in Medieval China.* Princeton: Princeton University Press, 1988.

———. "The Ritual Behind the Opera: A Fragmentary Ethnography of the Ghost Festival, A.D. 400–1900." In David Johnson, ed., *Ritual*

Opera, Operatic Ritual. Berkeley: Chinese Popular Culture Project, 1990: 191–223.

ter Haar, Barend J. "The Rise of the Guan Yu Cult: The Taoist Connection." In Jan A. M. De Meyer and Peter M. Engelfriet, eds., *Linked Faiths: Essays on Chinese Religions and Traditional Culture in Honour of Kristofer Schipper*. Leiden: E. J. Brill, 2000: 184–204.

Ting Ch'uan-ching. *A Compilation of Anecdotes of Sung Personalities*. Trans. Chu Djang and Jane Djang. Taipei: St. John's University Press, 1989.

Twitchett, Denis. "The Fan Clan's Charitable Estate, 1050–1760." In David S. Nivison and Arthur F. Wright, eds., *Confucianism in Action*. Stanford: Stanford University Press, 1959: 97–133.

————. "Documents on Clan Administration 1: The Rules of Administration of the Charitable Estate of the Fan Clan." *Asia Major* 3rd ser., 8 (1960): 1–35.

Unger, Roberto Mangabeira. *Politics: The Central Texts: Theory Against Fate*. London: Verso, 1997.

Van Straten, N. H. *Concepts of Health, Disease and Vitality in Traditional Chinese Society*. Wiesbaden: Franz Steiner, 1983.

Verellen, Franciscus. *Du Guangting (850–933): Taoïste de cour à la fin de la chine médiévale*. Paris: Mémoires de l'Institut des Hautes Études Chinoises 30, 1989.

Visser, Marinus de. *Ancient Buddhism in Japan: Sūtras and Ceremonies*. Leiden: E. J. Brill, 1935.

Vitiello, Giovanni. "Studio sul taoista Lu Xiujing (406–477)." *Annali dell'Instituto Universitario Orientale di Napoli* 47.3 (1987): 293–332.

Von Falkenhausen, Lothar. "Reflections on the Political Role of Spirit-Mediums in Early China: The *Wu* Officials in the *Zhou li*." *Early China* 20(1995): 279–300.

Von Glahn, Richard. "The Enchantment of Wealth: The God Wutong in the Social History of Jiangnan." *Harvard Journal of Asiatic Studies* 51.2 (1991): 651–714.

Wada Akio 和田昭夫. "Gohō dōji 護法童子." *Mikkyō Bunka* 104 (1973): 19–41.

Wakeman, Frederic, Jr. "Models of Historical Change: The Chinese State and Society, 1839–1989." In Lieberthal et al., eds., *Perspectives on Modern China: Four Anniversaries*. Armonk: M. E. Sharpe, 1991: 68–102.

————. "Civil Society in Late Imperial China." In Frederic Wakeman, Jr., and Wang Xi, eds., *China's Quest for Modernization*. Berkeley: Institute of East Asian Studies, University of California at Berkeley, Research Papers and Policy Studies 41, 1997: 325–351.

————. "Boundaries of the Public Sphere in Ming and Qing China." *Daedalus* 127.3 (Summer 1998): 167–189.

Waley, Arthur. *Ballads and Stories from Tun-Huang*. London: George Allen & Unwin, 1960.

———. *The Book of Songs: The Ancient Chinese Classic of Poetry*. New York: Grove Weidenfield, 1988.

Walleser, M. *The Life of Nāgārjuna from Tibetan and Chinese Sources*. Delhi: Nag, 1979.

Walton, Linda. "Southern Sung Academies as Sacred Places." In Ebrey and Gregory, eds., *Religion and Society in T'ang and Sung China*. Honolulu: University of Hawai'i Press, 1993: 335–363.

Wang Haihang 王海航 and Chen Yaolin 陳耀林. *Pilu si he Pilu si bihua* 毗盧寺和毗盧寺壁畫. Shijiazhuang: 1984.

Wang Qiugui 王秋桂. *Minsu quyi congshu* 民俗曲藝叢書, vols. 1–80. Taibei: Minsu quyi, 1993–.

Wilkerson, James R. "The 'Ritual Master' and His 'Temple Corporation' Rituals." In Lin Ru 林如, ed., *Minjian xinyang yu Zhongguo wenhua: Guoji yantao huilun wenji 2* 民間信仰與中國文化國際研討會論文集. Taibei: Hanxue yanjiu zhongxin, 1994: 471–522.

Wilkinson, Christopher. "The Tantric Ganesa: Texts Preserved in the Tibetan Canon." In Robert L. Brown, ed., *Ganesh: Studies of an Asian God*. Albany: State University of New York Press, 1991: 235–275.

Winkler, John L. *Auctor and Actor: A Narratological Reading of Apulius's The Golden Ass*. Berkeley: University of California Press, 1985.

Woodside, Alexander. "Emperors and the Chinese Political System." In Lieberthal et al., eds., *Perspectives on Modern China: Four Anniversaries*. Armonk: M. E. Sharpe, 1991: 5–30.

Wu Liancheng 吳連城. *Baoning si Mingdai shuilu hua* 寶寧寺明代水陸畫. Beijing: Wenwu chubanshe, 1985.

Wu Yongmeng 吳永猛. "Penghu gongmiao xiaofa de Pu An Zushi zhi shenyuan 澎湖宮廟小法的普唵祖師之探源." In *Donfang zongjiao yanjiu* 4: 165–181.

Wu Zimu 吳自牧. *Mengliang lu* 夢粱錄 (1274).

Wushang biyao 無上祕要 (late sixth century). HY 1130.

Wushang huanglu dazhai licheng yi 無上黃錄大齋立成儀. Jiang Shuyu 蔣叔輿 (1156–1217). HY 508.

Wushang jiuxiao yuqing dafan zuwei xiandu leiting yujing (twelfth century?). HY 15.

Wushang xuanyuan santianwang yudang dafa 無上玄元三天王玉堂大法. Lu Shizhong 路時中 (fl. 1158). HY 220.

Xianchun Lin'an zhi 咸淳臨安志. Song-Yuan difang zhi congshu, vol. 7. Taibei: Dahua shuju, 1980.

Xiaochu ji 小畜集. Wang Yucheng 王禹偁 (954–1001). *Wang Huangzhou Xiaochu ji* 玉黃州小畜集. Taibei: Sibu congkan (reprint ed.), 1936.

Xin Tangshu 新唐書. Song Qi 宋祁 and Ou Yangxiu 歐陽修. Beijing: Zhonghua shuju, 1974.

Xiuzhen shishu 修真十書. Anonymous (thirteenth century). HY 263.

Xu Daoling 許道齡. "Songlu zhongde shenpan zhidu." *Dongfang zazhi fugan* 4.4.

Xu Zizhi tongjian changbian 續資治通鑑長編. Li Tao 李燾. Taibei: Shijie shuju, 1961.

Xuantian shangdi qisheng lu 玄天上帝啓聖錄. Anonymous (late thirteenth–fourteenth century). HY 957.

Yamauchi Kōichi 山内宏一. "Hokusō no kokka to gyokkō 北宋の国家と玉皇." *Tōhōgaku* 62 (1981): 83–97.

Ye Mingsheng 葉明聲. "Fujiansheng Longyanshi Dongxiaozhen Lüshanjiao Guangjitan keyiben huibian 福建省龍巖市東肖鎮閭山教廣濟壇科儀本彙編." In Wang Qiugui 王秋桂, ed., *Zhongguo chuantong keyiben huibian* 中國傳統科儀本彙編. Taibei: Xinwenfeng, 1998.

Yi Run 儀潤. *Shuilu yigui* 水陸儀軌. Yangzhou: Yangzhou zangjing yuan, 1917.

———. *Shuilu yigui huiben* 水陸儀軌會本. Yangzhou: Yangzhou zangjing yuan, 1924.

Yijian zhi 夷堅志. Hong Mai 洪邁 (1123–1202). Beijing: Zhonghua shuju, 1981.

Yisheng baode zhuan 翊聖保德傳. Wang Qinruo 王欽若 (1016). HY 1275.

Yoritomi Motohiro 賴富本宏. *Chūgoku mikkyō no kenkyū* 中国密教の研究. Tokyo: Daitō shuppansha, 1975.

Yu Ji 虞集 (1272–1348). *Daoyuan xue gu lu* 道園學古錄. Shanghai: Shangwu yinshu guan, 1937.

Yü Chün-fang. *The Renewal of Buddhism in China: Chu-Hung and the Late Ming Synthesis.* New York: Columbia University Press, 1981.

Yuanshi 元史. Song Lian 宋濂 (1310–1381). Beijing: Zhonghua shuju, 1976.

Yunji qiqian 雲笈七籤. Zhang Junfang 張君房 (1028). HY 1026.

Zhang Xunliao 張勛燎. "Jiangxi Gao'an chutu Nan-Song Chunxi liunian Xu Yong mu 'Fengdu luoshan baku chaosheng zhengui shenxing' tu shike 江西高安出土南宋淳熙六年徐永墓‘鄷都羅山拔苦超生鎮鬼真形’圖石刻." *Daojiao wenhua yanjiu* 6. Shanghai: Guji chubanshe, 1995: 300–311.

Zhen Gao 真誥. Tao Hongjing 陶弘景 (456–536). HY 1010.

Zhengtong daozang 正統道藏 (1444–1445). Taibei: Xin Wenfeng chuban gongsi, 1990.

Zhi-zheng Jinling xinzhi 至正金陵新志. Song Yuan difang zhi congshu, vol. 3. Taibei: Dahua shuju, 1980.

Zhiqing zashuo 摭青雜説. Compiled by Wang Mingqing 王明清 (1127–ca.

1215). *Longwei bishu* 龍威祕書 vol. 4, fasc. 13 (1794). *Baibu congshu jicheng*. Taibei: Yiwen yin shu guan (reprint ed.), 1965–1970.

Zhongnan shan shuojingtai lidai zhenxian beiji 終南山説經臺歷代真仙碑記. Compiled by Zhu Xiangxian 朱象先 (fl. 1279–1308). HY 955.

Zhou Cheng 周城, ed. *Song Dongjing kao* 宋東京考. Beijing: Zhonghua shuju, 1988.

Zhou Yiliang. "Tantrism in China." *Harvard Journal of Asiatic Studies* 8 (1945): 241–332.

Zhouli zhengyi 周禮正義. Edited by Sun Yirang 孫詒讓. Taibei: Shangwu yinshu guan, 1965.

Zizhi tongjian changbian jishi benmo 資治通鑑長編紀事本末. Taibei: Wen-hai chubanshe, 1967.

INDEX

ABOUT THE AUTHOR

Edward L. Davis is associate professor of Chinese history at the University of Hawai'i at Manoa. He received his B.A. in modern European history from Harvard College and his Ph.D. in Chinese history from the University of California at Berkeley. His research interests focus on Middle Imperial China (750–1600 A.D.) and on the history of Chinese religions and culture. His previous publications include two essays on the cult to the Xu brothers in Fujian. He is co-editor of the *Encyclopedia of Contemporary Chinese Culture* and is currently at work on a history in 150 pages of Chinese religions from the Stone Age to the Computer Age.

CPSIA information can be obtained
at www.ICGtesting.com
Printed in the USA
JSHW070708251122
33759JS00001B/9